Globalisation and Economic Security in East Asia

What is the relationship between globalisation and economic security? This edited volume examines this key question through an empirical and conceptual analysis of the East Asian experience.

The contributors to this multidisciplinary volume examine whether the globalisation of the world economy has increased or decreased economic security for states, societies and individuals. They explore the different ways in which state and non-state actors understand the problem of economic insecurity, as well as how policymakers use national, regional and global institutions to help them govern in the interests of economic security. The East Asian region provides rich empirical material for the examination of global capitalism, and the insecurities it generates for societies and individuals.

This book will be of great interest to all students and scholars of international relations, the international political economy of East Asia, globalisation and non-traditional security studies.

Helen E. S. Nesadurai is Assistant Professor at the Institute of Defence and Strategic Studies, Nanyang Technological University, Singapore. She is the author of *Globalisation, Domestic Politics and Regionalism* (2003), which was also published by Routledge in the Routledge/Warwick Studies in Globalisation series.

Routledge/Warwick Studies in Globalisation

Edited by Richard Higgott and published in association with the Centre for the Study of Globalisation and Regionalisation, University of Warwick.

What is globalisation and does it matter? How can we measure it? What are its policy implications? The Centre for the Study of Globalisation and Regionalisation at the University of Warwick is an international site for the study of key questions such as these in the theory and practice of globalisation and regionalisation. Its agenda is avowedly interdisciplinary. The work of the Centre will be showcased in this new series.

This series comprises two strands:

Warwick Studies in Globalisation addresses the needs of students and teachers, and the titles will be published in hardback and paperback. Titles include:

Globalisation and the Asia-Pacific
Contested territories
Edited by Kris Olds, Peter Dicken,
Philip F. Kelly, Lily Kong and
Henry Wai-chung Yeung

Regulating the Global Information Society
Edited by Christopher Marsden

Banking on Knowledge
The genesis of the global development network
Edited by Diane Stone

Historical Materialism and Globalisation
Edited by Hazel Smith and Mark Rupert

Civil Society and Global Finance
Edited by Jan Aart Scholte with
Albrecht Schnabel

Towards a Global Polity
Edited by Morten Ougaard and
Richard Higgott

New Regionalisms in the Global Political Economy
Theories and cases
Edited by Shaun Breslin,
Christopher W. Hughes, Nicola Phillips
and Ben Rosamond

Routledge/Warwick Studies in Globalisation is a forum for innovative new research intended for a high-level specialist readership, and the titles will be available in hardback only. Titles include:

1 **Non-State Actors and Authority in the Global System**
Edited by Richard Higgott, Geoffrey
Underhill and Andreas Bieler

2 **Globalisation and Enlargement of the European Union**
Austrian and Swedish social forces in the struggle over membership
Andreas Bieler

3 **Rethinking Empowerment**
Gender and development in a global/local world
Edited by Jane L. Parpart, Shirin M. Rai
and Kathleen Staudt

4 **Globalising Intellectual Property Rights**
The TRIPs agreement
Duncan Matthews

Globalisation and Economic Security in East Asia

Governance and institutions

Edited by Helen E. S. Nesadurai

E·S·R·C
ECONOMIC
& SOCIAL
RESEARCH
COUNCIL

Centre FOR THE
Study OF
Globalisation AND
Regionalisation

Routledge
Taylor & Francis Group

LONDON AND NEW YORK

First published 2006
by Routledge
2 Park Square, Milton Park, Abingdon, Oxon OX14 4RN

Simultaneously published in the USA and Canada
by Routledge
270 Madison Ave, New York, NY 10016

Routledge is an imprint of the Taylor & Francis Group

Typeset in Baskerville by
Keystroke, Jacaranda Lodge, Wolverhampton
Printed and bound in Great Britain by
Antony Rowe Ltd, Chippenham, Wiltshire

British Library Cataloguing in Publication Data
A catalogue record for this book is available from the British Library

Library of Congress Cataloging in Publication Data
Globalisation and economic security in East Asia / edited by Helen Nesadurai.
  p. cm. – (Routledge/Warwick studies in globalisation ; 8)
  Includes bibliographical references and index.
1. East Asia–Foreign economic relations. 2. Economic security–East Asia.
3. Globalization–Economic aspects–East Asia. 4. East Asia–Economic policy.
5. East Asia–Economic conditions–21st century. I. Title: Globalization and
economic security in East Asia. II. Nesadurai, Helen Sharmini. III. Series.
  HF1600.5.G556 2005
  337.5–dc22   2005005280

ISBN10: 0–415–37350–6
ISBN13: 9–78–415–37350–0

Contents

Figures

Tables

Contributors

Mark Beeson is Senior Lecturer in International Relations, School of Political Science and International Studies, University of Queensland, Australia.

Mely Caballero-Anthony is Assistant Professor at the Institute of Defence and Strategic Studies (IDSS), Nanyang Technological University, Singapore.

Kevin Hewison is Professor at the Department of Asian Studies and Director of the Carolina Asia Center, University of North Carolina at Chapel Hill, USA. Prior to this, he was Director of the Southeast Asia Research Centre, City University of Hong Kong.

Richard Higgott is Professor of International Political Economy, Department of Politics and International Studies, University of Warwick, UK, and Director of the ESRC Centre for the Study of Globalisation and Regionalisation (CSGR) at the University of Warwick.

Miles Kahler is Rohr Professor of Pacific International Relations at the Graduate School of International Relations and Pacific Studies (IR/PS), and Director of the Institute for International, Comparative, and Area Studies (IICAS) at the University of California, San Diego, USA.

Hiro Katsumata is Research Fellow at the Institute of Defence and Strategic Studies (IDSS), Nanyang Technological University, Singapore.

Chyungly Lee is Associate Research Fellow at the Institute for International Relations, National Chengchi University, Taiwan.

Charles E. Morrison is President of the East-West Center, Honolulu, USA.

Helen E. S. Nesadurai is Assistant Professor at the Institute of Defence and Strategic Studies (IDSS), Nanyang Technological University, Singapore.

Pham Cao Phong is Deputy Director General, Institute for International Relations (IIR), Hanoi, Vietnam. Prior to this, he was the Assistant Director General at the Institute for International Relations.

Kurnya Roesad is an Economist with the World Bank based in Jakarta, Indonesia. Previously, he was Researcher, Economics Department, Centre for Strategic and International Studies (CSIS), Jakarta.

Wang Zhengyi is Professor and Chair, Department of International Political Economy, School of International Studies, Peking University, Beijing, People's Republic of China.

Henry Wai-chung Yeung is Associate Professor in Economic Geography, Department of Geography, National University of Singapore.

Foreword

Globalisation and Economic Security in East Asia was conceived as a means of exploring the relationship between globalisation and economic security, both conceptually and through an empirical analysis of the East Asian region. Its key questions include: (a) Is there a need to revisit traditional conceptions of economic security in the light of economic globalisation? (b) Has globalisation increased or decreased economic security for states, societies and individuals in East Asia? (c) What role might national, regional and global institutions play in helping policymakers govern in the interests of economic security?

These questions were first debated at a workshop organised by the Institute of Defence and Strategic Studies (IDSS) in Singapore on 11–12 September 2003. This volume is the fruit of that workshop, which benefited from the generous funding of the Sasakawa Peace Foundations of Japan and the United States. The workshop was, in fact, the third component of a larger, four-part project on Asia-Pacific security issues undertaken by IDSS with funding from the Sasakawa Peace Foundation. The first conference was held in December 2002 on the theme 'Evolving Approaches to Security in the Asia-Pacific'. The second workshop, which discussed 'United Nations Peacekeeping Operations and the Asia-Pacific Region', was co-hosted with the United Nations University in Tokyo in February 2003, while the fourth conference was held in Washington DC in November 2003 on the theme 'Reassessing Security Cooperation in the Asia-Pacific Region' in collaboration with the Mortara Center for International Studies, Georgetown University, USA. Together, the four books produced from these four conferences/ workshops constitute a major intellectual and policy contribution from the authors as well as IDSS to evolving security issues in the Asia Pacific/East Asian region.

While the four-part project as a whole was coordinated under the auspices of the institute's programme on Multilateralism and Regionalism, the workshop and book project on Globalisation and Economic Security also showcase the Institute's programme on international political economy (IPE). Many of the challenges and trends that affect economic security today lie at the interface between politics and economics – hence the emphasis by many of the authors in this volume on an IPE approach to their analysis. It is this sort of multidisciplinary approach to research, teaching and policy that IDSS believes is vital if we are to make sense of, and help find solutions to, the pressing issues of the day. It is hoped that this book makes a small contribution to that end.

Professor Amitav Acharya
Deputy Director and Head of Research,
Institute of Defence and Strategic Studies (IDSS),
Nanyang Technological University, Singapore

Acknowledgements

Many people have made possible the completion of this edited book, not least the volume's contributors. Their cheerful forbearance in the face of editorial demands is deeply appreciated. The insights that the authors brought to their writings have helped to take us some significant steps forward in our understanding of the pressing issue of economic (in)security in an age of globalisation, particularly as they pertain to East Asia.

Funding support from the Sasakawa Peace Foundation made possible the workshop held in Singapore on 11–12 September 2003 at which these papers were first deliberated, and is deeply appreciated. Thanks are also due to the forty participants to the workshop, whose active and valuable participation helped us clarify many issues, and especially in bridging academic theorising and the 'real world' of communities and individuals experiencing the effects of economic globalisation. We would also like to thank the project's advisers, panel chairs and discussants for their role in helping to bring this book to fruition: Amitav Acharya, Ng Chee Yuen, Vedi Hadiz, Manu Bhaskaran, Lee Lai To and Soedradjad Djiwandono. Heartfelt thanks are also due to Ambassador Barry Desker, Director of IDSS, for his total support and encouragement of this book project. The three anonymous reviewers for Routledge offered valuable advice and constructive criticism that has helped to strengthen the final manuscript. The book is a much better one as a result, and their contribution is deeply appreciated.

Some of the material in this book first appeared in a special issue of the journal *The Pacific Review*, 17 (4), 2004. Grateful thanks are due to Taylor & Francis (www. tandf.co.uk), publishers of *The Pacific Review*, for granting permission to reproduce Chapters 1, 2, 3, 4, 11 and 12 in this book.

The administrative staff of IDSS deserve special mention. The organisation of the September 2003 workshop and the production of the final manuscript would not have been possible without their efficient support. While their painstaking attention to detail helped ensure the smooth running of the conference, their cheery good humour and warm camaraderie made the exercise an extremely pleasant and stress-free experience. Finally, this book would not have at all been possible without the enthusiasm and commitment of the editorial team at Routledge. Especial thanks are due to Heidi Bagtazo, Editor of Politics and International Studies, and Harriet Brinton, Editorial Assistant, Politics and International Studies, for their part in making this book a reality.

Abbreviations

ABAC	APEC Business Advisory Council
ACD	Asian Cooperation Dialogue
ACFTA	ASEAN–China Free Trade Area
ADB	Asian Development Bank
AFTA	ASEAN Free Trade Area
AID	Agency for International Development
AMC	Asian Migrant Centre
AMF	Asian Monetary Fund
AMRC	Asian Monitor Resource Centre
APA	ASEAN People's Assembly
APEC	Asia-Pacific Economic Cooperation
APIAN	APEC International Assessment Network
APT	ASEAN Plus Three
ARENA	Asian Regional Exchange for New Alternatives
ARF	ASEAN Regional Forum
ASC	APEC Study Centres
ASEAN	Association of Southeast Asian Nations
ASEAN-ISIS	ASEAN Institutes of Strategic and International Studies
ASEM	Asia–Europe Meeting
ATM	automated teller machines
BDIPSS	Brunei Darussalam Institute of Policy and Strategic Studies
BULOG	national logistics agency (Indonesia)
CAEC	Council for Asia–Europe Cooperation
CAR	capital adequacy ratio
CAW	Committee for Asian Women
CCP	Chinese Communist Party
CEP	Comprehensive Economic Partnership
CGI	Consultative Group on Indonesia
CICP	Cambodian Institute for Cooperation and Peace
CIDA	Canadian International Development Agency
CMI	Chiang Mai Initiative
CODE-NGO	Caucus of Development NGO Network (Philippines)
CPF	Central Provident Fund (Singapore)

CPV	Communist Party of Vietnam
CSCAP	Council for Security Cooperation in the Asia Pacific
CSIS	Centre for Strategic and International Studies (Indonesia)
CSO	civil society organisation
DBS	Development Bank of Singapore
DPP	Democratic Progressive Party (Taiwan)
DPR	Dewan Perwakilan Rakyat (Indonesian parliament)
DSM	dispute settlement mechanism
EDB	Economic Development Board (Singapore)
EEZ	Exclusive Economic Zone
EU	European Union
FDI	foreign direct investment
FORUM ASIA	The Asian Forum for Human Rights and Development
FTAs	free trade agreements
G7	Group of Seven
G8	Group of Eight
G10	Group of Ten
G21	Group of Twenty-one
GATS	General Agreement on Trade in Services
GATT	General Agreement on Tariffs and Trade
GDP	gross domestic product
GFCF	gross fixed capital formation
GGT1	Global Governance Type 1
GGT2	Global Governance Type 2
GGT3	Global Governance Type 3
GIC	Government Investment Corporation
GLCs	government-linked corporations
HDR	Human Development Report
IAC	International Advisory Council
IBRA	Indonesian Bank Restructuring Agency
IDSS	Institute of Defence and Strategic Studies (Singapore)
IFI	international financial institution
IIR	Institute for International Relations (Vietnam)
IISS	International Institute for Strategic Studies (London)
IMF	International Monetary Fund
IPE	international political economy
IR	International Relations
ISDS	Institute for Strategic Development Studies (Philippines)
ISIS	Institute of Strategic and International Studies (Malaysia)
ISIS	Institute of Security and International Studies (Thailand)
JCIE	Japanese Center for International Exchange
JTC	Jurong Town Corporation
KKN	corruption, cronyism and nepotism (abbreviation in the Indonesian language)
KMT	Kuomintang

LDR	loan to deposit ratio
LOI	Letters of Intent
MAS	Monetary Authority of Singapore
MEFP	Memorandum of Economic and Financial Policies
MOFA	Ministry of Foreign Affairs (Japan)
MTNs	multilateral trade negotiations
NAFTA	North American Free Trade Area
NAMFREL	National Citizens' Movement for Free Elections
NGOs	non-governmental organisations
NGO-Cord	NGO Coordinating Committee for Rural Development
NIE	newly industrialising economy
NPL	non-performing loan
NTB	non-tariff barrier
NTUC	National Trade Union Congress (Singapore)
NWC	National Wage Council (Singapore)
OCBC	Overseas-Chinese Banking Corporation
ODA	official development assistance
OECD	Organisation for Economic Co-operation and Development
OUB	Overseas Union Bank
PAFTAD	Pacific Trade and Development Conference
PAP	People's Action Party (Singapore)
PBEC	Pacific Basin Economic Council
PECC	Pacific Economic Cooperation Council
PhilDHARRA	Philippine Partnership for the Development of Human Resources in Rural Areas
PLN	Perusahaan Listrik Negara (national electricity company, Indonesia)
PRC	People's Republic of China
PTAs	preferential trade agreements
QFB	Qualifying Full Banks
ROC	Republic of China (i.e. Taiwan)
Rp	rupiah (Indonesian currency)
S&P	Standard & Poor's
S11	September 11 (2001)
SARS	Severe Acute Respiratory Syndrome
SBI	Bank Indonesia Certificates
SEA-HDR	Southeast Asia Human Development Report
SEARICE	Southeast Asian Resource Institute for Community Education
SIIA	Singapore Institute of International Affairs
SMEs	small- and medium-sized enterprises
SOE	state-owned enterprise
TNCs	transnational corporations
TRIPS	Trade-Related Intellectual Property Rights
TRT	Thai Rak Thai (political party, Thailand)
UHS	Universal Health Scheme (Thailand)

UNDP	United Nations Development Programme
UOB	United Overseas Bank
VCF	Village and Community Fund (Thailand)
VND	Vietnamese dong (Vietnamese currency)
WALHI	*Wahana Lingkungan Hidup* (network of environmental NGOs in Indonesia)
WTO	World Trade Organization

Part I

Economic security and globalisation

Conceptual issues

1 Conceptualising economic security in an era of globalisation

What does the East Asian experience reveal?

Helen E. S. Nesadurai

Has globalisation of the world economy increased or decreased economic security for states, societies and individuals? What is the experience in East Asia more specifically, and what does that experience say about the nature and goals of governance and the role of national as well as regional intergovernmental institutions in that exercise? Do non-state regional governance mechanisms play any role in governance in the interests of economic security? Before we can even begin to address these questions, we need to ask what we mean by the term 'economic security', particularly in a world economy characterised by globalisation.

In the post-Cold War era, there has been considerable debate on what constitutes 'security', including the question of who or what is to be secured (the referent of security) as well as the sources of insecurity (Tickner, 1995; Baldwin, 1997; Buzan *et al.*, 1998). The issue of redefining *economic security* is thus also bound up with the larger debate in International Relations (IR) and Security Studies on reconceptualising security. Security studies specialists working within traditional neorealist frameworks tend to reject moves both to broaden the security agenda to include non-military sources of threats, such as poverty, environmental hazards, AIDS and economic recessions, or to focus on the security concerns of individuals rather than those of states (Walt, 1991). For noted security studies scholar Stephen Walt, such attempts would 'risk expanding "security studies" excessively' and thereby 'destroy its intellectual coherence and make it more difficult to devise solutions to any of these important problems' (ibid.: 213). Security studies scholars writing in the neorealist tradition generally subscribe to a narrow conception of economic security that is located within a traditional national security framework of analysis (Kolodziej, 1992: 422). Thus, the relationship between economic performance and military spending, the security implications (including the prospects of violent conflict arising from resource scarcity) and issues revolving around the use of economic instruments (trade and aid) in advancing foreign policy goals have loomed large in studies of economic security (Walt, 1991). Geo-economics also replaced geopolitics as the central preoccupation of the major powers in the 1990s, with economic power being recognised as crucial in determining the primacy or subordination of states in the international system (Luttwak, 1990; Huntington, 1993: 72; Moran, 1993).

That such concerns may be absolutely relevant to particular states is not at issue. The point is not to ignore understandings of economic security that speak to the experiences or conditions of other states and societies. More importantly, a notion of economic security that does not take into account the prevailing structural condition of economic globalisation may be far removed from the realities of contemporary life. Many scholars of globalisation would agree that contemporary economic globalisation, while bringing prosperity, appears also to be ushering in a period of economic volatility and uncertainty, with implications for how secure states, communities and individuals feel (Rodrik, 1997; Stiglitz, 2002). It is therefore not surprising that economic security concerns are now high on the national agendas of many states, including the United States.

Reconceptualising economic security

For scholars engaged in studies of development and for those adopting more critical approaches to IR and international political economy (IPE), the notion of 'economic insecurity' as the vulnerability of states, societies, groups and individuals to economic events, particularly economic shocks and crises that disrupt material well-being, is not such a radical shift (Scholte, 2000: 232–233). Moreover, scholars of public policy and public finance have long regarded economic security in terms of securing the individual against sudden income and consumption losses – through social security provision, for instance. Those working in such disciplines are perhaps untouched by the debates in IR/security studies over whether understandings of security should move away from statist preoccupations with violent conflict involving the use of military force. These disciplines have long subscribed to different conceptions of economic security centred on the economic and social life of individuals and societies. Even the White House website of the George W. Bush administration has an economic security portal that clearly defines economic security in terms of jobs.[1]

In examining the relationship between globalisation and economic security, we need to ask what dangers, if any, are posed by an integrating global market economy, who is to be secured and through what instruments. When exploring these issues, it is also important to avoid inflating the notion of economic security to include every economic risk and instance of economic dislocation, which could complicate policy design in an interdependent world economy and/or rationalise protection for chronically uncompetitive firms. This calls for more careful conceptualisation of the term 'economic security', although it is equally vital to avoid an overly narrow definition that normalises the particular security preoccupations of one or another state for *all* states and societies.

One way forward is to draw on insights from the broader social science literature in order to develop alternative conceptions of economic security. At the same time, it is important not to reject realist understandings of economic security, given that such concerns may be salient for some countries at certain points in time. The Taiwan experience, discussed in Chapter 7, is a case in point. Instead, realist versions of economic security should be seen, as suggested by David Baldwin (1997), as only *one* particular approach to economic security, one that regards the state as security referent to be secured from certain kinds of external threats (economic manipulation or a threat to its primacy in the international system). Instead, it is more productive to acknowledge that there exist other understandings and responses to the problem of economic security, depending on the historical, political and social contexts of states and their societies as well as the strategic environment in which they find themselves (Kolodziej, 1992: 422).

In line with Kolodziej's approach, this chapter first identifies alternative conceptualisations of economic security by drawing on theoretical perspectives from social science disciplines beyond neorealism. It then examines how policymakers and national or other communities of peoples have posed and responded to the problem of economic security/insecurity by reference to these various analytical categories. The point of departure is David Baldwin's general definition of security as 'a low probability of damage to acquired values', with economic security best seen as a different *form* of security aimed at ensuring minimal damage to a set of *economic* values (Baldwin, 1997: 13–23). From this general characterisation, more precise specifications of economic security with regard to its different dimensions can be articulated; 'security for whom', 'for which values', 'from what threats' and 'by what means' are four of the more crucial dimensions highlighted (ibid.: 12–18).

Integrating political economy considerations

Traditional conceptions of economic security are limited because 'economics is more than a source, or an instrument, of state power' (Goldfischer, 2002: 698). Perhaps more relevant to states and societies outside the context of superpower rivalry is the growing literature in IR/IPE that looks directly at the economic insecurities arising from the nature of capitalist production and the attendant conflicts that it produces *within* states (ibid.: 2002: 706). In doing so, this literature draws on insights from political economy in order to advance a notion of security that not only is cognisant of domestic distributional politics, but also takes into account the external structural context of globalisation. Accelerated globalisation since the 1990s has brought to the fore concerns over economic collapse and ecological disasters (Fierke, 2002: 130), while class antagonisms (Goldfischer, 2002: 706) and unfair land distributions and property rights allocations (Krause and Williams, 1996: 235) have triggered conflicts in many societies.

Departing from liberal precepts that the market is necessarily beneficial for all, and is thus both apolitical and non-conflictual, both Karl Marx and Karl Polanyi drew attention to the inherently *political* nature of markets. Markets are political constructs, with potential for allocating power and wealth between different groups depending on the norms and rules that authorities put in place to govern those markets (Polanyi, 1944; Crane and Amawi, 1997). This interpretation of the market has at least two implications in the context of our discussion on economic security: first, that distributional conflicts are part and parcel of a capitalist market economy; and second, that the manner in which market rules are written is crucial to governing in the interests of economic security.

The history of early Western capitalism reveals that market capitalism repeatedly opened schisms in society, including commercial rivalries, regional competition and class struggles in addition to interstate conflict. These histories suggest that we need to pay close attention to the variety of divisions that a capitalist economy produces and the implications of these divisions for the insecurities generated for individuals and groups in society and for intra- and interstate conflicts. With the growing transnationalisation of economic activity, the distributional implications of global capitalism for states as well as for different groups within and across states have become salient issues as well (Held and McGrew, 2002). These insecurities can, under certain circumstances, undermine social consensus within states, and possibly lead to violent conflict. Ultimately, such conflicts could spill over across national boundaries and lead to interstate tensions. Even if violent conflict is not the outcome, critical IR and IPE scholars share a normative commitment that these insecurities should be mitigated through suitable governance mechanisms (Cox, 1999).

A study of the many conflicts of the 1990s reveals the importance of opening up the black box of the state *and* tracing their links to economics. The ethnic conflict in Yugoslavia is said to have had its roots in economic dislocations beginning with the 1973 oil shock. The growing internal wealth disparities, including among the different states making up the Yugoslav federation, were themselves the outcome of the growth in national indebtedness and IMF-imposed austerity programmes. This led to new political antagonisms that tore the country apart during the 1990s, including by feeding into long-standing ethnic rivalries (Woodward, 1995; Kaldor, 1999: 37–39). Needless to say, insecurity in society and for individuals increased as a result. In Mexico, the armed uprising of indigenous people in the southern state of Chiapas in Mexico that began in 1994 has been linked to issues over land distribution and the property rights of the indigenous population (Krause and Williams, 1996: 235). Whereas the Constitution previously protected the communal lands held by the indigenous population, the Mexican authorities were obliged to implement a policy of land privatisation under the World Bank's structural adjustment programme, which itself was made a prerequisite for Mexico's accession to the North American Free Trade Area (NAFTA). Closer to home, in East Asia, it is no coincidence that social conflict and violence have broken out in parts of Indonesia, southern Thailand and the southern Philippines, and that these, despite taking on a religious and/or ethnic flavour, are deeply rooted in strong feelings and experiences of economic deprivation.[2]

These cases illustrate the critical importance of governance: first, in terms of how authorities deal with domestic struggles that break out over distributional issues; and second, and more fundamentally, how governance might be constructed in order to reduce such struggles in the first place. To put it another way, do national authorities govern in ways that ensure the economic security of individuals and society? Here, we need to recognise that different societies may well adopt distinct approaches to dealing with domestic insecurities and struggles (Goldfischer, 2002: 702–705). One central question is how privileged or ruling groups struggling to hold power and wealth respond to the distributional fallouts from economic activity.

Where repression may be the approach adopted in one setting, the solution in other contexts may be through more progressive governance mechanisms, including democratic reform, according rights to labour and other marginalised groups and social welfare systems, as well as by instituting credible domestic institutions for internal conflict management.

In this context, it is useful to recognise a historical definition of security, namely as a bond or pledge that provides assurance or safety for its holder in the face of danger (Der Derian, 1995: 28). When viewed in this way, security is clearly part and parcel of the social contract between state and citizens. To put this another way, the social contract may be regarded as a particular form of security practice if it results in significantly decreasing insecurities in society. Attempts to mitigate the domestic social conflicts that arise from economic insecurity by recrafting domestic social contracts have been evident in East Asia of late, illustrated in the chapters on Thailand (Chapter 3) and China (Chapter 4) in this book.

The comprehensive security approach

Does the increasing attention paid to poor and marginalised groups and individuals in East Asia suggest that comprehensive security approaches, which have long prevailed in this region, are giving way to society-centred approaches? In the former, the primary referent of security is the state (Acharya, 2001: 11). More specifically, it is the security of the prevailing regime or political system and survival of the incumbent government and its elite allies that is ultimately paramount (Alagappa, 1998: 624–625). Comprehensive security approaches explicitly link the economy directly to security by emphasising the crucial role of domestic socio-economic development as a means to a materially satisfied citizenry who would then be less vulnerable to internal and external subversion (Leifer, 1989: 3–4). Economic security has therefore long been a key component of security practice in East Asia, helping to legitimate and secure domestic regimes (Stubbs, 2001).

While political leaders may be paying greater attention to addressing the interests, needs and fears of citizens, as a number of the country cases discussed in this volume reveal, it is unclear to what extent this signals a deep normative shift towards human-centred security thinking and practice. The country cases suggest that the growing attention to human-centred approaches to economic security is driven by instrumental concerns with political and regime stability, a finding supported by Caballero-Anthony's discussion on continued resistance by segments of the Southeast Asian governing elite to non-elite calls to broaden understandings of economic security to embrace distributive and human rights concerns.

Although the idea of comprehensive security, especially as practised in Southeast Asia, goes beyond neorealist conceptions of security by acknowledging domestic sources of threats from non-military issue areas, this approach nevertheless reifies the state (or regime) as the main security referent *and* the main provider of security, especially through economic development. An emphasis on economic development does not necessarily mean that insecurities for groups and individuals within society are automatically reduced. State-centric approaches to security can conflict with the interests and security of *people*, especially if the state's agenda for economic development results in environmental degradation, worsens economic vulnerabilities and leads to further marginalisation of those whose needs and interests run counter to the state's conception of the national economic interest. It is in this context that the notion of human security, which emphasises the individual as the primary security referent, becomes increasingly salient.

Human security and economic security: convergent or divergent?

While comprehensive security speaks to the question of *what* threatens the state (or ruling regime), the central question for human security is '*whose* security?' (Acharya, 2001: 11). Having its formal genesis in the 1994 Human Development Report of the United Nations Development Programme (UNDP, 1994), the idea of human security emphasises the individual as the referent of security. The individual is to be made secure from two basic kinds of threats: freedom from fear and freedom from want. In the UNDP definition, human security comprises seven sub-components: economic security, food security, health security, environmental security, personal security, community security and political security. Human security, more precisely, encompasses 'protection from sudden and hurtful disruptions in the patterns of daily life – whether in homes, jobs or in communities' and 'safety from chronic threats such as hunger, disease and repression' (ibid.: 23).

Although economic security is clearly considered one of the means to attain human security in the UNDP approach, some scholars point out that conceptually the two may be contradictory (Leong Liew, 2000). More specifically, economic security for the individual, if we take this to mean security of employment, income and a given level of consumption, could well detract from *collective* economic security for the national community by going against the logic of a market economy and consequently undermining national economic growth prospects. The inverse relationship posited between human and economic security by some scholars depends, however, on the kind of economic model employed to infer these relationships. In the neoclassical view, for instance, the presence of economic insecurity for individuals provides incentives for people to seek work, while individual economic insecurity is a necessary by-product of the 'creative destruction' that is at the heart of the Schumpeterian model of capitalist progress. In both these models, economic security for the national community (in terms of national economic growth) is attained through processes that depend on some degree of economic *insecurity* for the individual (ibid.: 196). By extension, any attempts to ensure economic security for the individual could end up interfering with the very processes that generate growth and progress of the wider economy.

However, IPE and economic sociology offer us a somewhat different reading of the market economy, and, consequently, of the relationship between economic and human security. A central tenet in IPE theorising on the market, which draws on Karl Polanyi, is the idea that markets are embedded in society and require a supporting framework of institutions and laws in order to function effectively and fairly, in contrast to the neoclassical view of a desocialised market order (Polanyi, 1944). Writing from the perspective of economic sociology, Neil Fligstein (2001: 17–23) argues that markets are fundamentally social structures in which market actors seek *stabilisation* as their primary goal. Thus, economic sociology offers a rather different understanding of the market compared to the neoclassical or Schumpeterian models. In the former, market actors aim to promote the survival of their firms, and to this end they search for stable interactions with competitors, suppliers, workers, consumers and governments. Without this wider web of *stable social relations*, firms are unable to get a chance to become efficient producers, make profits *and* survive market competition. The point that economic actors (that is, firms) are dependent on the stability of wider social arrangements to remain competitive and make profits suggests that the relationship between economic security and human security can be mutually reinforcing.

That markets require stable social arrangements in order to function properly does not, however, tell us *how much* stability is necessary. Clearly, there should be some balance between market stability on the one hand, and the disruptions to economic activity that are part and parcel of dynamic change that allow countries to move up the development ladder on the other hand. It is also important that any conception of economic security address the issue of protectionism. For Buzan *et al.* (1998), the danger of the idea of economic security, of securitising the macro-economy, is that firms could end up being made the referent objects of security to be secured even from 'normal' market competition instrumentally posed as an existential threat to economic survival, in effect rationalising protectionism.

We can avoid potential misuse of the concept of economic security and address the question of how much stability is important in markets by taking guidance from the second element of the UNDP definition of human security – of 'protection from *sudden and hurtful disruptions*' in economic life. This involves making a distinction between 'normal' market risks and adverse market outcomes such as the cyclical decline of particular firms and economic sectors on the one hand, and sudden or even sustained economic disruptions that extend across the economy on the other hand that markedly increase uncertainty. In the latter situation, the normal economic adjustment mechanism, whereby rising sectors offset declining sectors, breaks down. Making such a distinction helps to conceptually limit the boundaries of economic security and makes it more difficult for the concept to be used to justify protectionism.

Securing market integrity

While there is certainly a case for seeing economic security and human security as complementary, and thus the individual as a key referent in economic security, it is equally important to ensure that the market itself is secured at the macro level. This is essentially a call to ensure the *integrity* of the market, what Leong Liew (2000: 200) terms 'market institutional security' in the form of secure property rights and contracts. Hernando de Soto (2000) argues persuasively that Western countries succeeded economically because of their superior system of property rights, which gives individuals access to much-needed capital with which to earn an income. De Soto argues that this has been denied to vast segments of the poor in parts of Asia, Africa and Latin America, who have little or no access to land and other economic resources that constitute potential capital resources through which to earn an income. Not only do absent or weak property rights regimes in these countries reinforce economic and social divisions, but also the growth potential of the economy is undermined. Secure property rights are thus vital not only for the broader economy, but for individual economic welfare as well. However, the allocation of property rights is not simply a technical exercise, since property rights can be assigned in ways that are considered unfair or unjust, or that exacerbate ecological damage. It is ultimately a political issue. More than being a case of merely allocating property rights, it is *how* they are assigned that is critical.

Aside from property rights, the development economist Dani Rodrik (2000) identifies four other types of market-supporting institutions that are critical for an effective market economy: regulatory institutions; institutions for macroeconomic stabilisation; institutions for social insurance; and institutions for conflict management. It is this ensemble of institutions working together that provide a high degree of economic security at the macro level. Rather than being something that emerges as an issue during major economic distress, market institutional security should be seen as something more fundamental, as the basic institutions of any market economy enabling individuals and firms to exploit the economic opportunities generated in a capitalist economic system legally and without fear. Moreover, the complementary nature of these institutions is crucial to enhancing the economic security of communities and individuals. Thus, while flexible labour markets help enhance economic competitiveness of the macro-economy, social insurance mechanisms help mitigate the insecurities people face in the cut and thrust of a market economy. Such institutions then become all the more critical to ensure economic security, given the structural context of globalisation, which is said to involve considerable *uncertainty* because there is little or no knowledge about the likelihood of future outcomes, especially in the light of weakly regulated financial markets (Zoellick, 1997/1998; Stiglitz, 2002).

Securing distributive equity

Additional rules that secure some minimal level of distributive equity are equally vital to ensuring the proper functioning of the market mechanism and to support human welfare. These should also be regarded as foundational to economic security, rather than as an issue that arises only in the context of severe economic distress, although the latter can certainly exacerbate social inequalities. Rodrik points out that deep pre-existing social divisions can trigger conflicts in society both when economic crises strike and in response to the adjustment policies adopted to deal with such crises. As a result, the economic costs of external economic shocks are magnified, while economic recovery is delayed (Rodrik, 1998).

The idea that distributive equity is important in securing the market economy comes from a range of sources. Adam Smith, in his *Theory of the Moral Sentiments*, emphasised the importance of equity in society as the minimum quality necessary before the free-market economy, as outlined in *Wealth of Nations*, is able to work as envisaged. Development economists have long pointed to the importance of distribution – to attain some minimal equity in assets and incomes – as key to sustaining growth, and therefore of providing for human welfare (Drèze and Sen, 1987). The growing consensus within the economics profession is that countries with an initial condition of relatively equitable distribution of assets and income tend to grow faster than countries with high initial inequality (Dagdeviren *et al.*, 2002). Moreover, redistributive growth strategies have been shown to be far superior in reducing poverty and inequality compared to the distribution-neutral growth strategies that have been a feature of development policy since the 1990s (MacEwan, 1999: 66–98; Rudra, 2004). Thus, even that most liberal of publications, *The Economist*, has recognised the salience of distributive equity and called for a 'mixed economy' approach to capitalism that includes safety nets, public services *and* moderate redistribution as a way to ensure capitalism's sustainability (Crook, 2001).

Economic security: varied conceptions

The discussion suggests that aside from economic power, which state elites may be intent on securing in the presence of interstate power political competition, there are three additional core economic values that states and communities should aim to secure in a world characterised by globalisation, namely, (a) streams of income and consumption necessary for basic human/family needs; (b) market integrity; and (c) distributive equity. Based on insights from the disciplines of IPE, development economics and economic sociology, these three values constitute an alternative conception of economic security, one that is able to accommodate the realities of global capitalism, and the distributional conflicts and insecurities it may produce within and across states.

In this alternative formulation, economic security clearly encompasses a micro and a macro component.[3] The former, centred on the individual as the referent of security, converges with the notion of human security, with economic security aiming for a secure stream of income for individuals as well as access to a level of consumption that provides for basic human/family needs. The macro component is directed at securing the integrity or robustness of the market to generate growth and welfare in society. This may be achieved by ensuring that the necessary market institutions exist, including a system of secure property rights and contracts that allow *fair* access to individuals to exploit economic opportunities. Economic security is also attained through securing distributive equity, which is now recognised as vital to ensuring the proper functioning of the market mechanism, to support human welfare and to ensure the political sustainability of capitalism. While this alternative conception of economic security speaks to the condition of states and societies beyond the world of interstate rivalry and power politics, this book nonetheless cautions against sacrificing such traditional realist understandings of economic security, which may be extremely salient for some countries at certain points in time. This book's study of Taiwan is instructive in this regard.

The utility of such an open-ended or eclectic approach to conceptualising economic security is supported by the empirical case studies of selected East Asian states in this volume. The different cases studied reveal a range of economic security preoccupations in different countries depending on the stage of development, the nature of domestic state–society relationships, and the external strategic environment. Nevertheless, policymakers in virtually all the cases examined are also paying very close attention to the socio-economic dimension of economic security, including distributive equity in view of the domestic challenges posed by globalisation. What the East Asian experience shows, as discussed in Part II of this volume, is that there is now in train a process of reviewing the relationship between globalisation and economic security. During much of the 1990s, the two were regarded as complementary, with integration into the global economy providing expanded opportunities for growth and wealth creation. The 1997–1998 Asian financial crisis revealed, however, that globalisation and economic security are related in more complex ways than previously experienced, with the *socially* disruptive effects and *political* consequences of enmeshment with the global market becoming increasingly evident.

Globalisation and economic security: the East Asian experience

In examining the link between globalisation and economic security, Miles Kahler in Chapter 2 calls for careful specification of the causal links between transnational economic activity and domestic economic and political outcomes, especially that of violent conflict. While Kahler is correct to call for caution in linking globalisation to insecurity, it is also becoming clear that participation in market activity under conditions of globalisation carries with it both risk and uncertainty, particularly in an age of weakly regulated global financial markets. During the 1997–1998 Asian financial crisis, the sharp and sudden rise in unemployment exacerbated economic disparities within society, widened poverty and deepened social inequality (Lee, 2000: 46). In Indonesia, the crisis led to considerable political violence. Some scholars caution, however, against exaggerating the *political/security* consequences of these developments, arguing that the political shifts and realignments experienced in countries such as Indonesia, South Korea and Thailand were accelerated or exacerbated by the crisis rather than caused by it (Haggard, 2000).

The fact that the financial crisis worsened long-standing ethnic, regional or class animosities in these countries only reinforces the point made in the preceding discussion that getting the governance right in the first instance is crucial to managing countries' insertion in the global economy. Economic security should constitute a central goal of economic governance rather than emerge on the political/policy agenda only when crises strike. Additionally, if globalisation has made it that much more difficult for all states to 'achieve distributive compromises that accommodate and attenuate class, communal and regional conflicts' (Thakur, 1997: 58), then domestic institutions to manage and contain the conflicts that economic integration generates become equally vital (Rodrik, 1997: 8–11). Kahler argues that institutions play a significant role in mediating between globalisation and economic security – that it is *how* globalisation is governed that is crucial in mitigating its adverse consequences. In this regard, the appropriate mix and type of institutions in place – national, regional and global – becomes central to globalisation's impact on economic security. In Chapter 2, Kahler also explores how institutions can offset the economic insecurities associated with globalisation in three ways: (a) by providing insurance; (b) by aiding policy credibility; and (c) by encouraging policy adaptation.

East Asian country responses to economic insecurity

In exploring how policymakers in East Asia have reviewed their understandings of, or approaches to, the question of economic security, this book undertakes six country studies in order to examine how the problem of economic security is posed in cases spanning a range of external and internal conditions. Thus, the book includes (a) studies of two countries directly affected by the Asian financial crisis and with high levels of domestic poverty and inequality (Thailand and Indonesia); (b) studies of two transition economies characterised by communist party political rule (Vietnam and China); and (c) studies of two countries affected by geopolitical/ geostrategic vulnerabilities (Taiwan and Singapore). The studies reveal that countries such as Singapore and Taiwan tend to subscribe to notions of economic security that see the economy as a vital means of empowering the 'vulnerable' state, although the sources of that vulnerability may differ. The transition economies have increasingly framed economic security in both realist/statist and social welfare terms. The end goal, nonetheless, remains to secure the political regime against challenges arising from the social upheavals generated by the transition process. Although Thailand and Indonesia had significant rural populations, had high levels of poverty and inequality, and were recipients of IMF rescue packages, they responded to problems of economic insecurity in different ways. Indonesia, given the near collapse of its economy, its consequent dependence on the IMF and its political turmoil and transformation, was primarily preoccupied with restoring the integrity of the economy and rebuilding domestic institutions. Thailand, with a well-functioning political system on the other hand, emphasised social protection for the poor, but for instrumental reasons, as a means to ensure the survival of domestic capitalists.

Kevin Hewison, writing in Chapter 3, shows how rising social conflict in Thailand due to the 1997–1998 financial crisis brought forth new political forces, which worked to recraft the social contract between Thai state and society by including an explicit commitment to social protection of the poor, a first for the country. Hewison notes, however, that the commitment to social protection was also an instrumental strategy to help domestic capital gain control of the state by building electoral support among Thailand's poor and working classes, which had suffered the most during the crisis. Nevertheless, this move was a departure from the long-standing approach to economic governance in Thailand based on the 'trickle-down' logic of the neoclassical economic model. Unfortunately, the new social contract remains fragile, not least because it depends on a level of spending that may well prove economically unsustainable if domestic capitalism does not become sufficiently productive. Rather than taking this to mean that emphasising social protection is poor economic practice, the Thai case instead reveals the integrated nature of the micro and macro components of economic security identified above.

As with Thailand, similar concerns in China with socio-economic security have prompted the Chinese authorities to rethink the relationship between globalisation and national security, which Wang Zhengyi analyses in Chapter 4. Where once economic growth and national security were viewed as two separate logics, the potentially adverse consequences of economic reform in the context of globalisation prompted a rethinking that now acknowledges a single, inextricably intertwined relationship between economics and security. In China, domestic socio-economic insecurities stem from unemployment and from a range of economic inequalities between the rural and urban sectors, between the coastal and inland areas, and between those working in the formal and informal sectors. These growing insecurities have the potential to undermine social and political stability and the continued legitimacy of the Chinese Communist Party (CCP) through the polarisations they are capable of generating. For the Chinese authorities, then, securing sustainable economic development defined in terms of broad-based economic growth *and* enhancing distributive equity within China in order to reduce economic and social polarisation has become a critical policy task.

The Singapore experience illustrates the critical importance of *domestic* institutions and strong state capacity in helping countries navigate globalisation processes. Despite being a city-state economy highly reliant on the global economy and therefore highly vulnerable to external shocks, Singapore has nevertheless successfully harnessed globalisation in ways that have ensured economic security for its citizens for over three decades. Henry Yeung accounts for this in Chapter 5 in terms of highly adaptive state institutions that were able to strategically harness foreign trade and investment for growth and development by constantly adjusting economic and other policies in ways that retained Singapore's attractiveness to global capital. Even the state's disciplining of labour did not prove too controversial in the light of the economic prosperity delivered as a result to its citizens, which constituted a central element of the government's social contract with citizens and the basis of its political legitimacy. Yeung notes, however, that the intense competitive pressures associated with globalisation have led to wage cuts, the introduction of flexible wages, cutbacks to the pension fund, and retrenchments, thereby raising questions about the sustainability of Singapore's traditional social contract.

The importance of having the right institutions of governance in managing a country's integration with the global economy and in addressing the pressures and risks arising from this integration is further illustrated in Chapter 6. Kurnya Roesad argues that Indonesia's articulation into the global economy during the 1990s was fragile largely because of a lack of effective domestic institutions to manage this process in ways that would secure the growth potential of the economy and check the growing corruption and cronyism. The latter eventually undermined investor sentiments, weakened market institutional integrity and prompted a domestic political backlash when crisis struck. As a result, economic security was severely compromised during the 1997–1998 economic crisis and has yet to recover. Not only was there a near collapse of the economy, but groups and individuals experienced a heightened degree of insecurity, particularly the already poor and marginalised. The crisis forced Indonesia to rely on an external institution, the IMF, to regain its policy credibility, although the IMF itself further undermined economic security through some very ill-conceived crisis adjustment responses. Nonetheless, the presence of the IMF has lent credibility to Indonesian economic governance, thus making economic security dependent on the relationship between the Indonesian government and the IMF.

While Indonesia had recourse to a global institution, the IMF, to help it regain economic security, notwithstanding the problematic aspects of that relationship, Taiwan, equally subject to the pressures, risks and uncertainties of globalisation, is unable to take advantage of either regional or global institutions to offset the declining capacity of the state to defend its economic security interests. As Chyungly Lee writes in Chapter 7, Taiwan's unqiue geostrategic situation makes the traditional notion of economic security extremely important. Sustaining Taiwan's national economic strength is crucial not only to help ensure continued economic growth and, therefore, society's welfare, but also because it is key to Taiwan's external manoeuvrability and will help counter the country's relative political and security weaknesses generated by China's diplomatic moves to isolate Taiwan internationally. However, Taiwan may be unable to rebuild the relative economic strength it once possessed, owing to the loss of its traditional competitive advantage in export production and the growing movement of Taiwanese capital to China. The latter in particular has contributed to a relative decline of Taiwanese economic presence in other parts of East Asia, which could otherwise have helped correct the growing imbalance in Taiwan–China economic relations, which is increasingly in China's favour. Unfortunately, Taiwan continues to be excluded from regional forums such as the ASEAN Plus Three process, which Taiwanese scholars and policymakers believe could help the country to become integrated into the wider East Asian regional economy.

Vietnamese policymakers too have come to emphasise the social welfare aspects of economic security, owing to the still underdeveloped nature of the country. Pham Cao Phong notes in Chapter 8 that considerable attention has been devoted to economic restructuring in order to develop the productive potential of the economy, including through economic integration with other countries, especially through Vietnam's participation in the ASEAN Free Trade Area (AFTA). Nevertheless, there is growing domestic concern that integration is bringing with it a series of challenges to Vietnam's economic security, including an externally imposed economic structure, continued underdevelopment of domestic industrial capacity, and overdependence on external economic actors. All these are viewed as threats to the development of a viable domestic economy that will help underpin social and political stability in the country. However, the still weak capacity of

Vietnamese state institutions reduces the extent to which Vietnamese policymakers are able to control the terms of their country's insertion into the global economy in the way their counterparts in Singapore have done.

Governance beyond the state: multilateral and regional institutions

While these country studies indicate the critical importance of domestic institutions in helping states navigate their encounter with globalisation, they are certainly not the only institutions that matter. In this context, multilateral and regional institutions may have useful roles to play, as is examined in Part III of this volume. In fact, multilateral institutions themselves are part and parcel of the globalisation phenomenon, embodying a set of prescriptions and proscriptions that have implications for how policymakers are able to respond to key economic security concerns.

Richard Higgott points out in Chapter 9 that the multilateral institutions have adopted a mode of governance that is not necessarily supportive of the economic security interests of societies. This is partly due to the United States, which is increasingly exercising its preponderant power through existing multilateral institutions such as the IMF to secure self-serving outcomes. For Higgott, the considerable power disparities in the global economy, which are replicated in the multilateral institutions, are a critical contemporary global governance issue. Without some attempt to mitigate these power disparities, the multilateral institutions and other authority structures in the world political economy may well end up serving the interests of the rich and powerful. In this regard, American interests lead Washington to endorse a form of global governance that is directed primarily at achieving the creation of global market integration as efficiently and as expeditiously as possible. Alternative understandings of global governance that endorse a commitment to other socio-political goals and that allow for departures from the neoliberal orthodoxy tend to be ignored, if not rejected as irrelevant. For critics of the neoliberal orthodoxy, economic security for states and societies has a better chance of being attained under an expanded notion of global governance than the narrower understanding preferred in mainstream US policy circles.

The problem of US hegemony and its implications for regional institution building in East Asia are further explored by Mark Beeson, who points out in Chapter 10 that there is an increasing tendency by the United States, especially since the September 11 attacks, to employ its preponderant power for securing self-serving economic, political and strategic interests. As a result, and given impatience with regional institutions such as the Asia-Pacific Economic Cooperation (APEC) forum, the United States has embarked on a series of bilateral economic agreements with countries in the region to secure its national interests. Bilateralism allows Washington undue bargaining leverage, given the still hegemonic position of the United States in the world economy, with the United States increasingly willing to employ direct political leverage to achieve American security and economic interests that may not always coincide with the interests and welfare of other societies. For Beeson, therefore, it is less the *extent* of American hegemony that is troubling than the *purposes* to which it is put.

The problem of US hegemony was clearly felt in the region when Washington vetoed Japan's initiative for the Asian Monetary Fund. This left member states with little option but to turn to the IMF, since regional intergovernmental institutions such as APEC and ASEAN were limited in their ability to address the regional financial crisis directly. The apparent failure of regional institutions and the problems caused by subscribing to IMF prescriptions created an impetus for regional institutional innovation, particularly for a regional self-help mechanism that could help regional states deal with future crises. Today, this takes the form of the Chiang Mai Initiative (CMI) of the ASEAN Plus Three process. The CMI, which comprises a series of bilateral swap arrangements, is best regarded as an insurance mechanism aimed at helping East Asian states to remain engaged with the global economy by providing a buffer between individual national economies and the vagaries of the global financial system (Kahler, this volume, Chapter 2; Ba, 2005). It helps fill gaps in existing global arrangements to govern global finance.

Aside from this particular institutional innovation, existing regional institutions have thus far not been successful in promoting policy adaptation among their members as a way of increasing their economic security, a point that Kahler emphasises in Chapter 2. This may not be too surprising, since the institutional inertia that tends to characterise formal, intergovernmental institutions makes it difficult for them to consider new ways of addressing problems, or even to identify new problem areas in the first place. In Chapter 11, Charles Morrison suggests that this role in providing the ideational drivers of change may be usefully undertaken by the 'Track 2' mechanisms that have long operated in the region, especially on a Pacific-wide basis. For Morrison, Track 2 processes involving policy networks of research institutes or individuals complement intergovernmental regional processes (Track 1) in a number of ways, particularly as a source of innovation and new ideas that may be difficult to achieve through national or regional bureaucracies. In this way, Track 1–Track 2 interactions helped policymakers find ways to respond to the 1997–1998 Asian financial crisis. However, since regional Track 2 networks are essentially elite networks sharing values and goals similar to those of the formal networks, they continue to champion ideas that draw on mainstream economic models rather than offer alternative approaches to the problems of globalisation.

Track 3 networks, involving non-governmental, non-elite groups, are more likely to promote alternative approaches and agendas, while they are also likely to differ from governments on the *objectives* of governance. Part of this stems from their championing of special constituencies, be they women's groups, environmental issues or human rights groups, which are often neglected in mainstream governance agendas. In Chapter 12, Mely Caballero-Anthony documents the emergence of a Track 3 network in Southeast Asia in the form of the ASEAN People's Assembly (APA). The APA champions approaches to economic security that challenge mainstream neoclassical approaches to economic governance that the Track 1 and Track 2 mechanisms tend to endorse. The civil society groups within this network have challenged the embrace of market governance and the neglect of issues such as distributive equity, justice and fairness. Caballero-Anthony's analysis also highlights the political struggles that accompanied the emergence of the APA, arising from its endorsement of a human-centred approach to economic security that challenged prevailing elite agendas on these matters, particularly the preoccupation of regional policymakers with rapid and high rates of economic growth, state-centric notions of security, and authoritarian approaches to domestic political governance.

The tensions involved in alternative conceptions of economic security, particularly of human-centred approaches, are further explored in the book's final chapter, on the regional politics of human security agendas. In evaluating Japan's contribution to economic security, Hiro Katsumata suggests that Japan may be caught between its two identities – as a member of the community of industrial nations embracing democracy, human rights and individual liberty on the one hand, and as a member of the East Asian region, where the commitment to such liberal political norms is more qualified. As a result, despite being a strong advocate of human security in the global arena, Tokyo has chosen to be pragmatic and has focused on the developmental aspects of human security while downplaying the human rights or 'freedom from fear' dimension. This was to avoid upsetting regional governments that find the concept of human security problematic. Nevertheless, Katsumata notes that Japan has still been able to contribute to economic security in the region by using its official development assistance to support development projects. Moreover, Japan's participation in the Chiang Mai Initiative renders this arrangement more credible as an insurance mechanism in the event of future financial crises. In that respect, Japan, far more than the United States is perceived as having contributed positively to regional economic security.

Conclusion

This chapter offers an alternative conception of economic security, defined as ensuring a low probability of damage to a set of three key economic values: (a) streams of income and consumption necessary for minimal human/family needs; (b) market integrity; and (c) distributive equity. While this alternative understanding of economic security speaks to a wider range of experiences and concerns beyond the world of interstate rivalry and competition, the book does not reject neorealist-based frameworks that emphasise the securing of national economic power. Instead, following Kolodziej (1992), this book advocates an open-ended or eclectic approach to conceptualising economic security, a methodological stand that acknowledges that a range of understandings, concerns and responses to the problem of economic security exist, depending on the historical, political and social contexts of states and their societies as well as the strategic environment in which they find themselves. The East Asian experience studied in this volume attests to the utility of such an approach.

The different chapters in this volume reveal that while economic insecurity has become a major preoccupation of East Asian states, especially since the financial crisis, governments have adopted distinct approaches to enhancing economic security for their respective societies. Moreover, while the problem of economic security in much of the region has largely been posed as one of ensuring sustainable economic growth *and* equitable social development, other, more realist conceptions of economic security have not become irrelevant. Taiwan is a case in point, revealing how economic and national security are closely intertwined, owing to the geostrategic realities of the China–Taiwan stand-off. While the growing concern in many states over equity and social welfare is to be welcomed, the attention paid to such issues also helps to secure governing regimes. Human-centred norms and approaches to [economic] security have yet to take root uniformly across East Asia. The studies also show that the diverse responses in East Asia to the problem of economic (in)security under conditions of globalisation are mediated by a country's particular stage of development, the nature of domestic state–society relations and the external strategic condition facing that country.

Two further areas of research remain to be explored. The first is the impact of political regime type on how economic security is perceived and the responses to it. The country studies in this volume suggest tentatively that there is no simple correlation between, on the one hand, broader approaches to economic security that encompass equity and social welfare notions, and, on the other, the nature of political systems, whether authoritarian, semi-democratic or democratic. For instance, democratic Thailand and authoritarian China have both embraced broader notions of economic security, and both for instrumental purposes. It is not possible, however, to draw generalisable conclusions on this question from these studies. This book's primary focus is to discuss alternative conceptions of economic security beyond neorealist frameworks, to examine how policymakers and other communities pose and respond to the problem of economic security, and the role of national, multilateral and non-state institutions in governing in the interests of economic security. This question about political dynamics is, however, an important one, and offers scope for further research.

A related issue, and one that similarly merits additional research, is the extent to which social welfare reform, adopted in parts of East Asia, is being accompanied by commitment to progressive governance mechanisms, including democratic reform, according rights to labour and other marginalised groups, and building credible institutions for internal conflict management such as judiciaries or other forms of arbitration. Adoption of the full range of such institutions is likely to indicate a stronger normative commitment to broader, human-centred notions of economic security. At present, the case studies suggest an instrumental use of social welfare policies to minimise the domestic political fallout from rising economic insecurities. How the ongoing political and economic shifts in East Asia will affect the approaches taken to enhance economic security remains a rich area for further study.

Notes

1   See www.whitehouse.gov/econ/.
2   Studies of these conflicts are documented in Higgott and Nesadurai (2002).

3 Leong Liew (2000: 193) also argues that economic security may be considered at the micro and macro levels, with the micro level encompassing both the human security and the market institutional integrity components while the macro component refers to the economic security of the state achieved through judicious use of trade and foreign policies in securing collective welfare for citizens. In this chapter, I categorise the institutional integrity of the market as a macro feature, as it allows individual welfare to be attained by guaranteeing economic opportunities for the overall economy. I also incorporate distributive equity as a key dimension of the macro component of economic security.

References

Acharya, Amitav (2001) 'Human Security: East versus West?', *IDSS Working Paper*, no. 17, Singapore: Institute of Defence and Strategic Studies.

Alagappa, Muthiah (1998) 'Asian Practice of Security: Key Features and Explanations', in Muthiah Alagappa (ed.) *Asian Security Practice: Material and Ideational Influences*, Stanford, CA: Stanford University Press, pp. 611–676.

Ba, Alice (2005) 'Contested Spaces: The Politics of Regional and Global Governance in Southeast Asia', in Matthew J. Hoffman and Alice D. Ba (eds) *Coherence and Contestation: Contending Perspective in Global Governance*, London and New York: Routledge, forthcoming.

Baldwin, David A. (1997) 'The Concept of Security', *Review of International Studies*, 23: 5–26.

Buzan, Barry, Waever, Ole and de Wilde, Jaap (1998) *Security: A New Framework for Analysis*, Boulder, CO: Lynne Rienner.

Cox, Robert (1999) 'Civil Society at the Turn of the Millennium: Prospects for an Alternative World Order', *Review of International Studies*, 25 (1): 3–28.

Crane, George and Amawi, Abla (1997) *The Theoretical Evolution of International Political Economy: A Reader*, 2nd edn, New York and Oxford: Oxford University Press.

Crook, Clive (2001) 'Globalisation and Its Critics: A Survey of Globalisation', *The Economist*, 29 September.

Dagdeviren, Hugo, van der Hoeven, Rolph and Weeks, John (2002) 'Redistribution Does Matter: Growth and Redistribution for Poverty Reduction', *UNU/WIDER Discussion Paper*, No. 2002/25, World Institute for Development Economics Research.

De Soto, Hernando (2000) *The Mystery of Capital*, London: Black Swan.

Der Derian, James (1995) 'The Value of Security: Hobbes, Marx, Nietzsche and Baudrillard', in Ronnie D. Lipschutz (ed.) *On Security*, New York: Columbia University Press, pp. 24–45.

Drèze, Jean and Sen, Amartya (1987) *Hunger and Public Action*, Oxford: Clarendon Press.

Fierke, Karin (2002) 'Meaning, Method and Practice: Assessing the Changing Security Agenda', in Stephanie Lawson (ed.) *The New Agenda for International Relations*, Cambridge: Polity Press, pp. 128–144.

Fligstein, Neil (2001) *The Architecture of Markets: An Economic Sociology of Twenty-first Century-Capitalist Societies*, Princeton, NJ: Princeton University Press.

Goldfischer, David (2002) 'E. H. Carr: A Historical Realist Approach for the Globalisation Era', *Review of International Studies*, 28: 697–717.

Haggard, Stephan (2000) *The Political Economy of the Asian Financial Crisis*, Washington, DC: Institute for International Economics.

Held, David and McGrew, Anthony (2002) 'Introduction', in David Held and Anthony McGrew (eds) *Governing Globalisation: Power, Authority and Global Governance*, Cambridge: Polity Press, pp. 1–21.

Higgott, Richard and Nesadurai, Helen E. S. (2002) 'Rethinking the Southeast Asian Development Model: Bringing Ethical and Governance Questions In', *ASEAN Economic Bulletin*, 19 (1): 27–39.

Huntington, Samuel (1993) 'Why International Primacy Matters', *International Security*, 17 (4): 68–83.

Kaldor, Mary (1999) *New and Old Wars: Organised Violence in a Global Era*, Stanford, CA: Stanford University Press.

Kolodziej, Edward A. (1992) 'Renaissance in Security Studies? Caveat Lector!', *International Studies Quarterly*, 36 (4): 421–438.

Krause, Keith and Williams, Michael C. (1996) 'Broadening the Agenda of Security Studies: Politics and Methods', *International Studies Quarterly*, 40 (2): 229–254.

Lee, Chyungly (2000) 'The Asian Turbulence: A Case Study in Economic Security', in Chyungly Lee (ed.) *Asia–Europe Cooperation after the 1997–98 Asian Turbulence*, Aldershot, UK: Ashgate, pp. 33–54.

Leifer, Michael (1989) *ASEAN and the Security of South-East Asia*, London: Routledge.

Leong Liew (2000) 'Human and Economic Security: Is There a Nexus?', in William T. Tow, Ramesh Thakur and In-Taek Hyun (eds) *Asia's Emerging Regional Order: Reconciling Traditional and Human Security*, Tokyo: United Nations University Press, pp. 192–208.

Luttwak, Edward (1990) 'From Geo-politics to Geo-economics', *The National Interest*, Summer: 17–23.

MacEwan, Arthur (1999) *Neo-liberalism or Democracy: Economic Strategy, Markets and Alternatives for the 21st Century*, London: Zed Books.

Moran, Theodore (1993) 'An Economics Agenda for Neo-realists', *International Security*, 18 (2): 211–215.

Polanyi, K. (1944) *The Great Transformation*, Boston, MA: Beacon.

Rodrik, Dani (1997) *Globalisation, Social Conflict and Economic Growth*, from the webpage of Dani Rodrik [Online] http://ksghome.harvard.edu/~.drodrik.academic.ksg/papers.html.

—— (1998) 'Where did all the growth go? External conflict, social conflict and growth collapses', from the webpage of Dani Rodrik (http://ksghome.harvard.edu/~.drodrik.academic.ksg/papers.html).

—— (2000) 'Development Strategies for the Next Century' from the webpage of Dani Rodrik (http://ksghome.harvard.edu/~.drodrik.academic.ksg/papers.html).

Rudra, Nita (2004) 'Openness, Welfare Spending and Inequality in the Developing World', *International Studies Quarterly*, 48 (3): 683–709.

Scholte, Jan Aart (2000) *Globalisation: A Critical Introduction*, New York: St Martin's Press.

Stiglitz, Joseph (2002) *Globalisation and Its Discontents*, London: Allen Lane (Penguin Books).

Stubbs, Richard (2001) 'Performance Legitimacy and "Soft Authoritarianism"', in Amitav Acharya, B. Michael Frolic and Richard Stubbs (eds) *Democracy, Human Rights and Civil Society in Southeast Asia*, Toronto: Joint Centre for Asia Pacific Studies, York University, pp. 37–54.

Thakur, Ramesh (1997) 'From National to Human Security', in Stuart Harris and Andrew Mack (eds) *Asia-Pacific Security: The Economics–Politics Nexus*, St Leonards, New South Wales: Allen & Unwin, pp. 52–80.

Tickner, J. Ann (1995) 'Re-visioning Security', in Ken Booth and Steve Smith (eds) *International Relations Theory Today*, University Park, PA: Pennsylvania State University Press, pp. 175–197.

UNDP (1994) *Human Development Report*, New York: United Nations Development Programme.

Walt, Stephen M. (1991) 'The Renaissance of Security Studies', *International Studies Quarterly*, 35 (2): 211–239.

Woodward, Susan (1995) *Balkan Tragedy: Chaos and Dissolution after the Cold War*, Washington, DC: Brookings Institution.

Zoellick, Robert C. (1997/1998) 'Economics and Security in the Changing Asia-Pacific', *Survival*, 39 (4): 29–51.

2 Economic security in an era of globalization

Definition and provision

Miles Kahler

Economic security has preoccupied national governments, in Asia and elsewhere, when economic shocks have been so unexpected and severe that existing social and political arrangements appear threatened. Contemporary globalization – economic integration at the global level that is no longer limited to the industrialized countries – accelerated during the 1980s, as programs of economic liberalization spread throughout the developing world. A sharp increase in capital flows to developing countries in the early 1990s reinforced positive views of globalization. That sunny perspective did not last the decade, however, as successive financial crises affected first Mexico, then East and Southeast Asia, Russia, and Argentina. Financial crises were succeeded in the new century by the international effects of an end to the US high-technology boom and its accompanying stock market bubble, the shock of 9/11 and the insecurity that followed (culminating in the Iraq war), and a US administration that appeared little interested in collaboration to mitigate the effects of globalization on smaller, more open economies.

The recent vicissitudes of societies in an increasingly integrated global economy have spurred renewed interest in economic security and forced its redefinition. This revised definition in turn has encouraged a search for policy prescriptions that will increase economic security in the new environment. Globalization, after undermining the old definition of economic security, is found at the center of a new definition that emphasizes the risks of unexpected shocks and economic volatility. The new definition must capture the causal consequences of globalization accurately and establish explicit benchmarks for assessing globalization's effects on economic security. The design of national, regional, and global institutions can then be evaluated in light of three available instruments for enhancing economic security: insurance, credibility, and adaptation.

Economic security is not a new concern of governments. Economic instruments have long been part of the toolkit of statecraft, a means to influence other states and their policies (Hirschman, 1980; Baldwin, 1985). Economic security in this traditional view was security from manipulation by other governments that wielded these instruments. Insecurity was vulnerability to other states. Economic inter-dependence was viewed with wariness, particularly among developing countries, because it risked an increase in such vulnerability. Industrialized countries gradually overcame their anxieties over economic vulnerability after 1945, a striking development given the past rivalries of these countries and their historic use of economic leverage against one another. Even more remarkable, given the speed of the transformation, was the economic opening of many developing economies after 1980. A complete accounting for that dramatic shift remains to be written; no simple explanation seems adequate for such a global shift to economic liberalization.[1] The Asia-Pacific economies joined this change in orientation toward the risks of economic vulnerability, a shift all the more striking for those (Taiwan, South Korea) that confronted threatening security environments.

Although this decline in concern over economic vulnerability had domestic political and economic sources, security calculations also promoted economic opening. That calculus still underpins support for globalization. Three considerations were of particular significance. First, governments, even those most wedded to a conventional view of international politics dominated by military force, saw positive gains to their national economic and technological base, and ultimately to their military power, through links to the global economy. Changes in military technology had opened an era of spin-on from the civilian economy rather than spin-off from the military sector. Those that rejected expanded international economic exchange risked conventional military inferiority.

Globalization had a second and more direct effect: reduction in vulnerability through diversification of suppliers and markets. The application of economic leverage and sanctions unilaterally became more difficult, even when the initiator, the United States, was the largest economy in the world. Although the United States has failed to give up its infatuation with economic sanctions, their effectiveness has declined in the absence of multilateral support, mirroring a decline in economic vulnerability on the part of other states. In addition, economic liberalization has meant that all governments have given up some of their leverage over private economic agents, reducing the effectiveness of economic instruments in their statecraft.

Finally, some of the states in the Asia-Pacific region began to accept that economic interdependence and integration might be promoted because of its positive security effects. Few states in the region endorsed the classical liberal view that growing economic integration would necessarily produce peaceful international outcomes. Nevertheless, several of the smaller and more economically dynamic countries in the region – South Korea, Taiwan, and Singapore – adopted strategies that deployed economic interdependence to advance their security goals in relation to larger or militarily threatening neighbors. At first, their strategies pointed toward explicit linkage, in which economic benefits were part of bargains to produce specific diplomatic outcomes. South Korea's *Nordpolitik* with the Soviet Union and then China was one successful example of such an exploitation of growing economic ties. As their neighbors also opened to the world economy, however, the ability to impose linkage declined and in some cases, such as those of Taiwan and China, could be reversed.

Economic interdependence could still provide security benefits, however. Domestic political constituencies that benefit from increased trade and investment might serve as a check on political elites that could disrupt those links by the use or threat of military force. In the longer run, economic integration could also aim at more profound regime transformation, inducing elites that endorsed a militarized view of security to accept a redefinition that produced a broader and less threatening assessment of national security. Kim Dae Jung's sunshine policy toward North Korea was based in part on such a long-run view of the effects of economic interdependence (Kahler and Kastner, 2004).

Anxiety over economic vulnerability to other states in the region – the traditional view of economic security – has declined over the past two decades, in part because of advancing economic integration. Even in the case of energy, a sector that had lain at the heart of traditional concepts of economic security, globalization and the growth in international markets began to undermine the old strategies. As Robert Manning has pointed out, despite national policies driven by concern over dependence and external manipulation, 'energy has the capacity to become an integrative force, creating a larger sense of shared interests and stake in cooperation' through market forces (2000: 202–203). Even when governments acted to reduce perceived vulnerability, as China appeared to do, their maneuvers could have only a limited effect on either the global oil market or the satisfaction of their country's own energy needs (Downs, 2000: 53–54).

Economic security redefined: the (perceived) perils of globalization

If globalization contributed to the erosion of an older definition of economic security, it also fostered a redefined concern over economic threats to national well-being. Recurrent financial crises during the 1990s struck emerging markets in Asia and elsewhere with particular force, to the surprise of both national elites and many financial market observers. These powerful shocks reinforced a more pessimistic view of a globalized world: economic openness might produce more economic insecurity. Renewed attention to the negative effects of globalization was reinforced by additional economic shocks that flowed from the terrorist attacks of 11 September 2001 and the Severe Acute Respiratory Syndrome (SARS) epidemic of 2003. The new century had dawned, it seemed, on an international landscape of diminished economic opportunity and heightened threat.

This swing from exaggerated optimism over the benefits of globalization to a more pessimistic assessment of insecurity in a globalized world was to be expected. Renewed economic insecurity, however, was not centered primarily on the threat of economic manipulation by rival states, as older anxieties had been. Instead, the new assessment linked globalization to economic security in two ways. Both emphasize the importance of nonstate actors and the new economic environment that they have created and exploited. Rather than concentrating solely on the vulnerability of states, both stress the vulnerability of individuals, groups, and societies as well as the internal political consequences of that vulnerability. Rather than external manipulation by other states, the undermining of state authority by nonstate networks and economic shocks is central.

The first of these connections between globalization and security was noted in the 1990s, but only became pressing in the wake of the terrorist attacks of 11 September 2001. Globalization had been defined by legitimate economic exchange (trade, investment, migration) and enabled by liberalizing policies. Now a harsh light was shed on the permissive role of globalization in the growth of illicit cross-border exchange. Globalization had led governments to emphasize the opening of borders; sorting desirable from undesirable cross-border exchange and movement had not been a priority. Those malign transactions and movements, parasitic on legitimate ones, encompassed the transport of illegal substances such as drugs and contraband, criminal and terrorist networks, illegal migration, environmentally damaging exotic species, and cross-border movement of pathogens, such as the SARS virus.

Negative cross-border effects associated with economic globalization can be labeled new security issues in their own right. They also have second-order effects on economic security. First, in response to these security threats, governments may reach for countermeasures that are economically damaging. In their efforts to sort good from bad cross-border flows, legitimate economic exchange may be taxed too heavily or even stifled in an effort to shut off threatening intrusions. The initial reactions of the United States to the 9/11 attacks suggest the possible costs of sharply reducing cross-border movement of people. For example, universities and colleges in the United States have voiced alarm over the threat posed by newly implemented security measures to the free flow of research and to the movement of students and scholars who conduct that research (Gates, 2003).

Second, these new sources of insecurity may themselves produce economic shocks, magnified through globalized communications and transportation networks and by the growth of sectors that are highly sensitive to such shocks. Air transport and tourism were both severely disrupted by the September 11 attacks, subsequent terrorist attacks in Southeast Asia, and the SARS epidemic. Agricultural exports have been sharply affected by even the rumor of disease that might affect livestock or plants: global communication networks far outstrip in their speed any collective ability to verify and respond to the outbreak.

Finally, economic insecurity in other societies may also reinforce or encourage illicit economic exchange that then produces further insecurity through avenues that have been widened by globalization. For example, in countries such as Indonesia, deep recession during the Asian financial crisis spurred entry into illegal exchange by those whose employment in the legal economy had disappeared.

Increased sensitivity of societies to illicit cross-border activity is only one of the sources of insecurity attributed to globalization. Even more prominent is added economic *volatility* that societies face as a result of external shocks. Critics of globalization, such as Dani Rodrik, argue that external openness has increased economic risk overall for developing countries, rather than offsetting domestic sources of economic risk through diversification and the spreading of shocks over a larger market (Rodrik, 1997: 55–57). International economic shocks associated with financial integration had occurred in earlier eras of globalization, but the expectations placed in governments by their societies were limited (Eichengreen and Fishlow, 1998). Perhaps the most severe economic shocks suffered by the developing countries – especially the poorest ones – have been declining terms of trade for their natural resource exports, an outcome unrelated to the latest wave of financial globalization.

For the industrializing economies of Asia, however, export-oriented manufacturing was meant to reduce vulnerability to external economic shocks by reducing dependence on exports of natural resource and agricultural products. What was not recognized during the golden years of export-oriented industrialization was vulnerability to financial shocks that could be associated with financial liberalization and the growth of global financial markets. In contrast to Latin America, the debt crisis of the 1980s had affected only a few economies in Asia. South Korea and the Philippines were forced to undertake adjustment programs when that earlier cycle of bank lending came to an abrupt halt. South Korea's rapid return to economic growth, however, stood in contrast to the plight of Latin American economies with weaker export sectors. Latin America's 'lost decade' seemed to reinforce the lesson that flexible, export-oriented, and diversified economies could surmount such financial shocks at relatively low cost. For a region certain of its economic invincibility, the Asian financial crisis of 1997–1998 brought home the hazards of a new international economic environment.[2] Economic vulnerability to other governments no longer loomed large among security threats. Even the new transnational security threats that accompanied more open borders paled in significance when compared to the risks brought home by the crisis. Instead, a new vulnerability to international markets and an awareness of the economic and political volatility imported through those markets became central to a redefinition of economic security.

Debate over the origins of the Asian financial crisis continues: the relative weight to be assigned to the actions of national governments, international market players, such as hedge funds, and international financial institutions (IFIs) remains a source of contention.[3] In evaluating the causal connection between globalization, particularly financial globalization, and economic insecurity, the record of the crisis and its outcomes merit careful assessment. The economic costs imposed by the crisis on the four most seriously affected Asian economies – Thailand, Malaysia, Indonesia, and South Korea – were large. Asset deflation was remarkable by any historical standard. Like the Mexican peso crisis that had preceded it, the Asian financial crisis produced sharp and painful recessions in these economies, followed, in all cases but that of Indonesia, by a relatively rapid recovery. Economic rebound was quickly complicated by a succession of events that also exacerbated economic insecurity: sharp decline in the US stock market, an end to the technology sector boom, a shallow US recession, the terrorist attacks of September 2001, and the SARS epidemic.

The effects of the financial crisis on other Asian economies were much less severe, despite regional contagion and globalized financial markets. Japan and China each faced their own internally induced financial crises, but the regional crisis had little effect on their overall economic performance. Australia, like China, transited the crisis with few ill effects on its economy, shielded by a policy mix that included a flexible exchange rate.

A regional financial crisis produced distinct national economic outcomes. The financial markets that had transmitted economic turmoil also served as a partial solution to the crisis. The diversified financial markets of the late 1990s and the first years of the new century were more forgiving of policy missteps than lenders had been in the less globalized financial markets of the early 1980s. Latin America had taken nearly an entire 'lost decade' to regain access to financial markets as its debt crisis persisted. The affected economies in Asia were able, after policy adjustments, to reenter global financial markets in the wake of the crisis, lowering their long-run economic costs. Foreign direct investment flows to the region continued throughout the crisis, marked by an increasing concentration on China.

The record of the Asian financial crisis suggests that the relationship between economic globalization and financial crisis is complex, dependent on national characteristics and policies as well as regional contagion effects. If one ventures beyond financial crisis to other economic and political outcomes that affect economic security, causal connections to globalization must be assessed even more carefully. Globalization has been linked to economic insecurity through its effects on economic inequality and the marginalization of some developing economies. Recent evaluations of those claims suggest that globalization appears to worsen international inequality when countries are taken as the unit of analysis (what might be called the sub-Saharan Africa effect). When individuals are taken as the unit of analysis, globalization appears to have more positive effects on global inequality (the China–India effect) (Bhatta, 2002; Fischer, 2003). Even when one is using countries as the unit of analysis, the question for many of the poor developing countries that have fared badly over the past two decades is why they have been marginalized and unable to participate in a globalized world economy. Part of the answer to that question lies in institutions – economic and political – that connect international and national economies.

The effects of globalization on political stability are also closely related to economic security through political institutions that provide a stable environment for economic growth. Economic volatility may undermine those institutions and the political basis for their effectiveness. Critics of globalization have pointed to the case of Indonesia, where the political effects of financial globalization and the Asian financial crisis appeared to be particularly severe: the collapse of the Suharto regime following policy changes enacted under external pressure.

Even limiting analysis to the most dramatic consequences of globalization – the risk of financial crises – its effects on domestic political development have often been overstated. Stephan Haggard's account (2000) of the Asian crisis and its political effects notes political trends and structural faults that may have been accelerated or exacerbated by the economic crisis; few were not caused by it, however. Constitutional revision in Thailand was affected by the crisis, but such revision had been broached well before its onset. South Korea confronted the crisis at a time of delicate political transition during the election and inauguration of Kim Dae Jung as president. Yet Korea surmounted the crisis rapidly and without damage to its political institutions. South Korea and Thailand demonstrate what Haggard calls 'the resilience of the democracies,' although these two cases also demonstrate that economic management varies across democracies. Even Indonesia, where a succession crisis loomed throughout the 1990s, managed its democratic transition under the worst possible economic circumstances without a political breakdown or civil war. Political violence increased in Malaysia and Indonesia during the crisis, but the relationship of that violence to the economic crisis (when compared to authoritarian regimes that had overstayed their welcome and long-standing separatist pressures) is not clear.

These examples from the Asian economic crisis – taken as a major case of economic volatility imposed by financial globalization – suggest that the causal links between globalization and domestic economic and political outcomes must be specified precisely. Other economic variables, such as industrialization or the introduction of market reforms, may be more disruptive than the effects of external economic opening and integration with the global economy. When certain domestic policy initiatives or poorly designed institutions, such as haphazard financial deregulation, are combined with economic opening, the effects of external shocks may be magnified. Institutional design at the national level is often the critical connection between positive and negative effects of globalization on economic security.

Careful assessment of competing explanations for observed outcomes must be coupled with an explicit recognition of the benchmark against which those outcomes are compared. Critics of the insecurity imposed by globalization on societies too often posit an implicit benchmark of no change at all. In other words, 'security' is expanded to mean the avoidance of any uncomfortable or politically risky change. The opponents of economic opening to the global market often deploy economic security in this overly expansive sense. Food security, for example, has been a powerful argument advanced for agricultural protection. Alternative strategies for ensuring adequate supplies of food from both domestic and international markets are set aside as economic security once again approaches its old sense of autarky.

Instead of treating economic security as a synonym for the status quo – a status quo that may hold instability in its future and certainly implies continuing economic change – judgments about economic security must weigh the effects of increased volatility (assuming that they cannot be reduced) introduced by globalization against the benefits of increased economic performance over time. The alternative to volatility may not be a smooth and equitably distributed pattern of economic growth, but rather an outcome embodied in its extreme form by North Korea or Myanmar: low volatility coupled with economic stagnation or decline. Rather than assuming that externally induced economic volatility or disturbance is necessarily to be avoided, a more appropriate – and difficult – calculation is determining each society's tolerance of such economic risks in light of future economic gain.

Political benchmarks for the calibration of economic security are even more difficult to determine. Estimating a 'politically sustainable' level of economic openness requires a definition of one's political vantage point – who will bear political costs – and, once again, the level and direction of political change. During successive financial crises in Latin America and during the Asian economic crisis of the late 1990s, an often-predicted backlash against globalization did not emerge as a full-fledged political movement. Indeed, as Haggard (2000) recounts, political opposition during the economic crisis often aligned itself, tacitly or explicitly, in favor of economic reforms proposed by the IFIs and other international actors. Such programs of reform were directed against collusive bargains between government and business that were associated with the onset of the crisis. Overall, publics have been willing to accept some of the costs associated with globalization, unless political paralysis (Indonesia, Argentina) or radical economic inequality and poverty (Venezuela) make those costs seem both interminable and inequitable.

Both the causal relationship between economic globalization and economic insecurity and the benchmarks for measuring that insecurity are closely associated with international and domestic institutions that intermediate between societies and the international economy. Domestic institutions may enhance the economic benefits of international opening and either magnify or reduce the effects of international economic shocks. International institutions, such as the International Monetary Fund (IMF) and World Bank, have been criticized for a prominent and single-minded attachment to international economic integration that omits attention to economic security. Regional institutions, on the other hand, were sharply criticized in the wake of the Asian financial crisis for their ineffectiveness. As globalization is examined with a new eye to its effects on national economic security, both the appropriate type and the mix – national, regional, global – of institutions become central to the provision of economic security under conditions of globalization.

Institutions and the provision of economic security under conditions of globalization

Globalization has produced new definitions of economic security centered on two types of unwanted transmissions across national borders: illicit flows that are more difficult to control and easier to disguise as legitimate economic transactions increase (terrorism, crime, pollution); and economic (largely financial) shocks that can undermine economic growth, increase inequality, and threaten political stability. Countering the first type of transmission involves identification, monitoring, and control at the national level, coupled with collaboration at the regional and global levels. Illicit flows often embody security threats independent of their effects on economic security. Economic security is reduced when countermeasures taken against these threats impose costs on legitimate economic exchange and reduce the levels of legitimate trade and investment.

More difficult to calculate and manage are the costs and risks associated with fluctuations in usually benign cross-border flows of goods, capital, and labor. It is this second dimension of economic insecurity that has drawn the most attention from policymakers. Institutions can offset the economic insecurity associated with globalization in three ways: providing *insurance*, adding to policy *credibility*, and encouraging *adaptation*. In the past, Asian governments managed their links to the international economy through institutions with high credibility: adopting a strategy of incremental economic liberalization and pragmatic economic policies, avoiding wide swings in policy that were more characteristic of Latin America. Policy credibility benefited both internal and external economic agents and encouraged a beneficial cycle of rapid economic growth. Credible economic policies adopted by national governments also reduced the need to borrow credibility from regional or global institutions, one reason that regional economic institutions in Asia were relatively weak.

Unfortunately, economic success encouraged institutional overreliance on credibility. As economic opening proceeded, both insurance and policy adaptation were undersupplied. Insurance against economic insecurity at the individual level in most Asian societies was left to individuals and families or, more broadly, to rapid economic growth and high individual savings rates. For national economies, insurance against economic shocks seemed unnecessary in a region that avoided high levels of external debt, maintained realistic exchange rates, and exercised fiscal prudence. Even when external shocks interrupted economic growth, as the 1982–1983 debt crisis did in South Korea, export-oriented industrial structures permitted rapid adjustment. Economic success during these decades of global economic liberalization bred confidence in existing institutions, and little adaptation of the engines of high-speed growth ensued. Regional and global institutions did not argue with success, generally endorsing the policies and institutions that seemed to produce unparalleled economic performance.

Financial crisis struck the region with particular severity in the late 1990s as policy credibility, the main pillar of economic security, temporarily wavered and, in cases such as that of Indonesia, crumbled. Democratizing societies such as Thailand and South Korea had not foreseen the effects of political opening on this critical contributor to their economic security. New institutions to add credibility in a democratic setting had not been put in place. Regional institutions such as the Association of Southeast Asian Nations (ASEAN) and Asia-Pacific Economic Cooperation (APEC) were unable to supply either insurance (in the form of financial support) against heightened economic risk, credibility, or pressure for policy adaptation (Cheng, 1998; Acharya, 1999). The crisis opened a new debate on the adequacy of institutions – national, regional, global – and their contribution to economic security.

National institutions will remain essential providers of economic security to their citizens under conditions of globalization. Globalization has not led to obsolescence or 'hollowing out' of national governance in favor of supranational institutions (Kahler and Lake, 2003). In order to provide economic security in the new environment, however, national institutions must evolve. As remarked earlier, the optimal design of such institutions is high on the international development agenda. Institutional links to the international economy are of central importance in determining globalization's negative and positive effects on economic growth and economic security.[4]

Three conclusions of particular importance for economic security follow from the links among globalization, economic growth, and national institutions. First, despite one view of market reforms that emerged in the 1980s (echoed later by the opponents of globalization), external economic liberalization does not imply an overall reduction in the functions of national governments or a shrinking of the public sector. As Peter Katzenstein (1985) and David Cameron (1978) pointed out in the case of Europe, small, open economies have cohabited with well-developed welfare states and large public sectors.[5] The insurance functions of national governments may increase under conditions of increasing economic openness.

Second, the institutional balance struck between policy credibility and adaptation to the global economy may change with democratization. Andrew MacIntyre (2003) has compared the supply of credible policy commitments and what he labels policy decisiveness during the Asian economic crisis. He emphasizes dispersal of decision-making power as a key institutional variable, one that is likely to increase with democratization. Democratization also changes each of the three instruments for provision of economic security. Individual and group demands for insurance are likely to increase. Policy credibility will require the invention or reinvention of institutions, such as central banks and regulatory bodies, with adequate delegated powers and broad accountability to the new electorate. Institutional and policy adaptation becomes more complicated under conditions of democratic account-ability. Institutional transparency is likely to increase with the transition from authoritarianism to democracy. Using increased transparency to build both credibility and enhanced abilities to adapt to changing international circumstances is a central challenge for new democratic regimes. As Haggard asserts, the key is 'changing institutions of governance to increase both their independence (from narrow interests) and their accountability (to the public at large)' (2000: 125).

Finally, the institutions of national governance do not provide economic security in isolation. Regional and global institutions can also provide insurance, enhance policy credibility, and encourage adaptation. Whether regional or global institu-tions can best provide economic security to Asia has emerged as an element in debates over the future of the region.

Regional and global institutions: substitutes or complements?

The Asian economic crisis revealed the shortcomings of regional institutions constructed over the preceding decades. They offered little economic security at a time of great need. The apparent failure of those institutions at a critical moment forced governments to turn to global financial institutions – particularly the IMF – that pressed politically controversial policy changes during the crisis. That experience in turn led to renewed interest in regional alternatives to the global institutions and their prescriptions. Although framing regional and global institu-tions as alternatives is understandable in light of this history, a more useful approach appraises the specific strengths and weaknesses of global and regional institutions in the provision of economic security. Multilateral institutions at the regional and global levels may also complement national strategies of economic security.

Global economic institutions and economic security

Insurance

The original design of the International Monetary Fund included insurance for national governments in the form of short-term balance-of-payments financing. This insurance was one part of an institutional design that aimed to avoid unnecessary and disruptive adjustments in national economies. Conditionality – an exchange of policy changes for increasing levels of financial support – addressed the problem of moral hazard, a significant issue in any insurance scheme. A key controversy that has long enveloped conditionality – and one that arose again in the Asian financial crisis – is the degree of policy change required for a given level of financial support. Although the IMF assembled large financial packages for Asian governments, many of those governments felt that the global financial institutions demanded unnecessarily sweeping and abrupt policy changes in exchange for their support.

A second form of insurance directed toward future financial crises was also controversial. The IFIs emphasized financial codes of conduct that encouraged regulatory convergence on what was defined as best regulatory and supervisory practice. These regulatory reforms were meant to insulate fragile financial systems against the type of collapse that had threatened (or ensued) in 1997–1998. However, the reforms also threatened the web of political relationships among financial institutions, corporations, and governments that defined economic policymaking in many Asian societies.

Credibility

Insurance of the latter kind was closely associated with one means of enhancing policy credibility that was endorsed by the IFIs: transparency and accountability to private market participants and to a government's own citizens. The new style of policymaking propounded by the IFIs collided with the collusive and opaque practices of government–business relations that defined for many the Asian model of governance.

Policy credibility could also be strengthened through international surveillance. Transparency and policy commitment would be guaranteed through external scrutiny by other governments in the framework of international economic organizations. The strengthening of surveillance provided yet another point of conflict between the global economic institutions and Asian governments. Such oversight was highly sensitive for Asian governments that, in their own regional organizations, had resisted what was seen as unwarranted intervention in domestic policy decisions. The norm of noninterference was widely held in the international politics of the region, enshrined in ASEAN and vigorously defended by states intent on defending a particular conception of national sovereignty. Weighing against these long-standing norms was a recognition that domestic policies and practices in neighboring economies could have large, negative spillovers on one's own economy, particularly the financial contagion spawned by weakly regulated banking systems and inappropriate macroeconomic policies.

Adaptation

Adaptation became the most difficult and uncertain territory of debate within the region and among institutions and governments outside. The IFIs argued for deep, structural policy changes during the Asian financial crisis, demands that were criticized by outside analysts for their timing as well as their content (Feldstein, 1998; Stiglitz, 2002). In the aftermath of the crisis, such changes were recommended for crisis prevention, reducing vulnerability to financial shocks and increasing policy credibility. Given their past, admirable record in making and defending credible policy commitments, Asian governments often preferred to take steps that aimed to restore credibility without changing their underlying model of economic policymaking. With the exception of specific improvements to financial regulation and supervision, no clear consensus had emerged on appropriate and necessary institutional adaptations required for greater economic security.

Regional institutions and new modalities of economic security

Although some regional institutions – notably APEC – drifted in the wake of the Asian financial crisis, new regional alternatives have emerged that promise to stake out new modalities of economic security. Most of these institutions did not include the United States or Australia, earlier proponents of Pacific-wide organization. Recent institution-building and innovation have tended to be 'Asia-only.' The relationship between these new institutions and the cooperative initiatives that they have produced on the one hand, and older regional and global institutions on the other, remains open.

Insurance

The Asian Monetary Fund (AMF), an initiative by Japan in 1997, might have provided financial insurance on terms less stringent than those imposed by the IMF. Although the AMF was not implemented, a similar appeal could be seen in the development of an Asian bilateral swap network under the Chiang Mai Initiative (CMI), part of the ASEAN plus Three (APT) process. A link to IMF conditionality in the CMI, however, suggests that this addition to economic security should be seen as a complement rather than a substitute for the IFIs, a useful financial supplement that could be mobilized as a first line of defense by governments in the region (Henning, 2002). New regional trading initiatives, such as the proliferation of proposed bilateral trade agreements, the China–ASEAN free trade initiative, and the Japan–ASEAN Comprehensive Economic Partnership (CEP) proposal can be seen as insurance against a different threat to economic security. Failure of the current round of global trade negotiations under the World Trade Organization

(WTO) could lead to a strengthening of regional trading blocs centered on Europe and North America.

Another new regional institution has recently promoted a different variety of insurance against financial shocks – adaptation of regional financial markets. The Asian Cooperation Dialogue (ACD), launched in 2002, has offered a plan to catalyze the development of a regional bond market. Parallel APEC and APT proposals support the ACD initiative. Deeper bond markets would provide a means of mobilizing Asian savings for regional borrowers. Bond market development would also reduce the dependence of Asian borrowers on bank lending (often centered outside the region), a dependence implicated in past financial crises (De Brouwer, 2003).

Credibility

Providing supplemental insurance against financial shocks has been one means for regional institutions to offer greater economic security. So far, however, regional governments have shown little enthusiasm for using regional institutions to complement their policy credibility. Building stronger (greater sanctioning power) and more intrusive regional institutions will probably be required if an institutional seal of approval is to carry any weight with market participants. Governments in the region have accepted a gradual and modest erosion of the norm of noninterference, defined as excluding any external scrutiny by neighboring governments. Modest steps toward mutual policy review were taken by ASEAN and the Asian Development Bank (ADB) in the wake of the financial crisis. Even more dramatic was the willingness of ASEAN to comment on the Myanmar political situation in the press statement that ended its 2003 summit (ASEAN, 2003). This willingness to admit greater collective scrutiny of domestic policies and practices is testimony to the strong regional effects that those internal decisions may have. In part, this movement also returns the norm of noninterference to its narrower and more useful role: banning the forceful interference of one government in the domestic affairs of another. That principle of legitimacy, so critical to the success of ASEAN, had been expanded over the years to encompass a much broader range of comment and scrutiny that was entirely peaceful and collective. Economic integration has forced and will continue to enforce a reexamination and redefinition of that norm in the interests of greater economic security.

Adaptation

Regional institutions have not so far used the third instrument for increasing economic security: promoting policy adaptation in the face of globalization. On the contrary, a minority in the region endorse regional institutions as one element in 'Asianization as a resistance movement' to globalization and its proponents outside the region. In this view, the new regionalism will permit Asian governments to formulate an alternative to globalization, one that calls for 'network capitalism instead of marketization, emphasizes regional economic integration rather than comparative advantage, stresses Asian Confucian values as compared to Western democratic ideals, and opts for regional cooperation to avoid global governance' (So, 2001: 152, 154). This view of regional institutions as a barrier to globalization and a substitute for global institutions has alarmed observers in the United States as well as others outside the region.

Fears that Asian institutions might serve as an alternative and exclusive mechanism of economic security, buffers for the region against unwanted change and competition from the global economy, are overdrawn. A healthy skepticism toward any claim of radical substitution and exclusion of globalization is justified for two reasons. First, even if Asian economies become less dependent on markets and investors outside the region, sources of economic instability are hardly limited to the global economy. Japan's financial disarray and similar fragility in China's banking system will continue to pose substantial threats to economic security in the region. The withdrawal of Japanese bank lending was responsible for a large share of the decline in private capital available to crisis-affected economies after 1997–1998. Policy missteps by neighboring states would be of even greater concern in a region more insulated from the global economy.

To guarantee a higher level of economic security through an 'Asianized' regional system would also require a level of regional institution-building that Asian governments have so far been unwilling to endorse. Rather than attempting to substitute for national or global institutions, the new regionalism will most effectively enhance economic security if it serves as a complement to both national governments and existing global institutions. In an era of globalization, national governments will continue to play an essential role as providers of social insurance against international economic instability. Asian governments have begun to improve their systems of social insurance, although fiscal constraints and aging populations will probably mean a public–private balance different from that in Europe and the United States (Haggard, 2000: 230–236). Global institutions continue to contribute to the policy credibility of member governments in the eyes of global market participants. It is a credibility supplement that national governments need in the new financial environment and one that regional institutions in Asia cannot provide.

Finally, on the knottiest issue in economic security – how much adaptation of institutions and policy is required for economic well-being in a globalized environment – regional institutions in Asia can insure that Asian views on this controversial issue are reflected in global economic institutions and other international forums (Stubbs, 2002). As important as the question of *which* adaptations are required, however, is determining the level of governance that is most likely to insure that beneficial adaptation. Here as well, no easy answer presents itself. National constituencies are critical actors in the debate over policy change and essential to the legitimacy of such change. Regional institutions, sensitive to local norms and practices, may provide a less visible and more effective means to influence the actions of neighboring governments. Global institutions can draw on best practice and advice from around the world, advice that, in the best of circumstances, is subjected to critical scrutiny from a wide audience. Developing a constructive means for these three levels of governance to shape the adaptation of policies and institutions is a final task for those who wish to improve economic security in Asia and elsewhere.

Conclusion: economic security or economic management?

In an era that is post-Cold War and post-Asian financial crisis, concerns over economic security have not disappeared; they have been transformed. Governments have become much less wary of economic vulnerability that might be manipulated by their neighbors or economic partners. Instead, governments have become more aware of unwanted and dangerous spillovers from more open borders and the risks of economic volatility posed by economic openness.

Redefinition of economic security has not led to a broader reversal of the region's trend toward greater economic openness. The new perspective on economic security has instead spurred a debate over appropriate measures to reduce costs and risks associated with openness while retaining gains from globalization. The final combination of national, regional, and global policies will vary from country to country, but the mix will remain. National policies will remain central, although those policies and the institutions that produce them will continue to adapt. Regional institutions may take on new life as complements to long-standing national and global institutions. A revived sense of regional identity may insure that global institutions reflect the economic importance of Asia for the first time.

Renewed attention to economic security is not misplaced, but it may be transitory, a preoccupation of societies that have benefited from economic openness but are now grappling with its negative consequences for the first time. What is now seen as economic security may, with the passage of time and the accumulation of institutional means to deal with these challenges, be retired to the more mundane and less alarming category of economic management.

Notes

1 Simmons and Elkins (2003) examine competing explanations for widespread external liberalization.
2 For an account of the effects of the Asian financial crisis on the economies of the region, see McLeod and Garnaut (1998).
3 For different views of the crisis, see Stiglitz (2002), Haggard (2000: 1–14), Goldstein (1998), and Radelet and Sachs (1998).
4 For two recent perspectives on the relationship and relative importance of institutions and economic integration as determinants of economic growth, see Rodrik *et al.* (2002) and Dollar and Kraay (2003).
5 For an analysis of the relationship between openness and public expenditure, see Rodrik (1997: 49–67).

References

Acharya, A. (1999) 'Realism, Institutionalism, and the Asian Economic Crisis,' *Contemporary Southeast Asia*, 21 (1): 1–29.

ASEAN (2003) Press Statement by the Chairperson of the Ninth ASEAN Summit and the Seventh ASEAN Plus Three Summit, Bali, Indonesia, 7 October [Online] http://www.aseansec.org/15259.htm.

Baldwin, D. A. (1985) *Economic Statecraft*, Princeton, NJ: Princeton University Press.

Bhatta, S. S. (2002) *Imagine There's No Country: Poverty, Inequality, and Growth in the Era of Globalization*, Washington, DC: Institute for International Economics.

Cameron, D. (1978) 'The Expansion of the Public Economy,' *American Political Science Review*, 72: 1243–1261.

Cheng, T. (1998) 'APEC and the Asian Financial Crisis: A Lost Opportunity for Institution-Building?' *Asian Journal of Political Science*, 6 (2): 21–32.

De Brouwer, G. (2003) 'Financial Markets, Institutions, and Integration in East Asia,' *Asian Economic Papers* 2 (1): 53–80.

Dollar, D. and Kraay, A. (2003) 'Institutions, Trade, and Growth: Revisiting the Evidence,' World Bank Policy Research Working Paper 3004, March.

Downs, E. S. (2000) *China's Quest for Energy Security*, Santa Monica, CA: Rand.

Eichengreen, B. and Fishlow, A. O. (1998) 'Contending with Capital Flows: What Is Different about the 1990s,' in M. Kahler (ed.) *Capital Flows and Financial Crises*, Ithaca, NY: Cornell University Press.

Feldstein, M. (1998) 'Refocusing the IMF,' *Foreign Affairs*, 77 (March/April): 20–33.

Fischer, Stanley (2003) 'Globalization and Its Challenges,' AEA Papers and Proceedings, *American Economic Review*, 93 (2) (May): 1–30.

Gates, R. M. (2003) 'Open Doors versus Closed Borders: The Challenge for Universities,' Address delivered at the 116th Annual Meeting of the National Association of State Universities and Land-Grant Colleges (NASULGC), 18 November [Online] http://www.nasulgc.org/AM2003Files/gatesAM2003.pdf.

Goldstein, M. (1998) *The Asian Financial Crisis: Causes, Cures, and Systemic Implications*, Washington, DC: Institute for International Economics.

Haggard, S. (2000) *The Political Economy of the Asian Financial Crisis*. Washington, DC: Institute for International Economics.

Henning, C. R. (2002) *East Asian Financial Cooperation*, Washington, DC: Institute for International Economics.

Hirschman, A. O. (1980) *National Power and the Structure of Foreign Trade*, Berkeley: University of California Press.

Kahler, M. and Kastner, S. (2004) 'Strategic Uses of Economic Interdependence', unpublished manuscript.

Kahler, M. and Lake, D. (2003) *Governance in a Global Economy: Political Authority in Transition*, Princeton, NJ: Princeton University Press.

Katzenstein, P. J. (1985) *Small States in World Markets: Industrial Policy in Europe*, Ithaca, NY: Cornell University Press.

MacIntyre, A. (2003) *The Power of Institutions: Political Architecture and Governance*, Ithaca, NY: Cornell University Press.

McLeod, R. H. and Garnaut, R. (eds) (1998) *East Asia in Crisis: From Being a Miracle to Needing One?* New York: Routledge.

Manning, R. (2000) *The Asian Energy Factor: Myths and Dilemmas of Energy, Security and the Pacific Future*, New York: Palgrave.

Radelet, S. and Sachs, J. D. (1998) 'The East Asian Financial Crisis: Diagnosis, Remedies, Prospects,' *Brookings Papers on Economic Activity*, 1.

Rodrik, D. (1997) *Has Globalization Gone Too Far?* Washington, DC: Institute for International Economics.

Rodrik, D., Subramanian, A., and Trebbi, F. (2002) 'Institutions Rule: The Primacy of Institutions over Geography and Integration in Economic Development,' unpublished paper, October.

Simmons, B. A. and Elkins, Z. (2003) 'Globalization and Policy Diffusion: Explaining Three Decades of Liberalization,' in M. Kahler and D. Lake (eds) *Governance in a Global Economy*, Princeton, NJ: Princeton University Press, pp. 275–304.

So, A. Y. (2001) 'The Globalization Project and East Asia: An Opportunity or a Trap?' in James C. Hsiung (ed.) *Twenty-first Century World Order and the Asia-Pacific*, New York: Palgrave, pp. 135–156.

Stiglitz, J. (2002) *Globalization and its Discontents*, New York: W. W. Norton.

Stubbs, R. (2002) 'ASEAN Plus Three: Emerging East Asian Regionalism,' *Asian Survey*, 42 (3): 440–455.

Part II

East Asian country responses to economic (in)security

3 Crafting Thailand's new social contract

Kevin Hewison

Introduction

In the first general election under Thailand's reformist 1997 Constitution, Thaksin Shinawatra led his newly founded Thai Rak Thai (Thai Love Thai, TRT) party to an unprecedented victory in January 2001. This was also the first election following the deep recession that began with the devaluation of the baht in July 1997. TRT ran a slick and well-financed campaign that the media cast as nationalist because its policy platform rejected the unpopular economic reform package brokered by the International Monetary Fund (IMF). TRT was also seen as populist because it directed its major campaign promises to rural and poor voters. In victory, TRT promised a new era for Thailand, captured in its slogan that declared the party would think in new ways for all Thais.

There is something to this slogan. TRT's election victory represents the most significant moment in the development of Thailand's political economy since the military coup led by General Sarit Thanarat in 1958. To support this assessment, this chapter argues that the Thaksin government represents the seizure of the state, via the ballot box, by big domestic capital. The outcome of this new political role for domestic business has been accompanied by the first 'renegotiation' of Thailand's social contract between Thailand's ruling class and its subordinate classes since Sarit's time. This chapter traces these developments, beginning with a brief account of the economic crisis and its social impacts.

The economic crisis

Much has already been written of the economic impact of Thailand's crisis (see Glassman, 1999; Hewison, 2000a; Pasuk and Baker, 2000). In this brief account, the aim is to address some misconceptions. The popular picture, especially outside Thailand, is that the crisis was a disaster for the country's corporate conglomerates and the middle class. Capitalists lost their business empires, while many in the middle class were thrown out of work. This led to remarkable fire-sales as the rich rid themselves of luxury cars and condominiums. There is considerable truth in this (see Hewison 2001). However, this picture of a 'new poor', when combined with oft-repeated stories of brave entrepreneurial souls 'fighting back' through various innovative business schemes – the failed stockbroker turned sandwich-maker was endlessly repeated in the international media – is but a partial depiction of the broader impacts. The principal impact of the crisis was on millions of workers and small farmers.

It is worth recalling that prior to the crisis, Thailand was seen as an economic success story. Analysts such as Warr and Nidhiprabah (1996: 3) argued that this achievement was due to good policies implemented by capable technocrats. They concluded that Thailand's success in achieving economic growth was no accident, but was a model approach that could be emulated by other developing countries. All that was necessary was for technocrats to make the right policy choices, keep control to a minimum and emphasise 'steadiness, predictability, and stability' (ibid.: 228, 236). But something went wrong with the orthodox success story in 1997, and suddenly Thailand was at the centre of a region-wide economic crisis. Reflecting on Thailand's quick slide from model to failure, Pasuk and Baker (1998: 318) observed how the same analysts who had lauded its policies and successes suddenly 'blamed the crash on inadequate institutions, corrupt politicians, and imperfect liberalization', all of which had long been elements of Thailand's political economy and conveniently ignored during the economic boom times of the early 1990s. The crisis seemed to make the blind see.

The international financial institutions were not exceptions, and demanded major reforms for the model pupil gone astray. The IMF's programmes to address the crisis in the region were explained by the then managing director, Michel Camdessus (1998). What was required was

> a set of forceful, far-reaching structural reforms to strengthen financial systems, increase transparency, open markets and . . . restore market confidence. . . . [N]on-viable financial institutions [had to be] . . . closed down, and other institutions . . . required to come up with restructuring plans and to comply . . . with internationally accepted best practices. . . . Other . . . changes [would] strengthen financial sector regulation and supervision, increase transparency in the corporate and government sectors, create a more level playing field for private sector activity, and increase competition.

He added that the proposed reforms would 'require a vast change in domestic business practices, corporate culture, and government behavior' – in other words, a fundamental transformation of the ways of doing business and politics was proposed, driven by a neoliberal agenda.[1]

The neoliberal consensus was that the causes of the crisis were to be located in poor policies, a weak state and weak corporate governance, inadequate institutions, cronyism, corruption, moral hazard, resource misallocation and failed liberal-isation. For neoliberals, the crisis reaffirmed the difference between 'right' and 'wrong' economic policies, and the need for 'sound' macroeconomic management that included further liberalisation, albeit with a 'better' framework. In Thailand, the post-crisis neoliberal approach, promoted by the IMF, World Bank, Asian Development Bank and a range of bilateral partners, emphasised expanded

liberalisation and more privatisation, fiscal austerity, deregulation and decentralisation. A fundamental concern was for the economic role of the state to be further
reduced.

Following the flotation of the baht, its subsequent and rapid devaluation, and
the flight of capital, the IMF had brokered a 'rescue package' with the short-lived
government of Chavalit Yongchaiyudh. The devaluation saw many companies
pushed into insolvency. Those that were not insolvent, together with many small
businesses, found that they were unable to access a banking system that had all
but collapsed (see Hewison, 2000a; Regnier, 2001). Thailand had little choice but
to accept the IMF's US$17 billion stand-by facility and its demands for austerity
and market-enhancing reform. The first Letter of Intent (LOI) between the IMF
and the Thai government indicated a concern for financial restructuring and
'stabilisation', and involved a tightening of monetary and fiscal policy. It also
announced a massive reform programme that demanded that wages be kept low,
the privatisation of state enterprises (especially targeting communications, transport
and energy), civil service reform, improvements to corporate governance, and
regulatory reform; eased restrictions on foreign investment; and increased private-
sector participation in infrastructure projects (IMF, first LOI, 14 August 1997). All
of this was to be supervised by the IMF. When the Chuan Leekpai-led coalition
government came to power in late 1997, the second LOI was issued and reaffirmed
the recovery strategy. Additional measures were announced for the accelerated
privatisation of major state enterprises (IMF, second LOI, 25 November 1997).

The outcome of the crisis and this reform strategy was a recession that had major
and negative political consequences. By mid-1998, local business was deeply
distressed. The crisis cut a swathe through the domestic business class, destroying
or weakening all the bank-based conglomerates that had long dominated the
domestic capitalist class (Suehiro, 1989; Hewison, 1981). It also crushed many of
the business groups that had mushroomed during the 1990s boom. With the
banking sector crippled by non-performing loans, even small enterprises found that
they had no access to capital. Foreign investment grew rapidly as joint-venture
partners were bought out and cheap acquisitions completed. This was especially
notable in the finance and industrial sectors.

While business struggled, the social impacts of the economic downturn became
clear. It is appropriate to outline these impacts briefly as a background to the
emergence of TRT and its alternative economic and social policies.

The social impacts of the economic crisis

There have been but a handful of studies of the social impacts of the crisis
(e.g. Pasuk and Baker, 2000: ch. 4; Kakwani, 1998; Warr, 2002). In addition,
the World Bank, which took the role of coordinating the 'donor response' to
these impacts, completed several studies. These included regular monitoring and
reporting of the economic and social impacts of the crisis. In this section, the Bank's
data will be used to explain the effects on poverty, employment and wages, and
inequality.

The economic crisis had a marked impact on poverty. Prior to the crisis, robust growth had seen absolute poverty reduced (see Hewison, 1997), but the crisis saw more than 1 million people fall below the poverty line of US$1 per day in 1997–1998. By 2000, more than 7 million people were below the World Bank's now higher poverty line of US$1.50 a day, or about 60 baht per day (World Bank, 1999a: 32; 2000b: 8).[2] The impact was especially hard in already disadvantaged areas, and the crisis meant that poverty re-emerged as a serious national problem (World Bank, 1999b: 7).

There were also significant and negative impacts on employment and wages. Unemployment and underemployment increased by almost seven percentage points, to about 10 per cent (or almost 3.5 million persons) in the year following the devaluation (World Bank, 1999b: 48). In addition, a further half-million people, 'mostly women', apparently 'opted' out of the workforce (World Bank, 2000a: 4). The largest group affected by increased unemployment were lower-skilled and semi-skilled urban workers, mostly in the construction, service and manufacturing sectors (World Bank, 1999b: 13). Managers and professionals in these sectors did not lose their jobs as readily as workers. Contradicting popular views regarding 'traditional' social safety nets in villages, many of the unemployed were found in rural areas. Rural unemployment doubled between 1997 and 1998, to over 1 million persons. The already poor northeast region accounted for almost 40 per cent of all unemployed, and its unemployment rate more than doubled to 8.2 per cent by 1998 (World Bank, 1999c: 9). World Bank (2000b: 11) analysts were surprised that agriculture did not provide 'the expected safety net, as employment levels in that sector . . . continued to fall' during the crisis. In fact, even during the crisis, people continued to leave farms, just as they had during the economic boom.

The crisis meant that real wages declined, and the World Bank (1999c: 10) concluded that this 'had a more substantial impact on welfare than pure un-employment'. For those in employment, average real monthly wages fell by 7.9 per cent between 1997 and 2000. In addition, the percentage of workers receiving overtime payments (a common way for low-paid workers to increase their take-home pay) declined substantially (World Bank, 2000b: 17). Wages declined for all occupational categories, but most substantially in the agricultural sector, manufacturing, sales, transport and clerical work. The most severely affected workers were those with primary school or lower education (that is, the 60 per cent of the population who had not been educated beyond primary school), and especially those in the north-east and central regions (World Bank, 2000c: 3). Strikingly, the World Bank (ibid.: 32) concluded that '*there was a shift in the distribution of aggregate wage earnings from groups with low pay to those with high pay*' (emphasis added). This involved shifts in the distribution of aggregate wages from rural to urban areas, from poor to relatively wealthy regions, from shop-floor workers to technical and professional workers, and from those in small enterprises to those in large establishments (ibid.: 32).

These shifts meant increased inequality. The richest 20 per cent of the population saw its share of wealth rise between 1996 and 1999, while that of all other quintiles declined (World Bank, 2001: 27). Part of the reason for this was that the poor had to transfer substantially higher proportions of their incomes to support their extended families than did the rich. The World Bank concluded that 'increased income inequality is positively and strongly associated with increased poverty', and that inequality would substantially reduce the impact of renewed economic growth on poverty reduction (ibid.: ix–xii). The source of inequality was *profits*:

> Although one-half of total personal income . . . is derived from wages and salaries, the contribution of . . . wages and salaries to overall inequality is only 27%. . . . On the other hand, even though non-farm profits . . . constitute only 22% of total income, their contribution to overall income inequality is significantly higher (56%).
>
> (ibid.: 30)

The World Bank (2001: 21, 48) concluded that it was the poor who were most severely affected by the economic crisis. Interestingly, and despite comments to the contrary, these negative employment, wages and inequality impacts did result in increased social conflict. Labour in Thailand has a long history of struggle, despite significant constraints on organising, and state and employer repression (see Hewison and Brown, 1994; Ungpakorn, 2001), and during the crisis, workers again responded vigorously to their deteriorating situation. While strikes are few, the number of officially reported grievances rose by 37.6 per cent when 1996 and 1998 are compared, and the amounts of money involved in these disputes increased by more than 47 per cent (Brown *et al.*, 2002). Most of these disputes were over wages owed or severance payments.[3]

From this account, it is clear that the crisis has seen a significant reduction of wages and an increase in inequality.[4] As in other crises, the effect of the reduction in wages has been to reduce the costs of production and increase profitability. This is why the World Bank (2000c: 6) decided that 'labour markets had worked well to cushion the effects of the crisis'. While all workers suffered during the crisis, it was the lowest-paid workers who suffered the most. Part of the reason that the market 'worked' is that workers were easily laid off. Because of minimal social security, laid-off workers then went in search of other jobs. While they did this, their family savings supported them. The result was that family savings were rapidly depleted, especially for the poor. So, this crisis saw a movement of wealth and savings from the already poor to the already wealthy.

It might have been thought that the World Bank's analysis could have led to recommendations that supported the then Bank vice president Joseph Stiglitz's suggestion that safety nets be expanded and institutionalised during recovery. This was not the case, and the World Bank championed neoliberal calls for further privatisation, increased foreign investment and reduced spending on social safety nets.[5] In fact, these recommendations were in line with the agenda of the IMF and Chuan government. With this background to the social impacts of the economic crisis, it is now appropriate to examine the broader political and policy responses.

Domestic capital, economic crisis and politics

As the crisis deepened in the wake of the devaluation and first LOI, a widespread and popular opposition to the IMF's strictures developed. This resulted in a loose alliance of workers, public intellectuals, non-governmental organisations (NGOs), politicians, domestic business and even the country's monarch. They were drawn together by a broadly nationalist opposition to a perceived loss of sovereignty over economic policymaking, negative social impacts of the crisis and a 'fire sale' of local assets (both private and state) to foreign interests (see Hewison, 2000b). Domestic business was especially vocal, complaining of high interest rates and a lack of liquidity in the economy. Domestic business joined with some economists in urging that more attention be given to domestic initiatives to 'save' the economy.

While the government began to take notice of these complaints, and the third and fourth LOIs gave more attention to negative social impacts, the real economy remained distressed. Despite growing political ferment, the government continued neoliberal reform. This steadfastness caused powerful elements of the local business class to conclude that the IMF-sponsored reforms would so weaken their control and reduce their wealth that the demise of the class was possible. The baht's devaluation caused many companies to close in all business sectors, and meant that domestic capital needed to restructure. This was required under domestic competitive pressures and in the face of aggressive competition from international investors, and resulted in mergers and acquisitions. The result has been a massive reorganisation of ownership and control, including the transfer of assets to foreign investors through debt-for-equity swaps, takeovers, investment in devalued local companies, and buy-outs of Thai partners (for details, see Hewison, 2001, 2002).

The impact of the crisis was widespread. Manufacturing firms struggled with overcapacity (*Nation*, 18 September 2003). Weighed down with foreign currency debts, hamstrung by a liquidity squeeze, facing a plunge in domestic demand and already reeling from weak exports from 1996, industrial investment collapsed. A range of financial, real estate and construction firms were dissolved. Land developers fared particularly badly. The finance sector was in tatters, with only a handful of finance and securities companies remaining after 1997. The retail sector was also heavily indebted, and slack local demand made recovery difficult. These processes meant that a large number of the businesses that had expanded during the boom of the 1990s were wiped out.

Perhaps the most significant impact for Thailand's political economy was on the once powerful banking families and their conglomerates. Before the crisis, domestic banking families controlled the partially liberalised finance sector, including thirteen of the sixteen commercial banks, where foreign holdings were limited to 25 per cent. The crisis continued the competitive reorganisation of banking capital, a process that had begun earlier. In the 1980s, several families had found it difficult to recover from internal conflicts and increased competitive pressures. Later, during the 1990s boom, small family banks, often acting as little more than family treasuries, had come under pressure. The crisis sounded the death knell for these troubled family-controlled banks, which were taken over either by the state or by foreign investors. By 1998, only five commercial banks remained outside state control and in majority Thai ownership, with each of these having foreign share-holdings of 40–49 per cent (Hewison, 2001). This was a remarkable transformation of the power relationships within the domestic capitalist class as the banking-based conglomerates had represented the most powerful fraction of domestic capital since 1957. Foreign owners and minority shareholders have changed the pattern of doing business in banking, but what is more significant is the break-up of the conglomerates as the families have attempted to protect their core banking interests. This suggests the end of the bank-based conglomerates' control that has been a central feature of Thailand's capitalist industrialisation.

In this context, it is not surprising that foreign capital was generally supportive of reform, carping only when the pace slowed. Meanwhile, domestic capital remained convinced that the IMF-sponsored reforms threatened their power and control, and evidenced a deep distrust of the Chuan government's role in the reform process. The government was seen to be implementing a programme that kept the IMF and its Western supporters on side and made international business 'comfortable', while conveying a reform message that suggested they blamed the domestic capitalist class for the crisis. The government appeared determined to restructure Thailand's capitalism in a manner that gave foreign investors a more powerful position. In the LOIs, the government gave special attention to those sectors protected from foreign competition, including real estate and telecommunications (IMF, LOI, 25 August 1998, 23 March 1999).

Business leaders pleaded that the government not ignore their plight, with little success (*Bangkok Post*, 10 April 1998). The Chuan government and the IMF were implementing a neoliberal agenda that sought to buttress a generalised notion of capitalism, rather than for domestic capital in particular. This contrasted with the outcomes during previous economic downturns. In these, foreign capital had retreated and domestic business had been able to expand, often with the support of the state. This time, the crisis made matters worse for domestic capital. This was a major contradiction: for more than three decades, international agencies and various Thai governments had supported the development of local business; now they seemed to be supporting its destruction.

The threat to the power of local business forced the domestic capitalist class to take direct control of the state, parliament and ministries. As noted above, they were supported by a much broader coalition that felt that Thai society was being shattered by both the crisis and neoliberal reform. In 1997, Chuan and the Democrats had seemed the only alternative to Chavalit's inept government. The Democrats appeared less hamstrung by the obligations of Chavalit's coalition of provincial-based politicians scrambling to recoup election expenses and to enrich themselves and their business cronies. However, by 1998 Thaksin had established a viable alternative party in TRT.[6]

More than any previous party, TRT represented the interests of big domestic business. Previously, the biggest business leaders had remained aloof from the somewhat grubby electoral politics; they had not needed to be directly involved, for government had long supported domestic business (Baker, forthcoming). It was the threat to their interests and power posed by neoliberal policy that caused the remaining tycoons to conclude that big *domestic* capital needed supportive government policies. This could only be achieved by taking control of the state.[7] Many business rivalries were put aside as big business coalesced around Thaksin. TRT thus became the vehicle through which to oppose the neoliberal agenda, to slow liberalisation in some areas, and to give back a competitive 'edge' to domestic business. This was symbolised in the TRT's runaway 2001 election victory.[8]

TRT, using techniques drawn from US campaign experience and marketing strategies, built an electoral platform that addressed the aspirations of many voters. Its slogan emphasised the theme that something new was required in politics: 'new thinking, new ways, for all Thais'. This inclusive slogan and a party platform tinged with nationalism and promising help for those suffering from the slump were especially appealing to poor, especially rural, voters. TRT also targeted small businesses, promising to make credit available for them. Such promises and policies showed that TRT was to follow a different reform path from that promoted by the Chuan government and the IMF. At this time, the broad domestic debate about the crisis seemed unable to distinguish between the suffering of the poor and that of domestic business.

In campaigning, Thaksin and TRT caught the mood of an electorate that had suffered the welfare declines described above. The party prepared a range of policies that included what is now termed a 'dual-track development strategy'. TRT policy documents (n.d.) describe this as a

> model [that] aims to strengthen domestic activities at the grass-roots level as well as promote the linkages between the domestic economy and the world economy. Such a balanced development will lead Thailand towards a high performance economy with sustainable, quality-oriented growth and economic stability.

The Party proclaimed these 'progressive policies designed to solve the economic hardship and creat[e] opportunities for the Thai common man' (TRT, n.d.). The emphasis on the domestic economy was reinforced by platforms that coalesced into three broad policies, summarised as 'wars' on poverty, corruption and drugs. Specific programmes and promises that attracted considerable support during the election included soft loans for every village in the country, a three-year debt moratorium for farmers and a 30-baht universal healthcare programme.[9]

Not only did these policies and promises deliver a handsome election victory, but they rejected the IMF-brokered policies of the Democrat-led government. As if to emphasise this, Thaksin declared that the IMF had harmed Thailand (Third World Network, 2001), and extolled the virtues of managed development, drawing on the examples of Malaysia and Singapore (Thaksin, 2001). In something of an innovation, not only did Thaksin and TRT make promises but, following the election, they moved quickly to implement them, emphasising the TRT's pledges to the poor.

These obligations to the poor should not conceal the fact that the TRT party dominated a government by and for the rich. Thaksin's first two cabinets included a range of business leaders who were forces in the post-crisis era, from powerful groups including his own Shin Corporation, Jasmine, Charoen Pokphand, Bangkok Entertainment, the Thai Military Bank, Thai Summit, and a range of others (see Baker, forthcoming). On achieving power, the government set about helping domestic business, including businesses associated with TRT's leaders, advisers and supporters. It did this by measures to protect domestic business and by strengthening the government itself.

To protect domestic business, the government immediately slowed the pace of liberalisation in a number of areas, including in the telecommunications sector, placed the privatisation of state enterprises on temporary hold, and evidenced a concern to limit foreign ownership, ignoring timetables set in the LOIs. The government also slowed moves to establish independent agencies in the media and telecoms sectors, and some of the investigations into the financial irregularities of the pre-crisis period were downplayed (Baker, forthcoming: 18–19). At the same time, state banks organised deals with bankrupt supporters and advisers to the government. The fact that serious conflicts of interest were involved in some of these moves was hidden in the language of economic nationalism.

While powerful, the nationalist shibboleth was unlikely to be a successful long-term strategy for maintaining political consensus. Thus, the government also strengthened its political control. Thaksin, his ministers and advisers attacked a range of potential and actual critics. The prime minister threatened a number of the independent agencies established under the 1997 Constitution. He and his party attempted to limit media criticism, both domestic and international, by haranguing and investigating journalists, controlling advertising budgets and using the extensive state- and Thaksin-controlled media to manage news. At the same time, TRT strengthened its parliamentary position by managing mergers with smaller parties, so that TRT controlled almost two-thirds of the seats in the Lower House. This limited parliamentary scrutiny of the government's work. In an authoritarian mould, Thaksin considered that an ideal parliament was one with a limited opposition, which would be united with government in working for the 'best interests of the people'. Indeed, he argued that adversarial politics was a betrayal of the people (Thaksin, 2002: 4). Thaksin hoped that his government might stay in power for twenty years, and was relentless in attacking critics, including NGOs, journalists and public intellectuals (*Bangkok Post*, 2 November 2003). The intention has been to make the government of tycoons 'safe' over the long term by minimising and managing opposition and criticism.

Renegotiating social contracts

As intimated above, the rise of TRT is not a simple case of domestic business seizing the state. Rather, Thaksin, TRT and domestic capital, operating within a representative parliamentary system, established TRT's political legitimacy through a new social contract that replaced the developmental social compact that had operated since the late 1950s.[10] The prime minister, Thaksin, has shown that he is aware of the process he has embarked upon, using the term 'social contract' to describe a relationship between political parties and 'the people'. While it is not exactly in the spirit of Rousseau's conceptualisation of the general will and general good, Thaksin felt that this contract required that parties dedicate themselves 'to solving the people's problems, improv[ing] their livelihood, and creat[ing] greater opportunities for them to enrich their lives' (Thaksin, 2002: 2). For us to understand the nature of the new social compact, it is necessary to outline the earlier social contract that underpinned Thailand's development in the period from the early 1960s.

Thailand's developmental social contract

In 1958, the military leader General Sarit Thanarat seized political power. While a military-led leadership was not new for Thailand, Sarit's coup established a government that set about altering the ways in which politics and economics had been organised. Sarit did this in the context of promises to improve the then struggling economy, proclaiming that his government would boost national income and improve standards of living (*Journal of the Thai Chamber of Commerce* [*nangsuphim ho kankha thai*], 13 March 1959: 130). He explained that his government's authoritarianism was required to deliver the political stability necessary for the expansion and strengthening of the middle class. As Thaksin and TRT would do four decades later, Sarit proclaimed that his government would build a 'new society for Thailand, a society that is happy' (*Journal of the Thai Chamber of Commerce*, 14 November 1960: 99–100).

The regime's economic approach represented a significant change over that of previous governments, evidencing a determination to promote private rather than state investment and encouraging foreign participation. The state's economic role was to be more limited, concentrating on the development of infrastructure. With substantial US and World Bank assistance, the regime developed an economic plan that heralded an unprecedented period of economic growth (Hewison, 1985). In politics, Sarit established a system of 'despotic paternalism', under which a highly authoritarian government established order and stability (Thak, 1979).

In summary, Thailand's developmental social contract amounted to a deal between the military leadership and domestic capital that demarcated their hegemony over the working and peasant classes. The military government would deliver political stability and support the expansion of private capital, while domestic capital was required to deliver increased economic growth and to modernise the economy. The subordinated classes, who had no role in establishing this developmental deal, were involved through an assumption that enhanced capitalist development would permit a gradual trickle-down of benefits to them and the expansion of a middle class. The position of rural areas and their populations changed over time. In the 1960s and 1970s, the peasantry was to be controlled to prevent any support for the communist insurgency and to shift development resources from agriculture to industry. When communism receded as a threat to the state and industrialisation expanded, rural areas became a source of workers for the expanding manufacturing sectors.

It was not until the 1973 uprising against military rule that this arrangement was challenged. At this time, the emphasis was on dismantling the authoritarian political element of the bargain through the establishment of constitutional and parliamentary politics. In 1976, however, the military led another coup, ending this democratic interlude. The military then retained control of the political process until 1989, when an elected politician became prime minister (see Hewison, 1993). The military returned yet again in 1991, but briefly, being ousted by a mass uprising in May 1992. This meant that the contract's authoritarian political element was effectively removed by the early 1990s. However, the economic development component was maintained by the economic boom, which continued until 1996. This period of rapid growth delivered significant benefits to all sectors of society, albeit highly unequally, as fast growth saw wealth disparities increase (Hewison, 2002). Growth continued to deliver rising living standards so that the social element of the developmental contract remained in place.

It was the 1997 economic crisis that finally destroyed the developmental social contract. As is demonstrated in the previous discussion of the social impacts of the crisis, the downturn meant that the trickle-down of benefits ended. More than this, when combined with the successful challenge to the political component of the contract, the deal struck in the early 1960s was, finally, dead.

Thaksin, TRT and a new social contract

Once TRT had secured its 2001 electoral victory, Thaksin set about delivering on the promises that had had him elected, and continued to develop and promote policies identified in the international media as both nationalist and populist. Thaksin and TRT have been reasonably comfortable with these labels, for they reinforce their marketing message to the Thai population: that TRT was different from the previous government and that Thailand had a sovereign government that was establishing a new path to prosperity.

While the political backlash against neoliberal economic policies had brought Thaksin into an alliance with 'anti-globalists' and others vehemently opposed to liberalisation, TRT did not fit well with these groups (see Hewison, 2000b). Thaksin has often spoken of his support for free trade, and some of TRT's policies were congruent with those favoured by the international financial institutions and international business. For example, both TRT and the World Bank favoured decentralisation, bureaucratic reform (including enhanced participation in decision-making) and the promotion of small and medium-scale enterprises. There were also reforms to corporate and bureaucratic governance that had the support of both domestic and foreign business. But foreign investors and international financial institutions were worried that the TRT government had abandoned the orthodox economic agenda. These concerns involved the government's lukewarm approach to foreign investment, privatisation and financial sector reform, and the potential for a budget blow-out as the government funded its election promises to the poor.

Clearly, TRT came to power through electoral policies that targeted the poor, made social welfare a significant part of its platform, and allocated government a central role in reducing poverty. While the World Bank and IMF fretted over the increased role for the state and the impact of aggressively expansionary economic policies, this approach delivered considerable political support for the TRT government. It also represented the establishment of a new social contract.

The IMF and the Chuan government, in appearing to abandon support for domestic business, had shown that they were not concerned to re-establish the developmental social contract, and this allowed TRT the opportunity to strike a new deal with the electorate. The deal was that if the electorate supported TRT, the TRT government would ensure enhanced social protection and economic opportunities for the relatively poor majority of the population. This side of the bargain was targeted directly at those who would elect the government in the 2001 polls: small farmers, the working class and those in the middle class who had been adversely affected by the economic crisis. The other side of the bargain was support and protection for domestic capital as it faced restructuring and significant competition, especially from foreign investors. These latter policies have been discussed elsewhere (see Robison *et al.*, 2002), whereas TRT's social protection policies have received scant attention. It is thus appropriate to examine how it is that a government that is representative of domestic capital has had to develop a social contract that potentially delivers state-supported social protection at a level never before considered possible for Thailand.

Interestingly, in the midst of competitive restructuring, the remaining elements of big local business were able to put aside their economic competition in order to cooperate politically. This was because they recognised that domestic capital needed a new social contract if it were to re-establish its economic power. In addition, domestic capital recognised that political and social unrest could result from crisis-induced rural stagnation, inequality and poverty; it was keen to avoid the situation seen in Indonesia with the overthrow of the Suharto regime.

The domestic capitalist class allocated a high priority to achieving direct control of the state at the 2001 elections. This was indicated by the large expenditures (more than US$3.6 billion) it allowed the TRT government to allocate to the five major election policies: the million-baht Village and Community Fund (VCF), the 30 baht Universal Health Scheme (UHS), the People's Bank, the one tambon–one product scheme and farmers' debt suspension. With the exception of the VCF, which was funded through loans from the Government Savings Bank, these programmes were funded from the normal government budget. The most significant of these programmes were the VCF and UHS, which accounted for about 90 per cent of the funding and claimed almost 52 million beneficiaries by late 2002 (Worawan, 2003: 3).

The VCF was central to domestic capital's election strategy. The scheme aimed to provide one-year, low-interest loans of up to 20,000 baht to individuals in every village and community in the country. This programme allowed TRT to demonstrate its concern for rural problems.[11] Such concerns had been expressed by previous administrations, but were seldom translated into policy and implementation. The loan scheme was part of a larger package of rural support that, for the first time, was not simply about propping up agriculture. Rather, TRT's aim is to develop entrepreneurs (see Baker, forthcoming). In this context, TRT's hope was that increased entrepreneurialism would create enhanced employment opportunities. These kinds of objectives meant that the scheme was uncontroversial for domestic capital. At the same time, it was anticipated that this spending would boost consumption, and domestic business was keen to receive the economic stimulus that would come from an injection of state funds.

The progress of the UHS has been more controversial. Even though Thailand's health system had been judged relatively successful in meeting the needs of the majority, health costs remained a significant expense for the poor. Where there was prolonged or serious illness within a poor family, the result was often a slide into deeper poverty. The divisions on healthcare had been indicated prior to the crisis, with, for example, the World Bank urging an expansion of the private sector's already substantial role (see Subbarao and Rudra, 1996). The crisis had seen the poor having to invest more in their health, and TRT's election promise of a cheap UHS was understandably popular. Essentially, the scheme permitted all Thai citizens to gain access to public hospital treatment for just 30 baht per consultation. The government paid hospitals 1,252 baht per registered person in the scheme (*Bangkok Post*, 14 January 2003). Worawan (2003: 3) estimated that the cost of the scheme to government was in excess of 63 billion baht in 2002.

The UHS has had a rockier political path than the VCF. The most obvious problem was that while the scheme was expensive for government, state hospitals complained that fixed government funding threatened their ability to provide adequate treatment. This was apparently confirmed in media reports about some patients being forced out of hospitals prior to the completion of their treatment. Health professionals argued that the scheme, with its emphasis on curative and institution-based health, was reversing gains that had been made in preventive healthcare, and was draining funds from health promotion activities (interviews, Bangkok, May 2002). Initially it seemed that the scheme would threaten the return to profitability of private health providers, but as overworked and poorly paid doctors fled the state system, along with wealthier patients, this seemed unlikely (*Bangkok Post*, 11 July 2003).

Nonetheless, the government began to look at ways to modify the scheme. One response was to bolster the funds available to government for the UHS by merging it with existing programmes like the Worker's Compensation and Social Security funds. This brought workers onto the streets in protest as they feared that their care would be downgraded once their funds were siphoned into the support of the UHS (*Bangkok Post*, 17 September 2002).

As the government sought ways to maintain its scheme, debate became increasingly political and polarised. The debate around the role of the state in healthcare provision was crystallised by the UHS and National Health Insurance bill. Much of the criticism came from medical professionals, and included the Medical Council, the Thai Medical Association, and associations representing nurses, dentists, pharmacists and private hospitals (*Bangkok Post*, 5 August 2002).

Interestingly, the government was supported by a range of domestic groups – including some who urged increased taxation to fund the scheme – and the World Health Organization and the International Labour Organization (*Bangkok Post*, 26 July 2002, 1 August 2002). Many in the private sector, including economists and some doctors, began to see the UHS as a step towards economic ruin and a welfare state (*Nation*, 29 July 2002, 3 September 2003). State doctors, who traditionally moonlight in private hospitals and in private practice, were opposed to increased workloads and working hours, and argued that the government was transforming a 'capitalist' health system into a socialised model of medicine (*Bangkok Post*, 9 January 2003, 30 August 2003).[12]

Even while making some concessions to the private sector, the TRT government is keenly aware that the UHS is a significant element in its popularity, and an essential component of the new social contract. It is for this reason that the government has continued to support the scheme, despite private-sector concerns. However, Thaksin attempted to ease anxiety by stating that he would never allow a 'welfare state'. He argued that his government was developing 'social capitalism', where the state's role would be reduced once the gap between the rich and the poor had been bridged (*Nation*, 2 October 2003; *Bangkok Post*, 5 October 2003). In the short term, however, maintaining this element of the new social contract was important for maintaining electoral support for the government of the rich in the 2004 election.

With this eye to the 2005 election, TRT has also begun to address the needs of workers under the new social contract.[13] Obviously, some of the earlier pro- grammes provided benefits to workers, but these had not been explicitly targeted to the working class, and elements of the UHS were seen to threaten hard-won benefits. In early 2003, Thaksin announced a new housing scheme for the urban poor, allocating a further 80 billion baht over five years (*Bangkok Post*, 16 January 2003). Further, in his 2003 Labour Day speech, Thaksin promised housing, land distribution, sponsored higher education for workers' children and higher wages for skilled workers. Most dramatically, he made a surprise announcement that, for the first time ever, a Thai government would support the introduction of unemployment benefits through the extension of the social security fund to all workers by January 2005, around the time of the next scheduled election (*Bangkok Post*, 2 May 2003, 3 November 2003).

Conclusions

The social and economic policies of Thaksin and the TRT government have been intimately related to domestic capital's struggle to re-establish its competitiveness following the economic crisis. Domestic capitalists saw Thaksin and TRT as vehicles to give an 'edge' back to their struggling businesses. The tycoons who had survived the crisis realised that domestic capital needed direct control of policy if it were to re-establish its power. In the past, the most powerful business families had generally remained aloof from formal electoral politics; they had not needed to be involved in the cut and thrust of electoral politics as government had adopted policies that were generally supportive of domestic business. However, the crisis had resulted in the Chuan government, which, supported by international organisations and investors, blamed domestic business for the downturn. Whereas these groups and government had always supported the development of local business, now they seemed to be supporting its destruction.

The threat posed to the power and profits of domestic capital meant that it had to take direct control of parliament, ministries and the state. Thaksin's 2001 election victory delivered a government that moved to implement its key policies, including measures for the poor. However, despite all its pro-poor rhetoric and policies, the TRT remained a government by and for the rich, and it immediately set about helping domestic businesses, including those of its own leaders.

This coalition of local businesspeople felt so threatened that it permitted – some might say forced – the TRT to promote social protection. The TRT and its supporters recognised that domestic capital could be rescued only if there was a new social contract. This yet to be fully embedded social contract involves the delivery of social and political stability through a bargain with the electorate. For the protection of domestic capital by the government of the remaining rich, TRT must deliver increased social security to the poor. Thaksin called this 'social capitalism', where the 'slaves of capitalism' – the poor – would be freed to pursue better lives (*Bangkok Post*, 2 October 2003). This is new for Thailand. It remains to be seen whether domestic capitalism, recovered from the crisis, can reform and become modern, progressive and productive enough to sustain this social contract.

Notes

Part of the research included in this chapter was funded by a City University of Hong Kong Grant. I am grateful to Jill Chung for research assistance.

1 The core elements of neoliberalism have been identified in a range of economic, social and related political policies that emphasise the market, liberalisation, deregulation, decentralisation, privatisation and a reduced role for the state. As neoliberalism has evolved, these elements have remained constant. In practice, a range of policies have been added, emphasised or modified in particular circumstances. These have included a minimalist welfare state, decentralised labour relations and a weakening of unions, fiscal discipline taking precedence over social policies, and a reduction of barriers to trade, especially tariff protection, and investment (see Portes, 1997: 238).

2 The official Thai poverty line was set outrageously low at 878 baht per person per month in 1998 and 886 baht in 1999. The latter is the equivalent of 75 US cents a day, less than 15 per cent of GDP per capita and less than a quarter of the official minimum wage (World Bank, 2001: 2–3).

3 Severance pay is legally mandated for laid-off workers. Unfortunately, World Bank (2000c: 5, 39) data show that less than 13 per cent of laid-off workers received such payments during the economic crisis, and most of these were in large firms (where still almost a half of laid-off workers got nothing). Workers in small firms had just a 3 per cent chance of receiving a severance payment.

4 Wages and employment were only one aspect of the impact on the poor and workers. For example, the government bail-out of commercial banks means that taxpayers are supporting some of the wealthiest capitalists (see Hewison, 2001).

5 It is worth noting the World Bank's recommendations for safety-net expenditures. It urged that the Thai government's already limited expenditures be *reduced* as recovery occurred, from about US$200 in 1999–2000 to about US$110 in 2000–2001 (World Bank, 2000b: 9–10). The centrality of liberalisation is indicated in the World Bank's programme, with more than US$2 billion allocated to these programmes (Shivakumar *et al.*, 2000: 20).

6 Thaksin was one of the few local businesspeople to come through the crisis relatively unscathed, although it is not clear how this was done. Certainly his telecommunications businesses provided cash flow even in the crisis period. It was alleged that when deputy prime minister under Chavalit, he may have benefited from early advice on the devaluation (see Thitinan, 2001: 327), but this allegation has always been vigorously denied. Thaksin is one of the most successful new magnates created by the economic boom, going from having small computer business interests in the early 1980s to being listed by *Forbes* magazine in 1996 as Thailand's fifth wealthiest person, with $2.1 billion (reported in *Bangkok Post*, 22 June 1998). In terms of holdings listed on the local stock market, Thaksin and his family had shares worth almost 37 billion baht in 2000, mostly in the broad communications sector (*Kan ngeon thanakhan* [Money and Banking], December 2000, p. 148). It is also noteworthy that Thaksin's business success was based on state concessions in telecommunications and related areas (see Ukrist, 2002). He had dabbled in national politics from 1994 to 1997, although he had not been particularly popular or successful as a minister. Thaksin also had excellent connections in the military (where relatives had powerful positions) and police (he had trained in the police and married a police general's daughter).

7 The provisions of the 1997 Constitution, including the system of party lists (where the candidates did not need to campaign), also made it more palatable for this elite to become more directly involved in politics.

8 It is worth noting that the former businesspeople who dominated parliamentary elections were provincial godfather figures. Many of these were very badly affected by the crisis, and were unable to provide funding to local candidates in the 2000–2001 elections. 'Money politics' was not dead, however. The elections showed that there remained pockets where local godfathers were influential. At the same time, TRT's platform promised a flow of funds to rural areas, amounting to money politics of the pork barrel type.

9 Other programmes included support for 'new entrepreneurs' and small and medium-sized enterprises, a 'people's bank', education reform, administrative and legal reform, and a new company to manage bad debts.

10 The pedigree of the term 'social contract' is often traced to Rousseau (2003). It usually denotes a belief that political structures and the legitimacy of the state derive from an explicit or implicit agreement by citizens to surrender some or all of their personal rights in order to secure stability and the protection of an organisation such as government (see D'Agostino, 1997). In this chapter, the term is modified to identify an arrangement where government makes an implicit or explicit promise to deliver benefits to citizens in exchange for political support.

11 The scheme also applied to urban areas, but rural Thailand was the main target. Data indicate that 2,339 urban communities received funding, compared with 71,102 villages. It is estimated that 73 per cent of loans were for agricultural purposes (Worawan, 2003: 5).

12 Caseloads, especially for outpatients, in state hospitals doubled or tripled following the introduction of the UHS (Worawan, 2003: 6).

13 Analysts do not usually consider Thailand's urban working class politically significant, but TRT recognised Thailand's changing demographics. At the same time, TRT's gradual return to neo-liberal policies (including privatisation and keeping wages low) meant a need to placate labour.

References

Baker, Chris (forthcoming) 'Pluto-Populism: Thaksin, Business and Popular Politics in Post-Crisis Thailand', in Eva-Lotta Hedman and John T. Sidel (eds) *Populism and Reformism in Southeast Asia: The Threat and Promise of New Politics*, New Haven, CT: Yale University Press.

Brown, Andrew, Bundit Thonachaisetavut and Hewison Kevin (2002) *Labour Relations and Regulation in Thailand: Theory and Practice*, Hong Kong: City University of Hong Kong, Southeast Asia Research Centre Working Papers Series No. 27, July.

Camdessus, Michel (1998) 'The IMF and Its Programs in Asia', Remarks by the Managing Director of the International Monetary Fund at the Council on Foreign Relations, New York, 6 February [Online] http://www.imf.org/external/np/speeches/1998/020698.htm (accessed 29 May 1999).

D'Agostino, Fred (1997) 'Contemporary Approaches to the Social Contract', Stanford Encyclopedia of Philosophy [Online] http://plato.stanford.edu/entries/contractarianism-contemporary/ (accessed 20 May 2003).

Glassman, James F. (1999) 'Thailand at the Margins: State Power, Uneven Development, and Industrial Transformation', PhD dissertation, University of Minnesota.

Hewison, Kevin (1981) 'The Financial Bourgeoisie in Thailand', *Journal of Contemporary Asia*, 11 (4): 395–412.

—— (1985) 'The State and Capitalist Development in Thailand', in Richard Higgott and Richard Robison (eds) *Southeast Asia: Essays in the Political Economy of Structural Change*, London: Routledge & Kegan Paul, pp. 266–294.

—— (1993) 'Of Regimes, State and Pluralities: Thai Politics Enters the 1990s', in K. Hewison, R. Robison and G. Rodan (eds) *Southeast Asia in the 1990s: Authoritarianism, Democracy and Capitalism*, Sydney: Allen & Unwin, pp. 159–189.

—— (1997) 'Thailand: Capitalist Development and the State', in Garry Rodan, Kevin Hewison and Richard Robison (eds) *The Political Economy of South-East Asia. An Introduction*, Melbourne: Oxford University Press, pp. 93–120.

—— (2000a) 'Thailand's Capitalism before and after the Economic Crisis', in R. Robison, M. Beeson, K. Jayasuriya and Hyuk-Rae Kim (eds) *Politics and Markets in the Wake of the Asian Crisis*, London: Routledge, pp. 192–211.

—— (2000b) 'Resisting Globalization: A Study of Localism in Thailand', *Pacific Review*, 13 (2): 279–296.

—— (2001) *Pathways to Recovery: Bankers, Business and Nationalism in Thailand*, Hong Kong: City University of Hong Kong, Southeast Asia Research Centre Working Papers Series No. 1, April.

—— (2002) 'Thailand: Boom, Bust, and Recovery', *Perspectives on Global Development and Technology*, 1 (3/4): 225–250.

Hewison, Kevin and Brown, Andrew (1994), 'Labour and Unions in an Industrialising Thailand', *Journal of Contemporary Asia*, 24 (4): 483–514.

International Monetary Fund, Letters of Intent. Government of Thailand Letters of Intent with the IMF, dated 14 August 1997, 25 November 1997, 24 February 1998, 26 May 1998, 25 August 1998, 1 December 1998, 23 March 1999, and 21 September 1999. All are available at http://www.imf.org/external/country/THA/index.htm.

Kakwani, N. (1998) *Impact of Economic Crisis on Employment, Unemployment and Real Income*, Bangkok: National Economic and Social Development Board.

Pasuk Phongpaichit and Baker, Chris (1998) *Thailand's Boom and Bust*, Chiang Mai: Silkworm Books.

—— (2000) *Thailand's Crisis*, Chiang Mai: Silkworm Books.

Portes, Alejandro (1997) 'Neoliberalism and the Sociology of Development: Emerging Trends and Unanticipated Facts', *Population and Development Review*, 23 (2): 229–259.

Regnier, Philippe (2001) 'Reform in Post-Crisis Thailand (1997–2001): Exploring the Contribution of Small Entrepreneurs to Socio-Economic Change, Democratization and Emerging Populist Governance', Draft paper presented to the EUROSEAS Conference, London, School of Oriental and African Studies, 6–8 September.

Robison, Richard, Rodan, Garry and Hewison, Kevin (2002) *Transplanting the Regulatory State in Southeast Asia: A Pathology of Rejection*, Hong Kong: City University of Hong Kong, Southeast Asia Research Centre Working Papers Series No. 33, September.

Rousseau, J.-J. (2003) *On the Social Contract*, Mineola, NY: Dover (originally published in 1762).

Shivakumar, J. *et al.* (2000) 'Social Capital and the Crisis', *Thailand Social Monitor*, Bangkok: World Bank, January.

Subbarao, K. and Rudra, K. (1996) *Protecting the Disadvantaged in a High Growth Economy: Safety Nets in Thailand*, Washington, DC: World Bank, July.

Suehiro, Akira (1989) *Capital Accumulation in Thailand 1855–1905*, Tokyo: Centre for East Asian Cultural Studies.

Thai Rak Thai (TRT) Party (n.d.) 'Thai Rak Thai Party Policy' [Online] http://www.thairakthai.or.th/policy_trt12.asp (accessed 28 October 2003).

Thak Chaloematiarana (1979) *Thailand: The Politics of Despotic Paternalism*, Bangkok: Thai Khadi Research Institute.

Thaksin Shinawatra (2001) 'Speech by His Excellency Pol. Lt. Col. Thaksin Shinawatra, Prime Minister of Thailand', 24 April, Putrajaya [Online] http://www.thaigov.go.th/news/speech/Thaksin/sp25apr01.htm (accessed 12 November 2001).

—— (2002) 'Keynote Speech' to the Second International Conference of Asian Political Parties, Bangkok, 23 November [Online] http://www.thaigov.go.th/news/speech/thaksin/sp23nov02-2.htm (accessed 26 November 2002).

Third World Network (2001) 'Thailand: Premier-elect for softening IMF terms' [Online] http://www.twnside.org.sg/title/elect.htm (accessed 29 October 2003).

Thitinan Pongsudhirak (2001) 'Crisis from Within: The Politics of Macroeconomic Management in Thailand, 1947–97', Ph.D. thesis, Department of International Relations, London School of Economics.

Ukrist Pathmanand (2002) 'From Shinawatra Group of Companies to the Thaksin Shinawatra Government: The Politics of Money and Power Merge', Paper presented to the International Conference on 'Crony Capitalism', Quezon City, University of the Philippines, 17–18 January.

Ungpakorn, Ji Giles (2001) 'The Political Economy of Class Struggle in Modern Thailand', *Historical Materialism*, 8: 153–183.

Warr, Peter G. (2002) 'Economic Recovery and Poverty Reduction in Thailand', *TDRI Quarterly Review*, 17 (2): 18–27.

Warr, Peter G. and Bhanupong Nidhiprabha (1996) *Thailand's Macroeconomic Miracle. Stable Adjustment and Sustained Growth*, Kuala Lumpur: Oxford University Press.

Worawan Chandoevwit (2003) 'Thailand's Grass Roots Policies', *TDRI Quarterly Bulletin*, 18 (2): 3–8.

World Bank (1999a) *Thailand Economic Monitor*, Bangkok: World Bank Thailand, October.

—— (1999b) 'Thailand Macroeconomic Update', 13 July.

—— (1999c) *Thailand Social Monitor: Challenge for Social Reform*, Bangkok: World Bank Thailand.

—— (2000a) *Thailand Economic Monitor*, Bangkok: World Bank Thailand, February.

—— (2000b) *Thailand Economic Monitor*, Bangkok: World Bank Thailand, June.

—— (2000c) *Thailand Social Monitor: Thai Workers and the Crisis*, Bangkok: World Bank Thailand.

—— (2001) *Social Monitor VI: Poverty and Public Policy*, Bangkok: World Bank Thailand.

4 China confronts globalization

Conceptualizing economic security and governance

Wang Zhengyi

Introduction

Economic growth and national security had been regarded as two separate logics rather than a single domain in China until the Asian financial crisis broke in 1997. Before the mid-1990s, economic reform and economic growth had been accorded high priority on the domestic policy agenda, while national security was primarily focused on ensuring territorial integrity and preventing subversion by hostile external forces. Partly because of the widening and deepening of global-ization and China's growing incorporation into the world economy since 1978, and partly as a result of the alarming outcomes of the Asian financial crisis that began in 1997, China's policymakers and scholars began reviewing the economics–security nexus. Governing insecurities resulting from economic growth, both conceptually and as policy practice, have received increased attention since the mid-1990s. The Chinese government has since developed a number of policy instruments and institutional mechanisms to help policymakers address these emerging economic insecurities.

Such concerns are subtly distinct from those often raised by critics of China's lack of political reform. Instead, these emerging worries are centred on whether China has the capacity both to sustain economic growth *and* to address the asso-ciated economic insecurities. In this regard, three questions will be discussed in this chapter. First, what prompted the conceptual shift over the past two decades from a view of economic growth and national security as two separate logics to one that sees them as a single domain? Second, what kinds of insecurities are raised by China's robust economic growth amid deepening globalization as well as by China's entry into the World Trade Organization (WTO), and in what ways do these insecurities challenge China's government, if at all? Third, what kinds of policy instruments and institutional mechanisms has the Chinese government adopted to mitigate these emerging economic insecurities while maintaining robust economic growth?

Economic growth and national security in China: from two separate logics to a single domain

The evolution, since China's economic opening in 1978, of the relationship between economic growth and national security, in both academic and official circles, may be divided into two stages. The first stage, between 1978 and 1992, saw economic growth and national security conceptualized as two separate logics. The second stage, from the mid-1990s, sees economics and security as a single domain, especially after the Asian economic crisis that began in 1997 and as a result of China's entry into the WTO.

Maintaining economic growth and security as two separate logics, 1978–1992

Compared to the Mao Zedong era, three forms of transitions have taken place in China since 1978 under Deng Xiaoping's leadership. These transitions include the shift from a centrally planned economy to a market-based one; from a rural, agricultural society to an urban, industrial one; and from a non-WTO nation to a WTO member nation. To prepare for the latter transition, economic reform was placed at the top of both the domestic and the international policy agendas. However, until the 1990s China's integration into the world economy was accompanied by gradual domestic economic reforms. This allowed national security and economic growth to be characterized as two separate logics.

At the Third Plenum of the Eleventh Central Committee in December 1978, China embarked on economic reforms aimed at improving its economic performance and raising people's living standards. Until 1992, domestic economic reform centered on a socialist-based, 'planned economy–market economy' relationship evolved gradually, and was accompanied by a process of ideological change. First, the ideas of 'planned economy' and 'market adjustment' were officially adopted at the Twelfth Party Congress in September 1982, with the former as primary and the latter as secondary. The notion of a 'planned commodity economy' was later adopted at the Third Plenum of the Twelfth Party Congress in October 1984, and subsequently explicated in terms of 'the state controls the market, and the market guides enterprises' at the Thirteenth Party Congress in October 1987. Finally, the idea of the 'establishment of a socialist market economy' was put forward at the Fourteenth Party Congress in November 1992 (Yabuki, 1995: 43).

During the evolution of these conceptions of economic reform, 'economic growth' and 'national security' had been regarded as two separate logics. In the economic domain, it was believed that as long as economic growth was the assured end result, whatever domestic economic reform and international cooperation seemed appropriate could be adopted. Three examples illustrate this thinking. First, the open door policy was maintained, and the number of 'Special Economic Zones' extended from four (Shenzhen, Zhuhai, Shantou and Xiamen) in 1978 to fourteen coastal cities in 1984 in order to attract foreign direct investment (FDI). Second, decentralization of fiscal authority was undertaken in 1980 and that of the trade regime in 1984, both of which played important roles in attracting FDI and promoting trade growth in many regions, especially in the coastal areas. Third, the political movements based on 'opposing bourgeois liberalization,' which took place in 1983, 1986, and 1989, were regarded as irrelevant to economic reform and confined strictly to the political and security domains. In Deng Xiaoping's words:

> As for the scope and focus of opposing bourgeois liberalization . . . Don't relate it with the following including the policy of economic reform, rural policy, scientific and technological studies, style and technique of literature and art, and everyday life of people. It has its particular definition.
>
> (Documents Research Division of the Central Committee of the Chinese Communist Party, 1987: 1208)

At the same time, national security, either as concept or policy, was strictly confined to the ideological and political domains and regarded as being independent of economic reform. Generally speaking, the concept of national security had two basic meanings domestically and internationally during the same period. Domestically, national security meant maintaining the leadership of the Chinese Communist Party (CCP) and the socialist system. Although Deng Xiaping indicated his approval of political reform in August 1980 and reiterated it in August 1986, the bottom line was to adhere to the 'Four Basic Principles' he had put forward in 1979, of which the most fundamental is the leadership of the CCP and socialism. In Deng's words, 'only if we make our country a modern, powerful socialist state can we more effectively consolidate the socialist system and cope with foreign aggression and subversion' (quoted in Zhao, 1996: 51).

Internationally, national security meant ensuring state sovereignty and territorial integrity. While promoting China's 'opening up' to the outside world, the 'Five Principles of Peaceful Coexistence' (mutual respect for sovereignty and territorial integrity, mutual nonaggression, noninterference in each other's internal affairs, equality and mutual benefit, and peaceful coexistence) are the basic principles that China uses in international affairs. In one word, national security was conceptualized as part of Chinese foreign policy and irrelevant to its foreign economic relations such as trade and FDI.

Seeking linkages between economic growth and security (from 1992)

Chinese economic reform entered a new phase with Deng Xiaoping's tour to south China in January–February 1992 followed by the Fourteenth Party Congress in November 1992. In the decade that followed, China sustained high economic growth, even maintaining the growth momentum during and after the Asian economic crisis. From 1991 to 2000, China registered an average annual growth rate of GDP of about 10.1 percent (Figure 4.1), and continued to register a robust annual GDP growth rate of 7.3 percent in 2001 and 7.6 per cent in 2002, while

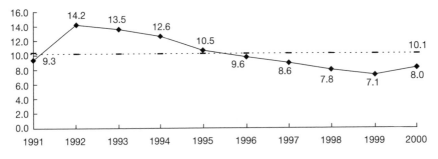

Figure 4.1 China's economic growth in the 1990s.

Source: Yu Yongding, 'A Review of China's Macroeconomic Development and Policies in the 1990s', *China and World Economy*, 2001, No. 6.

GDP per capita increased from $236 (Y 855) in 1985, $344 (Y 1,643) in 1990 to $909 (Y 7,543) in 2001 (National Bureau of Statistics of China, 2000: 51). The annual inflation rate was kept under 3 percent (Yu, 2001). As for other important economic indicators such as investment and trade, it is estimated that the Chinese mainland attracted $321 billion, or 45 percent of the $719 billion in FDI flowing into the East Asian region (comprising ASEAN, China, Japan, and South Korea) since 1990, while its share of total US imports has more than tripled to 8.4 percent since 1989 and exports to its neighbors soared 27.8 percent to $249 billion (Hawkins, 2002). China's macroeconomic performance is described either as 'a true economic miracle' (Yu, 2001) or as 'one of the few bright spots in the region' (Asian Development Bank, 2000).

Compared to economic reforms undertaken during the 1980s, economic growth in the 1990s was accompanied by the following three features. First, transformation of the economic structure has yet to be complete, especially with regard to reform of state-owned enterprises (SOEs) and banks, despite considerable government attention to these areas. Second, China's economy has increasingly come to depend on the world economy, especially on foreign trade and FDI. Figures show that foreign trade in the Chinese economy rose from 10 percent in 1978 to about 44 percent in 2001 (Figure 4.2), while FDI in China rose from $1 billion in 1983 to $47 billion in 2001 (Figure 4.3). Third, socioeconomic polarization has intensified with the deepening of domestic reforms and the process of China's incorporation into economic globalization.

These three features led Chinese scholars and policymakers to begin to reconceptualize the economics–security relationship and seek linkages between economic growth and national security, especially after the 1997 Asian economic crisis and China's entry into the WTO. As a result, national economic security has become the most popular topic for Chinese scholars and policymakers since the mid-1990s, and there are many writings on this subject.[1] It is especially noteworthy that 'national economic security and globalization' as a single concept was explicitly expressed in the *Documents of the 16th National Congress of the Communist Party of China*:

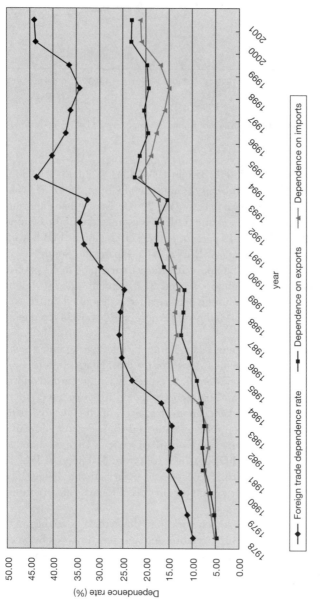

Figure 4.2 China's dependence on foreign trade, 1979–2001.

Source: National Bureau of Statistics of China, *China Statistical Yearbook 2002*, pp. 51 and 612.

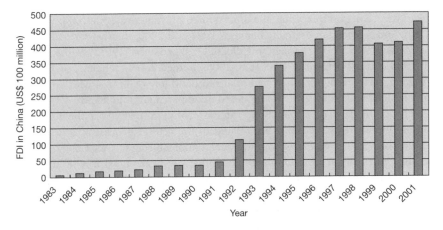

Figure 4.3 Foreign direct investment (FDI) in China, 1983–2001.

Source: National Bureau of Statistics of China, *China Statistical Yearbook 2002*, p. 629.

> In response to the new situation of *economic globalization* and *China's entry into the WTO*, we should take part in international economic and technological cooperation and competition on a wider scale, in more spheres and on a higher level, make the best use of both international and domestic markets, optimize the allocation of resources, expand the space for development, and accelerate reform and development by opening-up. . . . In opening wider to the outside world, we must pay great attention to safeguarding our *national economic security*.
>
> (Chinese Communist Party, 2002: 34, 35)

Economic insecurity in China: domestic and international sources

The three kinds of transitions taking place in China have increased risks and uncertainties in the Chinese economy and in its market-related society. The result has been a gradual diminution in the capacity of the state to govern, a phenomenon that now receives serious attention both domestically and internationally.[2] The economic insecurities that challenge China's capacity to govern its economy and society include (a) rising unemployment; (b) severe economic inequalities between coastal and interior provinces, rural and urban areas, and those working in the formal core of the economy and those in petty and informal economic activities; and (c) decentralization of authority in the Chinese economy and society.

Rising unemployment

The first challenge to governance comes from rising unemployment. Although the officially registered unemployment rate is 3.0–3.6 percent, a growing number of scholars have focused on China's real unemployment rate,[3] which since 1993 has risen sharply and to a much higher degree than the official, registered unemployment rate. For example, while the official unemployment rate was 3.0 percent in 1996, and 3.1 percent annually between 1997 and 2000, the real rate calculated by scholars was 5.1–6.0 percent in 1996, 6.8–7.8 percent in 1997, 7.9–8.3 percent in 1998 and 8.2 percent in 1999 (Lai, 2003). Some Chinese scholars, such as Hu Angang, have even computed high real rates and low real rates, with both rates much higher than the officially registered unemployment rate (Figure 4.4).

The rising real unemployment rate in China is related to the following developments. First, it is directly related to the reform process of state-owned enterprises (SOEs), especially in traditional manufacturing sectors. Long regarded as the central pillar of the Chinese economy, the SOEs now provide the basis of, and legitimize, the idea of a socialist market economy with Chinese characteristics. Therefore, the success of SOEs is a key indicator of the overall success of structural adjustment programs in China, and reflective of a smooth transition from a centrally planned economy to a market-dominated one. Because of their centrality in the Chinese political economy, the deficits of SOEs have been tolerated while the subsidies provided to deficit enterprises have increased yearly from 1985 to 1990, in the process maintaining the 'triangle debt' situation (Yabuki, 1995: 51–52). During the 1990s, approximately 40 percent of SOEs displayed chronic deficits, and over 20 percent of banks' portfolios consisted of nonperforming loans to money-losing SOEs (Economy, 1998: 12).

Second, unemployment was of a unique form called 'Xiagang' (lay-offs)[4] and was concentrated in the urban state-owned and collective-owned industrial sectors

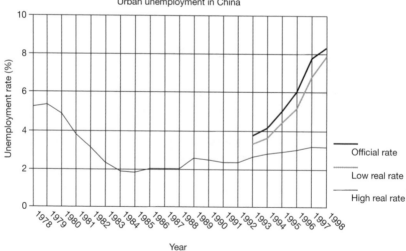

Figure 4.4 Urban employment insecurity.

Source: Hu Angang (1999) in Wang Shaoguang, 'Openness, Distributive Conflict, and Social Insurance: The Social and Political Implications of China's WTO Membership', http://www.gateway2china.com/report/CUHK_paper.htm.

in the 1980s and early 1990s. Since 1997, 'Xiagang' workers have no longer been registered as employed, and now constitute the main component of unemployment in China. This is the reason why China's officially registered unemployment rate provokes much debate and criticism from international organizations such as the International Labour Organization (International Labour Organization, 2001)[5] and the Asian Development Bank (Asia Times, 2000). The official estimate of urban unemployment at the end of 1999 was 5.8 million, about 3.1 percent of the urban labor force. However, this estimate covers only those registered with the Ministry of Labour and Social Security. It does not cover the 9.4 million Xiagang workers who were laid off as part of the SOE reforms but who have not found alternative employment. When Xiagang workers were included, urban employment was about 15 million, or about 8.2 percent of the urban labor force. Finally, a social security system for unemployed workers has only now been established. If unemployed workers were unable to find alternative work, they entered the ranks of the urban poor.

Moreover, the existing situation is unlikely to improve anytime soon with China's accession to the WTO and its integration with economic globalization, according to Hu Angang and Wang Shaoguang, because economic growth in China is entering a stage of so-called jobless growth. Their calculations, shown in Figure 4.5, reveal that in the 1980s, approximately a 0.32 percent increase in employment opportunities was created by every additional percentage point of GDP growth, but by the middle of the 1990s this relationship had changed. Now, job opportunities increased by only 0.14 percent with every additional percentage of GDP growth. During the late 1990s, the relationship worsened. For example, in 1999 only a 0.05 percent increase of employment accompanied the 7.1 GDP growth rate (Wang, 2000).

It is not surprising at all, therefore, that dealing with rising unemployment and creating more job opportunities is placed at the top of the CCP's agenda. In the

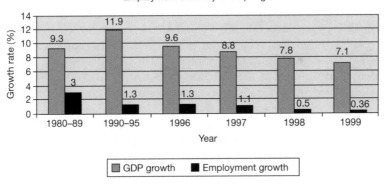

Figure 4.5 Growth of GDP and employment in China.

Source: Hu Angang (1999) in Wang Shaoguang, 'Openness, Distributive Conflict, and Social Insurance: The Social and Political Implications of China's WTO Membership', http://www.gateway2china. com/report/CUHK_paper.htm.

CCP's economic blueprint project, the task of creating work to improve people's livelihood is for the first time being treated as 'arduous' and 'important':

> *Doing everything possible to create more jobs, and improving the people's lives.* Employment has a vital bearing on people's livelihood. The task of increasing employment is arduous and important now and will remain so for a long time to come. It is a long-term strategy and policy of the state to expand employment. Party committees and governments at all levels must take it as their major responsibility to improve the business environment and create more jobs.
>
> (CCP, 2002: 33)

Continued inequalities

The presence of income polarization was regarded by Deng Xiaoping in the 1980s as one key criterion by which to differentiate capitalism from socialism:

> One of the features distinguishing socialism from capitalism is that socialism means common prosperity, not polarization of income. The wealth created belongs first to the state and second to the people; it is therefore impossible for a few bourgeoisie to emerge.
>
> (quoted in Hu, 1997: 131)

However, since the mid-1990s, continued inequalities in income distribution accompanying rising growth have become indisputable, and therefore a key challenge for the government.

There are three kinds of inequalities in China (International Labour Organization, 2001). The first is the inequality in income per capita between rural and urban households. As Table 4.1 shows, the difference in income per capita between urban and rural households increased from 2.5 in 1978 to 2.9 in 2001. The second is the growing inequality between coastal provinces and inland areas. Both foreign trade and FDI have been mainly concentrated in or near only a third of China's provinces (Figures 4.6 and 4.7). In particular, coastal provinces have benefited more from economic globalization than inland provinces, leading to greater job opportunities and higher incomes. The GDP per capita in the coastal provinces (Jiangsu, Zhejiang, Guangdong, Fujian, Shandong) is higher than that in the inland provinces (Figure 4.8), except for the three centrally administered cities, with Shanghai taking a lead at $4,500 (Y 37,382), Beijing ranking second at $3,000 (Y 25,523), and Tianjin third at $2,400 (Y 20,154).

The third is the growing inequality between those in the official core of the economy and those surviving in petty and informal economic activities. An Asian Development Bank study shows that 'about 230 million people (18.5 per cent of the population) still lives below the US$1-a-day poverty line while 670 million (53.7 per cent of the population) live below US$2-a-day' (Asia Times, 2000). Even in urban areas, about 12–15 million people (4–5 percent of the urban population) were living below the poverty line, assuming an urban poverty line of $200 (Y 1,700)

Table 4.1 Annual income per capita of urban and rural Chinese households and the related index

Year	Annual net income per capita of rural households		Annual disposable income per capita of urban households	
	US$	Index (1978 = 100)	US$	Index (1978 = 100)
1978	16.2	100	41.5	100
1980	23.1	139	57.8	127
1985	48.1	269	89.4	160
1986	51.3	278	108.8	183
1987	55.9	292	121.2	187
1988	65.9	311	142.9	183
1989	72.3	306	166.4	183
1990	**83.0**	**311**	**182.6**	**198**
1991	85.7	317	205.6	212
1992	94.8	336	245.1	233
1993	111.4	347	245.1	233
1994	147.6	364	422.8	277
1995	**190.8**	**384**	**517.9**	**290**
1996	232.9	418	585.1	302
1997	252.7	437	624	312
1998	261.4	456	656	330
1999	267.3	474	707.9	361
2000	**272.5**	**484**	**759.4**	**384**
2001	286.1	504	829.5	416

Source: National Bureau of Statistics of China, *China Statistical Yearbook 2002*, China Statistical Publishing House, 2002, p. 320.

per capita income per year, according to the Development Research Center of the State Council of China in 1997 (ibid.). There is, however, no official urban poverty line in China.

Decentralization of authority

The third kind of economic insecurity comes from the decentralization of authority in the Chinese economy as domestic reforms interact with economic globaliza- tion (Economy, 1998: 14; Saich, 2001: 152). This is not unique to China, given that decentralization of authority has taken place worldwide over the past 15 years (World Bank, 2000), but it is extremely serious for the CCP and the Chinese government, considering the imperative of governing a vast territory and a large population and given the historical legacy of authoritarian rule.

The decentralization of authority was the result of tensions in the financial relationship between the center and local authorities in the 1978–1980 period, with the former in deficit (by Y 356.3 million in 1978 and Y 382.3 in 1980) while the latter had been in surplus (Y 366.5 million in 1978 and Y 285.5 million in 1980) (Table 4.2). The decentralization of authority became an important policy

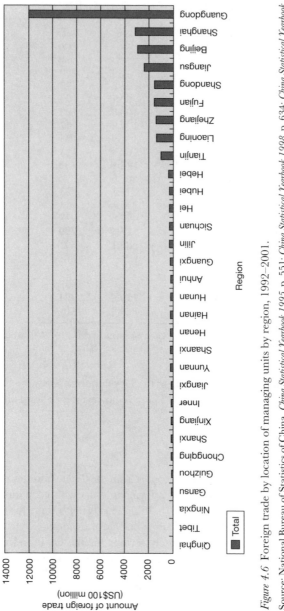

Figure 4.6 Foreign trade by location of managing units by region, 1992–2001.

Source: National Bureau of Statistics of China, *China Statistical Yearbook 1995*, p. 551; *China Statistical Yearbook 1998*, p. 634; *China Statistical Yearbook 1999*, p. 591; *China Statistical Yearbook 2002*, p. 626.

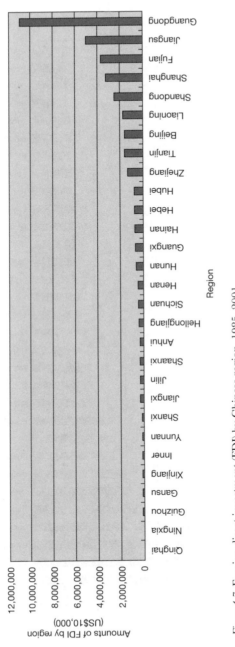

Figure 4.7 Foreign direct investment (FDI) by Chinese region, 1985–2001.

Source: National Bureau of Statistics of China, *China Statistical Yearbook 2002*, pp. 630 and 633.

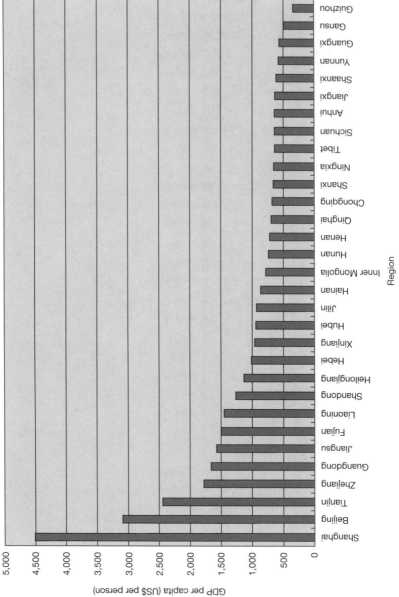

Figure 4.8 GDP per capita for all China's provinces, municipalities and autonomous regions, 2001.

Table 4.2 Relationship between central and local finance in China

Year	Budgetary revenue (100 million yuan)		Budgetary expenditure (100 million yuan)		Balance (100 million yuan)	
	Central government	Local government	Central government	Local government	Central government	Local government
1978	176	956	532	590	−356	367
1980	**284**	**875**	**667**	**590**	**−382**	**286**
1985	770	1,235	795	1,209	−26	26
1990	992	1,945	1,004	2,079	−12	−134
1991	938	2,211	1,091	2,296	−153	−85
1992	980	2,504	1,170	2,572	−191	−68
1993	956	3,391	1,312	3,330	−356	61
1994	**2,907**	**2,312**	**1,754**	**4,038**	**1,152**	**−1,727**
1995	3,257	2,986	1,995	4,828	1,261	−1,843
1996	3,661	3,747	2,151	5,786	1,510	−2,039
1997	4,227	4,424	2,533	6,701	1,694	−2,277
1998	4,892	4,984	3,126	7,673	1,766	−2,689
1999	5,849	5,595	4,152	9,035	1,697	−3,440
2000	6,989	6,406	5,520	10,367	1,469	−3,961
2001	8,583	7,803	5,768	13,135	2,815	−5,331

Source: National Bureau of Statistics of China, *China Statistical Yearbook 2002*, pp. 271 and 272.

instrument to balance the center–local relationship and to give local governments an incentive to encourage economic expansion. It began with the 1980 fiscal reform called 'Eating in Separate Kitchens', followed by decentralization of the foreign trade apparatus and other measures in 1984 (Shirk, 1993: 178–181). Decentralization was reconfirmed in 1993 with 'separate tax systems'[6] in the 'Decision of the Chinese Communist Party Central Committee on Some Issues concerning Establishment of a Socialist Market Economic Structure' adopted by the Third Plenum of the Fourteenth Central Committee of the Chinese Communist Party in Beijing in November 1993.

In retrospect, the decentralization of authority as a policy undoubtedly alleviated the tension between the center and the local authorities, but it also weakened the state's capacity to govern the macroeconomy. As a result of decentralization, the negative implications of the increase in local government's power emerged in the late 1980s and early 1990s. According to Susan Shirk, the most serious of these were (a) economic overheating accompanied by inflation, shortages, and budget and trade deficits; (b) segmentation of the national market by local protectionism; (c) competition among local governments for foreign trade and investment; and (d) local administrative interference and rent-seeking in enterprise management (1993: 182). Moreover, although the center's finances improved gradually from 1994 with implementation of the tax system reform already mentioned, the central government fiscal deficit has been maintained during the 1990s (National Bureau of Statistics of China, 2002: 265). This was because the central government has had to give fiscal subsidies to many inland provinces, which finally diminished and limited the state's capacity to govern the macroeconomy and deal with potential crises. For example, in the aftermath of the Asian crisis, the government followed an expansionary fiscal policy. Two fiscal stimulus packages ($12 billion in 1998 and $7.2 billion in 1999) were used to increase investment in infrastructure and pump-prime growth, as a result of which the fiscal deficit increased from less than 2 percent of GDP to 4.2 percent in 1999 (Asia Times, 2000).

How China confronts economic insecurity

With the emergence of economic insecurity from rising unemployment, continued distributional inequalities, and the decentralization of authority, a balance between reform, development, and stability is now at the top of the agenda of both the CCP and the Chinese government:

> *Ensuring stability as a principle of overriding importance, and balancing reform, development and stability.* Stability is a prerequisite for reform and development. We should take into full consideration the momentum of reform, the speed of development and the capacity of the general public to cope with changes. Continued improvement of the people's lives must be regarded as an important link in balancing reform, development and stability.
>
> (Chinese Communist Party, 2002: 11)

In order to confront economic insecurities, China has embarked on a series of adjustments since the mid-1990s, especially gradual institutional adjustments; establishing a social security system; and coordinating the development of the regional economy.

Gradual institutional adjustments

Balancing economic growth and political stability has been key to China's reform experience since 1978, an approach based not only on lessons learned from China's own experience during the Great Leap Forward in 1958 and the Cultural Revolution in the 1960s, but also on lessons learned from the collapse of the Soviet Union. Consequently, the gradual adjustment of institutions has become an important means of confronting domestic socioeconomic changes. Three kinds of institutional adjustments are significant in this regard, which have proceeded continuously since they were put forward by Deng Xiaoping in the mid-1980s (Deng Xiaoping, cited in Documents Research Division of the Central Committee of the Chinese Communist Party, 1987: 1106).

The first was to deal with party–government–enterprise relations by the idea of 'two separations'; that is, the 'separation of party from administration' (Dang Zheng Fen Kai) and 'separation of administration from enterprise' (Zheng Qi Fen Kai). The idea of 'two separations' originated from the political reforms proposed in the mid-1980s, and was aimed at avoiding overwhelming influence of the party on the day-to-day management of enterprises and returning more management power to enterprises. It finally failed because of unceasing ideological debates, economic troubles and political instability in the late 1980s, especially the Tiananmen demonstration in 1989. However, the 'macro adjustment and management' (Hong Guan Tiao Kong) policy has been emphasized repeatedly since the Third Plenum of the Fourteenth Central Committee in November 1993 in order to address the problems of economic decentralization, while sweeping economic reforms were also adopted under the 'socialist market economy' formulation (Saich, 2001: 71). Under the 'macro adjustment and management' policy, the restructuring of the financial system and enterprise systems has begun, paving the way for robust economic growth in the 1990s.

The second institutional adjustment involved balancing center–local relations through the 'decentralization of authority.' From a vertical system under strict central planning, there is now a gradual transition to a system of horizontal coordination within the government structure. Under the vertical system, the central government controlled the state and society, and socioeconomic development in each province followed the dictates of the central government while local governments, despite being counterparts in structure and function to the central government, had no room to make their own policy choices. In contrast, the horizontal coordination system under decentralization, which began in the mid-1980s, saw local governments gaining more decision-making power to approve foreign investment projects, set up special trade and investment zones, decide on tax rates for foreign investment firms, establish trading companies, provide export subsides, allocate foreign exchange at official rates, and offer access to the foreign exchange swap markets in addition to gaining extensive authority over the domestic economy (Shirk, 1994: 31). Not only did the local governments become challengers to the central government, they also became competitors with each other in the 1990s, forcing the central government to undertake tax reform in 1993 and tax rationalization in 1998 to prevent the levying of excessive fees and other taxes by local authorities (Saich, 2001: 75).

The third institutional adjustment was to improve efficiency and prevent corruption by the 'simplification of administrative structure,' which had been undertaken four times in the past since 1978 as part of political reform (in 1983, 1988, 1993, and 1998). This form of adjustment had significant socioeconomic implications. First, it indicated that both the CCP and the Chinese government were attempting to cope with economic and social changes and improve their efficiency. Second, and more importantly, along with the 'separation of party from administration' and 'separation of administration from enterprise' policies, it was aimed at preventing the rent-seeking that had been rampant both in the party system and in the government apparatus at all levels following China's open-door policy (Economy, 1998: 15). This was regarded as threatening the legitimacy of the CCP and undermining public confidence in the 'reform and open door policy' of the authorities.

In short, these three institutional adjustments, although adopted for political expediency, have helped shape China's socioeconomic transition and were conducive to robust economic growth.

Establishing a social security system

While institutional adjustments have paved the way for maintaining economic growth, deepening reform of the income distribution system and improving the social security system are other important instruments to help China adjust to growing economic insecurities. These two reforms were expressed explicitly for the first time at the Sixteenth National Congress of the Communist Party of China:

> *Deepening the reform of the income distribution system and improving the social security system.* Rationalizing the relations of income distribution has a bearing on the immediate interests of the general public and the display of their initiative. We should adjust and standardize the relations of distribution among the state, enterprises and individuals.
>
> (Chinese Communist Party, 2002: 33)

Rhetorically, China's government is optimistic about its ability to create employment. According to the State Council Information Office, 'by the end of 2001, employees in urban areas accounted for 32.8 per cent of the total, and those in rural areas for 67.2 per cent. The unemployment rate on record in urban areas was 3.6 per cent' (State Council Information Office, 2002). In reality, China's government feels great pressure from rising unemployment and takes this as a serious challenge to political and social stability:

> The Chinese government is also fully aware that the unemployment problem in both the rural and urban areas will remain sharp, and structural unemployment will become more serious for a long time to come. Labor relations are expected to become more complicated, the aging of the population and the increase of unemployment will put more pressure on social security, and promotion of social security in rural areas will still have a way to go.
>
> (State Council Information Office, 2002)

Since the Fifteenth Party Congress and the Ninth National People's Congress in September 1997 and March 1998 respectively, a series of mechanisms have been put into effect to counter socioeconomic instability from rising unemployment, including developing a market-oriented employment mechanism; making overall plans for urban and rural employment; optimizing the employment structure; establishing a reemployment service and training centers; and setting up a social security system.

Establishing a market-oriented employment mechanism

To cope with the transition from a planned economy to a market economy and the formation of new labor relations, the government has called for a market-oriented employment mechanism since the 1980s, based on the notion of 'labor finding employment on their own initiative, the market adjusting the demand for employment and the government promoting employment' (State Council Information Office, 2002).

Making overall plans for urban and rural employment

To address the serious lack of employment opportunities in rural areas with abundant labor, and to stem rural–urban labor migration, two basic policies have been proposed (State Council Information Office, 2002). The first is to encourage rural labor to find work locally, which is aided by approaches to make use of local resources through readjusting the structure of agriculture and that of the rural economy in the following ways: developing profitable and labor-intensive agriculture alongside nonagricultural industries in the rural areas; guiding township enterprises to develop through the construction of small cities and towns; enhancing the construction of rural infrastructure facilities; and promoting elementary education and vocational training in the rural areas. The second policy is to guide rural labor to find employment in other areas.

Optimizing the employment structure

Optimizing the employment structure involves restructuring primary, secondary, and tertiary industries and that of state-owned, collective, and private enterprises. While undertaking reform of the SOEs, the government has encouraged the development of tertiary and private industries, an aim that has seen progress through the 1980s and 1990s. The proportion of employment in primary industry has dropped markedly, while that in secondary and tertiary industries has increased rapidly. In 2000, employment in the primary, secondary, and tertiary industries was registered at 50 percent, 22.5 percent and 27.5 percent respectively, while employees of state and collective enterprises and institutions accounted for only 37.3 percent of total urban employees in 2001, down from 99.8 percent in 1978 (State Council Information Office, 2002).

Establishing reemployment service and training centers

From 1998, the government began implementing the first phase of the 'ten million in three years' reemployment training program aimed at training 10 million laid-off/jobless workers within three years. Official claims are that more than 13 million laid-off and unemployed persons nationwide had taken part in training between 1998 and 2000, while the reemployment rate after six months of training had reached 60 percent (State Council Information Office, 2002).

Setting up a social security system

Compared to the above measures, the social security system is regarded as fundamental to social stability and was thus given priority on the political agenda of both the CCP and the government. Beginning in 1998, Labor and Social Security

Departments have been established at all levels of government, while a National Social Security Fund was also set up, with funds coming from the central finance appropriation and other channels. The 'two guarantees' policy has been adopted since then. The first is a guarantee of the basic livelihood of laid-off personnel from SOEs, which involves a laid-off worker receiving an allowance for basic living expenses, and he or she is also paid social insurance premiums. The second is a guarantee of the basic livelihood for all retirees, in the form of full basic pensions.

Coordinating the development of the regional economy

Regional disparities and the resultant instabilities constitute the third set of economic security issues for both the CCP and the Chinese government. Of these, the development of the western region has become the most pressing:

> *Advancing the development of the western region and bringing about a coordinated development of regional economies.* The implementation of the strategy for the development of the western region has a bearing on the overall situation of national development, ethnic unity and stability in border areas.
>
> (Chinese Communist Party, 2002: 28)

The Western Region Development Program,[7] which began in 1999, is regarded as a great strategy to 'eliminate regional disparities gradually, consolidate the unity of ethnic groups, ensure border safety and social stability and promote social progress' (Office of the Leading Group for Western Region Development of the State Council, 2002). The main objectives of the Western Region Development Program during the Tenth Five-Year Plan period, as set out by the Office of the Leading Group for Western Region Development of the State Council of China, include:

> During the Tenth Five-Year Plan period, priority should be given to such key tasks as infrastructure construction, ecological improvement, environmental protection, industrial restructuring and developing science, technology and education. Efforts should be concentrated on the construction of key projects in the following fields: water conservancy, communications, telecommunications, energy, urban public utilities, ecology, science and technology, education and rural infrastructure.[8]

It is too early to evaluate the Western Region Development Program, but three points are clear. First, China's policymakers are aware of the potential threat posed by regional disparities to China's political and social stability, and they hope to diminish or eliminate these disparities through appropriate policies. Second, coordinating the development of the regional economy is regarded as an important mechanism to maintain China's economic growth by promoting domestic market demand. Among the main objectives and projects in the Western Region Development Program are water conservation, communications, telecommunications, energy, urban public utilities, ecology, science and technology, education, and rural infrastructure, which not only legitimate increased central government investment in these regions but are also vital for attracting FDI. From 1999 to 2002, the central government invested US$73 billion (Y 600 billion) in the western region for thirty-six infrastructural programs, while nearly US$4 billion (Y 30 billion) was provided for water conservation and ecology during 2001–2002 (Office of the Leading Group for Western Region Development of the State Council, 2002). Third, western regional development helps alleviate not only the emerging tensions between the central government and local governments in the inland provinces, who complain that they are accorded less preferential treatment than the coastal areas, but also the tensions between local governments in the coastal areas and those in the inland provinces. These latter tensions similarly arise from their different economic performance, economic opportunities, and policy privileges, including the extent of fiscal subsidies provided by the central government since the early 1980s.

Concluding remarks

There is no doubt that China has benefited from its open-door policy in the context of globalization since the early 1980s. The consensus, in fact, is that China has benefited far more from globalization than have other regions such as Latin America and Africa (Mittelman, 2000: 49–54). This is perhaps why China undertook a fifteen-year effort to apply for WTO entry and continues its open-door policy. However, globalization and China's gradual incorporation into the world economy pose risks for the Chinese domestic market (especially its economic structure) and its market-related society (for example, through polarization, rising disparities, and unemployment), as discussed earlier in the chapter. Far more important, however, is the diminishing capacity of the state to govern economic reforms and China's changing society.

It appears that the uncertainties and risks from rising unemployment, continued inequalities, and decentralization of authority will become more serious because of deepening globalization and China's WTO entry, even as China maintains its robust economic growth in the future. Therefore, governing in the interests of economic security is now placed at the top of the agenda of the CCP and the Chinese government, and institutional adjustments will continue in order to address these economic insecurities. While it is not possible to draw any definite conclusions that the institutional adjustments and other policy instruments adopted by China to maintain its economic growth and address these emerging economic insecurities have been fully successful, we are at least able to draw three kinds of lessons from China's experience in order to help us understand how difficult it is to govern in the interests of economic security in the context of globalization.

First, globalization has prompted a reconceptualization of the linkages between economic growth and national security, especially as the flow of capital and trade not only promotes economic growth, but also leads to subsequent changes in the nature and structure of national security. This has increasingly meant that intellectuals and policymakers have had to shift their focus from the traditional dichotomies between the domestic and international levels and between economic growth and (political and military) security.

Second, adjustments to national institutions and domestic policy instruments remain key measures by which individual states can attempt to address national economic insecurities arising from globalization. But the responses of different countries to national economic security may vary. From observing both the evolution of conceptions of economic security in China and Chinese approaches to addressing economic insecurity in the context of globalization, we may say that an approach based on gradualism has been successful, especially when compared to the 'shock therapy' chosen by the former Soviet Union and in light of the economic crisis in East Asia. But this does not mean that China will be immune from similar events.

Third, it is necessary for individual countries to establish a broader social-economic insurance network rather than depend solely on economic policy instruments to address economic insecurity. Because the economic insecurity from globalization emerges from the bottom, as in China, and through multiple channels due to globalization of the economy, the task of managing both the economy and society becomes that much more difficult for the state. The Chinese case shows that policy instruments may be efficient in the short term and in some domains, but for long-term socioeconomic security a more balanced social-economic insurance network to channel the risks of globalization needs to be developed. This can be achieved through state-led institutional adjustment or regional/global (formal and informal) cooperation, or a combination of national and regional/global institutions, if only to reduce the cost of institutional adjustment in individual countries and to ensure that the insecurities are addressed at source.

Notes

1   Among the many works on this issue are the following: 'Origin of Economic Security,' *Contemporary World and Socialism*, No. 4, 1997; 'A Survey of Opinions about Economic Security,' *Academic Tendency*, June 1998; 'National Economy and China's Economic Security,' *Forum on World Economy and Politics*, Vol. 2, 2000; and *Economic Globalization and National Economic Security*, The Economics Publishing House, 2000.

2   Among the studies undertaken on this issue are *China Confronts the Challenge of Globalization: Implications for Domestic Cohesion and International Cooperation*, Rockefeller Brothers Fund Inc., and Wang and Hu (1999). The surveys on this issue conducted by international organizations include International Labour Organization (2001).

3   See, for example, Wang (2000), Lai (2003), and International Labor Organization (2001).'

4   'Xiagang' staff and workers are those in urban state-owned and collective enterprises who become redundant while keeping welfare connections with their original units and receiving a minimum wage.

5   In terms of labor market security, conventional statistics are misleading. The unemployment rate typically mentioned is 3.1 percent. But, as it is easy to show, this is actually a residual, and is a fiction, which cannot even be used as a proxy for unemployment or for time-series analysis, let alone for international comparisons.

6   The taxes are divided into three parts in 'separate tax systems': central taxes needed to maintain the center's ability to exercise macro control on a national scale for the national benefit; regional taxes needed to meet regional needs; and shared taxes to directly support economic development at the central and local levels.

7   The Western Region Development Program covers six provinces, one municipality, and five autonomous regions, namely, Chongqing Municipality, Sichuan Province, Guizhou Province, Yunnan Province, Shanxi Province, Gansu Province, Qinghai Province, Ningxia Hui Autonomous Region, Xinjiang Uygur Autonomous Region, Tibet Autonomous Region, Inner Mongolia Autonomous Region, Guangxi Zhuang Autonomous Region.

8   Full details are to be found in 'Overall Plan of Western Region Development during the Tenth Five-Year Plan Period,' Office of the Leading Group for Western Region Development of the State Council (http://www.chinawest.gov.cn/).

References

Asia Times (2000) *Country Economic Review: People's Republic of China*, [Online] http://www.atimes.com/reports/BL23Ai01.html (accessed 5 March 2003).

Asian Development Bank (2000) 'China's Economic Prospects' [Online] http://www.adb.org/Documents/Speeches/2000/sp2000001.asp (accessed 5 March 2003).

Chinese Communist Party (2002) *Documents of the 16th National Congress of the Communist Party of China*, Beijing: Foreign Languages Press.

Documents Research Division of the Central Committee of the Chinese Communist Party (1987) *Selected Readings of Important Documents since the Third Plenum of the Eleventh Central Committee*, Beijing: People's Press.

Economy, Elizabeth (1998) *China Confronts the Challenge of Globalization: Implications for Domestic Cohesion and International Cooperation*, New York: Rockefeller Brothers Fund.

Hawkins, William R. (2002) 'The Chinese Economic Challenge and Its Geo-political Implications' [Online] http://www.tradealert.org (accessed 1 March 2003).

Hu Sheng (1997) *Reflections on China's Road to Development: Nine Essays by Hu Sheng, 1983–1996*, Beijing: Commercial Press.

International Labour Organization (2001) 'China: Labor Market and Income Insecurity' [Online] http://www.ilo.org (accessed 1 March 2003).

Lai Pingyao (2003) 'China's Economic Growth: New Trends and Implications,' *China and World Economy*, No. 1.

Mittelman, James H. (2000) *The Globalization Syndrome: Transformation and Resistance*, Princeton, NJ: Princeton University Press.

National Bureau of Statistics of China, *China Statistical Yearbook*, various years, Beijing: China Statistical Publishing House.

Office of the Leading Group for Western Region Development of the State Council (2002) 'Overall Plan of Western Region Development During the Tenth Five-Year Plan Period' [Online] http://www.chinawest.gov.cn/ (accessed 20 March 2003).

Saich, Tony (2001) *Governance and Politics of China*, New York: Palgrave.

Shirk, Susan L. (1993) *Political Logic of Economic Reform in China*, Berkeley: University of California Press.

—— (1994) *How China Opened Its Door: The Political Success of PRC's Foreign Trade and Investment Reforms*, Washington, DC: Brookings Institution.

State Council Information Office (2002) 'Labor and Social Security in China' [Online] http://www.china.org.cn (accessed 20 March 2003).

Wang Shaoguang (2000) 'Openness, Distributive Conflict, and Social Insurance: The

Social and Political Implication of China's WTO Membership' [Online] http://www. gateway2china.com/report/CUHK_paper.htm (accessed 25 February 2003).

Wang Shaoguang and Hu Angang (1999) *The Political Economy of Uneven Development: The Case of China*, Armonk, NY: M. E. Sharpe.

World Bank (2000) *World Development Report 1999/2000*, ch. 5, Oxford: Oxford University Press.

Yabuki, Susumu (1995) *China's New Political Economy: The Giant Awakes*, trans. Stephen M. Harner, Boulder, CO: Westview Press.

Yu Yongding (2001) 'A Review of China's Macroeconomic Development and Policies in the 1990s,' *China and World Economy*, No. 6.

Zhao Quansheng (1996) *Interpreting Chinese Foreign Policy*, Hong Kong: Oxford University Press.

5 Institutional capacity and Singapore's developmental state

Managing economic (in)security in the global economy

Henry Wai-Chung Yeung

Introduction

To date, an overwhelming body of literature has been devoted to 'globalisation' – both as a contested set of discourses and as a transformative force in the global economy. Boyer (2000: 294) argues that the constantly used term 'globalisation' is

> not an innocent one, since it suggests that nation-states, firms and, even more so, individuals are powerless in the face of an implacable determinism, since it comes from somewhere else, outside the control of national politics. This opinion, widely accepted, even by those who are politically opposed to globalization, merits systematic criticism.

As a set of discourses, globalisation encapsulates certain political agenda, in particular neoliberalism, to create its own conditions of existence (Yeung, 1998a, 2000a, 2002a; Kelly, 1999). As a set of material processes, globalisation is constituted by intensified flows – tangible and intangible – across societies on a global scale. It is, however, beyond the scope of this chapter to review this huge body of literature (see Hirst and Thompson, 1996; Mittelman, 1996; Held *et al.*, 1999; Olds *et al.*, 1999; Berger and Huntington, 2002; Dicken, 2003; Peck and Yeung, 2003).

In this chapter, I want to emphasise one critical dimension of globalisation: its transformative nature, which both strengthens state *capacity* under certain historically and geographically specific conditions, and reduces state *control* through the globalisation of economic activities orchestrated by global firms and extra-territorial institutions (see Sassen, 2000; Rieger and Leibfried, 2003). As explained by Wallerstein (1999: 32), the state is indispensable to capitalists, 'for they need the state, the strong state, far more than their official rhetoric has ever admitted. . . . [C]apitalists depend on the intervention of the states in such a multitude of ways that any true weakening of state authority is disastrous'. This is an important point, because it has often been assumed in the ultra-globalist literature that globalisation represents a single and uni-directional socio-spatial logic towards the homogenisation of national economies and state governance.

This view, however, fails to recognise that the very logic of globalisation itself is highly contested in a reflexive manner by multiple actors (e.g. firms, states, civil organisations, international institutions and so on) at different spatial scales (e.g. local, regional, national and global). Thus, globalisation operates as a set of complex and conflicting tendencies, the outcomes of which – for instance, about the power of the state – often cannot be predicted a priori but must be investigated empirically. As argued by Mittelman (2000: 55), 'globalization does not sideline the state but, rather, conduces it to accommodate domestic policies to the pressures generated by transnational capital'. Globalisation may lead to the demise of one state; but it may also contribute to the rise of another. As a set of tendencies, globalisation has no inherent 'goodness' or 'badness' for its players: social groups, labour unions, firms, and state institutions. It depends on the transformative capacity of these players, some of which are clearly better positioned than others to benefit from globalisation tendencies (Kapstein, 2000).

This chapter presents an empirical case study of the complex interactions between a city-state in Southeast Asia – Singapore – and globalisation processes. Singapore's case is significant because many of its characteristics (e.g. small size, economic openness and heavy reliance on foreign investments) make it particularly vulnerable to the detrimental effects of globalisation (e.g. external dependence and economic shocks). Singapore's experience in the past four decades since it became a modern nation-state in 1965, however, has been one of enormous benefit from its participation in globalisation processes. How then do we explain this anomaly in the midst of the globalisation debate and the growing concern with economic security in a global era? I show in this chapter that the relative success of Singapore clearly has something to do with how the state and its domestic institutions are able to adapt and respond to globalisation processes. In managing its participation in the global economy and avoiding the potential pitfalls of economic globalisation, the Singapore state has carved out a unique developmental trajectory premised on the relentless search for global capital, the direct involvement of state institutions in economic activities and the championing of policy credibility and consistency. The state is conceptualised as a set of contested institutional structures and social practices that possess specific power and authority to effect changes and to achieve specific policy goals. To Mitchell (1991: 90), the state should not be taken as 'essentially an actor, with the coherence, agency, and subjectivity this term presumes'. Instead, the state should be viewed as a network of institutional mechanisms that internalises the state–society distinction and maintains the social and political order (see also Jessop, 1990; Weiss, 1998, 2003; Brenner *et al.*, 2003).

In the case of Singapore, I would argue that the policy effectiveness of these institutional mechanisms contributes significantly to the state's capacity in meeting the challenges of globalisation. More specifically, this chapter focuses on two market sectors (labour and finance) that the state in Singapore is capable of governing in order for Singapore to be articulated beneficially into the global economy. My objective here is to demonstrate that the various state institutions involved in labour market and financial market governance are highly adaptive to the dynamic challenges of globalisation. In engaging with global forces, the state in Singapore is being constantly reconstituted through institutional changes. As a caveat, however, this chapter tends to emphasise less the *external* activities of the Singapore state that may contribute to Singapore's enlarging political-economic spaces, such as regional economic strategies and favourable global trade regimes underwritten by the United States. Apart from examining the policy changes occurring within key domestic institutions in their regulation of the labour and financial markets, this chapter also focuses on the developmental outcomes of these institutional changes; that is, minimising economic insecurity in relation to globalisation tendencies. This focus on state capacity does not necessarily imply that the state's performance legitimacy is automatically self-evident and self-sustaining. The now increasingly uncertain global economy looms large over the critical issue of whether state capacity, though having underscored past success, can continue to sustain Singapore's competitive position in the future global economy. I consider some of these future challenges in the concluding section of this chapter.

This chapter is organised into three sections. The next section discusses the role of the Singapore state in managing post-war development in a globalising era. In the second section, I focus on the state's governance of the labour and financial markets that allows Singapore to benefit from globalisation processes. The section takes a historical approach and describes certain strategic policy changes occurring among key domestic institutions involved in governance of both these markets. The concluding section revisits the globalisation debate and draws some implications from this study for understanding economic security in today's global political economy.

Unpacking the developmental state in Singapore: institutional capacity and political legitimacy

To understand the role of the Singapore state in effecting domestic governance, it is important to define in clearer terms its institutional capacity, which allows it to be highly adaptive and strategic in harnessing globalisation tendencies. Here, I simply take Weiss's (1998: 5) definition of state capacity as 'the ability of policy-making authorities to pursue domestic adjustment strategies that, in cooperation with organized economic groups, update or transform the industrial economy'. It is a negotiated product of institutions governing domestic activities. Although this chapter is concerned with state capacity that gives the state certain strategic advantages to respond to and benefit from globalisation processes, it does not ignore the strong pressures imposed by globalisation processes on certain states that are relatively weaker in their institutional capacity. But given the overwhelming attention paid by the ultra-globalist literature to the demise of the state, revisiting the constitution of state capacity and its realisation in specific geographical contexts may illuminate better the complex interdependency and interactions between globalisation processes and states. Before I examine the role of the Singapore state in governing firms through labour and financial market regulation in the next section, it is useful to offer a brief overview of Singapore's articulation into the global economy and the formation of important domestic institutions that condition this articulation.

Singapore's post-war economic development

Singapore has grown from a British colonial entrepôt in the late nineteenth and early twentieth centuries to a modern city-state specialising in high-value-added manufacturing activities and international financial and business services (Régnier, 1991; Huff, 1994; Perry *et al.*, 1997; Low, 1998; Pereira, 2000; Yeung, 2002b). With its independence and changing global economic systems, Singapore was able to attract a huge influx of foreign investment that took advantage of Singapore's explicit policies towards export-oriented industrialisation. This reliance on foreign capital worked very well in the first two decades of Singapore's industrialisation and plugged Singapore into the so-called new international division of labour (Fröbel *et al.*, 1980). This strategy of courting foreign capital was perceived as 'essential in view of the weak domestic technological base and the long lead-time needed to transform domestic entrepôt traders and small-scale entrepreneurs into a dynamic industrial entrepreneurial class able to compete in the global market' (Chia, 1997: 32).

The 1970s and the 1980s witnessed a massive expansion of foreign direct investment (FDI) from the United States, Japan and European countries (Mirza, 1986; Huff, 1994; McKendrick *et al.*, 2000). Net foreign investment commitments in Singapore's manufacturing sector grew tremendously from S$88.6 million in 1963 to S$6.3 billion in 1999, representing a more than seventyfold increase over a period of three and a half decades (Department of Statistics, various years a). Cumulative FDI in Singapore reached S$196 billion in 2000 (http://www.singstat. gov.sg, accessed 15 October 2003). Throughout the 1980s and into the early 1990s, Singapore attracted over 10 per cent of all FDI received by destinations outside the OECD (Perry *et al.*, 1997: 15). In an assessment of the importance of foreign capital in Singapore's economy, Huff (1995: table 6) estimates that foreign investment contributed some 22 per cent and 26 per cent of the gross fixed capital formation (GFCF) during the 1970–1979 and 1980–1992 periods respectively. This ratio of foreign investment to GFCF is certainly one of the highest among the Asian newly industrialising economies (NIEs). In 1997, Singapore played host to some 16,190 foreign transnational corporations (TNCs), over 300 of which were in the manufacturing sector (Department of Statistics, 2000: xi).

Since the 1980s, there has been a qualitative shift in the nature of foreign investment in Singapore as the island economy grew from being an offshore manufacturing base to being a regional control and coordination centre. Perry *et al.* (1997: 15) observe two major influences behind this transformation in FDI activities. First, the emergence of a 'regional focus' in the corporate strategy of many TNCs has resulted in the decentralisation of an extended range of business functions to enable fuller exploitation of the Southeast Asian regional market than had previously been attempted. Second, the regional decentralisation of foreign investment to nearby countries was a response to increasing labour costs, and unavailability of land and other factors of production. Singapore is well positioned as the apex in the emerging regional division of labour by assuming a key role as a distribution, testing, design and administrative centre for production that is spatially dispersed among a new 'periphery' of lower-cost countries (e.g. Indonesia, Malaysia, Thailand and the Philippines). The state-sanctioned 'growth triangle' concept also gained increasing currency because of its promise to expand significantly Singapore's regional economic space (Grundy-Warr *et al.*, 1999; Dent, 2002).

By the late 1980s, the Singapore state began to realise the limits of capital accumulation within Singapore and the need to expand its global reach in search of new sites for continuous capital accumulation (Yeung and Olds, 1998; Yeung, 1998b, 1999, 2002b; Pereira, 2003). Singapore faced increasing competition and rivalry with foreign capital because of the availability of more favourable investment locations in nearby countries. In short, global competition for investment had stepped up significantly by the late 1980s and the early 1990s (see Phelps and Raines, 2003). This anticipation of long-term limits to growth was later transformed into an official state policy for building an 'external wing' to Singapore's economy in the early 1990s. Singapore's regionalisation effort was officially launched in early 1993. Through it, both state-owned and private-sector enterprises were encouraged to regionalise their operations and invest in the Asian region and beyond. The state has not only created favourable conditions for this regionalisation effort, but also taken key initiatives to ensure its success. By the end of 2001, Singapore's total stock of foreign equity investment stood at S$257 billion, out of which S$131 billion was direct investment. China was the largest host country, accounting for 13 per cent of Singapore's direct investment abroad (http://www.singstat.gov.sg, accessed 25 August 2003). This relatively recent departure in Singapore's economic development strategies underscores the institutional capacity of the developmental state in steering the Singapore economy and domestic corporate activities.

Singapore's developmental state revisited

How do we explain the capacity of the state in Singapore to steer a pathway to economic development and to implement drastic restructuring policies that orient the city-state towards the global economy? To understand the formation of Singapore's developmental state, one has to unpack the political economy of its post-war development. Johnson (1982) and Wade (1990) have defined a developmental state as a state preoccupied with economic development through the establishment of elite economic bureaucracy to 'guide' the market (see also Woo-Cumings, 1999). A developmental state tends to engage numerous institutions for consultation and coordination with the private sector, and these consultations are an essential part of the process of policy formulation and implementation. While state bureaucrats 'rule', politicians 'reign'. The latter's function is not to make policy, but to create economic and political space for the bureaucracy to manoeuvre. They also act as a 'safety valve' by forcing the bureaucrats to respond to the needs of groups upon which the stability of the system rests; that is, to maintain the relative autonomy of the state while preserving political stability (Evans, 1995). In Singapore, this separation of 'ruling' and 'reigning' is accompanied by a form of 'soft authoritarianism' that maintains the needs of economic development vis-à-vis other claims and enjoys a virtual monopoly of political power in a single political party or institution over a long period of time (Mauzy and Milne, 2002).

To a certain extent, the rise of the developmental state in Singapore is influenced by immediate post-independence experience and subsequent political development. It has coincided with the ascent of the People's Action Party (PAP) to power and its enduring power in politics and government since independence. National economic development has become the primordial goal of the PAP government for the past forty years. The Singapore economy was very dependent on entrepôt trade for basic livelihood and employment under the British administration. Trade alone accounted for up to one-third of gross domestic product (GDP) at factor cost in 1957 (Rodan, 1989: 48) and 31 per cent of real GDP at 1968 prices in 1960. The development of manufacturing industries became the top priority of the newly elected PAP government in the immediate post-1959 period. Perry *et al.* (1997: 7) note that, as a consequence, 'the state gives much greater priority to transforming economic conditions than it does to changing aspects of the social order'.

The Singapore economy inherited by the PAP from the British administration was, however, weak in industrial bourgeoisie and lacked any significant manufacturing base. Indigenous entrepreneurship was not strong enough financially to shoulder the burden of industrialising Singapore. Moreover, the PAP-ruled state was suspicious of indigenous capitalists for fear of their pro-communist and pro-China attitudes (Régnier, 1993). The resource-deficient city-state subsequently chose to rely on foreign capital to accelerate economic growth in order to legitimise its political domination. In other words, the Singapore state realised the importance of harnessing global processes and orientating itself towards the global economy from the very beginning of its independence (Olds and Yeung, 2004). In his memoirs, the former prime minister Lee Kuan Yew (2000: 75) recalls that

> [s]ince our neighbours were out to reduce their ties with us, we had to link up with the developed world – America, Europe and Japan – and attract their manufacturers to produce in Singapore and export their products to the developed countries.

The state has since been building up its institutional capacity to realise its developmental strategies, irrespective of the 'arrival' of globalisation processes. In doing so, the PAP state founded several important developmental institutions that have evolved over time to become an indispensable part of its state capacity.

In 1961, the Economic Development Board (EDB) of Singapore was established as a one-stop investment promotion agency to assist foreign firms in their operations in Singapore. Working closely with the Ministry of Trade and Industry, the EDB has since played a key role in shaping the Singapore economy through its efforts to solve the unemployment problem, promote investment, train manpower and develop the industrial sector (Low *et al.*, 1993; Pereira, 2000; Koh, 2002). The main concern of the EDB was and still is in attracting foreign (preferably global) firms to invest in Singapore. Generous incentive schemes were offered to foreign firms to compensate for the lack of competitive advantage in Singapore during its early phase of industrialisation (e.g. the Pioneer Industries Ordinance in 1959 and the Economic Expansion Incentives Act in 1967). The establishment of the Jurong Town Corporation (JTC) in 1968 provided another institutional boost to the state's strategy of relying on foreign capital. The JTC was primarily responsible for the construction and management of industrial estates, the first of which was located in the Jurong area. These industrial estates were intended to provide low-cost production sites for foreign manufacturing firms. Since its establishment, the JTC has planned, developed and managed more than 6,000 hectares of industrial land, of which over two-thirds has remained under its ownership (Perry *et al.*, 1997: 158). It is also directly involved in the development of several high-tech clusters and science parks in Singapore (see Phillips and Yeung, 2003). Together, both statutory boards have worked well in attracting large inflows of foreign investment into Singapore throughout the past four decades.

Another key attribute of Singapore's developmental state is the close alliance of the PAP and the state bureaucracy (see also Haggard, 1999; Hamilton-Hart, 2000; Low, 2001). In a 1998 survey of PAP ministers, all 24 ministers and ministers of state had served the civil service and/or statutory boards except Lee Kuan Yew himself (former prime minister and senior minister and now minister mentor) and five others (*The Straits Times*, 26 April 1998). Since the first general election for a fully elected legislative assembly in 1959, the PAP has not lost to any single opposition party, thus ensuring a continuous domination of party ideology and preoccupation with economic development. There is a virtual monopoly of political power by the PAP in Singapore since its independence, and this has created a stable (albeit repressive) political environment and a significant space for a closer party–state alliance (Hill and Lian, 1995). To a certain extent, the PAP has become the state and has a significant role in 'guiding' developmental policies. The state bureaucracy, on the other hand, serves the general interests of Singapore exceptionally well by formulating development policies that enable the proliferation of foreign firms and state-owned enterprises. In particular, these development policies are situated in the context of labour market and financial market governance through which the institutional capacity of the Singapore state becomes most apparent.

Harnessing the global economy: the institutional regulation of labour and financial markets in Singapore

Other than creating appropriate institutions for promoting economic development (e.g. the EDB and JTC), the state employed other institutional measures to enhance Singapore's attractiveness to global capital. It did so in consultation with major TNCs. According to representatives of major TNCs interviewed by Dent (2003: 260), the transnational business community enjoys a 'symbiotic and consultative relationship' with the Singapore state. While these major TNCs 'do not directly shape the government's economic policies', they do offer feedback and comments that can be 'forthright, honest and brutal but non-political'. In this way, global executives are often invited by the state to 'sit around the strategic table to supplement the government's own thinking'. If these institutional measures and policy strategies make sense in the prevailing global economic conditions (and they often do), these executives will offer fine-tuning advice and ultimately endorsement. For example, Dent (2003) has examined how the EDB's International Advisory Council (IAC), first established in January 1995 and composed of fourteen top TNC executives, does not exert any discernible independent leverage over Singapore's economic policymakers, but rather offers minor suggestions on the state's pre-designed policy blueprints and strategies. In this sense, the state enjoys a significant degree of 'embedded autonomy' from domestic and international economic actors that allows the state to act decisively in accordance with changing global competitive dynamics. I now examine two key arenas in which the state harnesses the potential benefits of globalisation.

Labour market governance in an era of spatial flexibility

To begin, the rapid influx of foreign capital in the immediate post-independence era is largely explained by local labour market regulation in which labour movements were consciously suppressed and labour disciplined (Rodan, 1989; Huff, 1995, 1999; Yeung, 1999; Coe and Kelly, 2002; Sung, 2004). In a first move towards this goal, three labour organisations were brought together in late 1965 to ratify a 'Charter for Industrial Progress'. They were the National Trade Union Congress, the Singapore Manufacturers' Association and the Singapore Employers' Federation. Under this charter, 'all partners in the industrialization program, worker, employer, government, must pool their efforts and strive for a continuing increase in productivity and output in all enterprises' (quoted in Rodan, 1989: 91). The appeal of the charter was consistent with the ideological notions of self-sacrifice for the collective good and of economic problems being above class interests, both promulgated by Lee Kuan Yew's PAP. Through its political influence in the tripartite National Trade Union Congress (NTUC), which comprised representatives from the PAP government, labour and capital, the state was able to deny labour unions their traditional role as legitimate interest groups and to corporatise labour into the management needs of the state.[1]

The state further regulated the labour market by disciplining the labour force with the Trade Union (Amendment) Bill in 1966 and the Employment Act in 1968 and the Industrial Relations (Amendment) Act. These constitutional measures greatly weakened the scope for industrial action and marked the arrival of corporatism in Singapore. Rodan (1989: 93) observes that 'one thing was abundantly clear: militant trade unionism was finished in Singapore. Labor was now part of the corporate structure of the Singapore state'. These labour market regulations managed to achieve corporatist and non-militant labour relations, and resulted in the creation of a highly disciplined and depoliticised labour force in Singapore. They were deemed necessary because of Singapore's highly exposed economy and its lack of any natural resources (cf. other small states in Katzenstein, 1985).

Towards the mid-1970s, the low-cost export-oriented industrialisation strategy in Singapore faced increasing pressures from global competition because of contradictions in the labour market, where labour remained low in skill and productivity. Their relative low wages also made it difficult to sustain Singapore's export-led industrialisation because of insufficient mass consumption. The state intervened in the labour market through the National Wage Council (NWC), which is a state-related institution established to determine collective wages at the national level through its annual wage recommendations. The function of the NWC in the early phase of Singapore's industrialisation was to keep wage rises in check. This function was no longer appropriate by the mid-1970s, when Singapore faced increasing pressure for industrial restructuring in order to meet low-cost competition from regional economies. In 1979, a 'corrective' wage policy – alternatively known as the 'Second Industrial Revolution' in Singapore – was recommended by the NWC on the basis of the belief that artificially low labour costs in previous years had distorted the real market value of Singapore's scarce labour and contributed to high dependence of the economy on labour-intensive production established by foreign firms. The NWC recommended considerable increases in wages. A Skills Development Fund was proposed to aid the upgrading of labour skills and financed by a levy imposed on employers. This dramatic departure from a low-cost industrialisation strategy towards aiming to become a higher-value-added manufacturing and business centre demonstrates the pragmatic ideology of the NWC and the state in charting Singapore's economic development towards a more knowledge- and skill-intensive economy.

This 'Second Industrial Revolution' in Singapore aimed at shaking out inefficient users of labour by raising wages to induce rationalisation of production, which could take several forms. Some labour-intensive foreign manufacturers subsequently relocated their production facilities to other low-cost countries (Rodan, 1989; Ho, 1993, 1994; Chiu *et al.*, 1997). Others moved up the technological ladder by upgrading their value-added activities and automating their operations in Singapore. During this restructuring process, workers were allowed to operate a third shift (i.e. twenty-four-hour manufacturing operations were instituted) to offset the high fixed costs that resulted from capitalisation. These round-the-clock manufacturing operations also implied that there was a need to maintain flexible production arrangements.

Another dimension of labour-market restructuring during the 1980s was the increasing participation of foreign workers in Singapore's labour force. Firms were more willing to employ foreign labour because such labourers were perceived to have more positive work attitudes (including willingness to work extra hours and night shifts), higher education levels and relative youth. Between 1975 and 1979, foreign labour constituted one-third of the growth in the workforce. Between 1980 and 1984, foreign workers accounted for more than half the workforce increase in Singapore.[2] The original position of the state in the late 1970s and early 1980s was to view foreign workers as a temporary measure. But by the late 1980s, this view was replaced by one that allowed for a carefully controlled intake. The state has thereafter developed foreign-worker policies that are more indirect, using the foreign-worker levy and quotas to constrain the growth in the number of foreign workers. The size of the levy and quotas not only differ for skilled and unskilled workers, but also vary between different industries. These foreign-worker policies, however, generally favour high-tech and high-value-added foreign firms in Singapore (Hui, 1997; Coe and Kelly, 2000, 2002; Yeoh and Chang, 2001), as indicated in their relative ease in getting foreign-worker approval and quotas.

The rapid and flexible responses of the Singapore state and its domestic institutions (e.g. the NWC and the NTUC) to the 1997–1998 Asian economic crisis through politically unfriendly labour market regulation further underscore its still strong institutional capacity and political legitimacy. Singapore's political elite tried to deconstruct the Asian 'miracle' by distancing themselves from other Asian economies in which strong state intervention was turned into massive corruption and cronyism. They were also quick to point out that because of the PAP government's good governance, Singapore was relatively less troubled by the economic downturn. By naturalising globalisation processes and their negative impact on those Asian economies with weak and corrupt states, the political elite in Singapore were able to rally support from both labour and capital (Yeung, 2000b, 2000c; Kelly, 2001; Lai and Yeung, 2003). This support is crucial to maintain the political legitimacy of the corporatist state and is evident in the virtually uncontested implementation of the S$10 billion cost-cutting packages announced in late 1998. The National Wage Council recommended that the wages of Singapore's workforce be reduced by 5–8 per cent and the employers' contributions to the Central Provident Fund (CPF) be reduced from 20 per cent of gross salaries to 10 per cent (*The Straits Times*, 12 November 1998). Other non-wage measures included lower government taxes and charges to reduce business costs and to stimulate consumer demand.[3]

This significant wage cut was arrived at through state-coordinated deliberations by the NWC and political rallies to convince various labour unions and interest groups of its necessity. Speaking at the tripartite NTUC Ordinary Delegates Conference, Prime Minister Goh Chok Tong told union leaders that

> [i]nvestors are watching carefully how Asian countries respond to the crisis. They will watch whether government responses are rational, business-friendly and address the problems at hand. They will also see whether the people support necessary measures that are tough, painful and unpopular. Between 8 and 10 per cent, I recommend we bite the bullet and take a 10 per cent cut [in CPF]. This will give a strong and decisive signal to investors that Singaporeans are prepared to adopt tough measures to make their businesses competitive.
>
> (quoted in *The Straits Times*, 30 October 1998)[4]

Delegates at the NTUC Conference finally adopted a resolution to endorse the state's move to revive the economy through wage and CPF cuts. They pledged that the NTUC would give its 'full support to the Government in adopting whatever measures necessary to counteract the effects of the sharp economic downturn' (quoted in *The Straits Times*, 4 November 1998). Although this tripartite consensus among the state, capital and labour may be peculiar to Singapore's developmental state, it certainly shows the strength of the whole constituted by the credibility of individual constituents. The strong tripartite relationship contributes to the institutional capacity of the state to implement specific policy instruments (e.g. wage reduction and/or cuts in provident fund contributions) to counter the competitive pressures from globalisation. These packages have clearly contributed to rapid post-crisis economic recovery whereby growth rates increased from 0.5 per cent in 1998 to 5 per cent in 1999 and 10.1 per cent in 2000. They are likely to be a key set of policy instruments in addressing Singapore's 'competitiveness problem' – a lingering issue exacerbated by the recent war in Iraq and the SARS outbreak in the first half of 2003.

Financial market governance in an era of global finance

If Singapore's labour market can be effectively governed by strong state capacity in an era of globalisation (cf. larger states explained in Peck, 2000; Tickell and Peck, 2003), does the same observation hold for its financial markets, which are presumably much more volatile and globalised? Despite Singapore's role as a major international financial centre, the state has certain institutional capacity to manage and effect changes in its financial markets. The relationship between financial institutions, regulatory authorities and the state in Singapore is best characterised as 'interlocking networks of financial power and regulation' (Mitchell, 1991: 90). In fact, Hamilton-Hart (2000, 2002) argues that Singapore's state bureaucracy has little autonomy outside the financial sector, and the political leadership is entwined with leading members of the financial community. For example, several former and current ministers and top civil servants have links with local banks in various capacities as former chairmen and directors (e.g. the deputy prime minister, Tony Tan, with Overseas Chinese Banking Corporation; former cabinet minister S. Dhanabalan with the Development Bank of Singapore; and EDB chairman Philip Yeo with United Overseas Bank). Unlike the substantial autonomy enjoyed by central banks in many OECD countries, the senior management of Singapore's central bank, the Monetary Authority of Singapore (MAS), is appointed by the president of Singapore. The current chairman, Mr Goh Chok Tong, is also senior minister of Singapore (and a former prime minister). Given the relatively small pool of top leaders in Singapore, this close relationship between cabinet ministers, top civil servants and local banks contributes significantly to the institutional embeddedness of the Singapore state bureaucracy in its financial sector.

As will become evident, this institutional embeddedness has allowed for the emergence of major domestic banking institutions under the protectionist policies of the state, which is ironic given Singapore's continuous effort to be a global financial centre and a major player in financial globalisation. But this relatively stable relationship between domestic financial institutions and the state did not last for much longer. Primarily because of the intensification of global competition and the state's recognition of the need to develop Singapore as a leading international financial centre, financial market liberalisation was initiated through formal state policies before and in the aftermath of the Asian economic crisis. What makes the Singapore case different from that of other crisis-ridden economies in Asia is that this financial market liberalisation has proceeded gradually under the close supervision of such state institutions as the Ministry of Finance and the MAS.

When the Thai baht collapsed in July 1997, Singapore's financial sector was not completely liberalised to global competition. The MAS still held firm control of the sector and practised rather conservative financial-sector supervision, particularly after the Barings Bank debacle in 1995 (see Tickell, 1996). Indeed, under the chairmanship of the then deputy prime minister, Lee Hsien Loong (now prime minister), who preferred a more competitive financial sector, the MAS initiated major financial liberalisation programmes only in the aftermath of the 1997–1998 Asian crisis to take advantage of the impending influx of global capital. The state has therefore taken the opportunity offered by the crisis to liberalise further its financial markets, underscoring its institutional capacity in managing domestic economic affairs. As the former prime minister Lee Kuan Yew describes, '[w]hat we did was out of our own convictions, but it coincided with the IMF and US Treasury prescription on how to develop a financial free market' (Lee, 2000: 552–553).

Before we examine this process of financial market liberalisation, it is useful to review the nature of Singapore's financial market. As a major international financial centre today (Wu and Duk, 1995; Wu, 1997), Singapore has relatively high ratios of banks per 1,000 population (see Table 5.1). These banks, ranging from full-licence banks and deposit-taking banks to offshore banks, provide critical financial resources for the city-state to thrive in the global economy. In Singapore's early phase of industrialisation, state-owned enterprises participated directly in the capital accumulation process through the provision of credit and loans, subsidisation of labour costs, and expansion of land supply. The Singapore state established the Development Bank of Singapore (DBS) in 1968 as an industrial bank to provide long-term financing for the nascent domestic industrial sector. This had a tremendous 'demonstration effect' on Singapore's banking sector. A report by the director of DBS in 1969 observed that

> some banks are now beginning to grant term loans of, say, up to five years to industries. This step may have been taken as a result of the establishment of the Development Bank of Singapore. The provision of term loans may lead to opportunities for the more lucrative short-term financing. Unless banks want to lose business to Development Bank of Singapore, which also provides short-term loans, it may be to their interest to consider giving term loans to manufacturers.

> (quoted in Chiu *et al.*, 1997: 47–48)

Compared to other, similar financial centres (e.g. Hong Kong), a very important difference in Singapore's financial system is the role of the CPF. The establishment of the CPF Board in Singapore was intended to provide long-term security to its members and to initiate a compulsory national saving scheme to finance national development plans. These plans range from major infrastructural developments to public housing programmes. Excessive funds in the CPF are also invested in equities and other financial instruments through the Government Investment Corporation

Table 5.1 Financial markets and institutions in Singapore, 1960–1999 (S$million)

	Growth rate (%)				Annual figures				
	1962–70	1970–80	1980–90	1990–99	1962	1970	1980	1990	1999
Number of banks	—	—	4.1	0.9	—	—	97.0	141.0	154.0
Per 1,000 population	—	—	—	—	—	—	4.0	4.7	4.0
Total bank loans (S$)	21.8	75.7	16.9	15.5	731.1	2,167.7	20,206.9	57,696.4	147,178.0
Manufacturing (%)					12.8	34.1	21.6	13.0	7.9
General Commerce					51.6	31.3	39.3	23.7	13.5
Financial industries					6.7	3.6	10.4	17.2	14.3
Transport & Comm.					2.7	1.5	6.4	3.0	2.5
Construction					2.6	8.4	9.3	22.3	39.8
Individuals						13.1	7.0	13.4	14.7
Prime rates (%)						8.0	13.6	7.73	5.8 (1998)
Stock market turnover	—	85.9	51.9	11.4	—	746.9	7,806.1	36,756.0	74,479.4
Ratio to GDP at current prices (%)	—	—	—	—	—	12.9	31.1	55.3	52.7
Contributions to central provident fund (S$)	45.7	124.4	19.3	13.7	30.6	156.4	2,296.0	7,174.2	16,000.4
Ratio to GCF at current prices (%)	—	—	—	—	9.6	7.0	19.7	29.5	33.9

Source: Monetary Authority of Singapore (various years).

(GIC), which manages diverse financial portfolios for the Singapore government. The availability of these relatively cheap funds via the CPF (low-interest-rate savings) has enabled the state to engage in long-term development plans without relying on the foreign borrowing and foreign financing that have crippled some Southeast Asian economies during the recent economic crisis. From an initial rate of contribution at 5 per cent of gross monthly salaries in 1955, the CPF rates rose steadily over time to 25 per cent just before the 1985 recession and subsequently decreased to about 15–20 per cent. Measured in terms of their ratio to gross capital formation at current prices, contributions to the CPF increased significantly from 7 per cent in 1970 to 34 per cent in 1999 (see Table 5.1). In other words, some one-third of total national capital formation in Singapore today comes from this compulsory individual savings scheme. The effect of this state-enforced savings scheme is manifested in the channelling of a large share of potential investment capital from private capital markets to the CPF board and other state-owned sectors.

In the immediate aftermath of the Asian economic crisis, Singapore moved swiftly to further liberalise its financial sector in order to become more competitive in the regional and global financial markets. The then deputy prime minister and former chairman of MAS, Lee Hsien Loong, said that

> [i]t's very difficult to decide to change policies when they are working. But we got feedback from bankers and others that if you want to take the next stage up, then really you have to shift gears and allow more free play.
>
> (quoted in *The Straits Times*, 2 December 1998)

The state subsequently announced in May 1999 the most comprehensive liberalisation programme ever for the banking sector. The programme effectively forced local banks to take on global competition on their home turf, and this led to subsequent mergers and acquisitions among local banks (see Yeung, 2000c, 2004). The state argued that Singapore's small domestic banking market should allow for only two local banks, one of which had been designated to be the government-controlled DBS. Lee expected that '[t]here is room for consolidation, but we hope that there will be at least two Singapore institutions. . . . If we succeed in building up two such strong local banks, our financial system will have two pillars of strength and stability' (*The Straits Times*, 17 May 1999: 38; 18 May 1999: 49). Such responses came in 2001–2002 when the family-controlled Overseas-Chinese Banking Corporation (OCBC) bought into Keppel-TatLee Bank (previously owned by the government-linked Keppel Group), while another family-controlled bank, United Overseas Bank (UOB), initiated a friendly takeover of Overseas Union Bank (OUB) to become the largest local bank in Singapore. These two family-controlled banks, OCBC and UOB, were also aggressively expanding abroad by opening new branches and/or through acquisition.

In fact, the financial liberalisation programme had already begun in 1990 when the MAS raised foreign shareholdings of Singapore banks from 20 per cent to 40 per cent. Foreign banks could compete freely with local banks in wholesale domestic banking, offshore banking, and treasury and capital market activities. They accounted for more than one-third of resident deposits, 45 per cent of loans to resident borrowers and about 90 per cent of business with non-residents (*The Straits Times*, 17 May 1999: 38). On 17 May 1999, the Singapore government announced its further financial liberalisation programme: by 2001, six Qualifying Full Banks (QFB) licences will be issued to foreign banks. These banks will also be allowed to set up additional branches and off-premise automated teller machines (ATMs) and share an ATM network among themselves – practices previously disallowed (*The Straits Times*, 18 May 1999: 51). The MAS will increase the number of restricted banks from thirteen to eighteen by 2001 to cater to offshore banks, and give offshore banks greater flexibility in the Singapore dollar wholesale business.

This recent liberalisation of Singapore's banking sector has had a significant impact on local banks, which have experienced a larger squeeze on their interest margins with stiffer competition from twenty-two full-licence, thirteen restricted and ninety-eight offshore foreign banks in Singapore. These local banks had been well protected by the MAS for a long period: no new licences for full and restricted banks had been granted since 1970 and 1983 respectively. Then Deputy Prime Minister Lee again noted that

> [g]overnment protection and strict MAS supervision have enabled local banks to grow into sound, well-capitalised institutions. . . . The present situation is not sustainable. Even if the Government does not liberalise the banking industry, local banks will be unable to maintain the status quo. Globalisation and electronic delivery channels have altered fundamentally the competitive landscape. Further rapid developments in Internet banking will enable foreign banks to reach out extensively to domestic consumers, reducing and eventually neutralising the advantages of an extensive branch network and Government protection.
>
> (*The Straits Times*, 18 May 1999: 48)

Conclusion

This chapter shows that the state is often very much involved in managing the benefits and risks associated with globalisation processes. The success of this management, however, depends on its institutional capacity and political legitimacy. In the case of Singapore, its entrepôt status and the state's pursuit of an export-oriented industrialisation strategy have inevitably articulated the city-state into the global economy (see also Olds and Yeung, 2004). Right from its very beginning, modern Singapore has experienced economic openness and global forces. What surprises most neoliberal observers is that the Singaporean state, through its strategic manipulation of political legitimacy and building up of institutional capacity, has been able to harness these global forces to its own advantage. This conclusion does not, of course, imply that the Singapore state is not subject to the pressures and perils of globalisation. In fact, the slowdown of economic growth during the 2001–2003 period has led to a partial erosion of the performance legitimacy accumulated over three decades by the state. The implicit domestic social contract established between the PAP state and Singaporeans (both citizens and residents) has apparently witnessed some limits to its sustainability. The wave of wage cuts in 1999 and 2003 led to a series of questions about the complicated trade-off between continuous social protection and attracting global capital – both critical developmental goals of the PAP state. In short, there seems to be serious questioning of the continual viability of state capacity in managing growing economic insecurity in the twenty-first century global economy.

Yet it is important to point out that the Singapore state is not 'retreating' in the face of globalisation; it continues to strengthen its institutional capacity and political legitimacy, even in the aftermath of the 1997–1998 Asian economic crisis and the Iraq war and SARS outbreak in 2003. A stronger, not weaker, developmental state might indeed be a better cure for the 'globalisation syndrome' identified by Mittelman (2000). While this chapter does not intend to engage in the futile debate about the future of Singapore, it is important to note that Singapore's unique historical-geographical formation bestows on its stakeholders some natural advantages that are hard to replicate elsewhere. Insofar as the PAP state continues to engage actively the dynamic changes in the global economy, it is conceivable that the management of economic insecurity associated with globalisation can be both driven by the state *and* benefiting the state. The recent strategies of the state in enhancing job protection through wage cuts and reforming the CPF, enabling a smooth leadership transition towards a second-generation political elite and reconfiguring the state's involvement in economic activities through privatisation and corporatisation of government-linked corporations (GLCs) and statutory boards, must be seen as constituting such efforts to maintain its political legitimacy and economic stability. There is thus neither a single pathway nor a standard model to succeed in today's highly uncertain and insecure global economy. What matters most is the continual adjustments and adaptation of such economies as Singapore that are coordinated through state capacity and institutions. While neoliberalism and neoliberalisation seem to be at their heyday elsewhere now (see Tickell and Peck, 2003), this does not obliterate the significant developmental trajectory charted by the state. Quite the contrary: neoliberalism is indeed itself a product of conscious state effort to redirect the strategic orientation of economic development via the market mechanism.

More specifically, what emerges clearly from this chapter is that the developmental state in Singapore has always been placed its *political credibility* and *policy consistency* as top priority in its engagement with global capital and in managing economic security associated with globalisation. This institutional capacity is best observed in its labour and financial market governance. In both markets, the state has consistently managed flexibility and domestic interests to attract global capital. While globalisation has enabled capital to become increasingly mobile and 'placeless' – a phenomenon just too prematurely celebrated by the ultra-globalists (cf. Yeung 1998a, 2002a), some nodes in global networks are better able to pin down these global processes and benefit from capital's mobility. As shown in the Singapore example, this ability is predicated on the character and legitimacy of domestic institutions, not on the alleged external pressures created by globalisation. While the state and its myriad associated institutions cannot possibly guarantee the future success of Singapore's economic development, its accumulated capacity to effect changes and transformations can be crucial to the continuous remaking of the Singapore political economy into something that might just be more resilient and versatile in the face of apparently growing global competition and economic insecurity.

Notes

For their helpful comments on this chapter, I would like to thank Helen Nesadurai, Amitav Acharya, K. C. Ho, Gillian Koh, Linda Low, Bae Gyoon Park, James Sidaway and Evelyn Wong.

1   Notice the very similar call to put national interest above individual well-being in recent state discourses on the pending reduction in employer's contribution to the Central Provident Fund (CPF), effectively a form of wage cut, in order to reduce labour costs in Singapore. See Prime Minister Goh's 2003 National Day Rally Speech at http://www.straitstimes.com.sg (accessed 26 August 2003). Former Deputy Prime Minister Lee Hsien Loong has further noted that 'We don't like it but we have to do it. I think that sums up the attitude for many of us, including in government. . . . [The changes] are vital adjustments to make ourselves more competitive, and to prepare Singapore for the long term. If we don't do it, we will be in trouble. If we do this, it will be another part of getting Singapore competitive again' (*The Straits Times*, 25 August 2003).
2   Such a high ratio of foreign workers in job growth has become a key focus of heated debates. The Ministry of Manpower has reported that between 1992 and 1997, total employment increased by 470,000. Foreigners accounted for 60 per cent of this increase. Between 1997 and 2002, foreigners made up only 10 per cent of the 102,000 new jobs created (http://www.mom.gov.sg, accessed 26 August 2003).
3   A similar lack of contestation is expected to the latest state proposal to cut employer's contributions to the CPF.
4   Compare this quotation to Prime Minister Goh's 2003 National Day Rally Speech:

> I am aware that the CPF changes we are thinking of may be hard to swallow. For some of you, a cut in the CPF rate may be the difference between meeting and failing on your mortgage payments. . . . Our choices are: adjust, or lose more jobs. . . . I am convinced that we have to adjust and reform our CPF system. And the sooner we do it, the better. Otherwise, we will lose our competitiveness and many jobs, especially jobs held by older and lower skilled Singaporeans. We will also store up problems for the future. Singaporeans will retire and find that they do not have enough savings for their old age. But if we make these tough choices now, we will put right a major weakness in our CPF system. We also signal to investors that we are realistic and long-term in our thinking . . . show that we are willing to bring down our costs. . . . This will help us attract more investments and more jobs.
>
> (http://www.straitstimes.com.sg, accessed 26 August 2003)

Bibliography

Berger, Peter L. and Huntington, Samuel P. (eds) (2002) *Many Globalizations: Cultural Diversity in the Contemporary World*, Oxford: Oxford University Press.

Boyer, Robert (2000) 'The Political in the Era of Globalization and Finance: Focus on Some *Régulation* School Research', *International Journal of Urban and Regional Research*, 24 (2): 274–322.

Brenner, Neil, Jessop, Bob, Jones, Martin and MacLeod, Gordon (eds) (2003) *State/Space*, Oxford: Blackwell.

Chew, Yoke-Tong and Yeung, Henry Wai-chung (2001) 'The SME Advantage: Adding Local Touch to Foreign Transnational Corporations in Singapore', *Regional Studies*, 35 (5): 431–448.

Chia, Siow Yue (1997) 'Singapore: Advanced Production Base and Smart Hub of the Electronics Industry', in Wendy Dobson and Chia Siow Yue (eds) *Multinationals and East Asian Integration*, Ottawa: IDRC, pp. 31–61.

Chiu, Stephen W. K., Ho, Kong Chong and Lui, Tai-Lok (1997) *City-States in the Global Economy: Industrial Restructuring in Hong Kong and Singapore*, Boulder, CO: Westview.

Coe, Neil M. and Kelly, Philip F. (2000) 'Distance and Discourse in the Local Labour Market: The Case of Singapore', *Area*, 32 (4): 413–422.

—— (2002) 'Languages of Labour: Representational Strategies in Singapore's Labour Control Regime', *Political Geography*, 21 (3): 341–371.

Dent, Christopher M. (2002) *The Foreign Economic Policies of Singapore, South Korea and Taiwan*, Cheltenham, UK: Edward Elgar.

—— (2003) 'Transnational Capital, the State and Foreign Economic Policy: Singapore, South Korea and Taiwan', *Review of International Political Economy*, 10 (2): 246–277.

Department of Statistics (various years a) *Statistical Yearbook of Singapore*, Singapore: DOS.

—— (various years b) *Foreign Equity Investment in Singapore*, Singapore: DOS.

—— (various years c) *Report on the Census of Industrial Production*, Singapore: DOS.

—— (various years d) *Report on the Census of Services*, Singapore: DOS.

—— (various years e) *Singapore's Investment Abroad*, Singapore: DOS

—— (1992) *Singapore's Corporate Sector: Size, Composition and Financial Structure*, Singapore: DOS.

—— (2000) *Singapore's Corporate Sector 1996–1997*, Singapore: DOS.

Dicken, Peter (2003) *Global Shift: Reshaping the Global Economic Map in the 21st Century*, 4th edn, London: Sage.

Dicken, Peter and Kirkpatrick, Colin (1991) 'Services-Led Development in ASEAN: Transnational Regional Headquarters in Singapore', *The Pacific Review*, 4 (2): 174–184.

Economic Development Board (1993) *Growing with Enterprise: A National Report*, Singapore: EDB.

—— (various issues) *Annual Report*, Singapore: EDB.

Evans, Peter (1995) *Embedded Autonomy: States and Industrial Transformation*, Princeton, NJ: Princeton University Press.

Fröbel, Folker, Heinrichs, Jürgen, and Kreye, Otto (1980) *The New International Division of Labour*, Cambridge: Cambridge University Press.

Grundy-Warr, Carl, Peachey, Karen and Perry, Martin (1999) 'Fragmented Integration in the Singapore–Indonesian Border Zone: Southeast Asia's "Growth Triangle" against the Global Economy', *International Journal of Urban and Regional Research*, 23 (2): 304–328.

Haggard, Stephan (1999) 'An External View of Singapore's Developed Status', in Linda Low (ed.) *Singapore: Towards a Developed Status*, Singapore: Oxford University Press, pp. 345–375.

Hamilton-Hart, Natasha (2000) 'The Singapore State Revisited', *The Pacific Review*, 13 (2): 195–216.

—— (2002) *Asian States, Asian Bankers: Central Banking in Southeast Asia*, Ithaca, NY: Cornell University Press.

Held, David, McGrew, Anthony, Goldblatt, David and Perraton, Jonathan (1999) *Global Transformations: Politics, Economics and Culture*, Cambridge: Polity.

Henderson, Jeffrey (1989) *The Globalisation of High Technology Production*, London: Routledge.

Hill, Michael and Lian, Kwen Fee (1995) *The Politics of Nation Building and Citizenship in Singapore*, London: Routledge.

Hirst, Paul and Thompson, Grahame (1996) *Globalization in Question: The International Economy and the Possibilities of Governance*, Cambridge: Polity.

Ho, Kong Chong (1993) 'Industrial Restructuring and the Dynamics of City-State Adjustments', *Environment and Planning A*, 25 (1): 47–62.

—— (1994) 'Industrial Restructuring, the Singapore City-State, and the Regional Division of Labour', *Environment and Planning A*, 26 (1): 33–51.

Huff, W. G. (1994) *The Economic Growth of Singapore: Trade and Development in the Twentieth Century*, Cambridge: Cambridge University Press.

—— (1995) 'The Developmental State, Government, and Singapore's Economic Development since 1960', *World Development*, 23 (8): 1421–1438.

—— (1999) 'Turning the Corner in Singapore's Developmental State?', *Asian Survey*, 39 (2): 214–242.

Hui, Weng-Tat (1997) 'Regionalization, Economic Restructuring and Labour Migration in Singapore', *International Migration*, 35 (1): 109–130.

Jessop, Bob (1990) *State Theory: Putting Capitalist States in Their Place*, Cambridge: Polity Press.

Johnson, Chalmer (1982) *MITI and the Japanese Economic Miracle*, Stanford, CA: Stanford University Press.

Kapstein, Ethan B. (2000) 'Winners and Losers in the Global Economy', *International Organization*, 54 (2): 359–384.

Katzenstein, Peter (1985) *Small States in World Markets*, Ithaca, NY: Cornell University Press.

Kelly, Philip F. (1999) 'The Geographies and Politics of Globalization', *Progress in Human Geography*, 23 (3): 379–400.

—— (2001) 'Metaphors of Meltdown: Political Representations of Economic Space in the Asian Financial Crisis', *Environment and Planning D: Society and Space*, 19: 719–742.

Koh, Buck Song (ed.) (2002) *Heart Work: Stories of How EDB Steered the Singapore Economy from 1961 into the 21st Century*, Singapore: EDB.

Lai, Karen P. Y. and Yeung, Henry Wai-chung (2003) 'Contesting the State: Discourses of the Asian Economic Crisis and Mediating Strategies of Electronics Firms in Singapore', *Environment and Planning A*, 35 (3): 463–488.

Lee Kuan Yew (2000) *From Third World to First: The Singapore Story, 1965–2000*, Singapore: Times Editions.

Low, Linda (1998) *The Political Economy of a City-State: Government-Made Singapore*, Singapore: Oxford University Press.

—— (2001) 'The Singapore Developmental State in the New Economy and Polity', *The Pacific Review*, 14 (3): 411–441.

Low, Linda, Toh, Mun Heng, Soon, Teck Wong, Tan, Kong Yam and Hughes, Helen (1993) *Challenge and Response: Thirty Years of the Economic Development Board*, Singapore: Times Academic Press.

McKendrick, David G., Doner, Richard F. and Haggard, Stephan (2000) *From Silicon Valley to Singapore: Location and Competitive Advantage in the Hard Disk Drive Industry*, Stanford, CA: Stanford University Press.

Mathews, John A. (1999) 'A Silicon Island of the East: Creating a Semiconductor Industry in Singapore', *California Management Review*, 41 (2): 55–78.

Mauzy, Diane K. and Milne, R. S. (2002) *Singapore Politics under the People's Action Party*, London: Routledge.

Mirza, Hafiz (1986) *Multinationals and the Growth of the Singapore Economy*, London: Croom Helm.

Mitchell, Timothy (1991) 'The Limits of the State: Beyond Statist Approaches and Their Critics', *American Political Science Review*, 85 (1): 77–96.

Mittelman, James H. (ed.) (1996) *Globalization: Critical Reflections*, Boulder, CO: Lynne Rienner.

—— (2000) *The Globalization Syndrome: Transformation and Resistance*, Princeton, NJ: Princeton University Press.

Monetary Authority of Singapore (various years) *Annual Report*, Singapore: MAS.

Olds, Kris and Yeung, Henry Wai-chung (2004) 'Pathways to Global City Formation: A View from the Developmental City-State of Singapore', *Review of International Political Economy*, 11 (3): 489–521.

Olds, Kris, Dicken, Peter, Kelly, Philip, Kong, Lily and Yeung, Henry Wai-chung (eds) (1999) *Globalisation and the Asia-Pacific: Contested Territories*, London: Routledge.

Peck, Jamie A. (1996) *Work Place: The Social Regulation of Labor Markets*, New York: Guilford.

—— (2000) *Workfare States*, New York: Guilford.

Peck, Jamie and Yeung, Henry Wai-chung (eds) (2003) *Remaking the Global Economy: Economic-Geographical Perspectives*, London: Sage.

Pereira, Alexius A. (2000) 'State Collaboration with Transnational Corporations: The Case of Singapore's Industrial Programmes (1965–1999)', *Competition and Change*, 4 (4): 1–29.

—— (2003) *State Collaboration and Development Strategies in China: The Case of the China–Singapore Suzhou Industrial Park*, London: RoutledgeCurzon.

Perry, Martin and Tan, Boon Hui (1998) 'Global manufacturing and local linkage in Singapore', *Environment and Planning A*, 30 (9): 1603–1624.

Perry, Martin, Kong, Lily and Yeoh, Brenda (1997) *Singapore: A Developmental City State*, London: John Wiley.

Perry, Martin, Poon, Jessie and Yeung, Henry (1998a) 'Regional Offices in Singapore: Spatial and Strategic Influences in the Location of Corporate Control', *Review of Urban and Regional Development Studies*, 10 (1): 42–59.

Perry, Martin, Yeung, Henry and Poon, Jessie (1998b) 'Regional Office Mobility: The Case of Corporate Control in Singapore and Hong Kong', *Geoforum*, 29 (3): 237–255.

Phelps, Nicholas A. and Raines, Philip (eds) (2003) *The New Competition for Inward Investment: Companies, Institutions and Territorial Development*, Cheltenham, UK: Edward Elgar.

Phillips, Su-Ann Mae and Yeung, Henry Wai-chung (2003) 'A Place for R&D? The Singapore Science Park', *Urban Studies*, 40 (4): 707–732.

Régnier, Philippe (1991) *Singapore: City-State in South-East Asia*, Honolulu: University of Hawaii Press.

—— (1993) 'Spreading Singapore's Wings Worldwide: A Review of Traditional and New Investment Strategies', *The Pacific Review*, 6 (4): 305–312.

Rieger, Elmar and Leibfried, Stephan (2003) *Limits to Globalization: Welfare States and the World Economy*, Cambridge: Polity Press.

Rodan, Garry (1989) *The Political Economy of Singapore's Industralization: National State and International Capital*, London: Macmillan.

Sassen, Saskia (2000) 'Territory and Territoriality in the Global Economy', *International Sociology*, 15 (2): 372–393.

Sung, Johnny (2004) *Explaining the Economic Success of Singapore: The Developmental Worker as the Missing Link*, Cheltenham, UK: Edward Elgar.

Tickell, Adam T. (1996) 'Making a Melodrama out of a Crisis: Reinterpreting the Collapse of Barings Bank', *Environment and Planning D: Society and Space*, 14 (1): 5–33.

Tickell, Adam T. and Peck, Jamie A. (2003) 'Making Global Rules: Globalization or Neoliberalization?', in Jamie Peck and Henry Wai-chung Yeung (eds) *Remaking the Global Economy: Economic-Geographical Perspectives*, London: Sage, pp. 163–181.

Wade, Robert (1990) *Governing the Market: Economic Theory and the Role of Government in East Asian Industrialization*, Princeton, NJ: Princeton University Press.

Wallerstein, Immanuel (1999) 'States? Sovereignty? The Dilemmas of Capitalists in an Age of Transition', in David A. Smith, Dorothy J. Solinger and Steven C. Topik (eds) *States and Sovereignty in the Global Economy*, London: Routledge, pp. 20–33.

Wang, Jason H. J. and Yeung, Henry Wai-chung (2000) 'Strategies for Global Competition: Transnational Chemical Firms and Singapore's Chemical Cluster', *Environment and Planning A*, 32 (5): 847–869.

Weiss, Linda (1998) *The Myth of the Powerless State: Governing the Economy in a Global Era*, Cambridge: Polity.

—— (ed.) (2003) *States in the Global Economy: Bringing Domestic Institutions Back In*, Cambridge: Cambridge University Press.

Wong, Poh Kam (1995) 'Competing in the Global Electronics Industry: A Comparative Study of the Innovation Networks of Singapore and Taiwan', *Journal of Industry Studies*, 2 (2): 35–62.

Woo-Cumings, Meredith (ed.) (1999) *The Developmental State*, Ithaca, NY: Cornell University Press.

Wu, Friedrich (1997) 'Hong Kong and Singapore: A Tale of Two Asian Business Hubs', *Journal of Asian Business*, 13 (2): 1–17.

Wu, Friedrich and Duk, Sin Yue (1995) 'Hong Kong and Singapore: "Twin Capitals" for Overseas Chinese Capital', *Business and the Contemporary World*, 7 (3): 21–33.

Yeoh, Brenda S. A. and Chang, Tou Chuang (2001) 'Globalising Singapore: Debating Transnational Flows in the City', *Urban Studies*, 38 (7): 1025–1044.

Yeung, Henry Wai-chung (1998a) 'Capital, State and Space: Contesting the Borderless World', *Transactions of the Institute of British Geographers*, 23 (3): 291–309.

—— (1998b) 'The Political Economy of Transnational Corporations: A Study of the Regionalisation of Singaporean Firms', *Political Geography*, 17 (4): 389–416.

—— (1999) 'Regulating Investment Abroad? The Political Economy of the Regionalisation of Singaporean Firms', *Antipode*, 31 (3): 245–273.

—— (2000a) 'The Dynamics of Asian Business Systems in a Globalising Era', *Review of International Political Economy*, 7 (3): 399–432.

—— (2000b) 'State Intervention and Neoliberalism in the Globalising World Economy: Lessons from Singapore's Regionalisation Programme', *The Pacific Review*, 13 (1): 133–162.

—— (2000c) 'Economic Globalisation, Crisis, and the Emergence of Chinese Business Communities in Southeast Asia', *International Sociology*, 15 (2): 269–290.

—— (2000d) 'Local Politics and Foreign Ventures in China's Transitional Economy: The Political Economy of Singaporean Investments in China', *Political Geography*, 19 (7): 809–840.

—— (2002a) 'The Limits to Globalization Theory: A Geographic Perspective on Global Economic Change', *Economic Geography*, 78 (3): 285–305.

—— (2002b) *Entrepreneurship and the Internationalisation of Asian Firms: An Institutional Perspective*, Cheltenham, UK: Edward Elgar.

—— (2004) *Chinese Capitalism in a Global Era: Towards Hybrid Capitalism*, London: Routledge.

Yeung, Henry Wai-chung and Olds, Kris (1998) 'Singapore's Global Reach: Situating the City-State in the Global Economy', *International Journal of Urban Sciences*, 2 (1): 24–47.

Yeung, Henry Wai-chung, Poon, Jessie and Perry, Martin (2001) 'Towards a Regional Strategy: The Role of Regional Headquarters and Regional Offices in the Asia Pacific', *Urban Studies*, 38 (1): 157–183.

6 Globalisation, economic security and governance

The case of Indonesia

Kurnya Roesad

Introduction

Of the many fascinating snapshots taken during the economic and political crisis in Indonesia, three pictures remain vivid. The first picture shows Michel Camdesssus, then the managing director of the International Monetary Fund (IMF), standing behind President Soeharto to watch him sign the IMF Letter of Intent (LOI) on 15 January 1998. A couple of months later, on 21 May, a second picture shows President Soeharto standing in front of the world press announcing his resignation amid a free-falling rupiah, social turmoil and internal political struggles. The last image is one of jubilation by students in the compounds of the Parliament celebrating the fall of one of the longest-ruling dictators of the twentieth century.

Those scenes, of course, can mean different things to different people. To many, they serve as powerful metaphors for a state's submission of its economic security to the overwhelming forces of globalisation. Advocates of globalisation believe in the neoliberal dictum that the breakdown of Soeharto's authoritarian New Order regime was only the logical outcome of a long process in which economic liberalisation will ultimately lead to political liberalisation. The collapse of the economy was blamed entirely on the past policies of a rent-seeking 'developmental' state that ultimately faced unsustainable transaction and corruption costs. Repression of internal dissent and conflicts to justify development goals in the end proved too costly, as the demands from a politically conscious middle-class for greater freedom could not be ignored for ever, freedom itself being a developmental goal. According to this view, safeguarding a country's economic security necessitates the deepening of economic liberalisation and the adoption of democratic, transparent governance. Critics of globalisation, on the other hand, argue that the rapid opening up of the economy only resulted in the collapse of economic security, which had been achieved during the Soeharto era. A strong, interventionist state had been necessary to deliver material wealth and ensure a certain level of welfare for the people. The collapse of the Indonesian economy is, then, entirely blamed on external factors, notably an unregulated, extremely volatile international financial market. Consequently, resistance to further liberalisation of the domestic economy is a prerequisite to restore economic security and to reduce dependence on volatile international markets. Both sets of views were to be found in Indonesia.

Conventional wisdom now suggests that the collapse of economic security in 1997–1998 was a mix of domestic and external factors reinforcing each other to exacerbate what was initially an exchange rate and contagion problem to a full-blown economic crisis. The Indonesian case is also puzzling, as the same factors that were held responsible for the demise of the New Order – corruption, cronyism and nepotism (KKN in the Indonesian language), lack of transparency and democratic accountability – did not weaken the positive market sentiment towards Indonesia before 1997. Therefore, the question is one of identifying the factors contributing to the strong and capable state that had successfully delivered economic security before 1997, as well as the factors that contributed to the loss of economic security during the 'globalisation crisis' of 1997–1998.

In a world characterised by economic globalisation, economic security may be seen as a function of the state's capacity to pursue policies that maximise the benefits and minimise the risks of liberalising economic systems. These policies can be pitched at two levels.[1] At the macro level, the state employs macroeconomic policy instruments (fiscal and monetary policies), trade policies and foreign policies to maximise the collective economic security of its citizens. Increased trade and financial liberalisation are then thought to benefit state security as increased reliance on market forces fosters economic growth and overall welfare. At the micro level, economic security for the individual describes the social security aspects of economic welfare such as employment and minimum income schemes. Realist or nationalist notions of economic security, on the other hand, tend to see economic activities – production, exchange, consumption and investment – as subordinated to the goals of state-building, with the creation of national wealth also helping the state to secure relative gains and establish an advantageous position in the international system (Crane, 1998). Both these understandings of economic security were evident in Indonesia.

In the Indonesian case, two observations stand out. Before the crisis, the government's approach to globalisation was to engage in regional cooperation to maximise the benefits of economic liberalisation. Regional forums such as Asia-Pacific Economic Cooperation (APEC) and the Association of Southeast Asian Nations (ASEAN) provided the institutional framework for pushing forward liberalisation. After the onset of the Asian financial and economic crisis in 1997, a weakened Indonesian state relied increasingly on multilateral institutions such as the IMF and the World Bank to manage domestic responses to globalisation, while regional institutions were reduced to the role of bystanders.

This chapter makes the following argument: a strong Indonesian state used regional institutions to manage globalisation before 1997. In the post-crisis period, the situation was mixed. The state was able to utilise its still high level of policy credibility – based on past achievements by technocrats and the disciplining effect of the IMF, which ensured the adoption of sound macroeconomic policies – to deliver effective macroeconomic management. However, the state faced low credibility with regard to its microeconomic and structural reforms, largely owing to the fragmentation of both the political structure and the decision-making process within the government. Investors stayed away as the pace of reform slowed, particularly with regard to bank restructuring and privatisation. Consequently, the implications for economic security in Indonesia are also mixed.

Economic security before the Asian economic crisis: exploiting the benefits of globalisation

Indonesia's New Order regime under former President Soeharto had a sound record in managing macroeconomic crises and used market-friendly policies to maintain economic security. The government generally adopted orthodox adjustment and stabilisation measures, especially in the 1980s, when the country faced periods of falling oil prices (Azis, 1994). To diversify the economy and to reduce dependence on oil as a prime revenue earner, the government liberalised trade and investment regimes from the mid-1980s on. Recognising the benefits of participating in the global market, the government undertook substantial reforms from 1986 to 1990. A total of twenty deregulation packages were issued, with the aim of dismantling monopolies in the economy, including those covering plastics and steel imports (ibid.; Soesastro, 2000c).

After a period of 'reform fatigue' in the early 1990s, a second phase of substantial reform emerged in 1994 when policymakers realised that Indonesia was beginning to lose out in the competition for foreign direct investment (FDI) to other countries such as China, Vietnam and India (Soesastro, 2000c). 'Competitive liberalisation' and 'open regionalism' became key phrases in the policy lexicon during this period. Domestic liberalisation packages issued in mid-1996 and 1997 led to further market-friendly reforms. The Indonesian government, like other countries in the region, engaged in enhanced regional liberalisation processes, culminating in the decision at the 1995 ASEAN summit in Bangkok to accelerate implementation of the ASEAN Free Trade Area (AFTA). Overall, the AFTA process helped reduce Indonesian tariff levels substantially, with intra-ASEAN trade expanding until the onset of the crisis (Stubbs, 2000).

During the same period, however, the market-friendly technocrats who were the main economic advisers to Soeharto during much of the New Order regime gradually lost their dominant roles in economic policy debates. Economic nationalists, headed by the minister of research and technology, B. J. Habibie – later to be Soeharto's successor – gained in importance in the 1990s and pushed for the protection of several important sectors in order to develop strategic industries. In addition, a growing number of populist politicians advocated the promotion of distributive policies in favour of small- and medium-sized enterprises (SMEs), combined with an affirmative action programme to empower Malay (*pribumi*) Indonesians vis-à-vis the dominant Chinese conglomerates (Rinakit and Soesastro, 1998). A tug of war between these different groups dominated the domestic economic policy debate, resulting in a slowdown of economic reforms. President Soeharto balanced these competing interests skilfully and managed during his regime to apply a pragmatic approach to economic policies: when economic conditions were favourable, an inward, protectionist regime was installed. Once recessions set in, market-friendly policies were introduced to appease foreign investors. Thus, Indonesia pursued a two-pronged strategy: while export policy reforms were undertaken, import liberalisation was limited, thus giving rise to protected industries.

Advocates of the developmental state view suggest that selective intervention was also effective in achieving equity objectives. Timmer (1996) argues that the stabilisation of the rice price helped to mitigate rural poverty. Keeping prices constant while facing declining world prices led to increased profits and a rise in real rural wages. This required sophisticated intervention not only in rice markets, but also in credit and input markets to subsidise agricultural extension programmes. Coordination between the national logistics agency (BULOG) and other government agencies in setting floor and ceiling prices for rice and controlling rice imports was successful in making Indonesia self-sufficient in the commodity in 1985. While this policy had its costs in terms of efficiency losses to the economy, the point to note is that efficiency losses had sometimes to be weighed against equity considerations. Rice policy was certainly one factor explaining the dramatic decline in poverty rates during the New Order era.

Overall, this strategy of mixed interventions had beneficial impacts in terms of higher growth rates that helped to alleviate poverty. Growth averaged an annual 6.5 per cent in 1967–1996 while poverty rates fell from 28.6 per cent in 1980 to 11.3 per cent in 1996 (World Bank, 1999).

Globalisation crisis and the loss of economic security

The story of how the crisis unfolded in Indonesia and in other countries in the region is now well known.[2] Despite favourable macroeconomic indicators, institutional deficiencies, particularly in the financial sector, were building up. Financial liberalisation had lured short-term capital into the Indonesian economy in the 1990s. Domestic business received short-term loans and invested the money in long-term projects, particularly in the real estate and property sectors. Weaknesses in the domestic financial sector were long hidden by massive capital inflows and strong investor confidence in the economy. Financial authorities did not properly record capital flows. As a result, much of this short-term foreign capital was not channelled to financially productive activities that would have generated the capacity to repay the debt in the future. Many banks, for example, lent massively to sectors with a high proportion of non-performing loans without sufficient credit examination. In addition, many of these loans were allocated to specific corporate groups (Sato, 2000).[3]

Fixed exchange rate regimes in the region were another contributing factor. Borrowers in the region relied on the historical stability of the currency and neglected hedging against exchange rate risks. However, with the appreciation of the US dollar, the region's balance of payments positions deteriorated and speculators anticipated that governments could not sustain the fixed rates. Speculative attacks then brought currencies down. Once the rupiah depreciated, a re-evaluation of the Indonesian economy by investors took place. Weaknesses in the

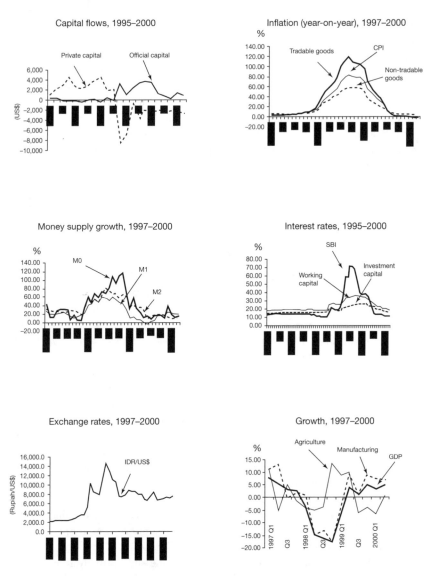

Figure 6.1 Macroeconomic trends in Indonesia, 1995–2000.

Source: Central Bureau of Statistics, Bank Indonesia.

financial sector were now fully exposed and this caused the massive pullout of capital (Johnson, 1998).[4]

The various dimensions of the crisis are illustrated in Figure 6.1. Capital outflows reached their peak in the fourth quarter of 1997, the capital account registering a deficit of US$1.8 billion by the end of 1999. An estimated US$30 billion left the country in 1998. Year-on-year inflation reached a record high of about 78 per cent in October 1998, while high interest rates did not help to attract capital inflows. High interest rates, frequently reaching 30–50 per cent in 1998–1999, and the depreciation of the rupiah (Rp) persisted for sustained periods during the crisis. The exchange rate in 1998 fluctuated between around 6,000 Rp/US$ in early January and over 16,000 Rp/US$ in June, and then stabilised to between 7,000 and 8,500 during the last quarter of the year. Indonesia's economy suffered a large contraction in 1998 and relative stagnation in 1999. The economy was most severely affected in the first half of 1998, with a reduction in quarter-on-quarter growth of 8 per cent in the first and 10.5 per cent in the second quarter. Year-on-year growth was at a low of −17.7 per cent in the fourth quarter of 1998. Lastly, the loss of economic security is reflected in increased poverty: the number of people living below the poverty line grew from 34.5 million in 1996 to 48.4 million in 1998 (World Bank, 2003).

The role of the IMF in managing the crisis

The failure of international and regional institutions to offer meaningful assistance during the Asian economic crisis has been thoroughly debated. In particular, the IMF's handling of the early phase of the crisis has been highlighted (Feldstein, 1998; Pangestu and Soesastro, 2002; Robison and Rosser, 1998; McQuillan and Montgomery, 1999), and three main criticisms have been levelled against the Fund.[5]

First, the IMF's advice to close sixteen commercial banks on 1 November 1997 created a run on the banks in the country as people rushed to withdraw deposits even from banks that were perceived to be healthy. The absence of a deposit guarantee scheme exacerbated the run on the banks. This sudden loss of confidence in the banking sector marked the starting point for the currency crisis to become a financial and banking crisis in Indonesia. It can be argued that without the banking crisis, the IMF would have been able to focus on shoring up Indonesia's balance-of-payments position by providing temporary liquidity support. Nasution argues that the government should have taken over the insolvent banks temporarily rather than have them closed down suddenly. This would have sustained credit to solvent borrowers and retained depositors' confidence.[6] Later, the ensuing banking crisis forced the government to provide liquidity support[7] and adopt a blanket guarantee, both of which raised the fiscal costs of the crisis.

Second, the content of the initial IMF programme and the analysis on which it was based was flawed. It was insufficient to deal only with the debt problems of the financial sector (Radelet and Sachs, 1998).[8] Jomo (2001) also argues that the IMF relied on 'old medicines for a new disease'. On the basis of its experience with Latin American economies with their chronic fiscal deficits and high inflation, the Fund applied the usual remedies to the East Asian economies hit by the crisis: orthodox austerity measures consisting of tight monetary and fiscal policies. These measures caused unnecessary economic contraction – a predictable outcome, given that most economies in the region ran no or only very small fiscal deficits. Later the IMF recognised that initial fiscal tightening was not warranted, and relaxed fiscal policies when severe output contraction was evident (Corden, 1999; Radelet and Sachs, 1998).

Third, the structural reforms failed to improve confidence. There was the perception that the proliferation of non-financial conditionalities distracted from core reform issues. Moreover, the Fund underestimated resistance to reform both from the public and from vested interests, which partly explains why the crisis was so severe.[9] The IMF argues in its internal evaluation report that the failure of the programme was due not to inadequate financing, but to non-implementation of key elements of the programme and failure to resolve the banking crisis, which subsequently led to the political crisis. Given the massive capital flight by domestic residents and the huge credibility gap, no reasonable amount of official financing could have saved the situation (IMF 2003).

Regaining economic security: sound macroeconomic policies, difficult microeconomic reforms

As the last of the crisis-affected Asian countries, Indonesia left the IMF economic reform programme in December 2003. Table 6.1 shows where Indonesia stands in comparison to other countries when they left their respective IMF-led programmes. Macroeconomic conditions are broadly in line with those in the other countries, and are better than in Brazil and Mexico. However, Thailand and Korea fared better than Indonesia when they graduated from their IMF programmes, particularly in terms of investment ratings. This is very much the story of Indonesia's economic recovery process: high macro policy credibility ensured sound macroeconomic management, but low policy credibility and the absence of institutional capacity in microeconomic and structural reforms have kept badly needed foreign investment away for the past six years.

Table 6.1 International comparison of major indicators upon IMF graduation

Country	Last loan	Credit rating (S&P)	Real GDP growth rate	Inflation	Budget balance (percentage of GDP)
Indonesia	Dec. 2003	B (current)	4.1	6.5	−1.9
Korea	May 1999	BBB	10.9	0.8	5.8
Thailand	June 1999	BBB−	4.4	0.3	6.7
Brazil	Dec. 1999	B+	0.8	8.9	5.0
Mexico	Dec. 1995	BB	−6.2	35.0	−0.2

Source: Updated from World Bank (2003).

Note: S&P: Standard & Poor's.

Macroeconomic stabilisation since 2000: a hesitant recovery

Table 6.2 reveals that macroeconomic conditions have improved steadily but slowly since 2000. Indonesia's macroeconomic environment stabilised in the first half of 2003 despite the uncertainties caused by the outbreak of SARS and the war in Iraq. Growth has remained moderate at an average of 3.3 per cent from 1999 to 2003. Inflation and interest rates have continuously declined, benefiting from a stronger rupiah and controlled money supply growth, with base money kept well below the indicative IMF-prescribed target since 2001. This provided room for Bank Indonesia to continuously lower its discount rate (the SBI rate, where SBI stands for Bank Indonesia Certificates). As the risk premium declined, heightened market sentiments led to capital inflow, reducing the pressure for domestic interest rates to increase. With a declining US dollar, the rupiah has gained strength, reducing imported inflation further. Moreover, higher international oil prices in the first quarter of 2003, caused by uncertainties during the build-up to the Iraq war, resulted in higher oil revenues, allowing a higher than expected current account surplus.

Against this background, fiscal risks associated with debt repayments have become less of a worry, at least in the short term. The government's track record in pursuing fiscal stabilisation has been impressive in the past few years. In the early years of the reform programme, there were fears that the high cost of banking recapitalisation would be unsustainable and the government would be tempted to monetise the deficits. These fears were unfounded, as the government debt-to-GDP ratio has consistently fallen since 1998. In addition, the rescheduling of domestic banking recapitalisation bonds ensured that debt repayments would not be massive in 2003–2004. A stronger rupiah, falling interest rates, higher oil export revenues and, above all, the reduction of fuel subsidies have helped to keep the budget deficit from burgeoning.

Despite moderate growth, the headcount poverty rate has also fallen since 2000. The reduction can be explained by stable and declining food and rice prices since 1999. As the poor spend a relatively large share of their income on food and a large chunk is spent on rice, poverty changes are fairly sensitive to price changes on those items (World Bank, 2003). Growth has, however, relied more on private consumption and government expenditure, a situation that is not sustainable in the long run. But higher growth depends on a country's capacity to attract more FDI and to increase exports. In this regard, Indonesia is slowly losing out in competitiveness when compared to other countries in the region, the worsening domestic investment climate also being partly due to the slow pace of reforms, particularly in asset sales and financial restructuring.

Undoubtedly the IMF played an important role in enforcing macroeconomic policy discipline on the government, which led to improved macroeconomic outcomes and restored partial confidence in the integrity of the macro-economy. Three factors are significant in this regard. First, the government adhered strictly to the tight fiscal and monetary policies prescribed by the IMF, which resulted in a stable macroeconomic environment, albeit with moderate growth. Second, and related to the previous point, the policy dialogue between the IMF and key economic ministries also improved significantly, especially after Megawati took over the

Table 6.2 Macroeconomic indicators for Indonesia, 1997–2003

	1997	1998	1999	2000[b]	2001	2002	2003[c]
Real GDP growth (y-o-y %)[a]	4.7	–13.1	0.8	4.9	3.1	3.7	3.9
Private consumption	7.8	–6.2	4.6	1.6	4.4	4.7	4.1
Government consumption	0.1	–15.4	0.7	6.5	9.0	12.8	9.6
Gross fixed investment	8.6	–33.0	–19.4	18.4	7.7	–0.2	0.0
Exports	7.8	11.2	–31.6	26.1	1.9	–1.2	0.7
Imports	14.7	–5.3	–40.7	25.9	8.1	–8.3	–5.7
Inflation	6.1	58.8	20.5	3.7	11.5	11.9	6.7[d]
Interest rates (1 month SBI)	14.5	49.3	23.1	12.5	16.6	13.5	8.4
FDI inflows (net, % of GDP)	2.2	–0.4	–2.0	–3.0	–2.3	—	—
Budget balance (% of GDP)	–0.5	–2.0	–2.3	–1.3	–2.9	–2.5	–1.9
Gov't debt to GDP ratio	23.6	74.1	96.8	87.9	85.7	80.0	68.9
Percentage of people below poverty line[e]	—	24.2	23.5	19.0	18.4	18.2	—

Source: Bank Indonesia, Central Bureau of Statistics, World Bank estimates.

Notes
a By expenditure, at constant 1993 prices.
b For nine months.
c Third-quarter figures.
d Jan.–Nov. figure.
e Based on Susenas and regular Susenas data.

presidency. The continued role of technocrats in economic decision-making also ensured consensus on getting the macroeconomic fundamentals right. Third, the IMF's stamp of approval on Indonesia's economic performance enabled donor countries grouped under the Consultative Group on Indonesia (CGI) to provide the external financing needed to reduce the budget deficit.

Political fragmentation and the lack of market-supporting institutions: bank restructuring and privatisation

In contrast to its macroeconomic achievements, the IMF could play only a modest role in pushing the government to accelerate the pace of structural reforms, particularly in bank restructuring and privatisation. Under Soeharto's New Order government, policy credibility in the macroeconomic field was the main pillar underpinning regime stability and economic security. This legacy is still alive, as Indonesia's technocrats still do exert considerable influence within governing circles. However, microeconomic and structural reforms require a modern market-supporting and transparent institutional framework, which is still lacking. This framework needs time to develop, and it involves distributing the costs of economic reforms among the different segments of society. At the same time, the democratisation process brought about a fragmentation of politics, which undermined the decisiveness of policy-making. Moreover, the dispersal of decision-making within the governing elite slowed down the decision-making process and has thus reduced the credibility of policy commitments. In addition, the decentralisation process also meant that local governments became powerful new political actors, thus increasing transaction costs further.

The rising number of interest groups – political parties, trade unions, NGOs – has increased populist opposition to privatisation and bank restructuring. It also increased pressure to abandon painful but necessary fiscal measures such as the reduction of fuel subsidies. During the Habibie presidency, the debate between those advocating an interventionist policy stance and those favouring a market-oriented approach to economic management intensified, but the interventionists eventually increased their influence. One of their main objectives was to establish a 'people's economy' (*ekonomi kerakyatan*) in which economic decision-making power would be dispersed to cooperatives and SMEs. Other issues raised by the interventionists included the fair distribution of land and the need for banks and financial institutions to favour SMEs and cooperatives when disbursing loans. During this time, the Ministry of Cooperatives and SMEs, under the high-profile minister Adi Sasono, received funds amounting to US$2.67 billion allocated from the budget. In addition, the minister called for bank assets taken over by the Indonesian Bank Restructuring Agency (IBRA) and revenues from privatisation of state enterprises to be distributed among cooperatives (Cameron, 1999).[10]

The government also had to face a frequently hostile Parliament in pushing through important bills supporting reforms. Bills to regulate labour and industrial relations, improve the investment climate, set up an Anti-Corruption Commission and establish a new Financial Authority have constantly been held up by the Parliament and were still not completed at the end of 2003. Neither was the government united in pushing for the implementation of economic reforms. Internal splits on privatisation and bank restructuring have been a constant trademark of all three governments since Soeharto's fall. The IMF – having learned from past experience in dealing with domestic resistance to economic restructuring – chose to tread carefully in this matter.

Banking restructuring

At the heart of the economic recovery process is bank restructuring. Without a functioning financial sector, Indonesia cannot resume a higher economic growth pattern, as much investment relies on a smooth supply of loans. Responding to the collapse of the domestic banking system, the government – with the enactment of Presidential Decree No. 27/1998 – established the Indonesian Bank Restructuring Agency (IBRA) to undertake the restructuring and recovery of the banking sector.[11]

The politically sensitive nature of asset sales and bank restructuring is clearly seen in the various cases of money politics, corruption and political interventions in crisis-management institutions like IBRA. These institutions constituted potential sources of financial resources for political funding. However, the IMF showed some resolve in enforcing greater will on the part of the government to continue with economic reforms. This, however, led to delays in signing new LOIs and even to the suspension of the programme on two occasions in the period after Soeharto's fall. The first suspension occurred when the Habibie government refused to publish the audit on Bank Bali, causing the suspension of the programme in September 1999. The second suspension occurred in November 2000 when President Abdurrahman Wahid's government failed to implement key targets. At that time, the government's economic team, led by Rizal Ramli, was openly critical of the IMF, maintaining that Indonesia should have more 'ownership' of the programme (Soesastro, 2003) (Table 6.3).

These suspensions were major blows to Indonesia's foreign credibility. Dick (2001) argues that it 'served the government's political agenda by showing the government as standing up to foreign pressures'. Although the IMF had become as much a hostage to the government as the government was to the IMF, the Fund did not give in. Yet in securing its objectives, the IMF was drawn more closely into the political process. In a sense, the IMF was the remaining voice for policy discipline and for restoring integrity to the economy. Dick (ibid.) argues that it remains an open question whether continuing IMF tutelage is a good or a bad thing. There is a kind of 'moral hazard' in the nature of the support programme. It 'creates perverse incentives for the government to act irresponsibly in public, while making excuses and apparent concessions in private'. It is not unusual for a government to evade responsibility by portraying the IMF as imposing harsh or unrealistic discipline (Soesastro, 2003).

After five years of financial-sector reforms, what are the main trends in this sector?[12] First, although a number of banks were closed and some merged, the

Table 6.3 Indonesia's IMF supported programmes, 31 October 1997–7 June 2002

Date	Agreement	Signatory(ies)	IMF review
Soeharto government			
31/10/1997	MEFP	MoF, GovBI[d]	
15/01/1998	Strengthened MEFP	Pres. Soeharto	
10/04/1998	Supplementary MEFP	Coord. Minister[e]	Completed
Habibie government			
24/06/1998	Supplementary MEFP	Coord. Minister[e]	Completed
29/07/1998	New MEFP[a]	Coord. Minister[e]	Completed
11/09/1998	Supplementary MEFP	Coord. Minister[e]	Completed
19/10/1998	Supplementary MEFP	Coord. Minister[e]	Completed
13/11/1998	Supplementary MEFP	Coord. Minister[e]	Completed
16/03/1999	Supplementary MEFP	Coord. Minister[e]	Completed
14/05/1999	Supplementary MEFP	Coord. Minister[e]	Completed
22/07/1999	Supplementary MEFP	Coord.Minister[e]	Suspended
Wahid government			
20/01/2000	New MEFP[b]	MoF, GovBI, Coord. Minister[b]	
17/05/2000	Supplementary MEFP	MoF, GovBI, Coord. Minister[b]	Completed
31/07/2000	Supplementary MEFP	MoF, Gov.BI, Coord. Minister[g]	Completed
(New Wahid cabinet)			
07/11/2000	Supplementary MEFP	GovBI, Coord. Min.[h]	Suspended
Megawati government			
27/08/2001	Extended MEFP[c]	MoF, GovBI, Coord. Minister[i]	Completed
13/12/2001	Extended MEFP[c]	MoF, GovBI, Coord. Minister[i]	Completed
09/04/2002	Supplementary MEFP	MoF, GovBi, Coord. Minister[i]	Completed
11/06/2002	Supplementary MEFP	MoF, GovBI, Coord. Minister[i]	Completed
20/11/2002	Supplementary MEFP	MoF, GovBI, Coord. Minister[i]	Completed
18/03/2003	Supplementary MEFP	MoF, GovBI, Coord. Minister[i]	—

Source: Soesastro (2003).

Notes
MEFP: Memorandum of Economic and Financial Policies.
MoF: Minister of Finance.
GovBI: Governor of Bank Indonesia.
Coord Minister: Coordinating Minister.
a   Second Arrangement.
b   Third Arrangement.
c   based on Third Arrangement.
d   Mari'e Muhammad and Soedradjad Djiwandono.
e   Ginandjar Kartasasmita.
f   Bambang Soedibjo, Sjahril Sabirin, Kwik Kian Gie.
g   Bambang Soedibjo, Anwar Nasution, Kwik Kian Gie.
h   Rizal Ramli, Anwar Nasution.
i   Boediono, Sjahril Sabirin, Dorodjatun Kuntjoro-Jakti.

Table 6.4 Bank asset and liabilities (trillion rupiah)

All commerical banks	1997	1998	1999	2000	2001	2002
Loans	408	540	245	287	321	381
Deposits	327	536	587	673	766	802
Capital	47	−99	−22	51	67	94
Total assets	529	762	789	985	1,040	1,060
LDR (%)	124.9	100.9	41.8	42.7	41.9	47.5

Source: Bank Indonesia, *Indonesian Financial Statistics*, various editions, as given in Anas *et al.* (2003).

Note
LDR: Loan to deposit ratio.

banking sector remains large. There are 141 commercial banks in the system, comprising 5 state-owned banks, 26 regional development banks, 76 private national banks, 24 joint venture banks and 10 foreign banks. Second, as shown in Table 6.4, total assets of commercial banks increased significantly, doubling in size. However, 38.3 per cent were in the form of government bonds issued for financing the bank recapitalisation programme, and 7 per cent were in the form of Bank Indonesia Certificates (SBI). This is especially true for major banks that were absorbed into the recapitalisation programme. Their assets increased significantly as a result of the recap bonds. The bank restructuring programme has also increased the government stake in the banking sector as a result of the closure and taking over of bad banks (Anas *et al.*, 2003).

Third, a troubling trend is that the banking sector has not regained its financial intermediation function. Essentially, banks are very risk-averse and still reluctant to lend to the private sector. They prefer to rely heavily on government funds, SBI and government bonds, which give high returns and lower risk compared to bank credits. As a result, the larger part of banks' interest income came from those assets. Bank loans are quite small compared to mobilised funds. At the beginning of 1999, the average loan to deposit ratio (LDR) of domestic banks fell to as low as 42 per cent – except for the A-category banks.[13] By December 2002, the LDR continued to remain below 50 per cent, compared to a high of 125 per cent in 1997 (Anas *et al.*, 2003).

Fourth, the amount of non-performing loans (NPLs) remains relatively high. In the early phase of the crisis, non-performing loans made up as much as 32 per cent of total loans in Indonesia. Peaking at 58.7 per cent in March 1999, NPLs then dropped to 8.3 per cent by the end of 2002, after IBRA cleaned them up from the commercial banks' balance sheets. However, non-performing loans of the recapitalised banks continued to be high, standing at 19 per cent in 2001, the latest year for which data were available at the time of writing. This indicates that the bank restructuring programme did little to improve the performance of the recapitalised banks (Anas *et al.*, 2003). Lastly, the continued existence of the blanket guarantee on bank deposits prevents much-needed bank mergers. While the blanket guarantee was effective in re-establishing public confidence in domestic banks, it nevertheless results in moral hazard. Under the IMF–LOI bank restructuring programme, the government is required to establish a market-oriented Deposit Insurance Institution. The plan was to have such an institution established in the year 2004, but progress remains slow.

Overall, IBRA's asset disposal was late and slow. Total loan assets were 321.1 trillion rupiah, out of which 219.5 trillion were sold, still leaving 101.6 trillion to be sold before IBRA's deadline in March 2004.[14] It was only from May 1999 when IBRA began its assets sale that in many cases IBRA had to take legal actions against shareholders of closed banks for allegedly misleading IBRA about their assets, including holding back assets which were pledged by the shareholders to cover the shortfalls of banks' assets below their liabilities. However, the result was mixed at best: in 2002 IBRA lost in 266 cases in court (IBRA, 2002). IBRA faced difficult and politically sensitive negotiations to reach agreements with top debtors such as Salim, Syamsul Nursalim and other conglomerates. In some instances, involving for instance Lippo Bank or Bank Internasional Indonesia, IBRA failed to exercise its supervision function.[15]

Privatisation and corporate governance

The government had also adopted a privatisation and deregulation process under the IMF-led economic policy agenda. Several important steps have been taken towards establishing a legal framework for a competitive market economy. For instance, the government has pushed through some important legislation to improve corporate and patent and trademark laws. More importantly, in a landmark decision against state monopolies and price controls, the Indonesian Parliament, DPR (Dewan Perwakilan Rakyat), passed a bill in October 2001 ending the monopoly of the national oil and gas company, Pertamina. This opened the domestic market to other national and international petroleum corporations. Other state monopolies are expected to be privatised or to lose their exclusive rights. They include the national electricity company, Perusahaan Listrik Negara (PLN), the telecommunications company, PT Telcom, and the national postal service.

However, after three years of the privatisation programme, progress in asset sales is proceeding slowly.[16] Initially, thirty state-owned companies were due to be privatised, but constant delays mean that the bulk of privatisation is to be implemented after the IMF programme ends in 2003. As a result, expected revenues from privatisation in 2003 have been revised downwards to 4 trillion rupiah from an initially targeted 8 trillion rupiah. The privatisation of Bank Mandiri, Bank Rakyat Indonesia and the gas distribution firm, PGN, was scheduled to make up the bulk of the proceeds in fiscal year 2003 (CSIS, 2003). The slow privatisation process is accompanied by the lack of implementation of clear regulations on key governance issues. First, efforts to combat corruption have been stalled. The setting up of an Anti-Corruption Committee, scheduled in 2002, was delayed by slow deliberation in the DPR and was not expected to be fully operational before December 2003. Second, market confidence in Indonesia's judicial system, and especially in the commercial court, is low. The latter has frequently issued inconsistent and controversial decisions in cases involving major business interests.[17]

Conclusion: the globalisation–economic security nexus reviewed

The simple premise of this chapter is that prior to the crisis in 1997–1998, a strong state was able successfully to control the country's integration into the global economy. After the crisis, a weak state had to rely on global institutions such as the IMF to regain economic security, particularly with respect to the integrity of the economy and its market institutions. What factors determined these two states of affairs?

Prior to the Asian crisis of 1997–1998, the New Order regime could be characterised as a patrimonial alliance between the state bureaucracy and business conglomerates. This structure generated costly rent-seeking activities and involved huge transaction costs. Scarce resources were directed to unproductive sectors. The question is why the long-run development performance under Soeharto's New Order regime was positive despite the pervasive role of the state. Conventional wisdom now suggests that selective intervention in the micro-economy was supplemented by orthodox macroeconomic prescriptions. Technocrats within the government managed to steer policies from an excessively interventionist stance when it mattered. Liberal policy periods interchanged with interventionist periods during Soeharto's reign. When macroeconomic stabilisation mattered, policy-makers acted, such as during the 1966–1973 period. When the oil boom generated huge revenues, import substitution strategies followed and resources were allocated to selected industries, as happened during 1973–1982. When the decline in oil revenues caused slower economic growth, market-oriented reforms were introduced, such as in 1982 and in the 1987–1995 period. Regional institutions such as ASEAN or APEC were also used to push for a 'controlled' trade liberalisation agenda. Investors too perceived the costs of corruption to be bearable so long as they could rely on a 'working' and predictable patronage system. But once doubts emerged about Soeharto's capacity to retain control over politics, investors pulled out on a massive scale, as happened during the height of the crisis in late 1997 and early 1998. Massive exchange rate depreciation and resulting inflation led to falling living standards. The power of (unregulated) capital flows and the market, therefore, coincided with the demands for democratic change once the legitimacy of the government – via successful development – was shattered.

After the crisis, economic security became a function of the relationship between the IMF and the government. While macroeconomic objectives could be achieved, microeconomic and structural reforms stalled, as the state's capacity to formulate coherent economic policies was influenced by more actors, including an assertive Parliament and a resurgent civil society. Thus, the economic reform process was also subject to the government's willingness to resist populist pressures, which on many occasions it failed to do. Political and economic reforms have been slow, especially legal reforms. The economic recovery programme was kept on track largely through the IMF-supported programme. However, the government's decision to leave the IMF programme at the end of 2003 will make it harder for the country to manage deficits and attract more FDI.

Indonesia's past growth experience depended to a significant extent on its capacity to increase exports and attract FDI. However, Indonesia is slowly losing out in the competitiveness game to other countries in the region, a situation that can only be improved by accelerating the process of privatisation and financial restructuring. But slow progress on economic reforms is also a natural 'price' to pay during a transition from an authoritarian system to a – hopefully – more democratic one. How to balance economic restructuring objectives with the social costs associated with reforms remains a legitimate concern for Indonesia's policy-makers. In this regard, the government's consistent and quick implementation of the reforms set out in its White Paper of September 2003 is of utmost importance.[18] The document shows the government's commitment to an action plan with a clear timetable for continued economic and governance reforms.

Ultimately, the biggest challenge for Indonesia is to develop a new governance model, one that balances the interests between state, market and society. Safeguarding economic security is therefore not just a function limited to state and market; it also requires the participation of civil society. Effective economic policies have to be channelled through democratic institutions, which are still being constructed. This process takes time, and the road to full economic recovery, and therefore towards regaining economic security, will remain a long one.

Notes

The views expressed in this chapter are the author's own and do not reflect those of the World Bank nor the Centre for Strategic and International Studies (CSIS), Jakarta.

1 The following builds on Liew (2000).
2 Corden (1999) and Schwarz and Paris (1999) provide good accounts of the crisis.
3 Regulations stated that Indonesian banks were not allowed to lend more than 20 per cent of their capital to a specific corporate group or a single borrower. In reality, some banks lent out 70 or 90 per cent of their total loans to specific corporate groups.
4 Interestingly, domestic investors seemed to have started the capital flight, whereas in Thailand, international investors started to pull out money.
5 The next section follows the argumentation in IMF (2003).
6 Quoted in Jomo (2001).
7 Known in Indonesia as BLBI, Bank Indonesia Liquidity Support, it is estimated at around 144.5 trillion rupiah.
8 During the period between the First and Second LOI (Letter of Intent) , October 1997 – January 1998, there was an expectation that difficulties in repaying the foreign debt would make it difficult to roll over debt and borrow foreign funds, which in turn caused further depreciation (Kunimune 1999).
9 There was a growing perception that Soeharto was not willing to implement the structural reforms devised by the IMF and the 'technocrats'. For instance, the September 1997 decision to reschedule the implementation of large projects was reversed for fifteen projects that were linked to the Soeharto family. Bank Andromeda, partly owned by a son of Soeharto, Bambang Trihatmodjo, and among the sixteen closed banks, reappeared under a different name, Bank Alfa, just a couple of weeks later. Another example was the approval of a private power plant project, Tanjung Jati-C, despite the earlier decision to shelve it because of the potential for financial losses for PLN and the already existing oversupply of electricity on Java (Soesastro and Basri, 1998).

10 The main points of 'people's democracy' were covered in Decree No. XVI/MPR/1998 on Political Economy within Economic Democracy issued at the November Special Session of the parliament (MPR).

11 IBRA was established as an *ad hoc* institution tasked with the following main functions: to administer the government's blanket guarantee programme; to monitor, manage and restructure banks taken over by IBRA; to restructure and dispose of loans in banks closed by IBRA; to manage shareholder settlement by former bank owners; and to recover state funds provided as liquidity support loans to banks (Anas *et al.* 2003).

12 The following closely follows Anas *et al.* (2003).

13 A-Category banks are banks with a capital adequacy ratio (CAR) greater than 4 per cent. The CAR for B-Category banks is 4 to –25 per cent, and for C-Category banks it is less than –25 per cent.

14 Data from Infobank quoted in Anas *et al.* (2003).

15 See Anas *et al.* (2003: 202–205).

16 Resistance to privatisation still remains strong, as evidenced by the street demonstrations against the largest privatisation deal to date when the government sold its stake in telecommunications firm Indosat to Singapore Technologies Telemedia in December 2002.

17 The most recent case is Bank Permata, where inconsistent rulings by the courts effectively failed to settle the debt claim and may result in the bank's second bailout by the government (various media reports June–August 2003.

18 Formally named the 'Economic Policy Package Pre- and Post-IMF' and issued as a presidential instruction on 15 September 2003. As of October 2003, the government had completed thirty-seven action plans out of a targeted fifty-four (World Bank, 2003: 8).

Bibliography

Anas, Titik, Suhut, Nancy K. and Amri, Puspa Delima (2003) 'The Indonesian Banking Sector: Five Years in Crisis?', *Indonesian Quarterly*, 31 (2): 197–208.

Azis, Iwan J. (1994), 'Indonesia', in John Williamson, *The Political Economy of Policy Reform*, Washington, DC: Institute for International Economics.

Baker, Richard W. and Morrison, Charles E. (2000) *Asia Pacific Security Outlook 2000*, Tokyo: Japan Center for International Exchange.

Booth, Anne (1999) 'Survey of Recent Developments', *Bulletin of Indonesian Economic Studies*, 35 (3): 3–38.

Bresnan, John (1999) 'The United States, the IMF and the Indonesian Financial Crisis', in Adam Schwarz and Jonathan Paris (eds) *The Politics of Post-Suharto Indonesia*, Singapore: Council of Foreign Relations, SNP Editions.

Cameron, Lisa (1999) 'Survey of Recent Developments', *Bulletin of Indonesian Economic Studies*, 35 (1): 3–40.

Corden, Max (1999) *The Asian Crisis: Is There a Way Out?*, Singapore: Institute for Southeast Asian Studies.

Crane, George T. (1998) 'Economic Nationalism: Bringing the Nation Back In', *Millennium*, 27 (1): 55–76.

CSIS (2003) 'Economic and Political Update', Jakarta: Centre for Strategic and International Studies, June.

Dick, Howard (2001) 'Survey of Recent Developments', *Bulletin of Indonesian Economic Studies*, 37 (1): 7–41.

Evans, Kevin (1998) 'Survey of Recent Developments', *Bulletin of Indonesian Economic Studies*, 34 (3): 5–35.

Fane, George (2000) 'Survey of Recent Developments', *Bulletin of Indonesian Economic Studies*, 36 (1): 13–44.

Feldstein, Martin (1998) 'Refocusing the IMF', *Foreign Affairs*, No. 2 (March/April): 20–33.

Feridhanusetyawan, Tubagus (1999) *Security Implications of the Economic Crisis for Indonesian Workers*, Research Paper, Jakarta: Centre for Strategic and International Studies.

Feridhanusetyawan, Tubagus and Anas, Titik (2000) 'Revisiting the Cause of the Indonesian Economic Crisis', in M. Ishida (ed.) *Economic Crisis in Indonesia*, Chiba, Japan: Institute of Developing Economies and Japan External Trade Organisation.

Gore, Charles (2000) 'The Rise and Fall of the Washington Consensus as a Paradigm for Developing Countries', *World Development*, 28(5): 789–804.

Haggard, Stephan and Kaufman, Robert R. (1992) *The Politics of Economic Adjustment*, Princeton, NJ: Princeton University Press.

IBRA (2002) *Laporan Tahunan 2002 dan Rencana Kerja 2003* (Annual Report 2002 and Work Plan for 2003), Jakarta: Indonesian Bank Reconstruction Agency.

IMF (2003) 'IMF and Recent Capital Account Crises', Evaluation report, Washington, DC: Independent Evaluation Office, International Monetary Fund, July.

Ishida, M. (2000) 'Economic Crisis in Indonesia', Chiba, Japan: Institute of Developing Economies and Japan External Trade Organisation.

Johnson, Colin (1998) 'Survey of Recent Developments', *Bulletin of Indonesian Economic Studies*, 34 (2): 3–60.

Jomo, K. S. (2001) *Growth after the Asian Crisis: What Remains of the East Asian Model?*, G-24 Discussion Paper Series No. 10: UNCTAD.

Kenward, Lloyd R. (2002) *From the Trenches: The First Year of the Indonesian Crisis of 1997/98 As Seen from the World Bank's Office in Jakarta*, Jakarta: Centre for Strategic and International Studies.

Khan, Mohsin (1986) *Macroeconomic Adjustment In Developing Countries: A Policy Perspective*, Policy Paper, Washington, DC: World Bank.

Kunimune, Kozo (ed.) (1999) *Asian Economic Crisis 97/98: Issues in Macroeconomic Imbalances, Capital Outflows and Financial Crises*, IDE Spot Survey, Tokyo: Institute of Developing Economies and Japan External Trade Organisation.

Liew, Leong (2000) 'Human and Economic Security: Is There a Nexus?', in William Tow, Ramesh Thakur and In-Taek Hyun (eds) *Asia's Emerging Regional Order. Reconciling Traditional and Human Security*, Tokyo: United Nations University Press, pp. 192–208.

McQuillan, Lawrence J. and Montgomery, Peter C. (1999) *The International Monetary Fund: Financial Medic to the World?*, Stanford, CA: Hoover Institution Press.

Pangestu, Mari and Hadi Soesastro (2002) 'The Role of the IMF in East Asia's Recovery: Lessons for the Future – Paper on Indonesia', in Tan King Yam (ed.), *Asian Economic Recovery – Policy Options for Growth and Stability*, Singapore: Institute of Policy Studies, pp. 157–186.

Pardede, Raden (1999) 'Survey of Recent Developments', *Bulletin of Indonesian Economic Studies*, 35 (2): 3–39.

Radelet, Steven and Sachs, Jeffrey (1998) 'The East Asian Financial Crisis: Diagnosis, Remedies, Prospects', mimeo, Harvard Institute for International Development. March.

Radelet, Steven C. and Wing Thye Woo (2000) 'Indonesia: A Troubled Beginning', in Wing Thye Woo, Jeffrey D. Sachs and Klaus Schwab (eds) *The Asian Financial Crisis: Lessons for a Resilient Asia*, Cambridge, MA: MIT Press, pp. 165–184.

Rinakit, S. and Soesastro, H. (1998) 'Indonesia', in Charles E. Morrison and Hadi Soesastro (eds) *Domestic Adjustments to Globalisation*, Tokyo: Japan Center for International Exchange, pp. 193–206.

Robison, R. and Rosser, A. (1998) 'Contesting Reform : Indonesia's New Order and the IMF', *World Development*, 26 (8): 1593–1606.

Rodrik, Dani (2000) *Institutions for High Quality Growth: What They Are and How to Acquire Them*, NBER Working Paper 7540.

Sato, Yuri (ed.) (2000) *Indonesia Entering a New Era: Abdurrahman Wahid Government and Its Challenge*, Chiba, Japan: Institute of Developing Economies and Japan External Trade Organisation.

Schwarz, Adam and Paris, Jonathan (1999) *The Politics of Post-Soeharto Indonesia*, Singapore: Council of Foreign Relations.

Soesastro, Hadi (2000a) 'The Indonesian Economy under Abdurrahman Wahid', in *Southeast Asian Affairs 2000*, Singapore: Institute of Southeast Asian Studies, pp. 134–144.

—— (2000b) 'Governance and the Crisis in Indonesia', in Peter Drysdale (ed.) *Reform and Recovery in East Asia: The Role of the State and Economic Enterprise*, London: Routledge, pp. 120–145.

—— (2000c) 'Globalization: Challenges for Indonesia', *Economic Reform Today*, No. 1: 51–54.

—— (2003) 'IMF and the Political Economy of Indonesia's Economic Recovery', *Indonesian Quarterly*, 31 (2).

Soesastro, Hadi and Basri, Chatib (1998), 'Survey of Recent Developments', *Bulletin of Indonesian Economic Studies*, 34 (1): 3–54.

Stubbs, Richard (2000) 'Signing On to Liberalisation: AFTA and the Politics of Regional Economic Cooperation', *The Pacific Review*, 13 (2): 297–318.

Timmer, Peter (1996) 'Does BULOG Stabilize Rice Prices? Should It Try?', *Bulletin of Indonesian Economic Studies*, 32 (2): 45–74.

Wade, R. (1998) 'The Asian Debt-and-Development Crisis of 1997–?: Causes and Consequences', *World Development*, 26 (8): 1535–1554.

World Bank (1999) *World Development Report 1998/99*, New York: Oxford University Press.

World Bank (2000) 'Indonesia: Seizing the Opportunity', *Economic Brief for the Consultative Group on Indonesia*, World Bank Office in Jakarta.

World Bank (2003) 'Indonesia: Beyond Macroeconomic Stability', *World Bank Brief for the Consultative Group on Indonesia*, World Bank Office in Jakarta.

7 Taiwan's economic security

Confronting the dual trends of globalization and governance

Chyungly Lee

The 1997–1998 Asian financial crises triggered economic, political and societal turmoil across East Asia and intensified debates on the impact of economic globalization on national and regional developments. More intriguingly to strategists and security experts, the Asian turbulence reopened debates on the concepts of *economic security* within the sphere of *non-traditional security* studies.[1] The paradigm of non-traditional security, as opposed to the traditional state-centric notion of national security, goes beyond state sovereignty and territorial integrity in identifying security objects to be protected. It also perceives national security threats from broader environments beyond military and political confrontations, and weighs nonmilitary approaches to security goals. The study of the economic–security nexus, which used to focus on the economic contributions to national defense capability and regional security landscapes, is now increasingly explored in the context of economic globalization and the emerging transnational governance in response to globalization.

Although there is no authoritative definition of globalization, it has been broadly accepted that the manifestations of economic globalization include the spatial reorganization of production, the interpenetration of industries across borders, the transnational spread of financial markets, and the liberalization of commodity exchanges (Mittelman, 1997: 2). Globalization refers to something more than 'interdependence.' It signifies both quantitative and qualitative changes in interactions between state and nonstate actors, and resets the stage from which these actors shape domestic and international orders. The evolution of global and regional governance, indicating the will and intent of managing common international affairs through ordered rule and collective action, reflects new dynamics in relations among state and nonstate actors, individuals, and institutions, as well as the public and private sectors.

In line with the dual trends of globalization and governance, economic security could be conceptualized either within a framework of national security, in which the national economy is one of the nontraditional security attributes of state-centered security and strategic interests, or within the realm of *human security*, in which individual economic welfare and 'freedom from want' are the primary objectives of people-centered security agendas. In both inquiries, states/governments retain their critical role in bridging the interests both of the nation and of non-state actors across borders. Taiwan, as an open economy and society, is fully exposed to the processes of economic globalization and a changing international environment as a result of the evolution of global and regional governance. Regretably, however, it is able to participate only partially in states-led modes of governance, whether global or regional, owing to diplomatic obstruction from China. Given the dual trends of globalization and governance, the Taiwanese government is thus confronting a double set of economic security challenges: the withering of the state's capacity to defend its economic security interests, and the lack of mechanisms through which Taiwan can participate in regional governance, which could help uphold the country's economic security interests.

This chapter addresses these concerns in some detail, beginning with a specification of key dimensions of Taiwan's economic security interests and their significance to Taiwan's grand strategy and national development. The next section highlights the imminent challenges to Taiwan's economic security interests in the process of globalization and the development of global and regional governance. The third section calls for better governance to enhance common economic security interests between Taiwan and other regional economies. The chapter concludes with some thoughts for policy considerations.

Conceptualizing Taiwan's economic security

Economic prosperity is one of the major elements of state power. While security is the oxygen (Nye, 1995: 90–91), economic growth and prosperity are the muscle (Lilly, 1996: viii), which in turn strengthens the physical conditions for attaining security goals. In a dynamic market-driven economy, fluctuations in economic cycles alert policymakers, but equilibrium may be resumed through the market mechanism. Such dynamics prevent economic depression and distress from turning into confidence crises or into threats to national security. Effective risk management may overcome the fear of collapse of the national economy. What causes security concerns, however, is the economic externalities arising from particular social and political systems and the uneven paths taken in resuming economic and sociopolitical order in the wake of economic crises. For instance, what led to security concerns in the case of the 1997–1998 Asian turbulence was not the economic disaster *per se*, but the link between economic issues and the internal security of devastated economies and the regional anxieties arising from security interdependence.

Conceptualizing economic security as a concept of national security beyond the notion of a safety net for the national economy requires specification of strategic goals and the security perceptions of individual states. Although the common objective of economic security across countries is to strengthen the economy and reduce vulnerability to changing environments, the strategic implications of the economic insecurities facing each country may vary. The goals and approaches adopted by individual states to eliminate the economic causes of national insecurity or their utilization of economic tools to enhance national security often depend on their respective levels of economic development as well as their internal economic

and non-economic structures. To those with strong economic and political structures and with a relatively superior international position, their economic strength
could be used as an instrument to leverage other countries and achieve the nation's
external policy goals. In contrast, for those states with relatively weak economic
and political structures, the internal imperative of defending political legitimacy
against disruptions from economic distress becomes more salient (Lee, 1999a).

During the takeoff stage of Taiwan's economic development in the 1950s and
1960s, regime legitimacy, to a great extent, was built upon the continuity of
economic growth. Disruption to economic growth might have induced internal
instability and resulted in political insecurity.[2] Through a strong state/government
and favorable access to the US market, Taiwan was able to manage its internal
state–market relations and generated national wealth through export-led economic
growth. The ruling party, the Kuomintang (KMT), was able to maintain political
security in Taiwan in part because of its successful strategy of economic
development. Following political reforms and democratization in the 1990s, regime
transformation in Taiwan has been undertaken peacefully.[3] While economic
distress now might result in political disputes among different political parties, it
is not likely to threaten regime legitimacy or provoke internal instability. However,
the economic determinants of Taiwan's external security remain crucial. The
strategic interests of sustaining Taiwan's relative economic superiority inevitably
lie with countering the country's relative political and security inferiority imposed
from the international environment, mainly as a result of diplomatic obstruction
and military threats from China.

Basic economic security interests

When the external relations of an individual state are primarily based on economic
engagements, either because of the constraints arising from geopolitical pressure
from other countries or because of strategic considerations of its own, then national
economic strength naturally becomes a central base of the state's international
capacity. Strengthening the national economy is an imperative not only for reasons
of domestic economic welfare, but also for stocking up resources for expanding its
economic ties with other countries. Japan's postwar policy, driven by the Yoshida
doctrine, and its comprehensive security strategy developed later greatly reflected
the considerations of Japan's basic economic security interests. Because of the
constitutional constraints that prevented Japan from pursuing military power,
developing economic ties became the main channel through which to extend the
country's international platform (Akao, 1983; Chapman *et al.*, 1982; Barnett, 1984).
In contrast to the case of Japan's economic security strategy, in which its own
proactive strategic considerations steered its external economic policy, Taiwan has
to develop its economic security strategy within the context of countering the
diminishing diplomatic space imposed by geopolitical pressures.

Taiwan is constantly under military threat from China against any actions the
latter perceives as pro-independence. Given the asymmetry of military capacities
between the two entities, the cross-Strait political stalemate will continue to be the

major cause of Taiwan's insecurity. The fact that the Taiwan Strait is a potential flashpoint of military confrontation has brought Taiwan's security under the spotlight of the regional security agenda. But the geopolitical and geostrategic concerns that neighboring countries have with regard to this issue do not necessarily lead to a favorable security environment for Taiwan. The rise of China and its increasing weight in regional security exacerbates anxiety. Given their geopolitical and strategic interests, any policy showdown for regional countries in the event that war breaks out between China and Taiwan will take the form of a zero-sum game, and the outcome will most likely be at Taiwan's expense. The alternative is for Taiwan to adopt a comprehensive approach to its security goal by building its national economic capacity and searching for international support in a broadened strategic context.

In addition to military threats to Taiwan's security, political tensions and diplomatic confrontations with China have impeded Taiwan from normalizing military or political ties with many countries and have excluded Taiwan from formal participation in most of the international institutions that require state membership. Instead, economic and other apolitical engagements have been the main arenas for building Taiwan's international capacities in the past. Economic capacity becomes the prime muscle through which Taiwan can play an international role. Until now, Taiwan's international bargaining chips have relied on the country's economic strengths. The economic–security nexus in Taiwan's national security is causal, and not merely a correlation. Sustaining economic strength is crucial not merely for people's welfare and internal security, but also to fuel Taiwan's external maneuverability.

Geo-economic security interests

An analytical framework based on geo-economic security would explore the influence of regional economic dynamism on the national economy and for its strategic and security implications. Geo-economic security interests are defined on the basis of *economic geography*,[4] in which it is economic *flows* and the functional relationship between places that delimit economic spaces, rather than physical geographical proximity. More importantly, a geo-economic analysis reflects realism in the economic agenda and incorporates the reality of geopolitical games into the conceptualization of economic security. Economic priorities previously subordinated to military concerns are consequently emerging and dominating the world political scene, with economic competition among international powers becoming increasingly critical in determining the primacy of states. The new concept of international rivalry thus consists of concerns with economic zero-sum games. The fear of a relative decline in power and the subsequent loss of strategic interests motivate a state's ambition to maintain its relative economic superiority and to develop 'an economic agenda for neorealists.'[5]

Nevertheless, the pursuit of geo-economic security interests is more likely when an economy is holding a relatively critical position in a particular geo-economic sphere. The competition between the United States and Japan over economic leadership in the Asia-Pacific in the 1980s, reflecting their respective geo-economic security interests in the region, has been well explored. More recent shifts in the Asia-Pacific economic geography, closely associated with China's relative gains in regional trade and investment shares in the post-Asian crisis period, have repositioned the Chinese economy in the structure of regional economic flows and manifested its significance to the regional geo-economic order. Such a shift has opened a new phase of geo-economic competition between Japan and China over economic security interests.

When Taiwan achieved its relative economic superiority in regional markets in the late 1980s, its pursuit of geo-economic security interests became possible. Taiwan's geo-economic security interests lay in the use of *economic leverage* to counterbalance the external political inferiority imposed by pressure from China. This concept should be distinguished from the so-called *economic diplomacy*, through which foreign aid or official development assistance (ODA) are the main instruments used to gain political support from friendly developing countries; such aid is often irrelevant to Taiwan's own economic capacities. In contrast, a geo-economic security goal stresses the deepening of economic leverage through expanding economic geographical boundaries and enlarging 'spaces as flows.' In other words, the expansion of substantive trade and investment flows with neighboring economies, not politically aimed economic ties, fortifies the basis of economic leverage.

Confronting the dual trends of globalization and governance

In the pursuit of economic security interests as the basis of Taiwan's international capacity, the sustainability of Taiwan's own economic growth becomes an imperative, while the extension of Taiwan's geo-economic security interests relies on maintaining Taiwan's economic leverage in the regional 'space as flows.' However, the dual trends of globalization and governance have posed three imminent difficulties for the Taiwanese government in strategic planning aimed at accomplishing the above two goals: the withering of state capacities against cross-Strait market dynamics, the loss of geo-economic leverage in the new regional economic geography, and the lack of access to states-led regional governance mechanisms.

Withering state capacity for safeguarding economic security interests

The export-oriented trajectory of Taiwan's industrialization, including the role of the state in the process, has been well documented. However, the economic techniques in the past, which highlighted the state's capacity for mobilizing resource allocations for designated economic goals, are no longer effective, given the increasing integration of the global economy. Global product and factor markets linked through trade, direct investment, and financial flows are greatly aided by deregulation of national markets and the liberalization of trade and capital movements. In the rapid path of economic globalization, Taiwan's economy faces three major challenges. First, Taiwan is losing both its competitive advantage in labor-intensive industries and its export market shares to less developed economies, while at the same time competing with developed economies and other newly industrializing economies (NIEs) over world markets in knowledge-intensive manufacturing. Second, to cope with such dual competitive pressures, Taiwan does not have the privilege of better terms of protection in the world trade regime. Third, the reorganization of production allowing economic resources to flow directly from the developed economies to less developing countries shrinks the room for Taiwan to play in either of these economies. These three challenges might be commonly faced by all NIEs, albeit to different degrees. However, the choice of mainland China in the late 1980s as a substitute market by many Taiwanese businesses eager to avert losses arising from the process of industrial restructuring has gradually given rise to unique economic security concerns for Taiwan.

The rise of the Chinese economy has generated market opportunities through which Taiwan has been able to cope with the difficulties associated with economic globalization. China and the United States are currently the two leading export markets for Taiwan. In fact, China surpassed the United States and became the largest market for Taiwan's exports, though marginally so, in 2000. The gap has, however, rapidly widened since then. In the third quarter of 2003, Taiwan's exports to China constituted 35.2 percent of Taiwan's total exports and almost double the share going to the US (at 18.6 percent) (Table 7.1). In terms of contribution to GDP, Taiwan's exports to Hong Kong and China constitute 9.6 percent and 8.6 percent of Taiwan's total GDP respectively in 2001. With 63 percent of Taiwan's exports to Hong Kong being reexported to China, Taiwan's total exports to China in 2001, including those reexported via Hong Kong, constituted 14.7 percent of Taiwan's total GDP (Table 7.2).

The impact of cross-Strait trade and investment relations to Taiwan's economy weighs not only on the trade surpluses directly generated from Taiwan's exports to China, but also on the profits gained from Taiwan's export-oriented foreign direct investment (FDI) in China. Chinese markets are considered to be opening windows to world markets for Taiwan's businesses, especially after China's entry to the WTO in December 2001. Taiwan's FDI in China increased dramatically in 2002. The share of Taiwan's FDI in China was 66.7 percent of Taiwan's total FDI outflows in 2002 and 71.3 percent from January to October 2003. There is also an increasing rate of approved FDI to China: 6.8 percent from 2000 to 2001, 38.6 percent from 2001 to 2002, and 52.9 percent from 2002 (first ten months) to 2003 (first ten months).[6] The manufacturing sector registering the largest FDI approval is the electronic and electric appliances sector, with a 31.1 percent cumulative share from 1991 to July 2003, followed by basic metals and metal products (8.7 percent).[7] Machineries and electrics, with a share of 54 percent of China's total export value in 2003 (January to October), is the most important exporting category.

Taiwan's economic outflows to China have essentially been market driven. The state government in Taiwan has been playing a responsive role and to a great extent

Table 7.1 Taiwan's exports to China and the United States (as a percentage of Taiwan's total exports)

	1994	1995	1996	1997	1998	1999	2000	2001	2002	2003 1st qtr	2003 2nd qtr	2003 3rd qtr
China	23.0	23.7	23.6	24.0	23.2	23.5	24.0	25.8	31.2	33.0	33.4	35.2
US	26.2	23.7	23.2	24.2	26.6	25.4	23.5	22.5	20.5	18.5	18.4	18.6

Source: Council for Economic Development and Planning, ROC: *Taiwan Statistical Data Book*, various years.

Note
a China includes Hong Kong.

Table 7.2 Shares of Taiwan's exports to China in Taiwan's total GDP (%)

	1992	1993	1994	1995	1996	1997	1998	1999	2000	2001	2002	2003 (1–7)
China	4.6	5.7	6.0	6.8	6.9	7.1	6.9	7.4	8.5	8.6	n.a.	n.a.
Hong Kong	7.3	8.2	8.7	9.9	9.6	9.9	9.3	9.0	10.1	9.6	n.a.	n.a.
HK's re-export to China (% of TW's export to HK)	55.6	62.2	61.1	59.6	61.5	60.8	62.7	63.5	60.3	63.7	69.4	74.4
Total	8.6	10.8	11.3	12.6	12.7	13.1	12.7	13.1	14.6	14.7	n.a.	n.a.

Source: Mainland Affairs Council, Executive Yuan, ROC: *Cross-Strait Economic Statistics Monthly*, July 2003.

trying to keep Taiwan's economy independent from China so that China will not use economic leverage to push for unification. Nevertheless, the economic flows keep growing. The average growth rate of Taiwan's exports to China was 29.2 percent from 1991 to 1996, while the average growth rate of Taiwan's contracted outflow of FDI to China was 24.6 percent from 1992 to 1996.[8] In September 1996, the 'no haste, be patient' guideline was unveiled to slow down Taiwan's FDI in China,[9] and to limit cross-Strait intra-industry trade for export-oriented investments. However, the average growth rate of Taiwan's export to China remained positive (5.5 percent) from 1997 to 2001. Taiwan's contracted outflow of FDI to China showed positive growth during the same period except in 1997. In November 2001, the Taiwanese government adjusted its cross-Strait economic guideline to 'active opening, effective management', in which the Chinese market is considered an essential link in the global deployment of Taiwanese industries. Exports to China surged in 2002, with a growth rate of 37.4 percent, and the contracted amount of Taiwan's FDI in China increased 33.4 percent in 2002, despite a slight drop in 2001 (Table 7.3).

The irresistible lure of the Chinese market in the global strategies of Taiwanese businesses will continue to drive cross-Strait economic interdependence. The escalating political tensions between Beijing and Taipei since 1996 seem to have

Table 7.3 Growth rate of Taiwan's economic outflows to China

	Estimate of Taiwan's exports to China[a]		Taiwan's outflow FDI to China[b]	
	Amount (US$ million)	Growth rate (%)	Contracted amount (US$ million)	Growth rate (%)
1991	7,494	70.5	2,873	
1992	9,696	29.4	5,543	92.9
1993	1,2726	31.3	9,965	79.8
1994	1,4652	15.1	5,395	−45.9
1995	17,886	22.1	5,777	7.1
1996	19,135	7.0	5,141	−11.0
1997	20,518	7.2	2,814	−45.3
1998	18,220	−11.2	2,982	6.0
1999	21,221	16.5	3,374	13.2
2000	26,144	23.2	4,042	19.8
2001	24,056	−8.0	6,914	71.1
2002	33,045	33.4	6,741	−2.5
2003 (Jan.–Oct.)	n.a.	n.a.	6,670	52.9

Source: Mainland Affairs Council, Executive Yuan, ROC: *Cross-Strait Economic Statistics Monthly*, July 2003.

Notes
a Data presented are calculated according to the formula of the Board of Foreign Trade (BOFT), ROC, i.e. Taiwan's exports to China + (Taiwan exports to HK (f.o.b.) – HK's imports from Taiwan (c.i.f.) + transit trade from Taiwan to China via Hong Kong).
b Official data from China. FDI: foreign direct investment.

low correlations with growing cross-Strait market integration. The military threats imposed by China in the 1996 missile crisis, the political tension that followed the adoption of the special 'state-to-state' theory in 1998, and the political impasse since the Democratic Progressive Party (DPP) took over the presidency in 2000 have not reversed the growing trend of cross-Strait economic integration. Warnings of market disruptions from the Taiwanese government and its policies of controlling investment flows have not slowed cross-Strait economic engagements. Such developments imply the erosion of Taiwan's state capacity to balance political and economic interests in cross-Strait relations and to safeguard Taiwan's economic security interests.

Developing economic ties with a political adversary often involves high risks of market disruptions caused by noneconomic factors. How seriously would Taiwan's economic sustainability and stability be threatened if severe market disruptions occurred in cross-Strait economic relations? The two cumulative effects of cross-Strait economic ties on Taiwan's industrial structure are the shrinking of labor-intensive industry, a large portion of which has moved westward to China, and the increasing value of the services sector, which however remains relatively weak in terms of international competitiveness. To overcome the withering role of the state in cross-Strait economic relations and to embrace economic globalization together with the rising Chinese economy, Taiwan reset its development goal to become a transpacific gateway to the Greater China market. It has reoriented its competitive strategies and is experiencing a qualitative change toward a knowledge-based economy in which the production, distribution, and use of knowledge are the main drivers of growth, wealth creation, and employment across all industries.[10] The harm resulting to the national economy from market disruption in labor-intensive industrial manufacturing will be marginalized if Taiwan succeeds in its industrial restructuring and builds up new types of manufacturing centers in Taiwan. The increasing value of the service sector will provide Taiwan with an opportunity to reorient its international competitiveness strategy toward a knowledge-based economy.

Declining geo-economic leverage in the new East Asian economic geography

One of the salient impacts of globalization on the economic geography of East Asia is the end of the Japan-led flying geese pattern of regional economic development. The flows of export-oriented FDI from the more developed economies to the less developed economies in the region used to be the driving force of regional economic growth. The rapid path of globalization now allows economic resources from developed economies worldwide to enter the less developed countries in the region directly, thereby shifting the boundaries of 'spaces as flows' in the region. Japan used to be the largest single-country source of FDI to the lower-income economies in East Asia. In 1993, Japan's FDI in China, Indonesia, Malaysia, Philippines, and Thailand accounted for 18.4 percent of total FDI inflows to these five countries, while the United States' share was 10.9 percent.[11] Nevertheless, as shown in Table

7.4, the cumulative amount of FDI from both the United States and Europe in three subregional growth areas in Southeast Asia from 1995 to 2001 surpassed Japan in all three instances, while the inflows from non-ASEAN NIEs accounted for only relatively marginal amounts.

Another phenomenon of the new East Asian geography is the rise of the Chinese economy, particularly after the 1997–1998 Asian economic crisis. China was never truly a part of the East Asian flying geese phenomenon in the past. Instead, the opening up of the Chinese economy has attracted economic resources worldwide. China has been the largest developing-country recipient of FDI and has enjoyed rapid growth under globalization. The rise of the Chinese economy soon became the major determinant delimiting East Asia's economic geography. China has gradually replaced the United States to become the largest export market for many East Asian economies and the chief driver of Asia's export growth. Japan's exports to China have posted record growth since 2000. In 2001, China overtook the United States to become Taiwan's largest export market. In 2003, China for the first time became the biggest export market for Singapore and South Korea.[12]

Besides growing trade and investment with the developed economies and the NIEs, China's trade and investment flows to the less developed countries in the region have also undermined the pattern of flying geese development. As a developing economy, China selects its outward FDI markets strategically. Compared to other emerging East Asian economies, China's manufacturing investment in the East ASEAN Growth Area, which includes provinces in Brunei, Indonesia, Malaysia, and the Philippines, was remarkably higher in the years 1995–2001

Table 7.4 Approved manufacturing investment projects in ASEAN subregional growth area, 1995–2001 by country of origin (selective) (US$)

	East ASEAN Growth Area (BIMP-EAGA)[a]	*Northern ASEAN Growth Area (IMT-GT)*[b]	*Southern ASEAN Growth Area (IMS-GT)*[c]
Japan	1,078,223,110	3,709,880,341	7,983,637,481
US	2,512,136,492	4,165,614,966	13,273,367,275
Europe	3,757,236,909	3,439,872,256	7,163,364,416
Emerging markets in East Asia			
China	1,271,689,369	57,684,554	6,884,211
South Korea	139,875,210	1,097,001,652	113,501,396
Hong Kong	728,633,787	84,363,541	96,465,116
Taiwan	136,279,496	625,249,338	2,986,296,820
ASEAN	4,021,527,218	1,928,396,613	3,862,182,608
Total	15,201,736,437	24,058,302,795	45,571,484,923

Source: ASEAN Secretariat FDI Database.

Notes
a BIMP-EAGA is Brunei, Indonesia, Malaysia, the Philippines – the East ASEAN Growth Area.
b IMI-GT is the Indonesia, Malaysia, Thailand Growth Triangle.
c IMS-GT is the Indonesia, Malaysia, Singapore Growth Triangle.

(Table 7.4). In development projects in the Greater Mekong subregion, which is home to 250 million people from Myanmar, Thailand, Laos, Vietnam, Cambodia, and China's Yunan province, China also plays an important role. In terms of ties with single countries, China is one of the very few countries to have investments in Laos and Myanmar.

Under the flying geese pattern of regional economic development, Taiwan, like other NIEs, has played a dual role in the region's economic growth.[13] On the one hand, Taiwan's FDI outflows toward the region provided sources of input for the growth of the region's lower-income economies. On the other hand, the increase in trade ties between the NIEs and the lower-income economies changed Taiwan's previous trade pattern of the 1970s and early 1980s, which had been based on an asymmetric dependence on imports from Japan and exports to the United States, and instead repositioned Taiwan to play a more significant role in East Asian economic interdependence. Such dual roles allowed Taiwan to have greater economic leverage over the region's developments.

In the new East Asian economic geography, as already discussed, Taiwan's economy is now strongly linked to the Chinese economy. The Taiwanese government has encouraged overseas Taiwanese investments to be shifted to Southeast Asia from mainland China to reduce the risks of overdependence on the Chinese market. Nevertheless, the apparent 'go South' policy, designated to diversify Taiwan's outward FDI markets in the region, has not been effective. FDI flows from Taiwan to Southeast Asia have not dramatically increased; rather, they have fluctuated (Table 7.5). The share of exports to the ASEAN-5 countries in Taiwan's GDP increased only marginally, from 4.2 percent in 1990 to 4.6 percent in 2001. The share of imports from the ASEAN-5 countries increased from 2.5 percent in 1990 to 5.5 percent in 2001.[14] Failing to extend trade and investment flows outside China could cause Taiwan to gradually lose its relative geo-economic strength, either directly against China or within a broader regional context.

The exclusiveness of East Asian states-led regional governance

Coping with the rising Chinese economy is certainly not a challenge unique to Taiwan. Japan today takes the prospect of losing its geo-economic security interests in East Asia even more seriously; other regional economies are also under pressure to make appropriate responses. However, it is being excluded from recent developments in states-led regional governance mechanisms in general, and the ASEAN Plus Three (APT) process in particular, that has deepened Taiwan's anxiety and its concerns with economic insecurity, particularly when such exclusion is motivated by political reasons. (The countries involved in APT are the ASEAN members – Indonesia, Malaysia, the Philippines, Singapore, Thailand, Brunei, Vietnam, Laos, Myanmar, and Cambodia – plus China, Japan, and South Korea.)

Since APT's first informal summit, held in November 1997, the APT cooperation process has, step by step, been formalized and expanded. The second informal

Table 7.5 Foreign direct investment in ASEAN countries, 1995–2002 (Jan.–June) by country of origin (US$ million)

	1995			1996			1997			1998		
	Japan	China	Taiwan	Japan	China	Taiwan	Japan	China	Taiwan	Japan	China	Taiwan
Brunei	6.1	—	0.8	7.4	—	0.3	7.2	—	0.4	6.9	—	0.4
Cambodia	n.a.	n.a.	n.a.	n.a.	n.a.	n.a.	n.a.	n.a.	n.a.	n.a.	n.a.	n.a.
Indonesia	1,750.9	5.7	(14.1)	1,828.6	—	19.5	1,597.2	8.0	7.7	(153.9)	(44.0)	(6.9)
Laos	0.9	1.5	1.1	0.4	0.4	0.1	4.1	2.7	0.2	7.0	2.8	0.1
Malaysia	450.1	13.5	186.9	390.8	6.5	(7.1)	490.5	23.0	56.2	308.0	3.4	54.1
Myanmar	0.4	3.1	—	15.6	2.2	—	18.9	0.4	—	33.5	2.6	—
Philippines	683.1	13.7	12.5	527.3	3.1	51.3	404.6	5.8	38.4	353.7	216.4	86.4
Singapore	680.8	105.7	303.6	1,503.2	84.5	254.2	2,505.6	14.6	291.3	1,633.2	84.2	115.0
Thailand	556.5	1.9	96.6	523.6	3.9	138.0	1,348.0	(7.8)	133.8	1,484.7	5.1	106.3
Vietnam	134.3	7.2	259.5	158.6	3.1	286.0	433.9	28.1	377.3	383.8	1.7	277.1
Total	4,263.0	152.3	846.9	4,955.4	103.7	742.3	6,810.0	74.9	905.4	4,056.9	272.2	632.4

	1999			2000			2001			2002 (1-6)		
	Japan	China	Taiwan	Japan	China	Taiwan	Japan	China	Taiwan	Japan	China	Taiwan
Brunei	5.6	—	n.a.	5.4	—	1.0	4.3	—	1.0	24.4	n.a.	—
Cambodia	n.a.	n.a.	n.a.	n.a.	n.a.	n.a.	n.a.	n.a.	n.a.	n.a.	(0.35)	(0.8)
Indonesia	(1134.8)	(1.2)	(20.5)	(1,717.4)	(2.81)	(4.9)	(1,101.5)	(1.5)	(7.5)	(246.9)	1.3	0.9
Laos	0.8	1.1	1.3	1.6	9.1	1.3	0.6	11.8	3.1	0.2	1.3	(39.5)
Malaysia	241.6	1.2	27.1	41.7	(1.0)	(24.4)	(715.1)	12.2	(20.7)	28.6	n.a.	n.a.
Myanmar	18.8	0.0	—	16.3	—	—	7.7	0.5	—	n.a.	—	15.1
Philippines	133	64.9	9.0	49.2	—	3.4	139.8	0.1	1.6	586.7	n.a.	n.a.
Singapore	1146.5	(27.4)	75.9	459.2	(7.1)	116.1	1104.2	99.9	87.9	n.a.	6.9	20.4
Thailand	488.4	(2.1)	121.5	869.9	7.2	159	1,373.7	1.0	55.0	307.1	1.4	23.6
Vietnam	400.5	7.0	121.6	139.2	21.0	230.9	87.5	24.2	215.4	39.1	10.4	19.7
Total	1300.3	43.6	335.8	(135.0)	26.4	481.7	900.5	148.3	335.8	739.2		

Source: ASEAN Secretariat FDI Database.

APT summit, held in December 1998 in Hanoi, reaffirmed the process as a priority for both Northeast and Southeast Asia. The agreements on establishing East Asian Deputy Finance Ministers' Meetings and on forming the East Asia Vision Group signal the intent to establish closer cooperation among APT members. The aspiration for cooperation for mutual interest continued to grow at the third informal APT summit in November 1999 in Manila, where the East Asian leaders adopted the Joint Statement on East Asia Cooperation. The 1999 summit was a great step toward regional governance. Since then, annual meetings of heads of state, ministers, and senior officials have become institutionalized.

The meeting of Finance Ministers in Chiang Mai in May 2000 was considered to be a milestone in the development of regional economic governance. APT members committed themselves to using the APT framework for regular and timely data and information exchange on capital flows, to review each other's financial policies in order to monitor regional finance, and to extend the existing ASEAN-5 currency swap system to all APT economies. With additional supportive bilateral swap arrangements and repurchase agreements adopted, a network of currency swaps in East Asia was created. In addition to such monetary and financial cooperation in the region, other development projects initiated and conducted at the state level, such as establishing a Human Resource Development Fund and the ASEAN Action Plan on Social Safety Nets, have also brought regional economies closer together.

Another regional development that has increased Taiwan's geo-economic insecurity is the 'ASEAN Plus One' arrangements. The APT cooperation process not only brings the economies of Northeast and Southeast Asia together, but also generates a momentum for ASEAN-10 as a whole to develop complementary ties with one or another of the Northeast Asian economies. The 'ASEAN Plus One' arrangement has opened a new platform for geo-economic competition among regional powers. In this context, China's offer to start a free trade agreement between China and ASEAN was an initiative of great historical significance. On 4 November 2002, China and ASEAN signed a Framework Agreement on Comprehensive Economic Cooperation to begin negotiations on the creation of an ASEAN–China Free Trade Area (ACFTA). The target date for the realization of the ACFTA is 2010 for the developed ASEAN countries, and 2015 for the new ASEAN members of Cambodia, Laos, Myanmar, and Vietnam. The agreement came into force on 1 July 2003.

China's strategic move to enhance its ties with the ASEAN economies seriously challenged Japan's geostrategic interests and prompted Japan to respond vigorously. After Japan's prime minister, Junichiro Koizumi, delivered a speech in Singapore in 2002 regarding Japan's proposals for further integration of the region, Japan signed the Framework for Comprehensive Economic Partnership with ASEAN in October 2003. The competition has extended to the broader geopolitical context in which ASEAN as a whole has taken steps to expand its diplomatic ties with non-ASEAN countries. The Joint Declaration of ASEAN and China on Cooperation in the Field of Non-Traditional Security Issues was issued in November 2002. A year later, China and India signed their accession to the ASEAN Treaty of Amity and Cooperation in Bali in October 2003, while Japan acceded to the Treaty in December 2003.

More broadly, recent developments in regional governance have gradually replaced what has been termed *de facto* East Asian regionalization, in which regional economic networks were driven by the private sector and market forces. Regional governance has also moved away from the so-called ASEAN Way approach to Asia-Pacific cooperation via the Asia-Pacific Economic Cooperation (APEC) process, based on voluntary commitments and flexible implementation by individual economies. These new developments towards rule-based cooperation enhance the role of governments in regional cooperation. However, they have created a new wave of political controversies over Taiwan's participation. Despite failing to persuade regional economies to accord Taiwan the status of a state, Taiwan has nevertheless been excluded from these cooperation processes. Cross-Strait political tension and diplomatic confrontation is now extended to the realm of economic governance. Taiwan's continued exclusion from rule-based regional governance not only threatens Taiwan's geo-economic security interests and its regional leverage, but also imperils Taiwan's basic economic security interests if market disruptions are caused by the lack of access to regional economic governance frameworks.

Better governance for common economic security interests

Taiwan is not the only economy to be excluded from state-led regional governance. The Hong Kong Special Administrative Region is not represented as a separate entity in the APT process either. It is apparent that, given the size and relative strengths of the Hong Kong and Taiwanese economies, as well as their record of capital flows to both ASEAN and China, failing to include them in regional cooperation processes will incur economic losses for the region in the long run. In fact, the accommodation of both Taiwan and China as members of the WTO has reaffirmed the pragmatic nature of the international economic regime, as does the coexistence of Taiwan and China in APEC. Searching for a better framework of regional governance to safeguard the region's common economic security interests remains a shared goal for all. However, in such a process Beijing's attitude will be key, given its rising market capacity and the perceptions of Chinese power among regional economies.

If the shared economic security interests arising from cross-Strait economic interdependence are not properly managed, China's economic security itself could be undermined. China is currently experiencing a transition from closed market socialism to open-economy capitalism. In the process, and in line with other developing countries, regime legitimacy and internal stability are two of the country's key security goals, which need to be secured from shocks from economic globalization and domestic inequalities resulting from free-market economic activity. Strengthening the institutional and legal infrastructures and enriching a healthy investment environment are being undertaken in order to reduce economic shocks from globalization, but balancing the path of economic growth against unequal distribution of the wealth remains a challenge to China's nationwide development. Failing to do so, in turn, would jeopardize regime legitimacy and internal stability.

To sustain China's export-led economic growth and to facilitate equal development between inland areas and the coastal regions, steady inputs of the sources of growth and stable manufacturing outputs are crucial. Taiwan's export-oriented FDI in China has greatly contributed to China's outward development. Total realized Taiwanese FDI, including indirect FDI from Hong Kong and the Virgin Islands, constituted approximately 54.4 percent of China's total FDI inflow in 2000, 54.0 percent in 2001, 53.5 percent in 2002, and 53.6 percent in the first half of 2003. Given the market shares of the second largest FDI source in China, 10.2 percent from the United States between 2000 to 2002 and 9.1 percent from Japan in the first half of 2003, it would not be possible to find an FDI substitute if any disruption in Taiwan's FDI flows to China occurred.[15] Nevertheless, the weight of Taiwan's role in China's economic security goes beyond the magnitude of economic impacts revealed by market shares. More importantly, the quality of cross-Strait economic interdependence is evolving through a process of integration in which the integrated markets are asymmetrically located in China. The externalities to local economic and social developments in the process have generated significant shared cross-Strait economic security interests, and consequently have substantially reduced the possibility for China to use economic sanctions against Taiwan.

Gradually, China-based Taiwanese businesses are ceasing to depend on imports of raw materials, parts, or intermediate products for manufacturing. The ratio of raw materials provided by Taiwan decreased from 52.5 percent in 1995 to 43.2 percent in 1999, while the ratio of raw materials provided locally increased from 35.4 percent in 1995 to 43.8 percent in 1999. The ratio of intermediate goods provided by imports from Taiwan decreased from 56.3 percent in 1995 to 46.6 percent in 1999, while the ratio of locally provided intermediate goods increased from 37.0 percent to 45.5 percent (Table 7.6). Developments in recent years have shown an even deeper integration of Taiwanese business into the local Chinese economy. Comparing the sources for manufacturing in 2000 and 1999, the prospective indices of imported raw materials and intermediate goods from Taiwan were −9.6 and −11.1 respectively; indices of these items provided by local Taiwanese businesses were 21.2 and 19.2, while indices for those provided by other local businesses were 1.8 and 15.6 (Table 7.7). The source indices in 2001 were also negative for imports from Taiwan, while more items were sourced from local businesses. In terms of destinations for final commodities, 46.6 per cent of China-based Taiwanese businesses have increased their sales in China's domestic market in 2000 from 1999. The localization of production and sales of China-based Taiwanese businesses could effectively boost China's development if it is well managed.

An early indication of the economic externalities to social developments in the integrated market comes from the direct consequences for local employment and changes in the labor force. Nineteen percent of China-based Taiwanese companies

Table 7.6 Sources of raw materials and intermediate goods for Taiwan's foreign direct investment in China (%)

	1995	1996	1997	1998	1999
Raw materials					
From Taiwan	52.5	50.3	45.2	49.8	43.2
From local Taiwan business	17.2	17.6	21.0	18.1	21.9
From other local businesses	18.2	19.5	21.0	19.9	22.0
From other imports	12.1	12.6	12.8	12.2	13.0
Intermediate goods					
From Taiwan	56.3	53.0	48.0	52.9	46.6
From local Taiwan business	18.3	18.6	22.1	20.6	24.0
From other local businesses	18.8	20.5	22.0	18.6	21.5
From other imports	6.8	7.9	8.0	8.0	7.9

Source: Statistical Bureau, Ministry of Economic Affairs: *Survey of External Manufacturing Investment*, years 1996–2000.

Table 7.7 Sources of raw materials and intermediate goods for Taiwan's foreign direct investment in China, changes 1999–2000 and 2000–2001 (%)

		2000–1999		2001–2000	
		Raw materials	Intermediate goods	Raw materials	Intermediate goods
From Taiwan	Total	100	100	100	100
	Increased	24.2	20.9	23.1	22.1
	The same	32.5	36.1	34.1	36.3
	Decreased	43.3	43.1	42.9	41.6
	Projected index[a]	–9.55	–11.1	–9.9	–9.7
From local Taiwanese business	Total	100	100	100	100
	Increased	51.9	47.7	47.4	42.6
	The same	38.5	43.0	39.7	42.8
	Decreased	9.6	9.4	12.9	14.6
	Projected index[a]	21.2	19.2	17.2	14.0
From other local businesses	Total	100	100	100	100
	Increased	25.0	42.9	43.3	38.6
	The same	53.6	45.4	45.3	47.5
	Decreased	21.4	11.7	11.4	13.8
	Projected index[a]	1.8	15.6	16.0	12.4
From other imports	Total	100	100	100	100
	Increased	31.0	23.5	29.3	23.3
	The same	49.3	53.2	51.2	53.7
	Decreased	19.7	23.3	19.5	23.0
	Projected index[a]	5.7	0.1	4.9	0.1

Source: Statistical Bureau, Ministry of Economic Affairs: *Survey of External Manufacturing Investment*, various years

Note
a   Projected index = (increasing rate – decreasing rate)/2

now consider it disadvantageous to recruit in Taiwan when opening overseas offices. On average, 75 percent of Taiwanese companies in China increased their recruitment of local managers, while only 3 percent reduced local employment at the manager level.[16] In other words, China-based Taiwanese companies have been gradually localized and have deepened their social relationship with local communities. In addition, the cultural commonalities across the Taiwan Strait have resulted in marriages and gradually changed the social structure where integrated markets are located. Despite its attraction of worldwide FDI to China, the deep economic and social integration in the process of China's opening up is primarily manifested in interactions with the Taiwanese business community.

The normalization of cross-Strait economic relations, stressing frequent and stable interactions to increase the capacities of both states to engage in crisis management, would be a big step in enhancing common economic security interests. As members of the WTO, Taiwan and China have both committed themselves to rule-based trade liberalization. However, while common bounds would facilitate the process of bilateral market liberalization, they will not necessarily lead to expectations of normalization of relations. Despite the rhetoric welcoming normalization of cross-Strait economic ties from both sides after their respective accessions to the WTO, the political impasse on the 'one China' issue continues to impede interactions at the level of national governments, and consequently prevents the possibility of building a comprehensive institutional framework for governance. While the private sector, civil society, and nongovernmental organizations (NGOs) have all been playing their respective roles in the multilayered cross-Strait 'diplomacy,' for overall strategic planning on promoting common economic security interests, efforts at the state government level remain critical.

Concluding remarks

Studying economic security is neither to devalue the traditional notion of national security, nor to exaggerate the neoliberal optimism that market forces can provide for economic well-being. The study instead examines the eroding capacity of the state both to mediate the quality and the quantity of transnational economic flows associated with the process of globalization, and to address challenges to a nation's development and strategic interests from both state and nonstate actors, on both the military and nonmilitary fronts. It has been widely acknowledged that economic measures might be more powerful than military means to resolve political tensions. That, however, is not the conclusion of this chapter. In principle, this study suggests defining economic security within the grand strategic framework of individual states rather than by the notion of national economic safety nets, and examining the nature of economic insecurity arising from economic trends and flows instead of those arising from the fear of political losses. The analysis reminds concerned parties of the merits of adopting pragmatic measures to address economic security concerns, rather than mere political rhetoric.

Economic strength is the primary non-military power base for Taiwan's internal and external policy objectives to counter military and diplomatic pressure from

China. Ironically, however, the increasing cross-Strait economic and social interdependence and the withering of Taiwan's state capacity to manage interdependence reveal a risk that Taiwan's economic power resources will be transferred to its political adversary. The optimal policies for Taiwan would be to use the Chinese market to facilitate Taiwan's industrial restructuring in order to sustain Taiwan's economic strength amid globalization, but without transmitting any part of this economic power base to China, and to deter diplomatic obstruction and military threats from China without the economic instrument being used as leverage.

Overlooking the positive local economic and social externalities of Taiwan's export-oriented FDI to China would underestimate Taiwan's economic leverage over China. The growth of China-based Taiwanese businesses is one of the major forces driving China's development. Moreover, promotion of China's inland development or other new growth areas cannot afford to exclude Taiwan's economic inputs. When other economies are still taking a wait-and-see attitude, Taiwan's businesses are willing to try their luck inland, especially given the absence of cultural barriers. For China, therefore, political rapprochement with Taiwan, which might elicit a cost internally, is obviously a better choice than military threats to win Taiwanese businesses.

While markets have their own momentum in generating business flows and profits, the promotion of common economic security interests, either across the Taiwan Strait or in East Asia, depends on the policy choices of governments in the region. Although the capacity of the Taiwanese government in removing geopolitical obstacles to Taiwan's economic security might be limited, given the dual trends of globalization and governance, that responsibility nevertheless remains salient. More research on creative and flexible measures to overcome these withering state capacities to manage cross-Strait common interests, to fortify favorable regional economic flows, and to participate in regional governance mechanisms is seriously needed for the pursuit of Taiwan's economic security.

Notes

1 For more discussion on the Asian turbulence as a case study of economic security, see Lee (2000).
2 The concept is similar to ASEAN's comprehensive security concept in which economic development is the foundation of national and regional resilience. For an example of related studies, see Jackson and Soesastro (1984).
3 The first direct presidential election took place in 1996. In the second presidential election in 2000, the candidate of the former opposition party, the Democratic Progressive Party (DPP), took over the presidency. The transfer was peaceful and successful.
4 Economic geography is primarily concerned with economic relationships between places that can be generalized into patterns of spatial interactions (see Hanink, 1994).
5 For related studies on geo-economics, see Luttwak (1993), O'Loughlin (1996), Huntington (1993), Moran (1993), and Lee (1999b).
6 Data provided by Investment Commission, Ministry of Economic Affairs, Republic of China (ROC).
7 Data excerpted from *Cross-Strait Economic Statistics Monthly*, July 2003 (Mainland Affairs Council, ROC), p. 28.

8 The contracted amount is chosen here to best indicate the incentives and expectations of Taiwanese businessmen concerning investing in China.

9 The policy, announced by former president Lee Teng-Hui, (a) classified domestic industries into three categories: forbidden, allowed, and with special permit; (b) set a strict guideline for high-tech industry and the basic infrastructure industry to limit investments in China; and (c) limited individual investment projects to an upper limit of $50 million.

10 Two ongoing policies are, first, to build up Taiwan as a center of global logistics operations, and second, to turn Taiwan into a high-value-added manufacturing center. The former is aimed at resuming Taiwan's status as a core trade and investment facilitator via institutions and building infrastructure. The latter stresses the development of competitive-edge technology and the upgrading of Taiwan's level of technological capacity in manufacturing. See Council for Economic Planning and Development, Taiwan, *Global Logistics Development*, 4 October 2000.

11 See the table in Barfield (1997: 26).

12 See Lee Kim Chew, 'Asian Exporters Ride China Wave,' *Straits Times*, 1 December 2003.

13 For more discussion, see Lee (1998).

14 Data excerpted from various volumes of *Taiwan Statistical Data Book*.

15 Data calculated from *Cross-Strait Economic Statistic Monthly*, July 2003 (Taipei: Mainland Affairs Council, ROC), originally from various volumes of *China Statistical Yearbook*, *China Foreign Economic Statistical Yearbook*, and *Intertrade*, published by the Ministry of Foreign Trade and Economic Cooperation, PRC.

16 Data cited here are based on the 2002 survey conducted by the Taipei Enterprise and Management Association.

References

Akao, Nobutoshi (ed.) (1983) *Japan's Economic Security*, New York: St. Martin's Press.

Barfield, Claude E. (1997) 'Trade, Investment, and Emerging US Policies for Asia,' in Claude E. Barfield (ed.) *Expanding US–Asian Trade and Investment: New Challenges and Policy Options*, Washington, DC: AEI Press.

Barnett, Robert (1984) *Beyond War: Japan's Concept of Comprehensive National Security*, Washington, DC: Pergamon Brassey's.

Chapman, J. W. M., Drifte, R., and Gow, I. T. M. (1982) *Japan's Quest for Comprehensive Security: Defense–Diplomacy–Dependence*, New York: St. Martin's Press.

Hanink, Dean M. (1994) *The International Economy: A Geographical Perspective*, New York: John Wiley.

Huntington, Samuel P. (1993) 'Why International Primacy Matters,' *International Security*, 17 (4): 68–83.

Jackson, Karl D. and Soesastro, Hadi (eds) (1984) *ASEAN Security and Economic Development*, Berkeley, CA: Institute of East Asian Studies.

Lee, Chyungly (1998) 'US Leadership in the Asia-Pacific Region,' *Issues and Studies*, 34 (4): 44–54.

—— (1999a) 'On Economic Security,' in Guy Wilson-Roberts (ed.) *An Asia-Pacific Security Crisis?*, Wellington, New Zealand: Center for Strategic Studies, pp. 67–84.

—— (1999b) 'Impact of the East Asian Financial Crisis on the Asia-Pacific Regional Order: A Geo-economic Perspective,' *Issues and Studies*, 35 (4): 109–132.

—— (2000) 'The Asian Turbulence: A Case Study in Economic Security', in Chyungly Lee (ed.) *Asia–Europe Cooperation after the 1997–1998 Asian Turbulence*, Aldershot, UK: Ashgate, pp. 33–54.

Lilly, James (1996) Preface to William Carpenter and David Wieneck (eds) *Asian Security Handbook*, Armonk, NY: M. E. Sharpe.

Luttwak, Edward (1993) *The Endangered American Dream: How to Stop the United States from Becoming a Third World Country and How to Win the Geo-economic Struggle for Economic Supremacy*, New York: Simon & Schuster.

Mittelman, James H. (1997) 'The Dynamics of Globalization,' in James H. Mittelman (ed.) *Globalization: Critical Reflections*, Boulder, CO: Lynne Rienner.

Moran, Theodore (1993) 'An Economics Agenda for Neo-realists,' *International Security*, 18 (2): 211–215.

Nye, Joseph (1995) 'The Case for Deep Engagement,' *Foreign Affairs*, 74 (4): 90–102.

O'Loughlin, John (1996) 'Geo-economic Competition and Trade Bloc Formation: United States, German, and Japanese Exports,' *Economic Geography*, 72 (April): 131–160.

8 Vietnam's economic security

Pham Cao Phong

Introduction

Vietnam's decision to engage in fundamental renovation of the country – *doimoi* – has involved a shift from a centrally planned economy towards a socialist-oriented market economy where individuals, private capitalists and households are significant components of the economy alongside state and collective ownership. The economic reform process has been accompanied by numerous legal, political and social reforms, while security and foreign policies have been reshaped as well. Despite the major changes experienced in Vietnam as a result, political stability and national security have been maintained, unlike in the former Soviet Union and Eastern Europe, while significant economic achievements have also resulted. Moreover, foreign economic cooperation has not only helped Vietnam develop its economy, but also created favourable conditions for Vietnam to strengthen its political relations with other countries, particularly the major powers, thus enhancing its role in the region and guaranteeing national security.

While affirming the benefits to Vietnam from external economic cooperation, this chapter nevertheless suggests that external economic cooperation also brings with it challenges and/or threats. The discussion that follows examines these issues from the perspective of two contrasting approaches to economic security that have prevailed in the literature: the comprehensive security approach and the human security perspective. The chapter argues that Vietnam's perspective on economic security conforms to neither of these approaches; rather, it is a combination of the two. For Vietnam, economic security is a key component of national security, which is conceptualized in terms of comprehensive security. Thus, economic security is considered both a security variable in its own right and a means to realize other security concerns, including satisfying people's needs and wants – the internal dimension of economic security or human security. The external dimension of economic security refers to Vietnam's ability to attain economic development free from excessive dependence on other countries and secure from external encroachments on Vietnam's sovereign economic affairs. Economic development through integration into the world economic system has become increasingly important as a means to secure overall economic security for Vietnam, including its internal, human security, dimension. Paradoxically, however, this has resulted in some difficulties for Vietnam in protecting itself from external pressures and encroachments on the country's sovereign economic affairs.

Revisiting theories of economic security

Although Buzan (1991: 433) had identified economic security as a key variable of *national* security in 1991, the 1994 Human Development Report of the United Nations Development Programme (UNDP) explicitly identified economic security as one of the seven elements of *human* security.[1] In the UNDP perspective,

> economic security can be described in human terms as the satisfaction of the economic needs and wants of the people. That is, on a broad definition of security, economic growth is a security goal in its own rights, for only so can societal welfare be assured.
>
> (Thakur, 1997: 61)

Clearly, the definition focuses on the human aspect of economic security, or on a combination of the economic and food security variables of human security, and suggests that human beings benefit from the fruits of economic development so that they enjoy 'freedom from want'.[2] If a state can meet its people's 'needs and wants', economic security is guaranteed. This perspective on economic security, therefore, shares some similarity with the notion of the welfare state, which emphasizes two key elements, namely, income transfers to meet material needs through family allowances, pensions and unemployment benefits, and social services such as healthcare and education, as proper measures to safeguard social security. Although its precise definitions may vary, a common point to all welfare states is the goal of equality, 'to eliminate destitution and individual misery', and 'to eliminate societal cleavages which might cause conflict and tension in society'; that is, to meet the needs of all members of society through *redistributive policies* (original emphasis) (Ringen, 1987: 6–8).[3]

This school of thought also applies to developing countries where there is a serious problem of satisfying people's 'needs and wants'. Starvation in Ethiopia and other African states cannot, under any circumstances, suggest that the economic security of those states is assured. In underdeveloped economies, feeding the population is of great concern to maintaining social security. Strikes in Argentina, Brazil and Venezuela in Latin America reveal that people's dissatisfaction in their material life can lead to social unrest, which, in turn, negatively affects economic activity.[4] In Laos, construction of the Theurn Hinboun Dam at the end of 1998 led to a reduction in the fish catch downstream by as much as 70 per cent, affecting the economic livelihood of the people living in the area (Osborne, 2000: 241–242). Furthermore, in a globalized world where 'weak states' are likely to be disadvantaged compared to 'strong states', realist thinking will see developing countries aiming to enhance national economic strength through sustainable development, including poverty elimination, so that these 'weak states' can become 'strong states' in the sense that they can, as Ngaire Woods (2000: 10–12) put it, control their integration process so as to have more choices in international economic relations to prevent the negative impacts of globalization.

However, a perspective on economic security that emphasizes the human dimension is unable to explain why economic security concerns continue to prevail in parts of the developed world where feeding populations is not an issue. Japan is a classic example. The country became increasingly concerned about its economic security following the oil crises during the 1970s, when the country had to cope with the unpredictable supply of raw materials and energy to fuel Japanese industry, which was heavily dependent on external sources of these inputs (Akao, 1983: 17). Japan, therefore, sees economic security as its ability to protect against external threats to its industrial development and economic well-being (Soeya, 1997: 199–205). In short, 'economic security is a state's ability to protect against perceived threats to its sovereign economic affairs and the absence of fear that such values will be attacked' (Lord, 2004: 5). The European Union similarly defines economic security in terms of securing access to raw materials, technology, export markets and overseas investment sites as well as the maintenance of macroeconomic stability (Afheldt, 1999: 174). In fact, it could be argued that in the march towards trade liberalization and economic integration, there will always be an inherent tendency towards protectionism of one kind or another. A state will tend to seek ways and means to protect against perceived threats to its sovereign economic affairs in a globalized world (Lord, 2004: 5).[5]

Developing states that are increasingly engaging with the global economy are similarly vulnerable to external threats to their economic security. Many of these countries are exporters of semi-processed products or agricultural products to the industrial world, and therefore are highly vulnerable to any conditions that weaken demand for these exports, including the development of substitutes, shifts in production technology in the industrial world, environmental and climate conditions, and even through depletion of the very products that are exported. Trade, therefore, is never an unalloyed good, as both trade generation and trade destruction can be generated by the process of economic integration and technological advancement. Like trade, foreign investments can similarly have negative effects on an economy, for instance by changing the economic structure of a country and its plan for balanced development. During colonial times, the economic structure of the colonies was set up to serve the interests of imperial centres. Even in the contemporary period, foreign investment may be directed at sectors that yield the greatest returns to the firm rather than to the host economy, in the process weakening the state's efforts to satisfy its people's 'needs and wants'.

Even poverty, often regarded as an internally generated problem, may well be triggered by external sources. In the case of Vietnam and Cambodia, for instance, deforestation or changes in river conditions upstream beyond national boundaries have the potential to undermine the economic livelihood of people downstream. The construction of dams in China could affect Cambodia's and Vietnam's lower delta, although the Chinese suggest that the dams will help reduce flooding and drought in those areas (Borton, 2002). Dupont argues that 'interrupting the natural cycle of the Mekong [River] could prove fatal for the fresh-water fishing industries of Cambodia and Vietnam' (Dupont, 2001: 129–130).

There are, therefore, two distinct approaches to economic security: one that is akin to the notion of the welfare state, but emphasizes the internal dimension of economic security, namely, the satisfaction of people's needs and wants so as to guarantee national security. The second emphasizes the external dimension of economic security, namely, the ability to protect against external threats to the economy and to sovereign economic affairs. Theo Peeters (1982: 35–37) argues that this particular perspective on economic security centred on foreign trade and investment has become dominant in security studies. Importantly, both these approaches are applicable to Vietnam.

Vietnam's economic security: issues and problems

Vietnam has long been a poor country, with poverty being a major challenge since independence in 1945. Nonetheless, the poverty problem was almost overcome during the Vietnam War period through assistance from Moscow and other socialist states. Weapons and the majority of consumer goods were provided by socialist states to meet the demands of the Vietnamese people in their struggle for the national liberation of Vietnam – then a socialist outpost in Southeast Asia.

The challenge of poverty and hunger

The position changed in the late 1980s and early 1990s owing to changes in the former Soviet Union and the Eastern European countries. Loans and aid to Vietnam, which had in some periods accounted for 38 per cent of Vietnam's total annual budget, were drastically reduced. In 1985, foreign sources accounted for 10.2 per cent of national expenditure, compared to 22.4 per cent for each of the five years between 1981 and 1985. Until 1989, much of Vietnam's fuel and 80 per cent of its fertilizer requirements came from the Soviet Union. However, in the first six months of 1991, bilateral trade between Vietnam and the Soviet Union was just 15 per cent of its 1990 level. Consequently, Vietnam had to secure a wide range of products, including oil and fertilizers, from the international market.

Furthermore, Vietnam was experiencing a socio-economic crisis at about the same time as foreign aid was declining, which led the country into economic crisis, accompanied by inflation, unstable production, increasing unemployment, and wages and salaries that were below subsistence levels. In 1978, rice production fell 4.5 million tons short of the country's requirements. In 1980, the rice harvest fell short once again, this time by 5 million tons. Strict food rationing was introduced as a result, which contributed to malnutrition among certain population groups. An acute food crisis in 1979–1980 forced a cautious effort at reform, although agriculture continued to be in crisis throughout the 1980s, failing to supply sufficient food for most of the decade (see Le Dang Doanh 1997: 45; Nguyen Sinh 1998; Williams 1992: 54; Nguyen Van Canh 1983: 28). Given these circumstances, economic security for Vietnam meant that it had to get out of the crisis quickly and stabilize the socio-economic situation, overcome poverty and underdevelopment, and improve living standards.

Although the crisis has long been over, Hanoi continues to experience economic difficulties. In moving from a centrally planned economy to a socialist-oriented market economy, issues pertaining to state-sector reform, employment, modernization of agricultural production, and infrastructure improvement, among others, require long lead times before they can be satisfactorily resolved. The Asian financial crisis, moreover, led to a slowing of economic growth from 8.2 per cent in 1997 to 5.8 per cent in 1998 and 4.8 per cent in 1999, undermining job creation. Hunger and poverty continue to exist, although national food security is now guaranteed. Although the average poverty rate has been reduced to 11 per cent, down from 13 per cent in 1999, poverty among minority groups remains a serious problem.[6] In fifty-two minority ethnic groups, poverty and hunger affect two-thirds of the population, while for the ethnic Kinh the ratio is 35–38 per cent. In other words, hunger and poverty among minority ethnic groups is 1.5–3 times larger than that of the majority group (Ha Que Lam, 2002: 61). There are three reasons – geographic, social and economic – for this situation.

Geographically, ethnic minorities live in remote areas with poor access to public and welfare services such as healthcare, education, cultural activities, information provision and credit provision, which tend to be concentrated in district and town centres. Road access to these areas is also poor at present.[7] *Socially*, their low educational attainment makes it difficult to apply scientific and technological advances in production, leading to low productivity. Furthermore, ethnic minorities continue to hold on to traditional customs, such as the adage of 'more children, more prosperity', which undermines development efforts by creating population pressures. Moreover, unequal labour migration within Vietnam has led to parts of the country having very high population densities and, consequently, reduced availability of land for cultivation, especially since they involve backward cultivation methods, further complicating the task of economic development. *Economically*, poverty of minority groups also derives from a lack of sustainable development in the mountainous and remote areas. The farming techniques employed often lead to deforestation, causing land erosion, depletion of water sources and subsequent droughts, and loss of aquatic resources. One study estimates that the total forest area already turned into wasteland and bare hills is as high as 50 per cent of existing forests (Ha Que Lam, 2002: 61).

Poverty can be found in other areas of Vietnam as well, arising from low income, low levels of educational attainment, ecological damage and poor agricultural management. Deliberate deforestation by foreign forces during wartime has had the long-term effect of producing acid soils and water leaching during the rainy seasons, which undermines agricultural and fishing activities in the delta (Osborne, 2000: 237). Then there is the problem of local groups who end up destroying forests in the process of earning a living. According to the World Bank's 'Vietnam Environment Monitor 2002', natural forest cover has shrunk from 43 to 29 per cent of the land area over the past five decades,[8] resulting in a national shortage of land for cultivation.[9] Deforestation is currently a major impediment to economic development in Vietnam, while deforestation and the change in the flow of the Mekong River are main causes of serious flooding in the South, which is the country's most important rice-growing area. For instance, the drought in the central region in 2001 led to more than 10,000 people suffering from hunger, while flooding in the South caused 262,000 households to be left homeless, with rice and shrimp fields destroyed and hunger becoming a critical problem.[10] In addition, the destruction of thousands of hectares of coffee trees, pineapples and other agricultural products by planters reveals that agricultural mismanagement is also a serious problem.

Given these circumstances, the most important task of economic management has been to address poverty and underdevelopment. In short, welfare and the needs of the people was regarded as a key aspect of economic security to help eliminate hunger and poverty, create more equitable development as well as ensure sustainable economic development of the country. One economic security measure would, therefore, be to facilitate economic development, particularly in the agricultural sector. In this regard, environmental security is also vital, since sustainable economic development cannot be achieved if environmental issues are neglected, especially deforestation and natural resource depletion. For the Vietnamese authorities, economic backwardness is regarded as the country's greatest threat and economic development a long-term issue and an integral part of Vietnam's transition process to socialism. The Political Report of the Sixth National Congress of the Communist Party of Vietnam (CPV) states:

> We must direct all our efforts at meeting the urgent and essential requirements of society, gradually stabilize and improve a step further the people's material and cultural life. Precisely speaking, we must ensure that the people get adequate food at a higher nutritional level than at present, and adequate clothing; we must satisfy better their needs for health protection and treatment of diseases, travelling, education and cultural enjoyment, for essential household necessities, and lessen the difficulties in housing, particularly in urban and concentrated industrial areas. These are the requirements of the fundamental economic law of socialism in the present conditions.
>
> (Communist Party of Vietnam, 1987: 45–46)

The imperative of national economic development

Vietnam therefore sees economic development as a critical means to combat poverty and improve living standards, and has adopted both internal reforms and external economic cooperation to achieve this goal. In the absence of its traditional sources of capital assistance from the Soviet bloc, Vietnam has had to diversify its economic cooperation, with the 1986 *doimoi* (renovation) also emphasizing integration into the regional and world economies (Nguyen Dy Nien, in Ministry of Foreign Affairs 1995: 33). Yet integration with the world economy has also brought a range of threats to the country's economic security arising from external trade and investment relations. In particular, Vietnam, which relies heavily on secure and reliable access for the country's main products to export markets, has had to contend with difficulties in ensuring markets for its output. With 75 per cent of its population living on agriculture,[11] Vietnam's main products that seek markets are rice, fisheries, vegetables and fruits, rubber, coffee, pepper, cashew nuts, tea, crude oil, footwear, garments and textiles, handicrafts and fine arts.

Vietnam's main problems in securing foreign markets stem from at least five factors. First, although Vietnam enjoys low tariffs, owing to its membership in the ASEAN Free Trade Area (AFTA) and privileges provided by the Bilateral Trade Agreement with the United States, Vietnam's exports are labour-intensive and therefore compete, often on unfavourable terms, with similar products from the other ASEAN members, with their difficulty in competing being exacerbated by low quality and poor price competitiveness. Second, the majority of Vietnamese products either lack trademarks or have had their trademarks counterfeited or stolen. Among others, Trung Nguyen, a famous coffee brand name, was stolen by a US company; Vinataba, a tobacco company, had to spend thousands of US dollars to buy back its trademark from Indonesia; and Phu Quoc, a fish sauce company, had to negotiate with a Thai company over its trademark. Third, Vietnam's still poorly developed legal system makes it difficult to respond to trade disputes and often results in unfair treatment by its trading partners. A case in point is the US investigation of Vietnamese catfish exports to the United States under US anti-dumping legislation. Although American agricultural exporters receive government subsidies for exports to Vietnam, it was not expected that Vietnam would counter with its own investigation, as Vietnam did not have anti-dumping legislation at that time. Fourth, the continued use of anti-trade measures such as anti-dumping, quotas and agricultural subsidies by developed states creates barriers to Vietnamese exports. Fifth, sudden changes in the import policies of other countries, particularly regarding agricultural products, lead to income losses for Vietnamese producers and exporters, as happened when Indonesia suddenly raised the import tax on rice.

Vietnam also faces a number of problems in ensuring secure *domestic* markets for its own products, and thus faces poorly developed market institutional security. First, goods smuggling is difficult to prevent in a country like Vietnam with a very long border, a problem that can be exacerbated by corrupt customs officials. Unfortunately, smuggled goods tend to be popular with low-income groups, but they undermine the development of a viable domestic manufacturing sector by discouraging foreign and domestic investors. Enterprises that conform to domestic regulations, including by paying taxes, are unable to compete with agencies engaged in smuggling, while serious health and consumer risks are also more likely with smuggled goods. Aside from smuggling, the presence of counterfeit products and money seriously undermines the development of a viable industrial base in Vietnam and a healthy business environment. The Vietnamese police in 2002 discovered a counterfeit ring operating in fourteen provinces throughout the country that was circulating counterfeit Vietnamese currency (the dong) worth US$66,666 that had been printed abroad.[12] Although Vietnam has built up a socialist-oriented market economy over the past ten years, Vietnamese entrepreneurs remain unfamiliar with the structures, processes and norms of a market economy. In particular, respect for property rights, either through registering trademarks or respecting those of others, remains weak. For instance, it is estimated that more than 90 per cent of all state-owned and private enterprises violate property rights by using counterfeit software.[13] The use of certain counterfeit products, notably building materials, agricultural and food products, often results in human and other disasters.

A third reason stems from Vietnam's participation in the global and regional economies, including its membership of regional organizations such as AFTA and Asia-Pacific Economic Cooperation (APEC). Although such participation allows Vietnam to enjoy preferential access to other markets, and thereby stimulates exports, it also has a downside in that Vietnam is obliged to open its domestic market to foreign products that compete with Vietnamese products. Although Vietnam, as a new ASEAN member, enjoys the privileges of a delayed tariff reduction schedule, it nevertheless had to begin implementing tariff cuts from 1996.[14] By 2006, all tariff lines will be at the 0–5 per cent level, with 56 per cent of tariff lines set at zero.[15] One Vietnamese writer likened Vietnam joining AFTA to a person swimming without a life jacket – and, moreover, as someone who did not even have sufficient time to practise with a life jacket (that is, to enjoy state protection).[16]

A key reason why Vietnamese products are unable to compete with imports is poor government management of industrial development. Little attention is paid to the marketing of Vietnamese products, while a more fundamental problem is excess capacity in certain factories and unprofitable state-owned enterprises.[17] For instance, thirty-eight out of the total forty-five sugar mills in the country are unprofitable.[18] Other contributory factors include the small scale of production, the high cost of imported materials, lack of skilled workers, low productivity due to the use of backward technology, and poor management of enterprises and other economic entities. Imports of agricultural products such as rice, fruits and fisheries have led to dramatic falls in price for similar Vietnamese products.[19] Eighty per cent of handicrafts, 80 per cent of toys and 60 per cent of chinaware sold in Vietnam are from China (Shutz and Ardrey, 1995: 140). These imports threaten Vietnam's fledgling industries, and thus work against the development of an indigenous economic base, considered crucial to Vietnam's economic and national security. Such threats will only increase when Vietnam becomes a member of the World Trade Organization (WTO).

Foreign direct investment and economic security

For a country concerned with building up its national economy as a means to national security, foreign direct investment (FDI) may pose a threat. There is no doubt that FDI is a major source of capital and technology, and contributes significantly to Vietnam's economic development by creating jobs, increasing government tax revenues, and stimulating structural change in the economy. However, FDI is also associated with vulnerabilities. Investment decisions made privately by foreign investors could result in an unequal distribution of investment among different localities. Among 4,324 foreign investment projects in Vietnam, only 3.1 per cent are found in the mountainous areas, while 73.7 per cent are located in the South, with the remainder being in the North.[20] This widens the development gap between regions, creating uneven development in the country.

The case of the Dung Quat oil refinery project in Quang Ngai province in the central region illustrates how the private interests of investors can diverge from social interests. While this project was aimed at developing the oil refinery industry in the country, it also fulfils social objectives in that the project, located in one of the poorer provinces, was expected to stimulate job opportunities for the local people and help address poverty in the region. The project was also expected to reduce labour migration to other parts of the country, with all its attendant problems. However, the project fell through, as its three foreign investors, Total of France, Petronas of Malaysia and Zarubezhneft of Russia, pulled out, claiming it was not profitable. The Vietnamese government had no choice but to become the sole investor in the project, having to borrow money in the process.[21]

Thus, reliance on FDI can paradoxically make it difficult for the government to achieve set developmental targets. Currently, the Vietnamese government provides incentives for foreign investment in labour-intensive sectors such as agriculture, forestry and fisheries in order to exploit the country's comparative advantage *and* help eliminate poverty in the countryside where 80 per cent of the population lives. However, these sectors have thus far absorbed only 9.7 per cent of the total FDI in Vietnam, while 70.7 per cent goes into construction and other industries, and the rest to services.[22] Again, these figures show how private investment decisions can often run counter to domestic planning targets.

While the case of the Dung Quat oil refinery project illustrates the pitfalls of relying on foreign investors to fulfil social goals, it reveals that the absence of FDI also poses problems for countries lacking the necessary domestic finance to undertake development. Moreover, Vietnam continues to encourage FDI as a means to help improve the competitiveness of Vietnamese companies. It should also be clear that economic interdependence can help reduce the likelihood that economic statecraft – sanctions, boycotts, market access limitations, foreign aid – will be used to pressure countries, owing to mutual dependence between states.[23] Even if these instruments are used, they are not likely to have catastrophic effects since other sources of capital and markets are available to the targeted country. This is an important consideration for Vietnam, a developing country that does not possess the capacity to employ economic statecraft in a globalized world to secure itself. It suggests that economic interdependence, while resulting in pitfalls, can also offer benefits.

Ensuring economic security

For the past few years, the Vietnamese government has done its best to guarantee economic security. Domestically, the government, with assistance from non-governmental organizations (NGOs), international organizations and other countries, has committed itself to eliminating hunger and alleviating poverty, reflected in Decrees Nos. 133 and 135. On 23 July 1998, the Vietnamese prime minister issued Decree No. 133/1998/QD-TTg, approving the Programme on Hunger Elimination and Poverty Alleviation. Eight days later, on 31 July 1998, he issued Decree No. 135/1998/QD-TTg to approve the Programme on Socio-economic Development for Extremely Difficulty-ridden Mountainous and Remote Areas (abbreviated as Programmes 133 and 135). The aim of these programmes is to improve the living standards of the ethnic minorities found in the mountainous and remote areas through addressing poverty and underdevelopment, thereby contributing to the country's sustainable development and therefore safeguarding Vietnam's economic security. In the past three years, the government has spent nearly VND 5,000 billion (equivalent to US$328.95 million) annually on hunger eradication and poverty reduction. That the government has spent more than 10 per cent of the country's GNP on these socio-economic programmes reveals its commitment to the internal dimension of economic security. The money has been spent on a wide range of projects in rehabilitation and resettlement, reforestation, and to develop electricity networks, transport and communications (television and radio) networks in mountainous areas. On the external side, the government has worked out a route map that will allow Vietnam the necessary time and flexibility to meet its AFTA commitments in ways that will not unduly jeopardize Vietnamese economic development.

The above discussion reveals that Vietnam emphasizes both the internal and external dimensions of economic security. For the former, attention is focused both on alleviating poverty and hunger – that is, meeting people's 'needs and wants' – *and* in securing sustainable economic development. Externally, economic security is seen in terms of protecting the sovereign economic affairs of the country against perceived external threats. Both these dimensions of economic security are, moreover, closely intertwined. Economic integration is now a priority, a crucial means to develop the economy and meet the goals of the internal dimension of economic security. However, integration itself can give rise to a situation of vulnerability for Vietnam through the negative effects of reliance on foreign trade and investment, as highlighted. Nevertheless, it is both these approaches to economic security that are seen to ensure Vietnam's overall national security, as seen in the Political Report of the Ninth Party Congress:

> To actively integrate into the world and the regional economic systems in the spirit of bringing into full play internal strength, improving the efficiency of international cooperation, guaranteeing independence, sovereignty and socialist orientation, safe-guarding national security, maintaining national cultural identity and protecting the environment.
>
> (Communist Party of Vietnam, 2001: 43)

The role of economic security in Vietnam's national security

According to noted security studies scholar David Baldwin (1995: 126), 'the end of the Cold War, like its beginning, raises the question of how important military security is in comparison with other goals of public policy'. In Baldwin's perspective, security should be understood in a broader sense. While the Cold War period saw national security defined as the survival of a state, the sources that threaten state survival may be varied. Thus, Baldwin (ibid.: 128) argues that

> a state without armed forces to protect it from external attack may not survive, but a state without breathable air or drinkable water will surely not survive. However, even the military approach to national security is now under-stood differently. Kolodziej (1992: 430) writes, 'balance of power, which must necessarily underlie any system of governance among states, must first be informed and strengthened – and surmounted by concert if not by collective security – to avoid war as a solution to conflict'.

Vietnam's security perceptions reflect these new approaches to security. Following unification in 1975, Vietnam concentrated on economic development as a means to attain prosperity and build an equal and civilized society. Vietnam therefore had altered its own perception of national security, from a military approach to the comprehensive approach, and from balance of power to cooperative security. Vietnam's Defence White Paper perceives threats to national security as coming from three dimensions: domestic threats (economic, political and social threats), external threats (sabotages under the pretext of 'human rights' and 'democracy' and territorial violations) and non-traditional threats (such as illegal immigration and emigration, and cross-border trafficking) (Ministry of Defence, 1998: 13–14).

The Ninth National Congress of the Communist Party of Vietnam has pinpointed four dangers that could jeopardize the country's security at present: 'our economy falling further behind many countries in the region and the world; deviation from the socialist orientation; corruption; and "peaceful evolution" attempts by hostile forces' (Communist Party of Vietnam, 2001: 15). Vietnam's 'Political Programme for National Construction in the Period of Transition to Socialism' reads, in part:

> The situation related to security and order remains very complicated. Hostile forces at home and abroad have collaborated with each other in exploiting the crisis of socialism and our mistakes and weaknesses to undermine our cause with threatening and dangerous manoeuvres. Our internal security, economic, ideological and cultural security, and border security leave much to be desired. Social order and public safety, especially in cities and towns, includes many problems to be solved; large-scale pilferage of socialist property, corruption, smuggling, and deterioration in ethical values, etc., are burning questions.
>
> (Communist Party of Vietnam, 1991: 88)

These documents reveal the importance Vietnam attaches to the domestic dimension of national security. For Vietnam, defending its national security is no longer an exercise that can be placed within the context of the bipolar world, as in the past. Rather, it is placed within an international order in which countries with different socio-political systems can live in friendship and cooperation. The collapse of the Soviet Union and the East European socialist countries placed Vietnam in a position where it could only maintain its national security by promoting friendship and cooperation with all other countries and by flexibly making good use of these relationships. Towards this end, Vietnam has, in the past few years, improved its relations with all countries in the world, including the major powers, a first in its modern history. Moreover, Vietnam has made good progress towards settling territorial disputes with neighbouring countries. It has signed agreements on overlapping areas with Thailand and Malaysia, as well as with Indonesia over the exclusive economic zone (EEZ). Vietnam and China have already signed the Land Border Treaty, the Agreement on Tonkin Gulf Demarcation and the Agreement on Fisheries Cooperation in the Tonkin Gulf. However, Vietnam remains on high alert for any external attempt to interfere in its internal affairs or provoke social chaos in the country.

Vietnam perceives that, as a developing country, remaining underdeveloped is the greatest threat to its national security. If the economy is not developed, living standards cannot be improved, and this could give rise to problems with social order and public safety, which hostile foreign forces can use to undermine Vietnam, in turn compromising Vietnam's national security and jeopardizing its avowed foreign policy goal of independence and sovereignty. This is why economic security is regarded as a central element in national security. More specifically, attainment of economic security through achieving economic development is seen as a means to political independence, which will enable Vietnam to resist external challenges and maintain domestic control over the country's sovereign affairs and the choices it makes in international economic relations. Second, economic security is also seen as a guarantee of internal political security. Unlike the Soviet Union, where *perestroika* began in the political field and led to social chaos and political instability, Vietnam has not sought to change its political system. Rather, Vietnam has undertaken adjustments to a range of internal and external policies, particularly economic policy. This was because the Vietnamese authorities regarded economic progress on poverty as central to maintaining political security and social order, which will then allow for further political and social reforms.

Thus, economic security became an important factor in the country's comprehensive development plan. Keenly aware of the experience of the former Soviet Union and the other East European socialist countries, and mindful that Vietnamese people's confidence in the leadership of the Communist Party of Vietnam (CPV) had eroded amid the crisis of the late 1980s (Communist Party of Vietnam, 1987: 18), the CPV adjusted the country's development agenda to emphasize economic security as the surest means to reduce the potential for social chaos. This would help to maintain political security and confidence in the CPV. Over the past few years, economic reforms have led to substantial economic achievements, and living standards have improved considerably, thereby restoring confidence in the CPV.

Economic security is also important for Vietnam as it creates conditions favourable for enhancing national defence and its military capacity. While paying considerable attention to economic security, Vietnam also feels the need to strengthen its military capability, for two reasons. First, there remain a number of sources of potential conflict and instability in the region, despite an overall trend towards peace and cooperation. Second, the collapse of the Soviet Union meant that Vietnam could not rely on Russia for military assistance in the event that it was needed. These two factors therefore made it imperative for Vietnam to maintain a military force capable of defending the homeland. Sustained economic growth and development will provide the resources needed for this task. In short, economic security has become the most important component in Vietnam's national security, and a precondition to enhancing political and military security.

Conclusion

Given that Vietnam is a very poor developing country that is only now beginning to integrate with the world economy, Vietnam perceives economic security in two dimensions. On the one hand, it is the ability to satisfy people's 'needs and wants' through sustainable economic development (the internal dimension). On the other, it is also the ability to maintain economic development free from dependence on other countries and secure from external challenges to its sovereign economic affairs (external dimension). However, economic security is also part of Vietnam's approach to the broader question of assuring national security through comprehensive means. Thus, it also safeguards other security variables – political and military security – in the process, leading to overall national security.

As long as Vietnam struggles against poverty, the internal dimension of economic security will be more important than the external dimension. However, as Vietnam increasingly integrates into the world economic system, it faces growing challenges and threats to its sovereign economic affairs, making the external dimension of economic security more salient. However, defending its economic security from such external pressures is not easy, simply because Vietnam is a new entrant into the world economic system as well as a developing nation, and consequently has to accept the rules of the game already established by the developed countries. Its capacity to employ traditional economic statecraft to secure itself from external threats is also limited. Thus, Vietnam may be depicted as being between a rock and a hard place: on the one hand, it needs to develop the economy; on the other hand, it desires to protect its economic security from external threats. These two goals do not always coincide, especially since Vietnam has chosen economic integration as a means to economic development. This has increased the country's sense of vulnerability to threats associated with foreign trade and investment relations. However, Vietnam has, in the past few years, tried to meet both these targets – developing the economy and safeguarding economic security – and has successfully managed this difficult balancing act.

Notes

Parts of this chapter have been presented to the 2002 International Studies Association Convention held in New Orleans. The generous financial support of the Institute of Defence and Strategic Studies (IDSS), Singapore, and the Sasakawa Peace Foundation in the form of the Sasakawa-IDSS Fellowship (December 2002 – January 2003) is gratefully acknowledged.

1 See Chapter 1 in this volume for a listing of the other six components.
2 Note that the definition of human security varies. While some scholars emphasise 'needs and wants', others focus on human rights. See Acharya (2001).
3 For further discussions on the welfare state, see Rose and Shiratori (1986) and Thane (1982).
4 For example, the demonstrations in Venezuela cost more than US$1 billion in only a couple of weeks (http://vnexpress.net/Vietnam/The-gioi/2002/12/3B9C397E).
5 Moreover, threats to economic security can also emerge from external political and security sources in addition to those arising from predominantly external *economic* conditions. The terrorist attacks of 11 September 2001 on the United States come to mind here. For the Southeast Asian states, any instability in the region, such as over contested claims in the South China Sea and terrorism, will negatively impact on economic development.
6 Poverty figures from different sources differ. According to the Asian Development Bank, the current poverty ratio is 29 per cent, down from 70 per cent in 1990 (http://www.undp.org.vn/undp/fact/base.htm, accessed June 2004), while World Bank figures show a poverty rate of 29 per cent in 2002 (http://www.worldbank.org.vn/news/press41_01.htm, accessed 20 February 2004).
7 http://www.mof.gov.vn/Default.aspx?tabid=612&ItemID=6413 (accessed 8 June 2004).
8 Forest cover has increased to 36.1 per cent in 2004 following four years of implementing the national reforestation programme (http://www.vneconomy.com.vn/vie/index. php?param=article&catid=0903&id=040521100749, accessed 8 June 2004).
9 http://web.worldbank.org/WBSITE/EXTERNAL/NEWS/.
10 Sources from http://vnexpress.net/Vietnam/Xa-hoi/2002/03/3B9BA9A4/ and http://vnexpress.net/Vietnam/Xa-hoi/2002/10/3B9COC7B/.
11 http://www.undp.org.vn/undp/fact/base.htm.
12 Sources from http://vnexpress.net/Vietnam/Phap-luat/2002/06/3B9BD57B and http://vnexpress.net/Vietnam/Phap-luat/2003/01/3B9C40FD.
13 http://www.vir.com.vn/Client/Dautu/dautu.asp?CatID=17&DocID=3023 (accessed 8 June 2004).
14 For details, see http://www.vneconomy.com.vn/index (accessed 6 December 2002) and http://vnexpress.net/Vietnam/Kinh-doanh/2002/08/3B9BF411.
15 See http://www.dei.gov.vn/vi/contents/b_world/c_international_economic_institutions/asean/eSC/a_afta/200311065634 (accessed 8 June 2004).
16 See Dao Huy Giam in http://www.mofa.gove.vn:8080/tbqt/2000_asean/18.htm.
17 Sources from http://www.vnn.vn/pls/news/ext_utls.htnoidung(7,90740,1).
18 Sources from http://www.vneconomy.com.vn/index (accessed 24 December 2002).
19 See http://vnn.vn/pls/news/Cate$.htnoidung(7,58340).
20 http://www.vneconomy.com.vn/vie/index.php?param=article&catid=03&id=031230183018 (accessed 31 May 2004).
21 Sources from http://vnexpress.net/Vietnam/Kinh-doanh/2002/12/3B9C3B36.
22 http://www.vneconomy.com.vn/vie/index.php?param=article&catid=03&id=040102101037.
23 On mutual dependence, see Kapstein (1992: 181).

Bibliography

Acharya, Amitav (2001) 'Human Security: East versus West?', Working Paper, Institute of Defence and Strategic Studies, Singapore [Online] http://www.idss.org.

Adams, Arthur B. (1936) *National Economic Security*, Norman, OK: University of Oklahoma Press.

Afheldt, Katja (1999) 'Economic Security: The EU's Stake in Sustainable Development in China', in Werner Draguhn and Robert Ash (eds) *China's Economic Security*, London: Curzon, pp. 142–162.

Akao, Nobushi (ed.) (1983) *Japan's Economic Security: Resources as a Factor in Foreign Policy*, Aldershot, UK Gower.

Baldwin, David A. (1985) *Economic Statecraft*, Princeton, NJ: Princeton University Press.

—— (1995) 'Security Studies and the End of the Cold War', *World Politics*, 48 (1): 117–141.

Borton, James (2002) 'Mother of Rivers: China's Dams Pose Threat to Way of Life for Nations Downstream', *The Washington Times*, 6 September 2002.

Burns, Eveline M. (1936) *Toward Social Security*, New York: Whittlesey House.

Buzan, Barry (1991) 'New Patterns of Global Security in the Twenty-first Century', *International Affairs*, 67 (3): 421–451.

—— (1994) 'The Interdependence of Security and Economic Issues in the "New World Order"', in Richard Stubbs and Geoffrey Underhill (eds) *Political Economy and the Changing Global Order*, Toronto: McClelland & Stewart.

Communist Party of Vietnam (1987) *6th National Congress Document*, Vietnam: Foreign Languages Publishing House.

—— (1991),*7th National Congress Document*, Hanoi: Foreign Languages Publishing House.

—— (1996) *Van kien Dai hoi Dai bieu toan quoc lan thu V* (5th National Congress Document), Hanoi: Nha xuat ban Chinh tri Quoc gia (National Political Publishing House).

—— (1998) *Van kien Dai hoi Dai bieu toan quoc lan thu VIII* (8th National Congress Document), Hanoi: Nha xuat ban Chinh tri Quoc gia (National Politics Publishing House).

—— (2001) *Van kien Dai hoi Dai bieu toan quoc lan thu IX* (9th National Congress Document), Hanoi: Nha xuat ban Chinh tri Quoc gia (National Politics Publishing House).

Dickens, David (1997) *No Better Alternative*, Wellington, New Zealand: Centre for Strategic Studies.

Dieter, Heribert (1998) 'Crises in Asia or Crisis of Globalisation?', Working Paper, Centre for the Study of Globalisation and Regionalisation, http://www.warwick.ac.uk/fac/soc/CSGR.

Dupont, Alan (2001) *East Asia Imperilled: Transnational Challenges to Security*, Cambridge: Cambridge University Press.

Friedmann, Robert R., Gilbert, Neil and Shere, Moshe (eds) (1987) *Modern Welfare States: A Comparative View of Trends and Prospects*, Brighton, UK: Wheatsheaf.

Ha Que Lam (2002) *Xoa doi giam ngheo o vung dan toc thieu so nuoc ta hien nay: thuc trang va giai phap* (Hunger elimination and poverty alleviation in Vietnam's ethnic groups: present situation and solution), Hanoi: Nha xuat ban chinh tri quoc gia (National Politics Publishing House).

Hirschman, Albert O. (1980) *National Power and the Structure of Foreign Trade*, Berkeley, CA: University of California Press.

Kapstein, Ethan Barnaby (1992) *The Political Economy of National Security*, New York: McGraw-Hill.

Knorr, Klaus (1997) 'Economic Interdependence and National Security', in Klaus Knorr and Frank N. Truger (eds) *Economic Issues and National Security*, Lawrence: Regents Press of Kansas.

Kolodziej, Edward A. (1992) 'A Renaissance in Security Studies? Caveat Lector!', *International Studies Quarterly*, 36 (4): 421–438.

Le Dang Doanh (1997) 'Foreign Investment and the Macroeconomy in Vietnam', in Tran Van Hoa (ed.) *Economic Development and Prospects in ASEAN*, New York: St Martin's Press, pp. 44–86.

Lord, Kristin (2004) 'Economic Security: Meaning and Challenge', in Jose V. Ciprut (ed.) *Of Fears and Foes: Complex Interactive Dimensions of Insecurity in an Evolving Global Political Economy*, Ithaca, NY: Cornell University Press.

Ministry of Defence (1998) *Vietnam: Consolidating National Defence, Safeguarding the Homeland* (Vietnam's Defence White Paper), Hanoi.

Ministry of Foreign Affairs (1995) *Hoi nhap quoc te va giu vung ban sac* (International integration and identity maintenance), Hanoi: Nha xuat ban chinh tri quoc gia (National Politics Publishing House).

Nau, Henry R. (1995) *Trade and Security*, Washington, DC: The American Enterprise Institute Press.

Nguyen Khac Than and Chu Van Cap (eds) (1996) *Nhung giai phap chinh tri – kinh te nham thu hut co hieu qua dau tu truc tiep nuoc ngoai vao* (Political and economical solutions to effectively attract foreign direct investment into Vietnam), Hanoi: Nha xuat ban Chinh tri Quoc gia (National Politics Publishing House).

Nguyen Mai (1998) 'Dau tu nuoc ngoai 1988–1997: danh gia tong quat' (General evaluation of foreign investment, 1988–1997), *Tap chi Cong san* (Communist Journal), No. 2, January.

Nguyen Sinh (1998) 'Kinh te Vietnam 12 nam doi moi 1986–1997' (Vietnam's economy in twelve years of renovation, 1986–1997), *Tap chi Cong san* (Communist Journal), No. 3, March.

Nguyen Van Canh (1983) *Vietnam under Communism, 1975–1982*, Stanford, CA: Hoover Institution Press.

Osborne, Milton (2000) *The Mekong: Turbulent Past, Uncertain Future*, St Leonards, NSW: Allen & Unwin.

Peeters, Theo (1982) 'National Economic Security and the Maintenance of the Welfare State', in A. M. Frans, Alting von Geusau and Jacques Pelkmans (eds) *National Economic Security: Perceptions, Threats and Policies*, Tilburg, Netherlands: The John F. Kennedy Institute, pp. 34–46.

Rana, Pradumna B. and Hamid, Naved (eds) *From Centrally Planned to Market Economies: The Asian Approach*, Vol. 3, New York: Oxford University Press.

Ringen, Stein (1987) *The Possibility of Politics: A Study in the Political Economy of the Welfare State*, Oxford: Clarendon Press.

Rose, Richard and Shiratori, Rei (eds) (1986) *The Welfare State, East and West*, New York: Oxford University Press.

Shultz, Clifford J. II and Ardrey, William J. IV (1995) 'Trends and Future Prospects for Sino-Vietnamese Relations: Are Trade and Commerce the Critical Factors for Peace', *Contemporary Southeast Asia*, 17 (2): 126–146.

Soeya, Yoshihide (1997) 'Japan's Economic Security', in Stuart Harris and Andrew Mack (eds) *Asia-Pacific Security: The Economics–Politics Nexus*, St Leonards, NSW: Allen & Unwin, pp. 195–205.

Thakur, Ramesh (1997) 'From National to Human Security', in Stuart Harris and Andrew

Mack (eds) *Asia-Pacific Security: The Economics–Politics Nexus*, St Leonards, NSW: Allen & Unwin, pp. 52–80.

Thane, Pat (1982) *The Foundations of the Welfare State*, Harlow, UK: Longmans.

Vo Thanh Nhu, Nguyen Cuong and Bui Le Ha (1998) *Quan he thuong mai – dau tu giua Vietnam va cac nuoc thanh vien ASEAN* (Trade and investment relations between Vietnam and ASEAN countries), Hanoi: Nha xuat ban Tai chinh (Finance Publishing House).

Walt, Stephen M. (1991) 'The Renaissance in Security Studies', *International Studies Quarterly*, 35 (2): 211–239.

Williams, Michael C. (1992) *Vietnam at the Crossroads*, New York: Council on Foreign Relations Press.

Woods, Ngaire (1994) *Economic Security for Americans*, New York: Columbia University Press.

—— (2000) *The Political Economy of Globalization*, New York: St Martin's Press.

Part III
Governance beyond the state

9   The limits to multilateral economic governance

Richard Higgott

Introduction

What are the problems and prospects for meaningful global governance in the contemporary era? This is an especially crucial question in the light of two key trends in the contemporary world political economy. First, it is quite clear that multilateral institutions are under considerable strain. Second, we are witnessing a contest in international economic governance between 'winners' and 'losers' under conditions of globalisation, with the international economic institutions coming under considerable criticism, especially from civil society and many developing states. In examining the problems and future prospects for multilateral economic governance in the light of these developments, this chapter adopts a three-pronged approach: (a) it discusses what we mean by 'governance' in the international economic context; (b) it examines the current health of the principal institutions of global economic governance, notably the World Trade Organization (WTO) and the International Monetary Fund (IMF); and (c) it raises some questions about prospects for their future reform.

The chapter is underpinned by two assumptions. The first is that the the strain faced by the multilateral institutions emanates in large part from the policy positions of the United States towards multilateralism in recent years. I do not suggest that the policies and practices of the United States are the only source of pressure on the international economic institutions, which face a range of problems of both a systemic and a structural nature under conditions of troubled globalisation. Moreover, the United States is not the only major state capable of playing fast and loose with the international institutions when it suits. But the role of a 'dominant America' is a determining factor in any discussion of both the theory and practice of international economic governance. We are in an era in which the United States possesses an unprecedented material preponderance (see Ikenberry, 2001; Jervis, 2003) and in which its foreign policy exhibits a strong unilateralist complexion. No understanding of the nature of multilateralism and global governance is complete without an acceptance of these 'givens'. This is not, however, to suggest that this preponderance is without limits or that unilateralism is without costs for the United States. Indeed, as the chapter suggests, some of the costs in the security domain that have only become apparent to the George W.

Bush administration in the post-Saddam era in Iraq have been visible in the economic domain for some time.

The second assumption is that the unfolding systemic contest in the domain of international economic governance between 'winners' and 'losers' of globalisation exacerbates tensions in the world political economy. While the transnationalisation of market forces increases aggregate economic wealth, it is also thought to exacerbate inequality. In so doing, it is not only reducing the capacity of international organisations to generate acceptable institutional processes that might mitigate growing inequality, but also spawning an accompanying political resentment. Whether globalisation is in fact enlarging the gap between rich and poor is an important issue (and one on which the jury is still out), but it is not relevant to this chapter. What is relevant is that it exacerbates political tensions in the global order.

The institutions of international economic governance, as currently constituted, reflect the interests of the powerful, not the poorer, states. Those global norms and rules that underwrote the institutional architecture of the last decades of the twentieth century (the Washington Consensus),[1] and attempts to reform these norms and rules in the domains of trade, investment, labour standards, the environment, transparency, capacity-building and, yes, 'governance' (a post-Washington Consensus) are still driven by 'Northern agendas'. The less powerful states remain 'rule-takers' within international economic institutions (Hurrell and Woods, 1999). But a process of political contest and transition is under way. It is too early to know the outcome of this process, but it may be that the rules on offer will either increasingly lack legitimacy and/or not be enforced by the poorer states. It is also possible that many states may simply lack the necessary governmental effectiveness to enforce them even should they so wish.

Either way, these processes have negative implications for a consensus-based evolution of global governance norms. The 'top-down' global governance agenda of the late 1990s and early twenty-first century is still driven by an understanding of governance as effectiveness and efficiency, not by one of democracy, accountability and justice. It has also generated new forms of resistance. Without a normative and practical commitment to stem the globalisation of inequality, the international order may be on the verge of the kind of combative politics that stalemated North–South global economic relations in the 1970s.

The chapter begins with a brief discussion of the concept of global governance. It then proceeds to examine US policy attitudes towards global governance by focusing on the relationship between unilateralism and multilateralism in the making of US foreign policy. The main portion of the chapter analyses the evolution of the multilateral economic institutions and the role of the United States on this process, while the conclusion looks at the limits to contemporary multilateralism in the light of the preceding discussion.

Globalisation and global governance

Although globalisation has many meanings, a simple economic definition suffices for the purposes of this chapter. In this essentially neoliberal understanding, globalisation is the tendency towards international economic integration, liberalisation and financial deregulation beyond the sovereignty of the territorial state. Global governance (not government) then refers to those arrangements – across a spectrum from weak to strong in influence – that various actors attempt to put in place to advance, retard, manage, regulate or mitigate market globalisation. The chapter expands on this definition to grasp the dynamics of the relationship between the market and the theory and practice of governance beyond the territorial state under conditions of globalisation. At the core of this relationship is a struggle over the continued pace of liberalisation. It is a political struggle about the distribution of global wealth, not merely a technical economic one about how best to produce that wealth. The struggle has become increasingly vocal since the currency crises of 1997 and the anti-globalisation backlash from the late 1990s (Higgott, 2000).

But the contemporary relationship between the state and the market has one important new dimension. Increasingly, the state–market relationship is also becoming part of the wider global security game, which has taken on a new and dramatic face since the turn of the century. The context is, of course, the world since 9/11. This is not to suggest that the world began anew at that time. Rather, it is to say that 9/11 brought into relief trends that had been developing in the global order in the closing years of the twentieth century. The key player is, inevitably, the United States, 'enjoying' a period of unparalleled global preponderance. This has implications for the evolution of global governance, given that the United States is uncomfortable with this concept. Global governance for large sections of the US policy community implies, at best, the opportunity for others to free-ride on its material support. At worst, it implies sovereignty dilution and unwanted entanglements.

US views notwithstanding, there is little doubt that demands for 'global governance' in world affairs have grown, especially within the international institutions and among influential players (state and non-state alike) in world affairs. This demand has been spurred by a number of factors:

- There is a growing dissatisfaction with traditional models of public policy that failed to capture the shift in the relationship between state authority and market power, identified by Strange (1988) and others.
- There is an increasing non-national manageability of policy problems and a consequent growing interest in the importance of new policy ideas on transnational economic governance. The methodological nationalism that underwrote much social science in the twentieth century is rapidly becoming redundant.
- Sovereignty has come to be seen more as a question of responsibility than one of absolute statist control over a specifically determined space. Major changes in conceptions of, and the role of, international law are also in train.

- The role of multilevel governance structures in certain policy areas, enhanced by the role and functions of specialised (both issue-specific and regional) agencies, has grown dramatically.
- Moves to flag up 'governance issues' have also been part of the attempt by the international financial institutions to dig themselves out of the intellectual corner into which their adherence to unfettered free market ideals had forced them in the 1990s. Nowhere is this better illustrated than in Joseph Stiglitz's (2002) broadside against the ideological blinkers that conditioned IMF policymaking during the financial crises that beset the closing stages of the twentieth century.
- Governance has now become a 'hosting metaphor' not only for transnational processes that require institutional responses, but also for identifying non-traditional actors (non-state actors such as non-governmental organisations [NGOs], global social movements and networks) that now participate in the governance of a globalised economy beyond the traditional confines of government. 'Global governance' thus becomes a mobilising agent to allow for the broadening and deepening of policy understanding beyond the traditional, exclusivist, international activities of states and their agents.

Within this context of the growing demand for global governance, we can identify three specific ways of thinking about global governance as a concept:

1   *Global governance as the enhancement of effectiveness and efficiency in the delivery of public goods – or Global Governance Type 1 (GGT1).* Collective-action problem-solving in international relations is often couched in terms of effective governance, with the international institutions seeing their role as consolidating or institutionalising the 'gains' made by processes of global economic integration (see Kaul *et al.*, 1999). It is rarely posed as a question of accountability and democracy, less still as a normative question of redistributive justice.

2   *Global governance as enhanced democracy – or Global Governance Type 2 (GGT2).* Understandings of global governance as exercises in accountability and democratic enhancement trail contemporary understandings of governance as exercises in effectiveness and efficiency. Nevertheless, the language of democracy and justice has taken on a more important rhetorical role in a global context. Indeed, the clamour for democratic engagement at the global level has become stronger even as the role of the nation-state as a vehicle for democratic engagement becomes more problematic. A key issue in this regard is the identification of agents that might advance the cause of greater accountability and transparency in the management of the international institutions while not undermining their effectiveness (Devetak and Higgott, 1999). For many, the incorporation of civil society actors into the policy process is a necessary condition for the legitimation of the global liberalising agenda (see Scholte, 2002). Most international economic institutions are, however, not good at reaching out to NGOs and see them as both boon and bane (Simmons, 1998). Once accepted as legitimate actors in the policy process, NGOs may well

challenge the governance functions of the institutions. There is still reluctance in the economic policy community to recognise that markets are socio-political constructions whose functioning (and legitimacy) depends on the possession of wide and deep support within civil society.

3   *Global governance as the emergence of an international managerial or bureaucratic class – Global Governance Type 3 (GGT3).* Although using different terminology, realists, liberals, constructivists and Marxists alike identify individuals or groups of individuals from the corporate, bureaucratic and intellectual-cum-research communities as increasingly significant strategic actors in transnational relations. These groups (epistemic communities, knowledge communities, policy networks or the like) represent the key players in the growth of a global market civilisation. Moreover, the globalisation of informational and technological elites is an essential part of the process of economic globalisation more generally.

Of these three conceptions of global governance, the need to enhance effective and efficient policymaking, driven by the international institutions, remains the prevailing view of global governance within these institutions. In fact, the 'Augmented Washington Consensus' (Rodrik, 2002a), which incorporates a set of socio-political norms in addition to existing neoliberal norms of economic governance, should be seen as an attempt to legitimate globalisation by mitigating its worst excesses. On this reading, global governance continues to reflect the ideology of neoliberal globalisation. Nevertheless, influential circles within the Bush administration have major problems with the very concept of global governance.

Multilateralism and unilateralism in US foreign policy

Perhaps the major problem the United States has with global governance is its potential to alter the structures of authority and power in the world political economy, as has already been occurring under conditions of economic globalisation over the past several decades. US concerns stem largely from the emergence of networks at the expense of hierarchies in contemporary global governance, given that networks pursue their activities (including waging unconventional war on states) by using systems of sprawling, horizontally interconnected networks of private power and authority (see Rosenau, 2002; Hall and Biersteker, 2002).

Economic globalisation is seen currently in the United States not only as an unalloyed economic benefit, but also – through the lenses of the country's national security agenda (United States Government, 2002) – as a 'security problem'. For the Bush administration, reconciling its security instincts with new patterns of globalisation, influenced not only by states, but by non-state actors, transnational forces and new kinds of threats, is hard. The blurring of the borders between the domestic and international in the policy process – a key characteristic of globalisation – has challenged its traditional understandings of national interest. This is not the case in all areas of transnational policymaking, of course. Multilateral norms in technical or functional contexts are digestible – indeed, often strongly advanced – by the United States. But where transnational decision-making clashes with US domestic law or runs up against a US conception of national security, things become difficult.

While the United States has a history of pragmatic involvement in the development of international institutions, it has always been ambivalent towards multilateralism. This is sometimes explained by American 'exceptionalism', a core belief of which is that conducting foreign policy through international institutions is but one option among many (Luck, 2003: 27). In this context, the United States is uneasy with discursive conference-style diplomacy (such as the 1998 Rome conference on the International Criminal Court) that attempts to take account of the voices of non-state actors in more open forum. These forums diminish the control of states in this process. Other forms of multilateral diplomatic activity, especially informal, internet-led, networked interaction, which is growing, also sits uneasily with the preferred modus operandi of the United States. As Wedgewood (2000: 35–40) has noted, Washington has not adjusted well to these new forms of diplomacy. Similarly, US policymakers, and not just Peter Spiro's (2000) 'new sovereigntists', are suspicious of multilateral regimes as resting places for a new global bureaucracy.

As Charles Kindleberger and others such as Susan Strange (1987) have noted, the United States has historically been a fairly altruistic hegemon, with the key explanatory variable being the ideological disposition of the regime of the day. Seemingly, the Bush administration has a policy preference for options other than cooperative, regularised, rule-governed multilateral endeavours. Rather, it has a preference for unilateral and bilateral options and short-term, issue-specific coalition-building, with freedom gained by acting usually being preferable to the constraint implied in the need to 'forum-shop' for the 'like-minded'. This might reflect the view of the contemporary administration in the United States. But recent extreme examples of what Daalder (2003) calls 'gratuitous unilateralism' should not encourage the view that the United States has repudiated multilateralism of late. Rather, it has become more selective and instrumental in its choice of issue areas. The United States will still accept 'legitimating' and burden-sharing multilateral engagement provided that engagement does not constrain its ability for manoeuvre (Patrick, 2002: 12–13).

If there has always been a historical ambivalence towards multilateralism, and a tension between it and unilateralism in US foreign policy, then unilateralism is in the ascendancy. Contemporary multilateralists in the United States, whether idealists such as Joseph Nye (2002) or realist managers such as Henry Kissinger (2001), have little influence over current US foreign policy. As exhibited by US involvement in Iraq, a fear remains that consensus-building will constrain the United States from acting freely in the pursuit of its stated goals. While this is understood in the context of US security policy, less well articulated are the contours of this unilateralist urge in US foreign economic policy involving similar changing US attitudes towards economic globalisation and the role of international economic institutions in managing the financial system and the trading regime. As the next section argues, the historical ambivalence that has characterised US security policy has also characterised US policy towards the multilateral economic institutions.

The United States and the multilateral economic institutions

Underwritten by the United States, the Bretton Woods institutions (the IMF and the World Bank) and the General Agreement on Tariffs and Trade (GATT) that were established after the Second World War were multilateral in both tone and practice. For sure, the United States saw these institutions as beneficial to its national interest and its view of world order, but it defined its interests broadly and in a sufficiently inclusive manner that other countries were keen to sign up to this vision. To locate US behaviour in historical context allows us to see how contemporary policy represents a break with the past.

In recent years, the incidence of the United States failing to ratify, demand exemptions from, opt out of, or retreat from existing multilateral commitments supported by many other members of the global policy community has increased notably. But US policy towards international economic institutions has also hardened since the growing anti-globalisation backlash against neoliberalism began in the second half of the 1990s. While the advent of the George W. Bush administration speeded up this process, the turning point took place before the administration came to office. Recent changes in US policies and behaviour on the key issues of economic globalisation, especially its increasingly assertive attitudes, following the Asian financial crises, towards reform of the key instruments of international economic management (the WTO, IMF and World Bank), are now well understood in terms of a US desire to set the rules of global economic management (see Stiglitz, 2002).

As I have suggested, globalisation is now seen not simply through rose-tinted neoliberal economic lenses, but also through the less rosy-coloured lenses of the national security agenda of the United States. In the context of the New Security Agenda, economic policy becomes an explicit arm of security policy. This trend can be seen across the spectrum of US policy towards the international economic institutions (the IMF, the World Bank), towards the WTO in the Doha round of multilateral trade negotiations, and in bilateral economic relations, as for example with its interest in preferential trading arrangements.

International finance and the International Monetary Fund

Given the differences in their institutional structure and decision-making process – especially the system of weighted voting, which gives the United States an effective veto – US control in the IMF and the World Bank is more assured than at the WTO. It is easier to secure more self-serving policy outcomes – as, for example, the recent stifling of the 2003 initiative by the IMF First Deputy Managing Director, Anne Krueger, to improve the management and regularisation of developing country sovereign debt restructuring.[2] The proposal was opposed by US banks and subsequently blocked by the US Treasury. But there are a series of more general problems facing the United States, and indeed other major powers, relating to the governance of the international financial institutions arising from the deregulatory, liberalising and asset-privatising trends that have been part and parcel of globalisation over the past few decades. Notably, the increased volatility in financial markets and the cycle of financial crises throughout the 1990s have led to the view that the system was (is) in need of reform. But this realisation also brought with it the vexatious question of how it is to be done.

Substantive change has come about in the activities of major international financial institutions (IFIs) in recent times that are changing their status as multi-lateral actors. The turning point for the IMF was, of course, 1971, when the United States, under Richard Nixon, closed the US$35 to the ounce gold window and effectively abandoned the Bretton Woods system of fixed exchange rates. In the 1970s, the United States began to use the Group of Seven (G7) and the Group of Ten (G10) as the vehicle for stabilising the global economy. Not only did this marginalise the IMF, it undermined its standing in the United States and signalled to other IMF members and officers 'that the organisation's status and role in the world economy would depend on the uses to which the United States would put it' (Woods, 2003: 94). Unsurprisingly, from that time on, the IMF took on a new mission with alacrity. At Washington's behest, the IMF's central role of managing exchange rate stability in the developed world was superseded. Instead, its contemporary role was to become the overseer of developing country macroeconomic rectitude. This was a role for which the Fund – given its bureaucratic capability and neoclassical technical economic expertise – felt it was institutionally and emotionally well equipped to conduct. This change of role was to have major implications for the understanding of global governance that began to emerge from that time forth.

Specifically, this change confirmed the priority of the first type of governance identified in the previous section – GGT1 – as the provision of effective and efficient public policy underwritten by a neoclassical orthodoxy. In privileging this role, however, it also laid the basis of that growing sense of discontent among those on the receiving end of the Fund's new policy remit; that is, those who felt that the second reading of global governance, GGT2 – as enhanced accountability and representation – was being denied to them. This change was underwritten by US will and power in the IMF, and we can see in it the seeds of much contemporary discontent with the institution. As Elliott and Hufbauer (2002: 382) put it,

> The power disparity between creditor and debtor countries conveyed by the Fund's weighted voting system, together with power disparity between the IMF and 'clients' facing a financial crisis, laid the groundwork for one of the backlashes now striking the multilateral world economy.

This backlash exists not only among that growing group of actors generically and indiscriminately described as 'the anti-globalisation movement', but also among the ruling elites of many developing countries for whom the 'clientalist' relationship with the Fund has proved costly in both political and (often personal) economic terms.

Mission creep took a further step forward during the recurrent financial crises of the 1980s and 1990s. The new conditionality regimes of the Fund and the Bank – with their emphasis on fiscal and monetary austerity and a flexible exchange rate, known as the Washington Consensus (see Williamson, 1990) – represented intrusions of a different magnitude as compared to the earlier mandates of these institutions. Moreover, with the end of the Cold War, and the clear recognition of its preponderance, the United States began to pay even less attention to the views of the other major partners in the IMF. The US emphasis on 'structural reform' was much more part of the late twentieth-century Anglo-American view of how to manage the global economy than either its European social democratic partners on the one hand or its major Asian (Japanese) partners, with their developmental-statist approach on the other, were comfortable with (see Albert, 1992; Garten, 1992). The absence of a need any longer to factor in Cold War considerations saw the United States push borrowers increasingly to accept stronger structural reform as part of their packages in return for IMF financial support (Elliott and Hufbauer, 2002: 383).

Nowhere was this better illustrated than in the IMF's 'Wall Street–Treasury'-driven policy towards Asia after the financial crises of 1997 in which the Anglo-American model was embedded in the conditions of the IMF loans. This was seen as an opportunity to put paid to the Asian developmental state model and establish the hegemony of the Anglo-American model (see Higgott, 1998; Higgott and Rhodes, 2000). But it was not only in Asia that the Fund worked closely with the US Treasury to develop these policy features. This also occurred subsequently with Brazil and Russia. The merits or otherwise of this much-criticised strategy (see, notably, Stiglitz, 2002) is not the salient point for this chapter. Rather, it is to note the overriding, albeit unsurprising, influence of the United States in this process, and the residue of bitterness that survives it to this day.

US unilateralism reached its zenith with the US allocation to the IMF after the 1997–1998 financial crises. This allocation was contingent on the creation of the International Financial Institution Advisory Commission to evaluate the structures and activities of the IMF and the World Bank. As Ngaire Woods points out, this Commission studiously declined to take evidence from, or hold consultations with, countries involved in, or affected by, the activities of the IMF. The initial assumptions of the Commission, and indeed the conclusions too, were that the United States needed to be 'tough' in the IMF in order to prevent other countries free-riding.

> The[se] instincts are not isolationist . . . but rather solidly unilateralist. The goal is for the US to bring the institutions, single-handedly under control. . . . The democratic rationale for the unilateralist approach is that the American people elect their government to look after their interests. Rather underplayed in this rationale is the fact that as the most powerful country in

the world the US is the only country which can (at least attempt to) unilaterally define multilateralism and international cooperation so as to meet its own ends.

(Woods, 2001a: 75–76)

This should come as no surprise. It is how one would expect a hegemon to behave. The new Bush administration appears to have conformed to this pattern (see Woods, 2003: 94). Nor should it come as a surprise that Bush administration policies provoked a backlash from the other major donors in the IMF. Even disregarding the views of those in the anti-globalisation movement, the degree to which the United States cast its influence over the IMF and World Bank in a manner disproportionate to all other members is, for most analysts and practitioners alike, a major contemporary global governance issue.[3] It is an issue that has accompanied us into the twenty-first century.

If the future governance of the Fund will turn on the role of the United States, this begs the question of what kind of governance that will be. The views of those of a unilateralist persuasion with influence in Washington during the early years of the first Bush administration are best captured in Elliott and Hufbauer's evocative phrase 'Our Fund or No Fund'. Should the United States find too much opposition to its values, interests and priorities, then it is not impossible that a momentum to withhold funding to the IMF could gain ground across a range of influential actors in the US public and private sector policy community (Elliott and Hufbauer, 2002: 394–395). Opposition to US positions is not impossible, however, given the strong views in almost all of the Fund's other major donors, and indeed developing country borrowers, that they should have a greater say in decision-making. In addition, discussions of the desirability and feasibility of alternative (regional) institutional sources of multilateral crisis lending – such as an Asian Monetary Fund or a lending facility by another name and over which the United States would have less influence – are in train (Deiter and Higgott, 2003).

Trade, multilateral trade negotiations and the WTO

Although the United States played a role in the formation of the GATT, which historically was successful in its agenda to lower tariffs, frustration set in over time. By the early 1980s, a view had emerged in the United States – not without evidence, it should be said (see Low, 1993: 70) – that the progressive reduction in tariffs over the life of GATT had opened up the US economy more than that of many of its trading partners. Poor sectoral coverage and the wide use of non-tariff barriers (NTBs) by US partners was seen to disadvantage the United States. Moreover, new sources of income – for example, from intellectual property – were underexploited, while services trade was a neglected area. In this context, it became apparent to members of the US trade policy community (both public and private) that existing GATT rules and procedures would not help redress this imbalance and that only unilateral action would be likely to offset it (see Elliott and Hufbauer, 2002: 400.)

US policy in this regard was two-pronged. In 1985, the United States advanced a policy of 'aggressive unilateralism' intended to prise open markets in the face of a mounting trade deficit with major partners (notably Japan), employing Article 301 to threaten unilateral retaliation against what it determined to be unfair trade practices (see Bhagwati and Patrick, 1990). The rhetoric often exceeded the activity, but the success of the strategy in adjusting the incentive structures of US trading partners is in no doubt (see Bayard and Elliott, 1994). The US policy of aggressive unilateralism made the second prong of its strategy – to pressure the other G7 states to mount a new trade round – seem more attractive. The Uruguay Round commenced in September 1986 and the agenda included new issues deemed essential to US interests. The Round was concluded in December 1993 and the WTO established in January 1995. While it continues the activities of the GATT, the WTO was a new organisation with a new remit, central to which were the new agreements on trade in services (GATS) and intellectual property rights (TRIPS) as well as a dispute settlement mechanism (DSM), all of which the United States was keen to secure.

That the United States led the agenda of the multilateral trade negotiations (MTN) is not to imply that it was not supported by other developed economies. If we leave agriculture out of the equation, it is quite clear that the Europeans and the Japanese were not unhappy with the outcome of the Round, not least because they felt that a new organisation would recommit the United States to a multilateral trade regime. A debate continues to this day in the United States as to whether the use of aggressive unilateral strategies helps renew the multilateral system embodied in the WTO (*pace* Bayard and Elliott, 1994) or simply jeopardises long-term support for an open multilateral trading regime (*pace* Bhagwati, 2002). It is also a question about hegemony and the degree to which it is benign/altruistic or selfish and destructive of a wider multilateral commitment. It remains one of the major issues of the day.

However, the WTO remit now intrudes more substantially into the domestic politics and economics of the contracting parties, including the United States, in a manner not fully appreciated during the Uruguay Round negotiations.[4] The DSM, keenly sought by the United States, applies to it as much as to other states, and thus makes the WTO an international site at which the United States cannot always be guaranteed to secure its own way. Indeed, it has already lost several disputes under the new settlement system, much to the alarm of groups in the United States. There was outrage in 2003 at the ruling that allowed the European Union to impose US$4 billion in trade sanctions on the United States as compensation in a dispute it won over US tax subsidies to exporters. The WTO ruling in November 2003 against the temporary steel tariffs imposed by the current Bush administration is a further case in point. There is a feeling that in signing on to the WTO – effectively swapping its aggressive unilateralist trade policy of the 1970s and 1980s for the 'multilateral assertiveness' of the DSM – the United States had failed to appreciate the manner in which the DSM would bite it as much as, if not more than, other contracting parties (Elliott and Hufbauer, 2002: 404–407).

Historically, US commitments to multilateralism have always been stronger in the economic domain than any other area of policy. But in the continual tension between unilateralism and multilateralism, the unilateralist urge is gaining the upper hand once again. Rhetorical commitment to a successful Doha round must be contrasted with an increasing recourse to bilateral free trade, or more accurately, preferential trade agreements (PTAs). In fact, the United States made it clear that a failure to progress the Doha round could lead to it striding out more firmly along the unilateral path. US trade representative Robert Zoellick noted ahead of the ministerial meeting that a failure at Cancún would see the US step up its efforts in the development of bilateral and regional free trade agreements (*The Straits Times*, 6 September 2003). This was confirmed when the Cancún ministerial meeting collapsed in September 2003 and the United States pledged to embark on further preferential trade agreements with partners that 'played a constructive role in Cancún' (*New Straits Times*, 16 September 2003).

Bilateral trading arrangements

An interest in bilateral trading arrangements has developed dramatically in US policy circles over the last few years. This interest is not, it should be said, simply a US phenomenon. But if the Europeans started it and other – smaller and weaker – states are now also exploring it, it is the zeal with which the interest in bilateral activities has been picked up by the United States that is the major cause for concern. The role of the United States, as the strongest partner in any bilateral relationship, is bound to be disproportionately influential. The United States is in a position to offer preferential access to the US market to secure concessions from weaker partners (Bhagwati and Panagiriya, 2003: 13).

Actions, rather than rhetoric, suggest that the United States currently attaches as much importance to its bilateral deals as it does to a successful conclusion of an acceptable MTN round – witness the rapid movement on bilateral deals with a range of countries, including Chile, Australia, Singapore, Morocco, and a number of Latin American states. In its defence, the current US administration argues that it is using its bilateral strategy to build what US trade representative Robert Zoellick calls a 'coalition of liberalisers, placing the US at the heart of a network of initiatives to open markets'. But there is a decidedly political element to the choice of partners in this process. As Zoellick, speaking at the Institute for International Economics in Washington, noted,

> A free trade agreement is not something that one has a right to. It's a privilege. But it is a privilege that must be earned via the support of US policy goals. . . . [The Bush administration] . . . expects cooperation – or better – on foreign policy and security issues.
>
> (quoted in *New Statesman*, 23 June 2003: 17)

By way of illustration, Zoellick noted that a free trade deal with New Zealand – given its historical ban on nuclear ship visits and, more recently, a failure to support the war in Iraq – was unlikely (*New Zealand Herald*, 24 May 2003). By contrast, the free trade agreement (FTA) with Australia, since the end of the war in Iraq, was 'fast-tracked'. Egypt's exclusion from talks on a Middle East Free Trade Zone was the US response to its failure to support the US case against the European Union on the issue of genetically modified foods (Watkins, 2003: 33). Political considerations are as important as economic ones in the development of bilateral trading agreements. Symbolically, Singapore, a strong coalition supporter, had its FTA signed in the White House with due dispatch. Chile, which was against the war in Iraq, had the signing of its agreement, the negotiations for which had begun prior to those with Singapore, delayed three months and signed in Miami!

The United States, however, is not the only party responsible for this trend. Such bilateral free trade deals undoubtedly prove popular to the policy elites of the smaller states that are offered them. Singapore, for example, is a strong defender of these initiatives, with the former prime minister Goh Chok Tong seeing his country's FTA with the United States as a strategic way of 'embedding the US in East Asian regionalism' (*Asia Inc*, August 2003: 10). But the important point here is that strong US use of the bilateral PTA, as reward for support of wider policy issues, reflects the linking of economics and security in a nexus that I call the 'securitisation' of US foreign economic policy (Higgott, 2003).

Given the interest of the Bush administration in the Free Trade Agreement of the Americas (itself a massive PTA), and the concerns about multilateralism identified above, it is no surprise that since 2000 there has been an increase in the tempo of bilateral negotiations in other parts of the world. From January 1995 to December 1999 alone, sixty-nine new regional trade agreements were notified to the WTO. Including previously existing arrangements, 113 were in power at the end of 1999. These figures do not include regional agreements still in negotiation stages and yet to be notified to the WTO. Nor do they reflect current developments in East Asia, where there is a strong interest in bilateral agreements, with at least fifty bilateral arrangements concluded, under negotiation or at the proposal stage (see Higgott, 2003: 28 for a listing).

The judgement that contemporary US foreign policy is unilateralist, and counterproductive, is not simply a European or leftist view. It is also criticised by major sections of the American politico-economic establishment, including the core of the US corporate community. For example, Jeffrey Garten, dean of the Yale Business School, a former Undersecretary for Commerce and Trade and a representative of the globalist wing of US capital, has cautioned that unilateralism is harmful not only to US business in particular, but to the health of economic globalisation in general (*Business Week*, 14 October 2002: 74–76). US unilateralism is similarly resisted by important sections of the 'global economic managerial elite'. Peter Sutherland, former director-general of the WTO, chairman of Goldman Sachs and co-chair of the Trilateral Commission, has argued that '[the United States] . . . no longer seems committed to the multilateralism . . . [it] did so much to foster' (quoted in Prestowitz, 2003: 9). Even important sections of the influential US policy community such as Clyde Prestowitz, president of the conservative Economic Strategy Institute and erstwhile prominent economic nationalist and

'Japan basher' of the late 1980s, find US unilateralism a problem. The thrust of Prestowitz's argument is captured in the title of his 2003 book, *Rogue Nation: American Unilateralism and the Failure of Good Intentions*.

Concluding thoughts: the limits of multilateralism

This chapter's arguments about US attitudes towards multilateral institutions, and the constraints on global governance beyond GGT1, have not been based simply on a reading of the Bush era. The relationship between US foreign policy and multilateralism over time has always been an exercise in what some call 'ambivalent engagement' (Patrick and Forman, 2002) and others call 'instrumental multi-lateralism' (Foot *et al.*, 2003). As Jervis (2003: 84) points out,

> The forceful and unilateral exercise of US power is not simply the by-product of September 11, the Bush administration and some shadowy neo-conservative cabal – it is the logical outcome of the current unrivalled position of the US in the international system.

In terms of governance as the effective and efficient management of the global economy (GGT1), the international economic institutions have served the interests of the United States well. This was the case during the bipolar Cold War era and in the present unipolar one. But this may not continue to be the case unless the United States takes greater account of the second understanding of governance offered – governance defined as accountability and representation (and justice) (GGT2). The continued globalisation of the economy – freer trade, freer capital flows, freer movement of technology – cannot continue without thought being given to how we develop structures of accountability and representation in these processes. Leaving it to the market will not do. Dani Rodrik (2002b) has identified what he calls 'the political trilemma' of the global economy, namely, the incompatibility of the continued existence of the nation-state (to ensure self-determination), the development of democratic politics beyond the state (to ensure that public policy is accountable) and the continuing economic integration of the global economy (to enhance living standards). At best, we can secure two of these three goals, never all of them.

The current neoliberal agenda, seen for example in the Doha MTN round-up to the disaster that was the Cancún ministerial meeting – with its emphasis on service trade, intellectual property and capital movements, and its refusal to address developing country concerns on the issue of agriculture – reflected the continued drive of the United States and Europe for enhanced (deep) global economic integration. But such integration sits at odds with the clamour for democratic politics within states and between states. It thus remains neither feasible nor desirable, says Rodrik, to continue towards global economic integration greater than is compatible with the desires of nation-states for representation in these processes. Thus, we need to think, more pragmatically, of what can be achieved. For Rodrik, the alternative is a renewed Bretton Woods Compromise: preserving some limits on integration, as built into original Bretton Woods arrangements, along with some more global rules to handle the integration that can be achieved. Those who would make different choices – towards tighter economic integration – must face up to the corollary: either tighter world government or less democracy. . . . [We might need to] scale down our ambitions with respect to global economic integration . . . [and] do a better job of writing the rules for a thinner version of globalization.

(2002b: 1–2)

The question, therefore, is whether we can have global economic integration without global governance. This is not to resist the central importance of market structures and activity, rather than to require an ethic of global governance that suggests GGT1 and GGT2 are not for de-linking.[5] In theory, the multilateral economic institutions should play the major role in this process. Unfortunately, the international economic institutions have a legitimacy deficit, acknowledged even by many officials within these organisations. This lack of accountability of the international economic institutions to all but their most powerful members is not new. Indeed, it has always existed.[6] What has made it no longer acceptable is the articulation of a series of telling and increasingly well-understood critiques, not all of which are just anti-globalisation rhetoric. To be specific, this chapter demonstrates the degree to which 'mission creep' by the international institutions, especially the WTO and the IMF, has generated resistance. The enhanced remits of the international institutions in the absence of major reform of the governance structures affecting GGT2 are the source of major backlash. Nothing demonstrates this better than the Cancún ministerial meeting, where the newly created G21 of developing countries, led by Brazil and India, flatly resisted US and European efforts to introduce new issues, especially on investment, into the negotiating agenda of the Round (*Financial Times*, 15 September 2003). The firmness of the stand by the developing countries in the face of considerable pressures from the major states represents something of a watershed since the birth of the WTO.

While there have been serious attempts to make decision-making procedures more transparent in the IFIs and the WTO (Woods, 2003), and momentum for reform continues, the point to note is that the reforms to date have focused on GGT1 and have been insufficiently substantial with regard to GGT2. These sorts of reforms will not ward off challenges to the credibility of these institutions. We need to remember that two out of the four ministerial meetings of the WTO since its inception in 1995 have ended in breakdown. Major rethinking about the way forward will have to take place.[7] If institutional change capable of address-ing legitimate demands for accountability and representation (GGT2) of the majority of smaller but weaker members of these institutions cannot be found, continued governance of the global economic order (GGT1) will become increas-ingly difficult to sustain despite the power of the United States and, in many common circumstances, the Europeans too.

Notes

1   A term originated by John Williamson to reflect shared opinion on how economies should be governed within the Washington international financial community that included not only the US administration, but also the major international financial institutions and think tanks such as the Institute for International Economics (IIE). See Williamson (1990).
2   For a description of the proposals, see Fisher and Krueger (2003).
3   See Woods and Narlikar (2001) for a review and analysis of this disproportionality.
4   For general discussion of the WTO and its operations, see Hoekman and Kostecki (2001).
5   See Brassett and Higgott (2004) for an elaboration of this argument.
6   Woods (2001b) and Woods and Narlikar (2001) have provided detailed empirical studies of the limits of accountability through their executive boards of the international institutions to their member governments.
7   See the articles by Verweij and Josling (2003), Howse and Nicolaidis (2003), King (2003) and Stiglitz (2003) in the special 2003 edition of *Governance*, 16 (1).

References

Albert, M. (1992) *Capitalism versus Capitalism*, London: Whurr.

Bayard, Thomas, O. and Elliott, Kimberly Ann (1994) *Reciprocity and Retaliation in US Trade Policy*, Washington, DC: Institute for International Economics.

Bhagwati, Jagdish (2002) *Free Trade Today*, Princeton, NJ: Princeton University Press.

Bhagwati, Jagdish and Panagariya, Arvind (2003) 'Bilateral Treaties Are a Sham', *Financial Times*, 14 July: 13.

Bhagwati, Jagdish and Patrick, Hugh (eds) (1990) *Aggressive Unilateralism: America's 301 Trade Policy and the World Trading System*, Ann Arbor, MI: University of Michigan Press.

Brassett, James and Higgott, Richard (2004) 'Building the Normative Foundations of a Global Polity', *Review of International Studies*, 29: 29–35.

Daalder, Ivo (2003) 'The End of Atlanticism', *Survival*, 45 (2): 142–166.

Deiter, Heribert and Richard Higgott (2003) 'Exploring Alternative Theories of Economic Regionalism: From Trade to Finance in Asian Co-operation', *Review of International Political Economy*, 10 (3): 430–454.

Devetak, Richard and Higgott, Richard (1999) 'Justic Unbound: Globalisation, States and the Transformation of the Social Bond', *International Affairs*, 75 (3): 483–498.

Elliott, Kimberly and Hufbauer, Gary (2002) 'Ambivalent Multilateralism and the Emerging Backlash: The IMF and the WTO', in Stewart Patrick and Shephard Forman (eds) *Multilateralism and US Foreign Policy: Ambivalent Engagement*, Boulder, CO: Lynne Rienner, pp. 377–414.

Fisher, Matthew and Krueger, Anne (2003) 'Building on a Decade of Experience: Crisis Prevention and Resolution', *International Crises: What Follows the Washington Consensus*, 6th Annual Conference, ESRC Centre for the Study of Globalisation and Regionalisation, Warwick University, UK, 11–13 July.

Foot, Rosemary, MacFarlane, Neil and Mastanduno, Michael (2003) 'Conclusion: Instrumental Multilateralism in US Foreign Policy', in Rosemary Foot, Neil MacFarlane and Michael Mastanduno (eds) *US Hegemony and International Organizations*, Oxford: Oxford University Press, 256–272.

Garten, Jeffrey (1992) *A Cold Peace: America, Japan, Germany and the Struggle for Supremacy*, New York: Time Books for the Twentieth Century Fund.

Hall, Rodney Bruce and Biersteker, Thomas J. (2002) (eds) *The Emergence of Private Authority in Global Governance*, Cambridge: Cambridge University Press.

Higgott, Richard (1998) 'The Asian Financial Crisis: A Case Study in the Politics of Resentment', *New Political Economy*, 3 (3): 333–356.

—— (2000) 'Contested Globalisation: The Changing Context and Normative Challenges', *Review of International Studies*, 26: 131-154.

—— (2003) 'American Unilateralism, Foreign Economic Policy and the "Securitisation" of Globalisation', University of Warwick, ESRC Centre for the Study of Globalisation and Regionalisation, Working Paper 124/03, available at www.csgr.org.

Higgott, Richard and Rhodes, Martin (2000) 'Beyond Liberalisation in the Asia Pacific', *The Pacific Review*, 13 (1): 1–20.

Hoekman, Bernard and Kostecki, Michel (2001) *The Political Economy of the World Trade System: The WTO and Beyond*, Oxford: Oxford University Press.

Howse, Robert and Nicolaidis, Kalypso (2003) 'Enhancing WTO Legitimacy: Constitutionalization or Subsidiarity', *Governance*, 16 (1): 73–94.

Hurrell, Andrew and Woods, Ngaire (eds) (1999) *Inequality, Globalization, and World Politics*, Oxford: Oxford University Press.

Ikenberry, John (2001) 'American Power and the Empire of Capitalist Democracy', *Review of International Studies*, 27: 191–212.

Jervis, Robert (2003) 'The Compulsive Empire', *Foreign Policy*, July–August: 83–87.

Kaul, Inge, Grunberg, Isabelle and Stern, Marc A. (1999) *Global Public Goods*, New York: Oxford University Press for the United Nations Development Programme.

King, Loren (2003) 'Deliberation, Legitimacy and Multilateral Democracy', *Governance*, 16 (1): 23–50.

Kissinger, Henry (2001) *Does America Need a Foreign Policy? Toward a New Diplomacy for the 21st Century*, New York: Simon & Schuster.

Low, Patrick (1993) *Trading Free: The GATT and US Trade Policy*, New York: Twentieth Century Books.

Luck, Edward (2003) 'American Exceptionalism and International Organization: Lessons from the 1990s', in Rosemary Foot, Neil MacFarlane and Michael Mastanduno (eds) *US Hegemony and International Organizations*, Oxford: Oxford University Press.

Nye, Joseph Jr (2002) *The Paradox of American Power: Why the World's Only Superpower Can't Go It Alone*, Oxford: Oxford University Press.

Patrick, Stewart (2002) 'Multilateralism and Its Discontents: The Causes and Consequences of US Ambivalence', in Stewart Patrick and Shepard Forman (eds) *Multilateralism in US Foreign Policy: Ambivalent Engagement*, Boulder, CO: Lynne Rienner.

Patrick, Stewart and Forman, Shepard (eds) (2002) *Multilateralism and US Foreign Policy: Ambivalent Engagement*, Boulder, CO: Lynne Rienner.

Prestowitz, Clyde (2003) *Rogue Nation: American Unilateralism and the Failure of Good Intentions*, New York: Basic Books.

Rodrik, Daniel (2002a) 'After Neoliberalism, What?', in *After Neoliberalism: Economic Policies that Work for the Poor*, Conference sponsored by the New Rules of Global Finance Coalition, Washington, DC, 23–24 May.

—— (2002b) 'Feasible Globalizations' [Online] http://ksghome.harvard.edu/~drodrik.

Rosenau, James N. (2002) 'Governance in the New Global Order', in David Held and Anthony McGrew (eds) *Governing Globalization: Power, Authority and Global Governance*, Cambridge: Polity Press, pp. 70–86.

Scholte, Jan Aart (2002) 'Civil Society and Governance in the Global Polity', in Morton

Ougaard and Richard Higgott (eds) *Towards a Global Polity*, London: Routledge, pp. 145–165.

Simmons, P. J. (1998) 'Learning to Live with NGOs', *Foreign Policy*, 111: 82–97.

Spiro, Peter (2000) 'The New Sovereigntists: American Exceptionalism and Its False Prophets', *Foreign Affairs*, 79 (6): 9–15.

Stiglitz, Joseph (2002) *Globalization and Its Discontents*, London: Penguin.

—— (2003) 'Democratizing the International Monetary Fund and the World Bank', *Governance*, 16 (1): 111–140.

Strange, Susan (1987) 'The Persistent Myth of Lost Hegemony', *International Organisation*, 41 (4): 551–574.

—— (1988) *The Retreat of the State*, Cambridge: Cambridge University Press.

United States Government (2002) *The National Security Strategy of the United States of America*, September [Online] www.whitehouse.gov/nsc/nss.html.

Verweij, Marco and Josling, Timothy (2003) 'Deliberately Democratizing Multilateral Organization', *Governance*, 16 (1): 1–22.

Watkins, Kevin (2003) 'Countdown to Cancun', *Prospect*, August: 28–35.

Wedgewood, Ruth (2000) 'Courting Disaster: The US Takes a Stand', *Foreign Service Journal*, 77(3): 34–41.

Williamson, John (1990) 'What Washington Means by Policy Reform', in John Williamson (ed.) *Latin American Adjustment: How Much Has Happened?*, Washington, DC: Institute for International Economics.

Woods, Ngaire (2001a) 'Who Should Govern the World Economy: The Challenges of Globalization and Governance', *Renewal*, 9 (2/3): 73–82.

—— (2001b) 'Making the IMF and the World Bank More Accountable', *International Affairs*, 77 (1): 83–100.

—— (2003) 'The United States and the International Financial Institutions: Power and Influence within the World Bank and the IMF', in Rosemary Foot, Neil MacFarlane and Michael Mastanduno (eds) *US Hegemony and International Organizations*, Oxford: Oxford University Press, pp. 92–114.

Woods, Ngaire and Narlikar, Amrita (2001) 'The WTO, the IMF and the World Bank: Accountable to Whom?', *International Social Science Journal*, 53 (170): 569–583.

10 Does hegemony still matter?

Revisiting regime formation in the Asia-Pacific

Mark Beeson

The Pacific political economy is in the midst of significant structural and institutional change. Over the past four decades the distribution of political and economic capabilities has shifted from a pattern that reflected American hegemonic presence toward a more complex balance of power. Economic and security issues have become more separate, reducing the nesting of these two issue-areas. Furthermore, an institutional basis for handling the regional political economy on a multilateral basis is rapidly being developed, with the result that the prior predominance of bilateral negotiations is eroding. Collectively, these changes constitute a substantial reorganization of the Pacific political economy.

(Crone, 1993: 501)

What a difference a decade makes. Writing as recently as 1993, Donald Crone in his widely cited paper detailed an apparently inexorable transformation that was occurring in what he described as the 'Pacific political economy'. Only just over a decade ago, US hegemony appeared to be in long-term decline. Crucially, the apparent waning of American power opened up a space for greater assertiveness on the part of what we might now prefer to describe as East Asian rather than Pacific powers. The change in language is in itself revealing: notions like the Pacific political economy, the Pacific Rim and even the Asia-Pacific have become not simply less fashionable, but indicative of an underlying transformation in relations between East Asia and North America and of the concomitant emergence of more narrowly conceived regional identities. At the core of this transformation has been a resurgence of American power and – crucially – a preparedness to use it in ways that are judged to further the United States' economic, political and, above all, strategic interests.

In less than a decade, expectations about the course of development in the Asia-Pacific region have changed in significant ways. The very idea of a coherent Asia-Pacific region has become problematic, and the expectation that it would be one characterised by increasingly multilateral processes and institutions, as Crone suggested, has become far less certain. At one level, this reflects a general disenchantment with the capacity of international organisations to fulfil the hopes of their supporters. At another level, however, the growing prominence and importance of bilateral and – in the United States' case – unilateral policy initiatives is the most tangible demonstration of the way relationships between key actors in the Asia-Pacific are being recalibrated and restructured. At the centre of this process is the increasingly assertive application of American power. As a consequence, bilateralism has become a more prominent part of a seemingly resurgent American hegemony. At the same time, the separation of economic and security issues that Crone took to be such a significant part of the evolving Pacific order also looks less entrenched than it did. Indeed, recent events suggest that we may need to embark on yet another re-evaluation of the relationship between economic security and its more traditional strategic counterpart.

This chapter explores the impact of the United States' evolving relationship with the countries of East Asia at a time when the country's foreign policy elite is prepared to act more forcefully and, where deemed necessary, unilaterally. After initially considering the transformation of America's own position in the inter-national system and the way in which hegemony might be understood as a consequence, the chapter draws on a number of theoretical perspectives in an attempt to illuminate the implications of changes in the wider geopolitical environment for East Asia in particular. The principal conclusion of this chapter can be stated at the outset: hegemony *does* matter, but its impact is more contra-dictory than might be expected. The United States' self-declared 'war on terror', its increased unilateralism and even the (re)fusion of economic and conventional security issues presents major challenges for the East Asian region, the consequences of which are difficult to predict and not necessarily in 'America's' long-term interest.

Regimes and hegemony: theorising institutional change in the Asia-Pacific region

When one is attempting to make sense of the apparently different patterns of international relations in the Asia-Pacific, there are some initial conceptual and linguistic hurdles to overcome, not the least of which is how to describe the area under discussion. A number of observers have highlighted the contested, discur-sively constructed nature of terms such as Asia-Pacific and Pacific Rim (see, for example, Dirlik, 1992). For my purposes, 'Asia-Pacific' is simply a shorthand way of referring to the broadly conceived economic, political and strategic interactions between the countries of East Asia,[1] the United States and – to a less significant extent – the rest of the Americas and Australasia. In other words, the conception of the Asia-Pacific used here is essentially geographic and descriptive. I do not assume that the Asia-Pacific is a coherent, unproblematic entity with a well-defined sense of identity. On the contrary, one of the purposes of this chapter is to consider whether there is any basis for a more substantial, institutionalised set of relationships within and across the Asia-Pacific. In this regard, Crone was right to highlight the importance of American hegemony, but it may not have the effect he anticipated.

American hegemony

It is remarkable how rapidly views about American power have changed. A decade or so ago, the US economy was widely considered to be in long-term decline and unable to compete with the competitive, increasingly prominent economies of East Asia. America's hegemonic position was seen as unsustainable and subject to 'imperial overstretch', as the United States' material circumstances seemed incapable of underwriting its geopolitical ambitions (Kennedy, 1988). Things could hardly be more different now. Despite the persistence of some very real doubts about the long-term health of the US economy (see Brenner, 2002), the conventional wisdom has it that America's overall position is historically unprecedented, unchallengeable in the foreseeable future, and provides the basis for a far more assertive, not to say unilateral, foreign policy (Bacevich, 2002).

Certainly when judged by the conventional measures of power – military might, political leverage, cultural influence and overall economic strength – the United States looks formidable and its position vis-à-vis potential rivals is unparalleled (Emmott, 2002). But even if we can accept that the United States is pre-eminent across a range of key variables and recognise that unique potential capacities accrue to American policymakers as a result, there is less agreement about either the best ways of conceptualising this power or about the purposes to which it may be put.

In the light of recent events and the role played by an increasingly assertive and unilateral United States, it is important to remember that one of the principal sources of concern for many policymakers and scholars alike during the 1980s and early 1990s was how the world would cope 'after hegemony' and the seemingly inexorable decline of American power (see Keohane, 1984). The key problem was considered to be establishing a new basis for international cooperation in the absence of a dominant power prepared, if necessary, to compel compliance for the collective good. Significantly, for scholars such as Crone and (especially) Robert Keohane, new regimes, or particular configurations of 'liberal arrangements for trade and international finance [established] as responses to the need for policy coordination created by the fact of interdependence' (Keohane 1984: 8), could provide the basis for a new international order in the absence of effective hegemonic power. Indeed, as hegemony declined, it was expected that the demand for international regimes would actually increase as states acting cooperatively sought to retain the advantages of reduced transaction costs that were formerly associated with effective regimes: increased multilateral cooperation could actually be an artefact of declining American power (Keohane 1982).

Two aspects of these older debates are worth emphasising, as they provide an interesting counterpoint to the contemporary period. First, those analysts who were sceptical about the degree of American decline have been vindicated (Strange, 1987; see also Snidal, 1985); whatever problems the international system may currently be experiencing, they are plainly not simply a consequence of any lack of will or capacity on the part of the United States. This is an especially important consideration when we recall that it was the particular nature of American hegemony that was considered to be the critical determinant of the sort of international order or regime that characterised the post-war era. Ruggie, for example, argued that 'when we look closely at the post-World War II situation . . . we find that it was less the fact of American *hegemony* that accounts for the explosion of multilateral arrangements than it was the fact of *American* hegemony' (Ruggie, 1992: 593). In other words, as far as observers like Ruggie and Ikenberry were concerned, what was distinctive about American power was that it was an expression of underlying values and interests that coalesced in the creation of a distinctive, liberal international order characterised first and foremost by openness and institutionalised multilateralism. This leads to a second critical point: much of the apparent legitimacy of the American-inspired international order, and the key reason why other states have either supported it or not sought to 'balance' against the United States, flows from what Deudney and Ikenberry (1999) describe as the 'penetrated' nature of American hegemony: a system of transnational relations generates pay-offs for other 'bandwagoning' nations and allows continuing access to centres of power in the United States.

As we saw earlier, there was a widespread expectation that the number and importance of institutionalised regimes would actually increase in the aftermath of declining American hegemony. An important question to ask in the light of an apparent resurgence and reassertion of US power, therefore, is whether regimes generally and multilateral ones in particular are likely to decrease in number and importance.

World orders are a consequence of the complex interplay between institutions, ideas and political power (Cox, 1981; Rosenau, 1992). At particular moments in history, this means that specific ideas may play an especially influential role in determining events and actually helping to constitute the institutional structures associated with specific regimes.[2] Crucially, the wider geopolitical context can help determine which ideas are influential at any time: the role played by American and British economists and technocrats in the aftermath of the Second World War in shaping the new international institutional architecture designed to entrench an 'open', liberal trade regime is a clear example of the power of particular ideas at moments of fluidity (Ikenberry, 1993). It is also clear that the role and guiding principles of particular institutions can evolve significantly over time as circumstances change and new ideas become more influential or are seen as more appropriate (Barnett and Finnemore, 1999). The evolving role of the International Monetary Fund (IMF), for example, as it moved from being the manager of a system of regulated exchange rates to proselytising on behalf of a market-determined order, is evidence of this possibility (see Pauly, 1997). Such changes can be explained by the complex nature of institutions and their role as mediators and crystallisations of international power relations.

For much of the post-war period, American hegemony was shaped and con-strained by the overarching strategic imperatives of the Cold War. The existence of a credible ideological and – in the initial phases of the Cold War, at least – economic competitor in the form of the Soviet Union constrained American options in profoundly important ways (Cronin, 1996). The possibility that its putative allies might defect to the communist camp meant that the United States was prepared to tolerate political practices and economic policies on the part of client states of which it did not necessarily approve. In short, American hegemony – as far as its allies were concerned, at least – was generally more benevolent than coercive,[3] and its impact on the specific institutional structures of East Asia was less direct as a consequence. At an ideational level, the impact of American hegemony in this period, in the economic and political sphere at least, was uneven and limited: neoliberal, market-oriented reform was – and still is, to a lesser extent – actively resisted in East Asia, much to the frustration of generations of American policymakers.[4] Indeed, it is important to recognise that even during the heyday of the American-led multilateral order, American policymakers consistently resorted to direct *bilateral* pressure to cajole key trading partners such as Japan into accepting 'voluntary' export restraints and the like (Lincoln, 1999).

Yet the long-term impact of American hegemony in the Cold War period was to create a distinctive political and economic space within which industrialisation across much of East Asia could take off. Throughout the Cold War period, the economic and strategic dimensions of American foreign policy were deeply intertwined, but both dimensions of policy had distinctive characteristics. The multilateral system epitomised by the Bretton Woods institutions that oversaw the reconstruction of successful capitalist economies in Europe and ultimately East Asia, created positive spillovers that were a crucial component of a more generalised struggle with communism, in which the viability of the Western economic system was crucial. By contrast, the strategic component of America's relationships in East Asia was predicated on an overwhelmingly bilateral basis, in which America provided the central cog around which the Asian security system revolved. For complex historical and cultural reasons, the United States did not regard the countries of East Asia as equals, and consequently constructed a very different order to that which prevailed in Europe (Hemmer and Katzenstein, 2002). It is a system that is still essentially in place, the emergence of regionally based security organisations notwithstanding (Hara, 1999). As Grieco (1999) points out, there is a significant degree of 'path dependency' in America's strategic policy, something that delimits the entire strategic trajectory of the region. This is especially the case given the low-profile but highly influential roles played by senior American military personnel embedded across much of the 'American empire' (see Bacevich, 2002: chapter 7).

Despite the overt and covert influence that flows from the United States' dominant military position, in the period before the Cold War was unambiguously concluded, American foreign economic policy and security policy had begun to proceed on 'separate diplomatic and institutional tracks' (Mastanduno, 1998: 843). This institutionalised separation came to characterise America's more assertive, results-oriented approach to foreign economic policy in particular (see Bhagwati and Patrick, 1990), and reflected an influential idea that, especially following the aftermath of the Cold War, geo-economics had decisively, and possibly permanently, trumped geopolitics (Luttwak, 1990). The emerging strategic doctrine of the administration of George W. Bush has been, however, a powerful reminder of just how important 'traditional' security policy can be,[5] and of the manner in which it has become inextricably re-entwined with other policy initiatives. The significance of this reconfiguration of American foreign policy priorities and the recombining of economic and military security issues is captured by Edward Rhodes, who argues that 'the liberal order the United States aims to create will, ultimately, rest on American military hegemony, not on the combined will and might of the liberal world. . . . Consensus is desirable, but it is not necessary' (2003: 136).

As a result of these changes, there are some noteworthy similarities and differences between pre- and post-September 11 (S11) American hegemony, which we might expect to influence political and economic regimes in East Asia, and the more broadly conceived Asia-Pacific region. On the one hand, the United States is plainly a good deal more powerful than much of the declinist literature led us to believe, and the basic assumptions that informed analyses by observers like Crone only a decade or so ago are therefore no longer appropriate.[6] On the other hand, however, the striking parallels between the strategic imperatives of the Cold War and the 'war on terror' might intuitively lead us to expect that the US approach to economic foreign policy might revert to its former style and become less coercive in an effort to keep key allies on side. After all, it was from the 1980s onwards that American economic policy became increasingly assertive as the importance of strategic issues appeared to decline, so it is reasonable to expect that the re-emergence of security issues might create a similarly favourable and multilaterally based situation. While some aspects of American economic policy do appear to be becoming somewhat less coercive, and its support for particular regimes has become less conditioned by human rights concerns, the most notable feature of economic policy is that it has become increasingly bilateral. To see why, we need to look at the evolution of the new international order in the Asia-Pacific in more detail.

The emerging Asia-Pacific economic and security order

What is most noteworthy about the emerging order in the Asia-Pacific is that, while there is recognition on the part of the United States that security issues are fundamentally connected to broader questions about international economic development, inequality and governance (Purdum and Sanger, 2002), there has been an overwhelming emphasis on the military aspects of American foreign policy. The desire to maintain freedom of operation militarily has led the United States to eschew multilateral entanglements in favour of direct, frequently bilateral interactions that permit maximum leverage and freedom of movement – a pattern that has been prominent in American foreign policy over the past fifty years or so (see the remarkably critical discussion provided in Prestowitz, 2003). It is within this overall context that the recent move to bilateralism has achieved such prominence, but the seeds of this approach have been germinating for some time (see Joffe, 2002).

The rise of economic bilateralism

The rise to prominence of the discourse surrounding 'globalisation' helped to entrench the idea that certain features of the contemporary international order not only were unambiguous ontological realities, but also had effects that could be managed only through multilateral auspices. The increased integration of formerly discrete national economic spaces as a consequence of higher levels of direct investment, greater short-term capital flows and increased trade were widely thought to make transnational regime formation an ever more essential and functional part of international relations – with or without the intervention of a hegemonic power (Keohane, 1982). The declining influence of a number of prominent multilateral trade regimes and organisations is therefore significant and surprising. However, possible answers to this puzzle pre-date the current obsession with the 'war on terror'.

One of the principal causes of the declining importance of multilateral agencies in managing and promoting reform in the economic sphere at least, has been widespread disenchantment with a number of key organisations. The most conspicuous failure in this regard in a regional context is the Asia-Pacific Economic Cooperation (APEC) forum, an organisation in which great hopes were invested, especially regarding trade liberalisation and regional economic integration, but about which there has been long-standing scepticism (Higgott, 1993). From its inception in 1989, APEC contained what ultimately proved to be irreconcilable tensions. The initial obstacle of regional definition – what exactly is the 'Asia-Pacific', and which countries should be included as a consequence? – was never satisfactorily resolved. The addition of ever more members – including Russia, a country with only the most marginal claims to membership as the organisation was originally conceived – further diluted any coherence APEC might have had and made the development of policy extremely difficult as a consequence. More fundamentally, perhaps, the very different, highly institutionalised patterns of political and economic organisation that are associated with East Asia's distinctive models of development made the rapid adoption of all APEC's ambitious liberalisation and reform timetable difficult to achieve.[7]

Whatever problems the economies of East Asia may have experienced since the crisis that began in 1997, it is important to recognise that for decades close relationships between business and government, state interventionism, non-transparency, protectionism and the panoply of measures associated with East Asia's developmental states were not simply highly effective parts of the region's remarkable economic expansion, but widely considered legitimate elements of East Asia's political systems, too. Although there is no intention of exploring the merits of state-led development or its possible relationship to 'crony capitalism' here (but see Beeson, 2004a), it is important to stress one thing: East Asian patterns of political and economic organisation are institutionally embedded and will not disappear rapidly. The entrenched patterns of power and interest that characterise many of the political economies of the East Asian region present powerful obstacles to the sorts of neoliberal reforms championed by APEC. Given APEC's inability to impose a multilateral trade liberalisation agenda because of its own institutional shortcomings and consequent lack of political leverage,[8] it becomes easier to understand why governments across the Asia-Pacific might have adopted alternative strategies. Indeed, APEC's perceived failings further contributed to its demise, for, as John Ravenhill perceptively points out, 'with most foreign affairs bureaucracies severely stretched, allocation of resources is inevitably a zero-sum game. The correlation between the lack of supply of leadership to APEC since 1998, and the growth of bilateralism is surely no coincidence' (Ravenhill, 2003: 312).

It is highly significant that in the flurry of bilateral deals that are either under consideration or – less frequently – actually completed, most are between countries that are not significant trade partners (Ravenhill, 2003: 309). The economic benefits of such agreements would therefore seem to be less critical than their possible domestic and international political importance. At the broadest international level, a confluence of circumstances has given the pursuit of preferential trading agreements what has been described as 'its own self-sustaining momentum' (Dent, 2003: 7): disenchantment with the capacity of key institutions such as APEC and the World Trade Organization (WTO) to deliver on trade liberalisation, combined with concerns about the relative gains that might accrue to competitors who have already achieved such agreements, has added a sense of urgency to the bilateral push. At a regional level in East Asia the bilateral momentum has been enhanced by the competing leadership ambitions of Japan and China. China in particular has energetically pursued a free trade agreement with the ASEAN grouping, not simply as a way of establishing its leadership credentials vis-à-vis Japan, but as a way of countering the United States' hegemonic presence in the region and attempting to reassure the smaller ASEAN states about its non-aggressive intentions (Ba, 2003). As a consequence, it has encouraged the US to seek its own bilateral deals with individual ASEAN members (Vatikiotis and Hiebert, 2003). Significantly, America's economic position in the region has been bolstered by increased investment by US multinationals on the one hand, and the declining importance of Japan on the other (Hsiao *et al.*, 2003).

Japan has directly responded to China's attempts to cement its place in East Asia's diplomatic hierarchy with its own ASEAN-oriented trade initiatives (Shanahan, 2002: 2), but they have had less impact as a consequence of Japan's own economic and leadership problems (Wall, 2002). This is not to say that bilateral deals are not potentially attractive to many Japanese policymakers, however; on the contrary, bilateral deals offer a way of circumventing or managing the potential pain associated with comprehensive, multilaterally based trade liberalisation initiatives that would inevitably impact on politically sensitive economic sectors such as agriculture. It is revealing that the bilateral deal that Japan had least trouble in securing was with Singapore – a country with no agricultural sector.

It would seem, therefore, that bilateralism is an approach that is in keeping with the times, as the noteworthy congruence that has developed between America's strategic and economic objectives seems to suggest. However, an overemphasis on America's increased predilection for unilateralism and bilateralism seriously underestimates the enduring impact of the United States' influence and role at the centre of the existent multilateral structures that govern global trade in particular and the international order more generally.

The direct and indirect impact of hegemony

Some of the most persuasive arguments advanced to explain the United States' increased interest in using bilateral leverage – in the economic sphere, at least – have centred on the American foreign policy elite's supposed disenchantment with APEC and the WTO (Dent, 2003: 19). As we have seen, in APEC's case this thesis looks quite plausible. As far as the WTO is concerned, however, the argument is more complex, the WTO's well-documented failure to advance its liberalisation agenda notwithstanding (Davis, 2003: 16). When seen in a larger geopolitical and historical context, the most significant development in the East Asian region may well prove to be China's accession to the WTO: as the last significant alternative to an increasingly pervasive neoliberal, capitalist world order dominated by the United States, China's embrace of the market and voluntary abandonment of socialism marks a transformation of truly world-historical proportions.[9]

For all China's well-known suspicions of American hegemony (Deng, 2001), it is revealing that China's elites consider that they have little choice other than to embrace 'globalisation' and hope to glean enhanced legitimacy from accelerated economic development as a consequence (Garrett, 2001). The implications of the WTO-inspired reform process cannot be overestimated as it necessitates fundamental changes to China's constitution, opens up hitherto protected parts of its domestic economy to international competition, and, in the long term, it will systematically reconfigure domestic interests and attitudes to international economic engagement (not to mention 'communism') as a consequence (Fewsmith, 2001). While it may be possible to argue that change at this world-historical level involving long-term transformation in underlying modes of production reflects the impact of deeper structural forces, they are synonymous with the American-led post-war international order. Indeed, the apparent congruence between American capitalism and 'globalisation' reinforces American hegemony and makes the survival of alternative political and economic orders increasingly precarious (Ikenberry, 2001).

It is precisely this longer-term, more diffuse and institutionalised 'structural power' that helps to explain why neoliberalism and Western economic practices more generally have become so dominant (see Gill, 1995; Cox, 1987; on structural power, see Strange, 1988). This is not to dismiss or underestimate the continuing differences that characterise capitalist organisation across the world generally and within the Asia-Pacific in particular (see Coates, 2000), but the differences within the increasingly pervasive capitalist system are less significant in this context than are differences between it and alternative economic models (Strange, 1997). It is this more indirect aspect of hegemonic influence that has been a critically important element of American power and that has been instrumental in consolidating the long-term dominance of capitalism as the overarching system within which specific regimes and institutions are nested. A preoccupation with short-term changes in the content and approach of different administrations, or even towards specific issue areas or regions, can obscure the remarkable continuity that has underpinned American foreign policy in particular and American hegemony more generally (Bacevich, 2002).

Nevertheless, apparently short-term policy changes are important and can have profound, unforeseen long-term consequences.[10] In this context, recent changes in American foreign policy in the aftermath of S11 have been especially significant. Perhaps the most important consequence of the emerging Bush doctrine as far as the Asia-Pacific is concerned has been the reintegration of economic and security policy, and the application of direct political leverage to achieve a range of interconnected economic and (especially) strategic goals. The privileging of strategic issues and the willingness to use direct pressure to ensure compliance with its goals may mean that – in the short term, at least – ensuring widespread ideational consensus and legitimacy is less important as far as the United States is concerned than is ensuring compliance.[11]

Across East Asia generally and Southeast Asia in particular, the George W. Bush administration has placed direct pressure on a number of governments to play an active part in the 'war on terror' (Lague, 2003; Beeson, 2004b). Unsurprisingly, Indonesia and the Philippines have been at the forefront of such efforts and, in a striking echo of the Cold War period, the United States has placed strengthening military ties ahead of other 'human security' issues (see, respectively, Donnan, 2003; Sheehan and Plott, 2001: 24). What is especially noteworthy about this evolving policy, however, has been the way the administration has used economic leverage to secure strategic goals. In Thailand, for example, the government of Thaksin Shinawatra has recently adopted a much more active anti-terror policy – something that is widely seen as being part of its push for a bilateral trade agreement with the United States (Crispin, 2003). Nor are such initiatives confined to the Southeast Asian corner of the Asia-Pacific: Australia has self-consciously wedded its high-profile support for, and participation in, American-led military activities to a concerted push for a bilateral free trade agreement (Beeson, 2003a). The very different attitude that the United States displays towards New Zealand, which has adopted a more independent position towards American security policy, confirms that the United States is self-consciously linking economic and strategic issues as part of its post-S11 approach to foreign policy (Hartcher, 2003: 23).

Thus, by accident or design, directly or indirectly, American power is inevitably shaping the strategic and economic architecture of the broadly conceived Asia-Pacific region. However, it is important to acknowledge that there are limits to American power, and that these are not confined to the Middle East. The United States' ability to influence North Korea's behaviour has plainly been limited, and any long-term resolution of the crisis on the peninsula will necessarily involve the cooperation of other countries, especially China (Johnston, 2004). Yet despite the limits to American influence, and the competing regional leadership claims of both China and Japan, American foreign policy may actually be inadvertently encouraging the development of a greater sense of East Asian, rather than Asia-Pacific, regional identity (Beeson, 2003b). In some ways, this is unsurprising: the inherent artificiality of the 'Asia-Pacific' has always meant that its status and ideational purchase were contested and uncertain. By contrast, the idea of 'East Asia', and the ASEAN Plus Three (APT) grouping, which gives political expression to it, can claim to be slightly more authentic expressions of broad underlying historical experiences in the region.[12]

One of the key determinants of APT's longevity and effectiveness is likely to hinge on its capacity to provide what Miles Kahler (this volume, Chapter 2) describes as 'insurance'. While US-led processes of 'globalisation' may have been associated with the economic crisis of the late 1990s, it is a moot point whether APT can provide mechanisms capable of insulating the region from destabilising, externally generated forces. Not only are there formidable technical obstacles in the way of monetary cooperation, for example, but Japan and China are plainly nervous about the open-ended nature of the commitment any such arrangements might imply (Ravenhill, 2002). On the one hand, therefore, American hegemony is encouraging greater regional cooperation as a defensive response to unwelcome intrusion and pressure. On the other hand, however, the nature of contemporary international economic processes and the pervasive role American power and values play in their management mean that it will be difficult for the countries of East Asia either to disengage from global structures or to create alternatives that are intrinsically more secure.

Whether there is sufficient political support and institutional capacity within the region to make the APT an important actor is unknowable at this stage, but the emergence of the APT should not surprise us: if the apparent decline of American hegemony in the 1980s and early 1990s was associated with a redistribution of power within the overall international system that encouraged more cooperative, multilateral forms of institutionalisation, it is to be expected that a resurgent, more assertive and unilateral United States should encourage a similar reconfiguration of the international order. Indeed, generations of realist international relations scholars have predicted precisely that: unipolarity *ought* to generate 'balancing' behaviour as states seek to counter American pre-eminence (see, for example, Waltz, 1993; Mearsheimer, 1994–1995). That it has not happened to any significant degree thus far would seem to be a consequence of the United States' pivotal role in the contemporary intentional system and a recognition that 'band-wagoning' may be more rational than balancing (Ikenberry, 1998), and that there are specific historical and material constraints in East Asia that make such behaviour either unlikely or ineffective (Beeson and Berger, 2003). Whether this strategic calculus will remain operative in the face of a fusion of American strategic and economic interests, and the single-minded pursuit of a more narrowly conceived national interest, remains to be seen.

Concluding remarks

The Pacific case suggests that there is an optimum power stratification for regime formation that falls away on either side; too much, as well as too little, hegemony may affect cooperation negatively.

(Crone, 1993: 525)

If Crone – and just about everyone else – was wrong about the way hegemony was going to develop, his conclusion about its possible importance still looks about right. Hegemony *does* still matter and decisively influences inter- and even intra-regional relations as a consequence; this is especially the case when most agree that the United States' lead in critical areas of hegemonic power and influence has actually expanded rather than contracted over the past decade. What is less clear is how American hegemony will affect the East Asian region in the longer term; whether it will revert to a more multilateral basis if and when the preoccupation with the 'war on terror' abates; and whether economic and military security will remain so intertwined. All of these questions are unknowable, of course, but by comparing past and contemporary patterns of hegemonic influence in the Asia-Pacific we can at least identify the factors that are likely to shape future outcomes.

In the short term, at least, the United States' reintegration of economic and military security issues looks likely to force compliance on the part of even the most powerful countries across the world. Even if East Asia – or Western Europe, for that matter – were united and had clear, widely supported regional responses to the multifaceted economic, political and strategic challenges American power inevitably throws up, there are plainly limits to any region's capacity to counter American power. In such circumstances, and given the current Bush administration's frequently doctrinaire predilection for the assertion of American power,[13] we might expect that US policy will continue to display a preference for unilateral rather than multilateral approaches to key issues. And yet one thing that emerges from even a brief review of the course of America's hegemonic influence is just how quickly things can change: already the limits of unilateralism and military adventurism are becoming apparent in Iraq, and the United States has begun to re-embrace multilateralism as a consequence (Reid, 2003: 11).

For all the hyperbole about American power, therefore, it has limits. As in the late 1980s and early 1990s, doubts remain about the strength of America's domestic economy and its long-term capacity to underwrite the United States' increasingly unilateral and militarised foreign policy. Whatever the limits to American power may be, though, for East Asia the short-term implications of the United States current policy stance are not auspicious: the United States is no longer constrained by the threat of defection by allies or client states that characterised the Cold War period, nor – to judge by the rise of bilateral preferential trade agreements – are American policymakers as wedded to the idea and normative importance of economic liberalism as they once were. While neoliberalism may not have ever achieved the ideational support or legitimacy in East Asia that American policymakers might have wished, the fact that the Americans themselves have moved away from it may be equally discomforting for East Asians if the United States uses its direct bilateral leverage to secure favourable deals.

Paradoxically, therefore, American policy may be actively undermining the foundations of its own hegemonic position. The United States' willingness and capacity to explicitly link economic and military security demonstrates just how pivotal hegemony remains. The principal insight that a comparative analysis of the evolution of American hegemony and its impact on the Asia-Pacific reveals is that we cannot assume that either an increase or a diminution in American power will affect the prevailing institutional and ideational order in predictable or inevitable ways. On the contrary, what recent events demonstrate is that American power may underwrite a liberal, multilaterally based order, or it may not. In other words, it is not a question so much of the *extent* of American hegemony, but of the purposes to which it is put.

While this will strike some as a remarkably trite observation, it is worth emphasising, nevertheless: much influential North American scholarship, and much of the debate about American hegemony and its impact on the world, has been predicated on the assumption that American power is ultimately a force for good and the indispensable basis for the creation of an open, liberal international order. Given the United States' historic willingness to flout the norms and values that constituted the very economic and strategic regimes it helped create, this was always a contestable contention. In the post-S11 era, it is increasingly looking like normatively inspired, remarkably uncritical, wishful thinking. We need to recognise that, as Crone pointed out just over a decade ago, too much hegemony can be potentially just as damaging to the prospects for international cooperation as too little.

Notes

Thanks to Bill Tow, Donald Crone and Hugo Radice for commenting on an earlier version of this paper. The usual caveats apply.

1 'East Asia' refers to the countries of Northeast Asia – Japan, Korea, China and Taiwan – plus the members of ASEAN.
2 A classic example can be observed in the transition from Keynesian to monetarist ideas in the 1970s. See Hall (1992).
3 For a discussion of 'benevolent' and coercive forms of leadership, see Snidal (1985: 588).
4 The great significance of the East Asian economic crisis was to create a situation in which the United States could try to force the sorts of reforms it had discursively championed to little effect. See Bello (1998).
5 This is especially the case given the United States' declared intention of acting 'pre-emptively' where it judges that to do so is in its interests. See White House (2002).
6 Although, as noted earlier, there are enduring doubts about the underlying strength of the American economy, especially as a consequence of the transformation in the overall budgetary position. See Eccleston and Dalton (2003: 6).
7 It was expected that trade barriers would be dismantled in the developed APEC economies by 2010, and in the rest by 2020.
8 In addition to APEC's voluntarist, consensually based decision-making style noted above, it lacks an effective secretariat to implement or devise policy.
9 On different ways of conceptualising historical change, see Tilly (1984: 61).
10 The Nixon government's decision to break the link between the value of the dollar and gold is a classic example of this possibility. See Gowa (1983).
11 In this context, Kaldor (2003) may be right to emphasise that the Bush doctrine will be unable to defeat terrorism decisively, but wrong to assume that the United States cannot compel allies and subordinate states to comply with the overall direction of American policy.
12 For a more detailed discussion of this point, see Stubbs (2002).

13 For an influential articulation of the case for a more assertive, unilateral US foreign policy, see Kagan (2003).

References

Ba, Alice D (2003) 'China and Asean: Renavigating Relations for a 21st-century Asia', *Asian Survey*, 43 (4): 622–647.

Bacevich, Andrew J. (2002) *American Empire: The Realities and Consequences of U.S. Diplomacy*, Cambridge, MA: Harvard University Press.

Barnett, M. N. and Finnemore, M. (1999) 'The Politics, Power, and Pathologies of International Organizations', *International Organization*, 53 (4): 699–732.

Beeson, Mark (2003a) 'Australia's Relationship with the United States: The Case for Greater Independence', *Australian Journal of Political Science*, 38 (3): 387–405.

—— (2003b) 'ASEAN Plus Three and the Rise of Reactionary Regionalism', *Contemporary Southeast Asia*, 25 (2): 251–268.

—— (2004a) 'The Rise and Fall (?) of the Developmental State: The Vicissitudes and Implications of East Asian Interventionism', in Linda Low (ed.) *Developmental States: Relevant, Redundant or Reconfigured?*, New York: Nova Science Publishers, pp. 29–40.

—— (2004b) 'US Hegemony and Southeast Asia: The Impact of, and Limits to, American Power and Influence', *Critical Asian Studies*, 36 (3): 323–354.

Beeson, Mark and Berger, Mark T. (2003) 'The Paradoxes of Paramountcy: Regional Rivalries and the Dynamics of American Hegemony in East Asia', *Global Change, Peace and Security*, 15 (1): 27–42.

Bello, W. (1998) 'East Asia: On the Eve of the Great Transformation?', *Review of International Political Economy*, 5 (3): 424–444.

Bhagwati, J. and Patrick, H. T. (eds) (1990) *Aggressive Unilateralism: America's Trade Policy and the World Trading System*, New York: Harvester Wheatsheaf.

Brenner, Robert (2002) *The Boom and the Bubble*, London: Verso.

Coates, D. (2000) *Models of Capitalism*, Oxford: Polity Press.

Cox, Robert W. (1981) 'Social Forces, States and World Orders: Beyond International Relations Theory', *Millennium*, 10 (2): 126–55

—— (1987) *Production, Power, and World Order: Social Forces in the Making of History*, New York: Columbia University Press.

Crispin, Shawn (2003) 'Targets of a New Anti-terror War', *Far Eastern Economic Review*, 10 July: 12–14.

Crone, Donald (1993) 'Does Hegemony Matter? The Reorganization of the Pacific Political Economy', *World Politics*, 45 (4): 501–525.

Cronin, James E. (1996) *The World the Cold War Made: Order, Chaos, and the Return of History*, London: Routledge.

Davis, Mark (2003) 'WTO: Little to Show for Lots of Talking', *Australian Financial Review*, 11 July: 16.

Deng, Yong (2001) 'Hegemon on the Offensive: Chinese perspectives on U.S. Global Strategy', *Political Science Quarterly*, 116 (3): 343–365.

Dent, Christopher M. (2003) 'Networking the Region? The Emergence and Impact of Asia-Pacific Bilateral Free Trade Agreement Projects', *The Pacific Review*, 16 (1): 1–28.

Deudney, Daniel and Ikenberry, G. John (1999) 'Realism, Structural Liberalism, and the Western Order', in Ethan B. Kapstein and Michael Mastanduno (eds) *Unipolar Politics: Realism and State Strategies after the Cold War*, New York: Columbia University Press, pp. 103–130.

Dirlik, A. (1992) 'The Asia-Pacific Idea: Reality and Representation in the Invention of Regional Structure', *Journal of World History*, 3 (1): 55–79.

Donnan, Shawn (2003) 'U.S. military funds for Jakarta prompt concern', *Financial Times*, online version, 24 January.

Eccleston, Roy and Dalton, Rodney (2003) 'War Cost Adds to Fiscal Pain for Bush', *The Australian*, 17 July: 6.

Emmott, Bill (2002) 'Present at the Creation: A Survey of America's Role in the World', *The Economist*, 29 June.

Fewsmith, J. (2001) 'The Political and Social Implications of China's Accession to the WTO', *China Quarterly*, 167: 573–591.

Garrett, B. (2001) 'China Faces, Debates, the Contradictions of Globalization', *Asian Survey*, 41 (3): 409–427.

Gill, Stephen (1995) 'Globalisation, market civilisation, and disciplinary neoliberalism', *Millennium*, 24 (3): 399–423.

Gowa, J. (1983) *Closing the Gold Window: Domestic Politics and the End of Bretton Woods*, Ithaca, NY: Cornell.

Grieco, Joseph M. (1999) 'Realism and Regionalism: American Power and German and Japanese Institutional Strategies during and after the Cold War', in E. B. Kapstein and Michael Mastanduno (eds) *Unipolar Politics: Realism and State Strategies after the Cold War*, New York: Columbia University Press, pp. 319–353.

Hall, P. (1992) 'The Movement from Keynesianism to Monetarism: Institutional Analysis and British Economic Policy in the 1970s', in Sven Steinmo, Kathleen Thelan and Frank Longstreth (eds) *Structuring Politics: Historical Institutionalism in Comparative Analysis*, Cambridge: Cambridge University Press, pp. 90–113.

Hara, K. (1999) 'Rethinking the "Cold War" in the Asia-Pacific', *Pacific Review*, 12 (4): 515–536.

Hartcher, Peter (2003) 'Stop Bluffing: For Bush It's Quid Pro Quo', *Australian Financial Review*, 19 July: 23.

Hemmer, Christopher and Katzenstein, Peter J. (2002) 'Why Is There No NATO in Asia? Collective Identity, Regionalism, and the Origins of Multilateralism', *International Organization*, 56 (3): 575–607.

Higgott, R. (1993) 'APEC – A Sceptical View', in A. Mack and J. Ravenhill (eds) *Pacific Cooperation: Building Economic and Security Regimes in the Asia-Pacific Region*, Sydney: Allen & Unwin, pp. 66–97.

Hsiao, Frank S. T., Hsiao, Mei-chu W. and Yamashita, Akio (2003) 'The Impact of the US Economy on the Asia-Pacific Region: Does It Matter?', *Journal of Asian Economics*, 14: 219–241.

Ikenberry, G. J. (1993) 'Creating Yesterday's New World Order: Keynesian "New Thinking" and the Anglo-American Postwar Settlement', in J. Goldstein and R. Keohane (eds) *Ideas and Foreign Policy: Beliefs, Institutions, and Political Change*, Ithaca, NY: Cornell University Press, pp. 57–86.

—— (1998) 'Institutions, Strategic Restraint, and the Persistence of the American Postwar Order', *International Security*, 23 (3): 43–78.

—— (2001) 'American Power and the Empire of Capitalist Democracy', *Review of International Studies*, 27: 191–212.

Joffe, J. (2002) 'Defying History and Theory: The United States as "the Last Remaining Superpower"', in G. J. Ikenberry (ed.) *America Unrivaled: The Future of the Balance of Power*, Ithaca, NY: Cornell University Press, pp. 155–180.

Johnston, Alastair I. (2004) 'Beijing's Security Behaviour in the Asia-Pacific', in J. J. Suh,

P. J. Katzenstein and Allen Carlson (eds) *Rethinking Security in East Asia: Identity, Power, and Efficiency*, Stanford, CA: Stanford University Press, pp. 34–96.

Kagan, Robert (2003) *Of Paradise and Power: America and Europe in the New World Order*, New York: Knopf.

Kaldor, Mary (2003) 'American Power: From "Compellance" to Cosmopolitanism?', *International Affairs*, 79: 1–22.

Kennedy, Paul (1988) *The Rise and Fall of Great Powers: Economic Change and Military Conflict from 1500 to 2000*, London: Fontana.

Keohane, Robert O. (1982) 'The Demand for International Regimes', *International Organization*, 36 (2): 325–355.

—— (1984) *After Hegemony: Cooperation and Discord in the World Political Economy*, Princeton, NJ: Princeton University Press.

Lague, David (2003) 'Uncle Sam Wants You', *Far Eastern Economic Review*, July: 14–18.

Lincoln, Edward J. (1999) *Troubled Times: U.S.–Japan Trade Relations in the 1990s*, Washington, DC: Brookings Institution.

Luttwak, Edward (1990) 'From Geopolitics to Geo-economics', *The National Interest*, Summer: 17–23.

Mastanduno, Michael (1998) 'Economics and Security Statecraft and Scholarship', *International Organization*, 52 (4): 825–854.

Mearsheimer, J. J. (1994–1995) 'The False Promise of Institutions', *International Security*, 19 (3): 5–49.

Pauly, L. W. (1997) *Who Elected the Bankers? Surveillance and Control in the World Economy*, Ithaca, NY: Cornell.

Prestowitz, Clyde (2003) *Rogue Nation: American Unilateralism and the Failure of Good Intentions*, New York: Basic Books.

Purdum, Todd and Sanger, David (2002) '2 top officials offer stern talk on U.S. policy', *The New York Times*, 2 February, Online version.

Ravenhill, J. (2002) 'A Three Bloc World? The New East Asian Regionalism', *International Relations of the Asia Pacific*, 2: 167–195.

—— (2003) 'The New Bilateralism in the Asia Pacific', *Third World Quarterly*, 24 (2): 299–317.

Reid, Tim (2003) 'Washington Tries to Put Iraq under UN Mandate', *The Weekend Australian*, 19–20 July: 11.

Rhodes, Edward (2003) 'The Imperial Logic of Bush's Liberal Agenda', *Survival*, 45 (1): 131–154.

Rosenau, James (1992) 'Governance, Order, and Change in World Politics', in J. N. Rosenau and E.-O. Czempiel (eds) *Governance without Government: Order and Change in World Politics*, Cambridge: Cambridge University Press, pp. 1–29.

Ruggie, J. G. (1992) 'Multilateralism: The Anatomy of an Institution', *International Organization*, 46 (3): 561–598.

Shanahan, Dennis (2002) 'Japan Free Trade Thrust to Foil China', *The Australian*, 2 May: 2.

Sheehan, Deidre and Plott, David (2001) 'A War Grows', *Far Eastern Economic Review*, 11 October: 24.

Snidal, Duncan (1985) 'The Limits of Hegemonic Stability Theory', *International Organization*, 39 (4): 579–614.

Strange, Susan (1987) 'The Persistent Myth of Lost Hegemony', *International Organisation*, 41 (4): 551–574.

—— (1988) *States and Markets*, New York: Pinter.

—— (1997) 'The Future of Global Capitalism; or, Will Divergence Persist Forever?', in C. Crouch and W. Streeck (eds) *Political Economy of Modern Capitalism: Mapping Convergence and Diversity*, London: Sage, pp. 183–191.

Stubbs, Richard (2002) 'ASEAN Plus Three: Emerging East Asian Regionalism?', *Asian Survey*, 42 (3),: 440–455.

Tilly, Charles (1984) *Big Structures, Large Processes, Huge Comparisons*, New York: Russell Sage Foundation.

Vatikiotis, Michael and Hiebert, Murray (2003) 'China's Tight Embrace', *Far Eastern Economic Review*, 17 July: 28–30.

Wall, David (2002) 'Koizumi Trade Pitch Misses', *The Japan Times*, 21 April, online version.

Waltz, K. N. (1993) 'The Emerging Structure of International Politics', *International Security*, 18 (2): 44–79.

White House (2002) *The National Security Strategy of the United States of America*, Washington, DC.

11 Track 1/Track 2 symbiosis in Asia-Pacific regionalism

Charles E. Morrison

Introduction

This chapter is addressed to the topic of how Track 2 international policy networks contribute to economic security. There are at least three prior questions. The first concerns the meaning and measurement of economic security. For example, do lower trade barriers and enhanced direct investment flows contribute to economic security? Many would argue that they do, more definitely in the longer term, by increasing the efficiency of production, widening consumer choices, and raising aggregate income levels. But others are less sure, or even argue to the contrary, pointing to short-term adjustment problems or the dangers of longer-term exploitation. Without dismissing the legitimacy and importance of this question, this chapter accepts a neoclassical economic view that trade and capital liberalization, when combined with measures to facilitate adjustments for industries, firms and individuals, improves economic security.

A second threshold question is whether 'Track 1', or intergovernmental, regional processes significantly enhance economic liberalization or otherwise contribute to the economic welfare of the people of the region. How different would the economic prosperity and security of the region be if there were no ASEAN, APEC (Asia-Pacific Economic Cooperation forum), ASEM (Asia-Europe Meeting) or ASEAN Plus Three processes, for example? In the early and mid-1990s, there were high hopes for regional processes as new drivers of trade and investment liberalization. But much of the regional cooperation 'bubble' burst with the 1997–1998 Asian economic crisis. APEC, for example, has difficulty in showing what it has achieved in trade liberalization above the substantial liberalization already occurring as the result of the Uruguay Round of GATT/WTO negotiations ('WTO Plus').

Again, this question is largely beyond the scope of this chapter. For the purpose of this discussion, I assume that regional institutions make at least a marginal difference, but I believe that both national policy and global institutions have been more important in economic development than the regional institutions noted in the previous paragraph. We assume, therefore, that Track 2 may contribute to economic security if it strengthens Track 1. But it may also contribute to economic security by encouraging national economic and social changes as well as regional and global processes. We also assume that Track 2 efforts that reduce tensions between countries provide a supportive environment for economic activity and security.

A third preliminary question concerns the meaning of 'Track 2.' The use of the term 'track' is inconsistent in the specialist and popular literature,[1] and even within a single definition, the boundaries of different 'tracks' are sometimes quite fuzzy. For the purpose of this project, Track 1 refers to intergovernmental processes, Track 2 to parallel policy-relevant activity by international policy networks with significant access to governments, even at times through formal channels such as the Pacific Economic Cooperation Council's (PECC's) observer status in APEC.[2] Track 2 networks consist of institutions and individuals who have generally close relationships with governments. The vast majority of Track 2 participants share the objectives of the Track 1 processes or at least those of their own government or a part of their own government (such as the foreign ministry). Many individuals in Track 2 processes have served in government itself or as government advisers. In the United States, where a 'revolving door' has operated for years between the government and the Washington-oriented think tanks, many of the Track 2 participants are either former government officials or officials-in-waiting. In Asia, there may be less rotation in and out of government, but the government/ nongovernmental roles are often less distinct. The same individual might be the head of an independent or quasi-independent research organization, an influential 'talking head' and writer of opinion articles, an adviser to a ministry, and a speech-writer for the prime minister. Many of the policy institutes are also dependent upon government funding or on private funding that values access to government. Some, like the Japan Institute for International Affairs, the Korea Institute of International Economic Policy, or Vietnam's Institute of International Relations, are fully governmental entities, although outside the bureaucracy proper.[3] Like Track 1, Track 2 institutes and policy networks generally argue that they are serving a broad, undifferentiated public good rather than acting on behalf of a specific industrial sector or interest group.

In contrast, Track 3 nongovernmental groups typically have less association with governments and are more likely to differ with government not just on approaches, but also on basic objectives. Track 3 participants also argue that they are promoting a public good, but often they are advocacy groups catering to a narrower con-stituency. Most do not hesitate to identify this constituency, be it women, specific trade associations, or environmental interests.

Some international networks do not clearly fall in one track or another. For example, governments created the 1991–1993 APEC Eminent Persons Group and the APEC Business Advisory Council (ABAC), chose the members, and gave them specific mandates to provide input into the intergovernmental APEC process. As both groups made independent recommendations, we regard them as Track 2 institutions, feeding directly into the governments.[4] A larger business group, the Pacific Basin Economic Council (PBEC), does not have a seat at the APEC table like either PECC or ABAC, but strives to be 'an independent voice of business.' As a Track 2 institution, it may thus be a little closer to Track 3 than to Track 1, feeding in views from a constituency rather than seeking to complement or substitute for the intergovernmental process. Many Track 2 institutions uncomfortably balance a desire for independence from government against their need for government financial resources and their interest in influencing government policies.

The Track 1–Track 2 symbiosis

Since the mid-1960s, countries in Asia and the Pacific have engaged in various forms of regional cooperation. Track 2 international policy networks started at about the same time and progressed hand in hand with Track 1. By the 1990s, in both the regional economic and the security cooperation processes, the two tracks had become deeply and symbiotically interconnected, so much so that the distinction between them is often blurred. Track 1 cooperation simply would never have developed as it did without the ideas and the consensus- and support-building activities of Track 2. Track 2 would have been a sterile exercise but for its impact on Track 1. In fact, almost by definition Track 2 cannot exist without a Track 1. However, despite the symbiosis between Tracks 1 and 2, there are often tensions in the relationships. While in some ways Track 1 gives Track 2 continuing life, in other ways it sucks resources and attention away, leaving little space for truly independent Track 2 processes. Track 2 provides Track 1 with valuable intellectual resources, but it can also crowd Track 1, demanding a pace of action that is difficult for Track 1 to deliver and then criticizing the results. Track 1 also protects its prerogatives as the official relationship among governments. As Barry Desker has noted, a stronger relationship between the two tracks would require 'a change of attitude in many official establishments' (2003: 355).

The chart in the Appendix maps some regional and global organizations and policy networks along four different dimensions. One concerns the track – governmental or nongovernment. A second dimension is the geographical scope of cooperation (subregional, regional, global), and the third the functional scope – whether for a specific purpose or sector or more general economic or even economic and political cooperation. Finally, the date of the creation of each activity indicates the temporal dimension.

As indicated by proximity on the chart, general regional economic and political cooperation is almost always associated with a second track activity: ASEAN with the ASEAN-Institutes of Strategic and International Studies (ASEAN-ISIS), APEC with PECC, ASEM with the Council for Asia–Europe Cooperation (CAEC), and the ASEAN Regional Forum (ARF) with the Council for Security Cooperation in the Asia Pacific (CSCAP). In some instances, notably ASEAN, the intergovernmental cooperation came first, but in other cases, most notably that of APEC, Track 2 led the way to intergovernmental cooperation. In all cases, it can be argued that intergovernmental cooperation has been significantly deepened and strengthened through its interaction with Track 2. It has become almost *de rigueur* that every Track 1 should have a corresponding Track 2. Hence, with ASEAN Plus Three (or the East Asian group), which so far lacks a clear Track 2 analogue, it is only a matter of time before a Track 2 group is established, through either self-designation by appropriate institutions or appointment by Track 1.

Why Track 2?

Why has Track 2 become so essential in regional economic policymaking and diplomacy? What does it offer that could not be done by Track 1 itself? This may seem puzzling in that many Asian governments have been reluctant to share policymaking in the domestic context with organizations from outside government. Moreover, government officials are often skeptical or even disdainful of Track 2, which they often see as full of 'wannabes' or 'has-beens' seeking to play intergovernmental roles themselves and dispensing unsolicited advice. Because of their independent roles and media visibility, Track 2 personalities can often jump protocol hurdles to have direct influence on Track 1 or affect the political environment around Track 1, again to the annoyance of officials. Perhaps the most striking example came when C. Fred Bergsten, chair of the APEC Eminent Persons Group, persuaded President Soeharto in 1994 to support free trade and investment in the region as an APEC goal, thus reversing an established position of the Indonesian bureaucracy. But despite the annoyances, Track 2 is often (although not necessarily) valuable to governments, even those not noted for providing much space for nongovernmental groups.

Perhaps most importantly, Track 2 constitutes the most reliable support group outside the government proper for Track 1 processes. To be sustained, government processes need appreciative audiences that help establish and maintain a positive value for regional cooperation, and reward politicians and policymakers for their efforts. In many areas of foreign policy, these audiences are very small despite the relatively significant media attention paid to these issues. Aside from small and often inconsistent support from large businesses, international policy networks provide a significant source of encouragement and reinforcement for Track 1 processes.

Second, Track 2 provides a source of innovation and ideas that is difficult to achieve through the bureaucracy. Particularly at the leader and ministerial levels, Track 1 has a tremendous need for new concepts, mainly because it is politically driven. Politicians themselves may initiate the ideas, but more frequently than not they are consumers looking for inputs from the private sector. And even when the politicians are the initiators, they need Track 2 to flesh out, repackage, and legitimize their ideas. Probably no part of the private sector is more attuned to generating foreign policy ideas than the Track 2 international policy institutions and networks. These, in fact, have an entirely complementary interest with political leaders in pushing forward new ideas. With some exceptions, where Track 2 is an artificial creation of government-dominated systems to provide analogues for Track 2 in other countries (such as North Korea's Institute of Peace and Disarmament), Track 2 lives off its ability to bring big ideas into the policy process. As in the case of leaders, some of this may be ego driven, but it is also a matter of funding. Track 2 participants also sometimes find that their ideas gain more visibility and weight through Track 2 than if they were at similar levels in Track 1.

The essence of the Track 1–Track 2 symbiosis consists of Track 2 policy and institutional entrepreneurs seeking Track 1 'champions', and Track 1 policy entrepreneurs seeking Track 2 'validators' and allies. While much of this symbiosis occurs within a national context, there are also transnational alliances. In Singapore's case within ASEAN, for example, it is not just Singaporean leaders who want to inject ideas into regional processes, but also the Singaporean bureaucracy. The Singaporean bureaucracy often finds that projection through an international policy network provides both a preliminary testing ground and a regionally more acceptable projection vehicle.[5] This leads Singaporean government officials into alliances with Track 2 policy institutes based in neighboring countries, with which viewpoints may be more readily shared than with Track 1 counterparts.

Track 2 not only is a useful innovator of ideas in the first instance, but often serves as a 'test bed' for such ideas among government-surrogates. This is particularly important for sensitive security topics. A Track 2 precursor to the six-party talks on North Korea held in August 2003, for example, took place in March several months earlier under the guise of the Northeast Asia Cooperation Dialogue, a Track 2 process only a stone's throw away from Track 1. Another such Track 2 was the Canadian-sponsored and Indonesian-chaired Workshop Series on Managing Potential Conflicts in the South China Sea. Carolina Hernandez has gone a step farther, suggesting that the ASEAN-ISIS group could prepare the way for harmonization of ASEAN foreign and security policies on such issues as the Spratlys, hardly a task that Track 1 is prepared to address, but one which it could tolerate (Hernandez, 2000: 121).

Track 2 seems to have played a highly unusual role in the development and work program of the ASEAN Regional Forum (ARF). The ARF concept emerged with the ASEAN-ISIS group in 1991. At its second meeting in Brunei in August 1995, the ARF considered and adopted much of a concept paper that had been prepared in an interactive Track 1/Track 2 processes. The chair's closing statement, representing a consensus among the governments, explicitly acknowledged that 'the ARF process would move along two tracks' – one carried out by governments and the other by 'strategic institutes and relevant non-governmental organizations to which all ARF participants should be eligible'. The ARF chair would serve as a link.[6] Subsequent annual statements of the ARF chair took note of the Track 2 activities, some of which have been carried out by national or small groups of national institutes and others by CSCAP. In a number of areas, particularly confidence-building measures and preventive diplomacy, Track 2 pioneered the way, allowing government officials to become more familiar with the concepts and the processes in informal, noncommittal sessions. As Ralph Cossa (1998) has noted,

> the preventive diplomacy effort provides a working example of how Tracks 1 and 2 complement each other – the ARF ministers at the Track 1 level first identifying preventive diplomacy as a potential future role of the ARF and then calling for an independent Track 2 assessment as to how to bring this about. Track 2 participants, not being bound by current government positions, have the license to pursue more innovative and forward-leaning approaches and solutions.

Third, aside from innovation and flexibility, Track 2 provides sources of expertise and institutional memories beyond those available to Track 1. Government officials are rarely in a position to carry out the analysis needed for projects, and this is even truer in the case of intergovernmental Asia-Pacific organizations. Unlike in the Organization for Economic Co-operation and Development (OECD), the UN system, or the European Union, there is virtually no Asia-Pacific regional in-house research capability.[7] ASEAN, founded several years before ASEAN-ISIS, suffered for several years from an acute shortage of intellectual resources from which to generate and carry through projects, its first initiatives in the trade policy area coming only with UN help.[8] Although it is the most comprehensive Asia-Pacific economic cooperation organization, APEC has deliberately limited itself to only a modest secretariat in Singapore, primarily tasked to arrange meetings, handle publications and public relations, negotiate contracts, and maintain archives. For serious analytical work, APEC must rely on contracted or voluntary resources from the outside. Moreover, while Track 1 officials rotate in their positions, Track 2 participants typically remain committed to their institutions and activities for long periods of time, thus reinforcing their relative position as sources of expertise and becoming the institutional memory of many Track 1 activities.

Given the sensitivities of the governments of APEC member economies, the regional PECC and APEC Study Center networks are in much better positions to supply these resources than national institutions. For this reason, after the Bogor vision of 'free trade and investment in the region' was adopted and APEC officials began to map existing trade barriers, they turned to PECC to conduct the study. Although the PECC work for APEC included individuals from both developing and developed economies in leading positions, they all shared a commitment to freer trade. Frustrated by the governmental constraints (at first the officials did not want the barriers to be identified with particular governments), the pressure from PECC to expand the envelope, and the development of trust between the scholars involved on the PECC side and the officials on the APEC side, the PECC contributions gradually became more robust and more valuable to APEC. In the case of services trade, for example, PECC played a dominant role for two or three years in APEC, building basic understanding of the economic, technical, and legal issues involved.

By traditional international organizational standards, APEC is open and participatory, with an informative website, public documents, and a relatively high degree of nongovernmental involvement in the activities of some of its working groups. Apart from the more quasi-official Track 2 processes described later in this chapter, the APEC committees have spawned hundred of projects involving small networks of committed individuals, some of them mixes of government officials and specialists outside the government. Some APEC forums have been even been led by nongovernmental personnel – for example, the Business Management Network in the APEC Human Resource Development Working Group. Since APEC itself has only very limited funding, these projects are often supported by national funds based on the APEC endorsement. The networks around such projects are multinational, but they may have only hazy notions of the larger APEC processes, their commitments being to their own specific project.

Fourth, as the preceding discussion implies, Track 2's most important longer-term role may be a transformational one, helping Track 1 procedures become stylistically and procedurally a little more like Track 2 itself. Over time, at least at the level of senior officials and above, Track 1 is becoming less patient with traditional protocol and formalities. This is reflected in a current debate within APEC about how the organization might be streamlined, with much more time given to leaders and ministers for informal discussion and a reversal of procedures that currently favor bottom-up rather than top-down agenda setting. It is perhaps an exaggeration to suggest that this has that much to do with Track 2, but in fact most APEC senior officials have significant exposure to the more informal Track 2 procedures. One suspects that officials' participation in Track 2 and mixed Track 1/Track 2 procedures, particularly in the case of the newer ASEAN members and the transitional economies, has helped attune them to a more informal style of interaction and exploration of ideas.

Asia-Pacific Track 2 networks

Track 2 exists in a bewildering array of forms. Some activities are *ad hoc* one-time events, and some 'international policy networks' are more among individuals than among institutions, particularly those focused around discrete projects. This chapter concentrates on the sustained activities supported by networks of institutional actors as most likely to have a longer-term impact on regional institution-building and economic security. In this section, we examine some of the more prominent of these networks.

The Pacific Trade and Development Conference (PAFTAD)

PAFTAD started as an almost purely academic professional network, and since it has remained so, it should be regarded more as a professional than a policy network. However, because PAFTAD played a significant role in incubating what eventually became the intergovernmental APEC organization, it is useful to consider it here. In the 1960s, the concept of a Pacific freer trade and development organization originated with Professor Kiyoshi Kojima, a trade economist at Hitotsubashi University.[9] Kojima's ideas received intellectual and some political support in Australia, the United States and elsewhere. Among those attracted were the foreign minister, later prime minister, Takeo Miki, who made the concept the centerpiece of several foreign policy speeches in the late 1960s. Another prominent Japanese advocate was Saburo Okita, the head of the Japan Economic Research Center, who served as an adviser to a later prime minister, Masayoshi Ohira, and was briefly foreign minister. PAFTAD was formally launched in 1968 with support from the Japanese government as a venue for consideration of Kojima's proposal. But the concept did not fall on truly fertile ground until 1979, when two PAFTAD members, Peter Drysdale of Australia and Hugh Patrick of the United States, were commissioned by the US Senate Foreign Relations Committee to make a policy-oriented report on the prospects for institutionalized regional economic cooperation

(Woods, 1993: 59). The Drysdale–Patrick report precipitated a renewed interest in the concept in Australia, the United States, and Japan (largely through the influence of Okita). It led to an Australian–Japanese meeting to which government officials as well as interested academic and business community leaders were invited to discuss the possibilities for a governmental organization. The meeting was a partial failure in the sense that it did not immediately result in movement toward the proposed regional governmental organization, owing to skepticism in some ASEAN countries, but it did lead to the establishment of the Pacific Economic Cooperation Conference, which was the more direct progenitor of APEC, as described in what follows.

The PAFTAD network continues to hold periodic academic meetings, focused around important economic issues. It continues to be an important intellectual network, having more substantive depth than the later, more policy-oriented networks such as PECC. However, PAFTAD's influence is indirect, mediated through the individual standing of its own members and through the filtering of information, analysis, and ideas into other networks with a more direct access to governments. For example, a number of PAFTAD habitués became members of APEC's Eminent Persons Group, known mostly for suggesting that 'free trade and investment' be the primary goal of APEC.

The Pacific Basin Economic Council and the APEC Business Advisory Council

Like PAFTAD, the Pacific Basin Economic Council (PBEC) dates from the mid-1960s, the creation of American and Japan businesspersons who saw it as a venue for business leaders to meet, exchange views, and do business on the side. Some of these leaders, notably Noboru Gotoh, were also very interested in the Pacific community concept and promoted it through PBEC and their involvement in the later PECC.

Developed from a bilateral Japanese–Australian business network, PBEC originally was confined to the more developed economies of the region: Australia, Canada, Japan, New Zealand, and the United States. As the regional economy grew, PBEC also expanded, with South Korea and Taiwan becoming particularly active. The organization, however, hardly qualified as a 'policy network,' since it lacked analytical capacity or interest (despite being housed at the Stanford Research Institute in its earlier years). The interest in policy issues evolved gradually from the 1970s onward. Once APEC was created in 1989, PBEC members became more interested in how they could more directly influence policymakers. By the early 1990s, the organization had styled itself 'the voice of business,' established a separate secretariat (first in San Francisco, later in Honolulu), raised a small capital fund (mainly from Taiwanese and Korean sources), sought to develop more active subcommittees, and issued reports. PBEC also sought a 'seat' or observer status at the APEC table, analogous to PECC's. In this it failed, as the business community was already represented through the tripartite PECC and as APEC later created its own business advisory council, the APEC Business Advisory Council (ABAC).

PBEC has undergone periodic crises of relevance throughout its history. In the middle 1990s, it had some 1,000 business members, including many small business-people, organized in chapters around the region, including Latin American Pacific countries. However, it began to decline in the later 1990s and is currently facing another identity and funding crisis. Some chapters have become inactive, partici-pation in meetings has dropped, and with meeting revenues failing to match current expenses, PBEC has been forced to borrow against its special fund for its operating expenses. While some members want to continue the traditional business conference format, others are looking for rejuvenation through a more clear-cut policy role, perhaps by cooperating or combining with PECC and/or the ABAC and by formats permitting more targeted approaches to political leaders by the members who contribute the most.

While PBEC participants often cite idiosyncratic reasons, such as tactical mistakes or personalities, for the association's current problems, broader, more fun-damental factors are probably more important. First, PBEC may have expanded its footprint too rapidly, particularly in Latin America, in the process losing some of its identity. One reaction has been to start new, more exclusive business groups with sharper geographical focus. Second, there were an increasing number of business conferences in Asia, including incursions by the Davos-based World Economic Forum. Third, the creation of ABAC provided an influential and very time-consuming venue for PBEC's most dedicated Asia-Pacific regionalists or potential members. These now had direct access to government leaders through the ABAC, making PBEC less important to them. It also appeared duplicative, raising questions among business leaders as to why they should support both PBEC and ABAC.

The APEC leaders established ABAC in November 1995. Probably seeking more a business constituency rather than business counsel, the governments agreed that each would designate three representatives to ABAC. ABAC would meet several times a year, make annual reports to the APEC leaders and ministers and issue periodic statements on issues of topical concern.[10] ABAC also typically joins the host government's chamber of commerce or other national business institutions at a 'CEO summit' at the time of the APEC leaders' meeting. ABAC is supported by secretariats, including an international secretariat in Manila and national organizations based in government institutions or nongovernment business organizations, which have been active in developing the group's reports. The reports cover a broad range of topics, including such items as global trade and investment, corporate governance and transparency, regulatory frameworks, labor movements, e-commerce, and cargo security.

However, there is little evidence that the network, as a group, has had much independent influence on policy.[11] A significant problem lies in the different percep-tions of government and business interests. Perhaps stirred by an APEC slogan dating from the 1996 leaders' meeting in Manila ('APEC Means Business') and the lack of similar APEC-sponsored advisory groups for other social segments, the business leaders expect the governments to privilege and be responsive to their interests. However, from the governments' point of view, business is only one constituency (albeit a very important one) and the expectations of the business community need to be considered against a broader set of political interests. Moreover, being a voluntary rather than a negotiating entity, APEC is simply not well structured to meet business expectations. Even when accepted by APEC, most of the recommendations must be implemented through national action or other, negotiating entities.

The Pacific Economic Cooperation Council

PECC is probably the region's most influential Track 2 policy network. However, it suffers from a lack of clarity as to its mission and from domination by projects, some policy-relevant and others less so, that seem to have acquired an almost permanent home in the organization. PECC traces its origin back to the Australian–Japanese-sponsored Canberra conference of 1980. Even after the 'failure' of that meeting, some of the more influential participants from business and academia determined to continue the conference series (PECC was then called the Pacific Economic Cooperation Conference) with the explicit purpose of fostering inter-governmental cooperation. From its beginnings, PECC was 'tripartite,' standing for academia, business, and governmental members acting in their personal capacities. This formula allowed PECC to acquire significant resources from government and government-related institutes as well as from business. Evolving an elaborate network of working groups, PECC made explicit policy recommendations to the governments, including recommendations for 'open regionalism.'

Until 1989, there was no intergovernmental process to deal with the recommendations, so PECC's primary policy role was to act as a kind of quasi-governmental regional organization in place of a real one. PECC kept alive the idea of inter-governmental cooperation until such time as the governments were ready to move. Therefore, the establishment of APEC in 1989 was the crowning achievement of PECC. But it also called into question PECC's future role and rationale. A provision in APEC that PECC (as well as the governmental ASEAN and Pacific Island Forum) should have observer status in the new APEC appeared to provide the continuing rationale. Although PECC had achieved its mission, it would have a continuing role as a kibitzer and helper in the APEC process, as outlined here. Many in PECC, however, aspire to a broader regional role beyond APEC and argue that PECC should have an independently determined agenda.

The way forward for PECC as an organization is not very clear. There is a small, independent secretariat in Singapore as well as committees in the various PECC economies. The secretariat derives virtually all its funds from member dues, and the large majority of these have ultimately come from government sources. Following the creation of APEC, these funds generally came from the same budgets that fund the Track 1 activities. Governments might well ask why they should provide general funds for PECC when PECC support can be contracted out on an 'as-needed' basis. But without a general base of support, PECC may not continue to be there when APEC needs it. Moreover, some in PECC complain that the governments pick up for themselves any areas in which PECC may have developed an interesting and promising agenda, in the process diverting intellectual resources and funding to the intergovernment activity and starving PECC of independent work.

The lack of a regular source of funding beyond nationally generated resources gives rise to another PECC problem: the proliferation as 'PECC activities' projects that are based in one or another national economy but which are not very related to government agendas. In an effort to contain this, PECC rationalized its structure in 2001, establishing a set of core activities in the areas of trade, finance, and community building. However, since the groups in all areas are basically self-financed, there is little organizational discipline over them. They are in essence supply rather than demand driven and therefore often of little interest at the higher levels of APEC. PECC is currently grappling with this question as it seeks to develop a role as the analytical base of APEC.

APEC Study Centers

The APEC Study Centers (ASC) were established pursuant to an American initiative proposed at the first leaders' meeting in Blake Island in 1993. The stated purpose was to harness the resources of higher education and advanced research groups for the APEC process. However, the network appears to have had its origin in the political imperative of White House initiatives, since there was no known advance process of deliberation and study. In fact, there was considerable confusion afterwards as to what functions APEC Study Centers were to fulfill. Taiwan, for example, at first designated vocational education institutions as APEC Study Centers before reversing course and housing the APEC Study Center with the Taiwan Institute of Economic Research. The United States itself initially convened a group of university-based Agency for International Development (AID) contractors, although in time its ASC network became dominated by international trade economists already connected with PECC and PAFTAD. Although the ASC had its origins in a US proposal, the US government was the only one not to provide some government subsidy to its centers. For the most part, the APEC Study Center network simply added more confusion to the webs of non- and quasi-governmental research and educational institutions associated with the regional economic cooperation processes. For some fortunate scholars, it has provided a source of government funding for trade and economic development work or an institutional platform for participation in the broader APEC processes.

In some cases, the APEC Study Centers did provide a tool for broadening intellectual awareness of the APEC process. In Japan, the lead institution was the Institute of Developing Economies, whose then director, Ippei Yamazawa, was already well connected to the APEC process as a leading participant in the PAFTAD, the PECC, and the former APEC Eminent Persons Group. However, APEC Study Center money was also distributed to a number of national universities in Japan, generally supporting academic publications in the Asian study field. Most of these had no connection to the APEC process itself, but ASC designation may have contributed to awareness of APEC in the academic community. In the

United States, Richard Feinberg, a University of California – San Diego professor with a government policy background, used the APEC Study Center at his institution to develop a project – APEC International Assessment Network (APIAN) – and network to monitor compliance with the Bogor goals. This project could have just as easily been associated with PECC (indeed, many of its participants were also prominent in PECC), but, almost by chance, Feinberg's base was an APEC Study Center. The project eventually turned to the APEC mission and organization. Since the government officials themselves were mulling these issues over, it has become very timely, and may have some significant policy influence.

ASEAN-ISIS

Most of the networks discussed in this chapter have either an economic or a political-security orientation. The ASEAN-ISIS network of Southeast Asian think tanks is an exception, working closely with both ASEAN and the ARF. The ASEAN-ISIS institutes also participate in the larger networks such as CSCAP and CAEC. In the Indonesian and Malaysian cases, the ASEAN-ISIS organizations also lead the two countries' PECC committees. Because ASEAN-ISIS is well organized and has exceptional experienced leadership, Southeast Asia is more effective in the international policy networks than its collective economic size might suggest.

As a network, ASEAN-ISIS dates from 1984, although its charter was not adopted until 1988 (Hernandez, 1993: 1–3). The core institutions are Indonesia's Center for Strategic and International Studies, Malaysia's Institute of Strategic and International Studies, and the Institute of Security and International Studies at Chulalongkorn University, Thailand. Other institutions were created in the university sector (as in the Philippines), as a nongovernmental organization (NGO) (Cambodia), or designated or created in the foreign ministries (Brunei, Vietnam, Myanmar, and Laos) to fill out the network as ASEAN itself expanded. The establishment of the network not only promoted cooperation among the institutes themselves, but also allows the member institutes to relate more effectively to the expanded ASEAN secretariat. ASEAN-ISIS has regular briefings with ASEAN senior officials and regularly sends memoranda on ASEAN issues. It has been particularly effective in influencing ASEAN's institutional development, including its expansion from six to ten members and, as seen in the next subsection, the creation of the ASEAN Regional Forum.

The Council for Security Cooperation in the Asia Pacific

Turning from the economically oriented activities to Asia-Pacific security activities, the principal mechanism for Track 1 consultations is the ASEAN Regional Forum. As I have noted, the ARF originated in an ASEAN-ISIS memorandum, but the ASEAN-ISIS group had asked a Japanese official sitting in its meeting, Yukio Satoh, to seek the support of the Japanese government. Satoh did his job so well that the idea was prematurely injected into a speech by the Japanese foreign minister, Taro Nakayama, prior to its review and adoption by the ASEAN leaders, but despite this hiccup the way was already prepared. Some governments were initially quite skeptical (this included the United States and China), but they were not in a position to resist, given the strong and united ASEAN initiative.

Because the ARF has become much more than an ASEAN organization, the ASEAN-ISIS group not only continues its own relationship with ARF but also works through the larger CSCAP, which it played an intimate role in creating and which includes policy institutes from most of the ARF member countries. CSCAP grew out of a series of conferences on regional security issues in the early 1990s and was formally launched in 1993 as the security analogue to PECC. It developed working groups on comprehensive security, maritime security, and confidence-building measures as well as the North Pacific dialogue referred to earlier. A study group on transnational crime has dealt with some significant economic security issues and is one of the principal vehicles through which CSCAP is broadening its reach into counterterrorism. The manner in which CSCAP has been integrated into the ARF process has already been described.

The Council for Asia–Europe Cooperation

The Council for Asia–Europe Cooperation (CAEC) was established in 1996 by policy institutes that sought to play a role in influencing the Europe–Asia Meeting (ASEM). In this case, the initiative came from the Japanese Ministry of Foreign Affairs, which inserted a recommendation for intellectual collaboration in a speech by Prime Minister Hashimoto. The ministry provided most of the budget, but turned to a nongovernmental policy institute, the Japanese Center for International Exchange (JCIE), to handle the program. The London-based International Institute for Strategic Studies (IISS) was designated as the European secretariat, later to be replaced by the Center for Asia-Pacific Studies at the University of Trier.

CAEC failed to be recognized in any official sense as ASEM's Track 2 policy network, as it was plagued from the beginning by a membership problem. The Japanese and many others wanted to include Australian and New Zealand members in their network, but some Asian governments (notably those of Malaysia and China) were adamantly opposed, saying that Australia and New Zealand were not Asian and fearing that a deeper intergovernmental embrace of the Track 2 group would create an expectation that they were to eventually join the Track 1 meeting as 'Asian' members. However, ASEM has not tried to create a competing network. Instead, it developed the Asia Europe Foundation to support intellectual activities involving Asian and European policy institutes. The Foundation has supported some activities of the CAEC that do not involve Australian and New Zealand participation.

In contrast to the programs associated with the APEC, CAEC has been broad-gauged, covering political as well as economic issues. One CAEC project looked at the implications of the Asian economic crisis.[12] Current projects address issues of global governance (including the new security agenda), energy security, and a review of European–Asian cooperation seven years after the creation of ASEM.

The challenges ahead

Track 2 processes have played a critical role in driving forward the Track 1 processes as sources of ideas, expertise, and historical memory and test beds for co-operation. They may also serve as models for Track 1 interaction itself. Formed in a more recent era than the global or transatlantic institutions, Asia-Pacific institutions are comparatively open to nongovernmental participation, allowing such groups as the ASEAN-ISIS, PECC, and CSCAP to become embedded in the ASEAN, APEC, and ARF processes. Some APEC meetings, for example, involve dozens of nongovernmental participants as observers or virtual full participants in APEC working groups and projects. However, a significant wall between the governmental and nongovernmental sides remains.

Are there any problems with this picture? Two potential dangers may be cited: overdependence and 'irrational exuberance.'

In its eagerness to be involved with policymaking, some would argue that the mainstream Track 2 has become too much like Track 1. According to this line of reasoning, an 'embedded' Track 2, like the journalists embedded in coalition forces during the Iraq war, becomes co-opted in the intergovernmental processes and fails to sufficiently question basic assumptions or maintain an independent agenda.[13] Moreover, the parts of Track 2 that are more independent have allowed their networks to be infiltrated by Track 1, thus accepting governmental institutions and government officials temporarily wearing academic hats as legitimate Track 2 components. It can also be argued that the work programs of Track 2 institutions have become overly absorbed in the Track 1 agendas. This diverts Track 2 from broader or more intellectual issues that may not be of much interest to Track 1, and because Track 1 typically underfunds the Track 2 inputs, it may threaten the financial viability of Track 2 itself.

Track 2 defenders would argue, however, that it is only through an embedding process that Track 2 can have a significant influence on Track 1. They would argue that Track 1 has forward and retrograde elements. By their closeness to Track 1, Track 2 institutions are sensitive to these differences and are able to ally with the forward elements in Track 1. They could point to many instances where Track 2 institutions have differed with or questioned judgments and have helped steer Track 1 into a different direction. Even in the case of Track 2 government entities, Track 2 advocates argue that by projecting norms of independence and experimentation, they gradually influence these entities to become more independent in their thinking. Track 2 has not become distorted by state preferences according to this line of argumentation; to the contrary, it can shape these preferences precisely because of its closeness. The more critical function can be played by Track 3.

Financial considerations may ultimately force Track 2 to shift emphasis to national issues as opposed to regional ones. The financial resources going to Track 2 international policy networks are dependent on the excitement generated by regional cooperation processes among funding agencies, whether governments, corporations, or foundations. As the initial excitement in Asia-Pacific regionalism tended to wear thinner after the 1997–1998 Asian financial crisis, the funding stream has become drier, creating financial problems for PBEC and PECC in particular, because they had established their own secretariats and central funds rather than simply relying on host organizations. On the other hand, ASEAN-ISIS and CSCAP depend on the viability of the component organizations, which are engaged in a variety of activities beyond their involvement in Track 1 regional institutions.

The drying of the funding stream may expose a reverse dependency by Track 1 on Track 2 for relatively cheap labor. There is a tendency for governments to sometimes assume that Track 2 is so anxious to be involved that it does not need to be paid for its work. While there are some in the academic world who are quite willing to contribute their expertise cheaply (often because their base salaries are being paid by their home institutions), this becomes less true if the work program has been established by the governments rather than themselves or their networks or if it has less political and psychological benefits. In this sense, Track 2 is a quixotic partner for Track 1, becoming involved when and where it wants but not necessarily capable of being relied upon except at a significantly higher price.

The funding dilemmas reflect the danger of 'irrational exuberance.' Track 2, like Track 1, has an incentive to magnify the potentials and achievements of regional cooperation processes. Moreover, Track 2 does not have some of the inbuilt cautions of Track 1, which after all is ultimately responsible for policy decisions and their implementation. Some of the big ideas promoted for regional cooperation, including the belief that APEC could be a driving force for global free trade and the transformational impacts of ASEAN on the newer members in the 1990s, have proved overly optimistic. Track 2 has perhaps overestimated the value of elites (as Track 2 participants are) rubbing shoulders with each other and strengthening their understanding. In the Asia-Pacific context, Track 2 appears to have undervalued the importance of legally binding commitments. As valuable as Track 2 is in developing norms and acting as a voice of the 'regional community,' this work can be very fragilely rooted in deeper governmental understanding, processes, and commitments.

What does all this have to do with economic security? As noted above, the regional economic organizations have been typically categorized into economic or security functions. Events are rendering these functional barriers increasingly problematic. Just as happened for ASEAN and the Group of Eight before it, APEC has been driven first by the 1999 crisis in East Timor and then the post-September 11 'war on terror' toward a political as well as an economic agenda.[14] At the same time, since the Asian economic crisis and the September 11 attacks, ARF and CSCAP have had to more explicitly recognize the economic roots of security. The term 'economic security' may not resonate with the mainstream thinking in either the economic or the security dialogues, but both have relevant activity. The liberalization, facilitation, and cooperation agenda in APEC contributes to the strengthening of the region's economies, particularly those in the developing part of the world. Of more relevance, however, is the work on financial systems, regulatory structures, corporate governance, and transparency, which is intended to build the institutions' need to help integrate emerging economies into the rest of the global economy without systemic breakdowns. Work in ASEAN, ARF, and CSCAP on such issues as terrorism, maritime security, and transnational crimes is also important from an economic security perspective. The past half-decade does not suggest that regional organizations or networks are going to eliminate business cycles or economic and trade adjustments associated with growth and globalization, although they may mitigate effects. But it does clearly show that both economic and political events can have catastrophic consequences affecting the livelihood of tens of millions of individuals. These issues should clearly have top priority in regional dialogues.

Appendix A: Global and regional organizations and Track 2 networks

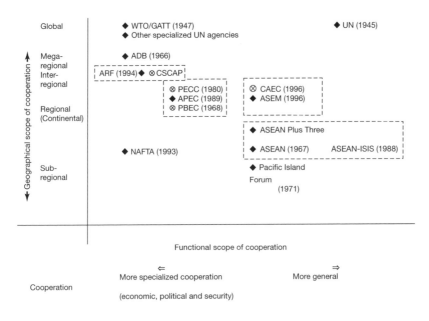

Key

◆   Intergovernmental (Track 1)

⊗   Nongovernmental (Track 2)

ADB: Asian Development Bank
APEC: Asia-Pacific Economic Cooperation
ARF: ASEAN Regional Forum
ASEAN: Association of Southeast Asian Nations
ASEAN-ISIS: ASEAN Institutes of Strategic and International Studies
ASEM: Asia Europe Meeting
CAEC: Council for Asia–Europe Cooperation

CSCAP: Council for Security Cooperation in the Asia Pacific
NAFTA: North America Free Trade Agreement
PBEC: Pacific Basin Economic Council
PECC: Pacific Economic Cooperation Council

Notes

1 The term was apparently invented by a former American foreign service officer, Joseph Montville, to refer to negotiations by nonstate actors on issues normally in the official diplomatic sphere. In some conflict resolution literature as well as popular terminology, however, 'Track 2' is used much more broadly, referring to almost any nongovernmental efforts to resolve conflicts, including grassroots dialogues.

2 PECC, ASEAN, and the Pacific Island Forum have formal observer status in the APEC process. The latter two are organizations of member governments and thus clearly in Track 1. PECC includes government officials acting in their private capacities, but it has been led by policy institutes. Its inclusion reflects that important PECC role in giving birth to the APEC process.

3 It can be argued that very few Asia-Pacific Track 2 institutions associated with intergovernmental processes are truly independent of government, but the policy space they occupy is smaller or larger depending on the personalities and standing of their key leaders, the nature of the issue, and the nature of the governments. Where Track 2 has been dominated by former officials, it can appear even less flexible than Track 1, as it can be stuck in past positions rejected by the Track 1 counterpart.

4 Commissioned research work for Track 1 is frequently done by individuals and individuals associated with Track 2 policy networks. However, depending on the degree of flexibility allowed by the contract, we would regard this as part of the Track 1 process.

5 Based on discussions with Track 2 leaders in other ASEAN countries.

6 See the ASEAN Regional Forum, Documents Series 1994–2002 from the ASEAN Secretariat (2003: 11).

7 One partial exception is the Pacific Island Forum. The ASEAN Secretariat has also gradually expanded its capabilities.

8 Based on interviews conducted at the national secretariats for ASEAN in 1969.

9 Kojima's 1965 concept of a Pacific Free Trade Area was apparently sparked by his participation in a 1964 East-West Center conference on Economic Cooperation for Development and Trade in the Pacific. See Lawrence Woods (1993: 41). Woods provides the best history of Asia-Pacific economic organizations, including PAFTAD, PBEC, and PECC, up to the early 1990s.

10 For example, statements at the 2003 meetings have dealt with SARS (in May) and support for the Doha round (in August).

11 There are frequent complaints by ABAC members that their reports are treated in a perfunctory manner by the ministers.

12 See the Report of the Council for Asia–Europe Cooperation (CAEC 2000).

13 For critique of the 'cooperative' rather than 'collaborative' approach, see Witte *et al.* (2000: 4).

14 One complication for APEC is the membership of Taiwan, referred to in APEC as 'Chinese Taipei.' China is adamantly opposed to Taiwan's participation as a political entity in political discussions, including the APEC leaders' meeting. This issue has also been extended into Track 2 networks, preventing Taiwan from organizing a committee.

References

ASEAN Secretariat (2003) *ASEAN Regional Forum, Documents Series 1994–2002*, Jakarta: ASEAN Secretariat.

CAEC (2000) 'Asia–Europe Cooperation: Beyond the Financial Crisis,' *Report of the Council for Asia–Europe Cooperation*, Les Cahiers de l'Ifri 31, Paris: French Institute of International Relations.

Cossa, Ralph A. (1998) 'Track Two Diplomacy: Promoting Regional Peace, Stability,' in *U.S. Foreign Policy Agenda*, USIA Electronic Journal, Vol. 3 (1), January.

Desker, Barry (2003) 'The ARF: Meeting the Challenges of the 21st Century,' in *Asia Pacific Security: Uncertainty in a Changing World Order*, Kuala Lumpur: ISIS Malaysia.

Hernandez, Carolina G. (1993) 'The Role of the ASEAN-ISIS,' *ASEAN-ISIS Monitor*.

—— (2000) 'Challenges for Society and Politics,' in Simon S. C. Tay, Jesus Estanislao, and Hadi Soesastro (eds) *A New ASEAN in a New Millenium*, Jakarta: Centre for Strategic and International Studies.

Witte, Jan Martin, Reinicke, Wolfgang H., and Benner, Thorsten (2000) 'Beyond Multilateralism: Global Public Policy Networks,' *Politik und Gesellschaft Online*, Vol. 2/2000.

Woods, Lawrence T. (1993) *Asia-Pacific Diplomacy: Nongovernmental Organizations and International Relations*, Vancouver: UBC Press.

12 Non-state regional governance mechanisms for economic security

The case of the ASEAN Peoples' Assembly

Mely Caballero-Anthony

Introduction

This chapter speaks to the broad question on how civil society organisations (CSOs) address the question of economic security. In particular, it looks at how these organisations, often referred to as Track 3, fit into the agenda of improving global governance by examining CSOs as part of the multilevel system of governance: organisations that are actively engaged in the overall quest of achieving human security. In doing so, this chapter brings into focus the dynamics between actors and processes in the constantly evolving conceptualisations of security.

Civil society and the rethinking of security: convergence or divergence?

There are discernible trajectories in the rapid growth of civil society and the current widespread calls for the reconceptualisation of security. This trend can be found in Southeast Asia, where there has been a dramatic increase in the number of civil society organisations, particularly in the early 1990s, which have called attention to human developmental issues and challenged the prevailing models of economic models that many states in the region have adopted. This trend can be juxtaposed with the ongoing momentum to rethink the prevailing concepts of security conventionally rooted in threats to state/military security and instead promote human security (see Commission on Human Security, 2003). The concept of human security that calls for the protection of the vital core of human lives essentially shifts the focus of security that privileged the macro-level concerns of state and economic development to that of the micro-level issues of individual development and empowerment.[1]

Several factors have led to these trends. The most commonly cited are the structural changes in the international environment brought on by the end of the Cold War, as well as the varying and complex forces of globalisation, which have had serious repercussions on the political, security and economic configurations in the global environment. The impacts of these changes come in many forms, not least the series of unexpected crises that have hit societies and states around the world. So far, the most significant crisis experienced recently in the region was the 1997–1998 Asian financial crisis. The ravaging onslaught of the economic crisis destabilised many governments and societies in a place once described as one of the most peaceful and fastest-growing regions in the world. Over this period, CSOs have been at the forefront of calls to improve the plight of the poor and the disadvantaged, the minorities and displaced persons, women and children who have been victims of conflicts, and the many pressing concerns of communities left behind in the rapidly changing global environment. CSOs have asked questions, fought for their causes and challenged the governance of states and institutions.

The evolving dynamics in the development of civil society on one hand and the reconceptualisation of security beyond the traditional notions of state/military security on the other are not mutually exclusive. One could argue that these two ongoing dynamics are essentially interlinked by a common need to broaden both the subjects and the objects of security. Thus, the idea in plotting these complementary trajectories is to reflect a critical fact; that is, security viewed comprehensively can be meaningfully attained only if it is defined by several actors of society, apart from the state. In this context, the role of civil society becomes a critical criterion since its inclusion in the 'ideal' multi-actor/multilevel approach in the attainment of security provides an alternative voice and creates added political space for different sectors of the society to be included in the processes of redefining security.

Thus, what we have in this region are two processes that are perceptibly moving in tandem. More significantly, these emerging processes reflect commonalities in agenda-setting and provide alternative modalities of state–society engagement aimed at highlighting the security concerns of individuals and communities and bringing these concerns to the international arena. These concerns could range from economic, political, environmental, food, health, personal and community security.[2] The importance of these processes therefore cannot be overstated.

Take the issue of economic security. Given the almost seamless nexus between politics and economics, alternative perspectives and approaches to economic development are increasingly getting the attention of the global community. These alternative modalities have questioned the prevailing canons of neoliberal policies on trade and development, which presuppose that the opening up of the social space at the economic level would result in a similar process at the political level and vice versa, and also that the consequence of this spatial opening would be the realisation of economic security, defined loosely as the economic well-being of the state. (It is also presumed that managing the economy is vital to attain national security.) Against this neoliberal perspective, the role of civil society organisations is seen to be fostering this process of political and economic pluralisation by acting essentially as a barrier against strong state involvement in both political and economic spheres. But there has to be more to this rather sanguine scenario.

The problem with this neat and simplistic perspective is the underlying assumption that the role of civil society is already fulfilled once these 'spaces' are opened up for them to contest the power of the state and market. This view does not go far enough to understand the context in which civil society organisations develop and the impact that this context can have on the trajectory that civil society takes. More significantly, it fails to identify and appreciate some of the avenues of actions that civil society organisations can take, and choose to take, in different regional settings.

To be sure, identifying some of these problems raises several issues with regard to the role of civil society in promoting alternative discourses on matters of political, social and economic development. Moreover, there is also the question of how the development of civil society becomes part of the ongoing debates on the future of security in the region (Lizee, 2000). In grappling with a number of complex issues and teasing out some of the underlying relationships between actors and processes, two central themes are addressed in this chapter:

1   How do civil society organisations relate to the actors and processes that are currently engaged in the reconceptualisation of security in the region?
2   To what extent does this configuration between actors contribute to governance for economic security?

The chapter analyses the above issues by looking at the emerging transnational civil society organisation called the ASEAN People's Assembly (APA). APA was established in 2000 under the initiative of the ASEAN Institutes of Strategic and International Studies (ASEAN-ISIS) network, a Track 2 organisation in Southeast Asia.[3] In examining APA and locating it within the emerging regional mechanisms for governance and security, this chapter has as its main objective the analysis of the dynamics between actors and processes that are interacting in the ongoing enterprise of promoting human security in the region.

The chapter is in three parts. The first briefly examines the concept of civil society and discusses some of the conceptual problems in identifying civil society organisations. The second part identifies some of the civil society organisations found in the ASEAN region that are involved in the broad subjects of development, global governance and security. The third part traces the genesis of the ASEAN People's Assembly and examines the implications of this new configuration of Tracks 2 and 3 processes in the efforts at building regional mechanisms for economic security.

Understanding civil society

The dramatic growth of civil society and its critical role in filling the space between the state and market belie the fact that the very notion of 'civil society' is a contested concept (Keane, 1995; Hall, 1995).[4] Within the Asian context, the definition of civil society differs among those who have studied the emergence of civil society in the region. One definition, for example, looks as civil society as 'non-profit voluntary organizations' that are engaged in developmental work (Serrano, 1994). Another definition, which uses the same description of the concept, refers to civil society as NGOs, research institutes and philanthropic associations (Yamamoto, 1995). A third definition referred to civil society as 'the broader sphere beyond the state and private interests composed of non-governmental and non-commercial citizens and organizations devoted to social good' (Coronel-Ferrer, 1997: 1–15).

In a recent work that attempted to trace the evolution of civil society and its relevance to Southeast Asia, Lee (2004) ascribes the indeterminate characteristic of this concept to the descriptive (what is), as well as the normative (what ought to be), dimensions that this concept carries. As a consequence, 'its usage has been subject to intense and endless debate'. This indeterminate nature of civil society is not altogether surprising, given that from its early roots, which can be traced back to the eighteenth century, the term 'civil society' has carried several different meanings, depending on the context in which this term was introduced. In Hegel's *Philosophy of Right*, civil society refers to the realm between the family and the state where individuals are free to associate to pursue their needs and interests. The Hegelian idea of civil society is (as paraphrased)

> an arena in which modern man legitimately gratifies his self-interest and develops his individuality, but also learns the value of group action, social solidarity and the dependence of his welfare on others, which educate him for citizenship and prepare him for participation in the political arena of the state.
>
> (Kumar, 1993)

While some thinkers have built on Hegel's notion of civil society, distinguishing it as a 'romantic alternative to the institutions of modernity', others, like Karl Marx, basically rejected this idea. Marx's *Das Kapital* found no place for populations and citizens to organise freely. From this historical context, one notes that the development of civil society in Eastern Europe emerged out of a history of oppression and intolerance of dissent. This historical experience largely informed one dominant view about civil society; that is, a 'conflict view that places civic societies as sites for resistance against two forces: the state and the market'. The East European-inspired conflict view of civil society regards the state in a largely antagonistic manner and argues for the emancipation and empowerment of individuals and disadvantaged groups. The efforts at opening spaces for these individuals to organise and articulate their interest eventually led to the story of democratisation in Eastern Europe. Within the prism of the conflict view of civil society, a democratic state is predicated largely on the presence of advocacy and public interest groups. Civil society is therefore a necessary countervailing force to the state that has elicited so much fear and distrust (Fine, 1997: 11).

The alternative to the conflict view of civil society is drawn from Robert Putnam's work, which identifies civil society as sites where social capital is generated and developed, rather than as sites for resistance. Putnam, who studied civil associations in northern Italy, claimed that civil societies helped to establish democracy, while the absence of such could weaken it. According to Putnam,

> Civil associations contribute to the effectiveness and stability of democratic governments . . . because of their 'internal' effects on the individual and because of their 'external' effects on the wider polity. Internally, associations instil in their members habits of cooperation, solidarity and public spiritedness.

> . . . Participation in civil organizations inculcates skills of cooperation as well as a sense of shared responsibility for the collective endeavors.
>
> (1993: 89–90)

Unlike the conflict view of civil society, Putnam's social capital approach does not pit civil society against the state. Civil society and state are not locked in an adversarial relationship since citizens trust and have confidence in the liberal democratic state, which is perceived to be reasonably responsive to the needs of its citizenry. Therefore, where the two views of civil society differ is in how they perceive the nature of the relationship between state and civil society (Lee, 2004).

These two dominant, albeit contrasting, views on civil society are instructive in understanding the nature of civil societies found in Asia. This has not, however, resolved its conceptual ambiguity. Some scholars have argued that while civil society in the sense of opposition to the state is well developed in parts of Asia, such as India, civil society in the sense of associational groups working with the state is not. Different human communities are concerned with establishing their own versions of civil society in their own differing ways, and 'therefore the search for the replication of a universal (i.e., Western) model of civil society all over the world should be abandoned' (Niraya, 2001: 124). Suffice it to say that despite the conceptual and philosophical ambiguities of civil society, this has not stopped many academics, activists and policymakers from using and promoting civil society. The most likely reason, perhaps, is the very desirability of civil society and the idea that its creation is a valuable goal or desideratum. Moreover, civil society carries with it the normative aspect that subscribes to the principle that it is accessible to all citizens. Being an arena of free engagement, deliberation, discussion and dialogue thereby mandates its democratic character, 'not only because it has the potential to ensure [political] accountability but also because it is a genuinely participatory sphere, open to all' (ibid.: 126).

Civil society organisations in Southeast Asia

Given the interest that the formation of civil society has generated in Asia, particularly in Southeast Asia, it is no wonder that there has been a rapid proliferation of CSOs. This trend was particularly notable in the late 1980s and early 1990s, when the region was in the throes of rapid structural and societal transformations. For the purpose of this chapter, I shall adopt a very broad definition of civil society to refer to non-governmental organisations (NGOs),[5] advocacy groups and a variety of social movements that have, in one way or another, expressed their views on various issues, including the rights of ethnic groups, the environment and economic displacement, to name but a few. This broad definition, however, includes the specific characteristic of CSOs being non-profit-making and voluntary, and they would also have to be 'transformative and innovative', with emphasis on their alternative views of development, governance and security. Against these parameters, business groups (which are organised for the sole purpose of profit) and political parties are not included.

To get a picture of the development of CSOs in Southeast Asia, the following statistics of a recent study on NGOs/CSOs in the region are instructive. Thailand has 19,878 registered NGOs, Malaysia 14,000 and the Philippines 70,200. The number in Indonesia showed a massive increase from 10,000 in 1996 to 70,000 in 2000, while in Singapore the number of CSOs, represented by registered charities and social organisations, is placed at 4,562 (Hadiwinata, 2003: 1). Another study, which included socialist states such as China and Vietnam, reported that there are more than 200,000 registered NGOs in China and about 600 at the provincial level, and several thousand at district and community level in Vietnam (Yamamoto, 2000: 43).

Most of these CSOs share common concerns essentially rooted in helping and assisting local communities, alleviating the miserable living conditions of the poor and underprivileged, and looking into the plight of abused women and children, among others. CSOs also share the common objective of empowering these groups to fight for social justice, human rights, improved environmental conditions and a better quality of life. Often, CSOs reflect the wide array of challenges faced by individuals and communities in areas related to poverty, economic and social injustice, women's and children's rights, minority rights, the environment and its resources (both land and water), and so on that neither the government nor the market is able to address adequately. And in less democratic societies, civil societies essentially come in two different forms: those that concentrate on activities geared towards community development to promote the idea of people-centred development, and those that focus on organising specifically defined constituencies to generate social movements (Hadiwinata, 2003: 25).

While it is beyond the scope of a single chapter to provide a comprehensive picture of the various types of civil societies found in Southeast Asia, a few NGOs are discussed below to characterise the different features of CSOs found in the region. Some are locally (national) based, while the others are regionally based.

In Thailand, the Assembly of the Poor is one of the more active and significant CSOs at the forefront of fighting for the interests of poor farmers in the country. This is in spite of the fact that it is a loosely structured CSO and lacks legal status. One of its recent achievements was to force the Thai government to negotiate with the Thai farmers who were displaced as a result of land appropriation for building dams and industrial estates. It did this by mobilising thousands of poor farmers countrywide to participate in a 'sit-in' protest in front of the Government House to demand for fair compensation. The Assembly of the Poor is an example of CSOs in the region that are fighting for distributive justice and good governance (Bunbongkarn, 2001: 66–88; Jumbala, 2000: 61–75).

There are also the pro-democracy groups – PollWatch and the Confederation for Democracy – which have played a significant part in the democratisation and political reform of Thailand since 1992. PollWatch was created in March 1992 to serve as an election-monitoring mechanism. Its activities raised the level of public concern over the proliferation of vote-buying and money politics in election campaigns, which contributed to popular demand for political reforms. Similarly, the Confederation for Democracy was a loosely organised group that fought against military rule in 1991 and 1992. It became the key organiser of the urban middle-class uprising in May 1992 that eventually brought an end to military rule in Thailand (Bunbongkarn, 2001).

The work and experience of PollWatch and the Confederation for Democracy have their own equivalent in the Philippines. The National Citizens' Movement for Free Elections (NAMFREL), along with several other CSOs in the Philippines, is notable for its contribution to the process of democratisation in the country during the martial law period under the Marcos regime. NAMFREL was founded in 1983 by concerned individuals and activists to restore public faith in the electoral process in the country, which had been restored after its suspension in 1972. NAMFREL mobilised more than half a million volunteers in poll-watching activities during the 1986 elections. It became a powerful symbol of the power of civil society when thousands of its volunteers staged a dramatic walk-out – captured live on Philippines television – when the counting of votes was reportedly rigged. This was one of the events that precipitated the People Power Movement in 1986 that brought down the Marcos dictatorship.

Many of the CSOs in the Philippines have also established coalitions and networks within the country to strengthen their work and improve their engagement strategies with the government. Some of these include the Caucus of Development NGO Network (CODE-NGO), the Philippine Partnership for the Development of Human Resources in Rural Areas (PhilDHARRA) and the NGO Coordinating Committee for Rural Development (NGO-Cord). The consolidation of NGOs in the country is part of the growing trend to improve their strategies for more recognition and access to state authorities in their advocacy work. The consolidation is done in an *ad hoc*, issue-defined manner (Ronas, 2000: 49–60). Other examples of national coalitions in other countries include the NGO-Coordinating Committee for Rural Development (NGO-Cord) in Thailand, the Environmental Protection Society of Malaysia, and the *Wahana Lingkungan Hidup* (WALHI), a network of concerned environmental NGOs in Indonesia (Yamamoto, 2000).

Southeast Asia is also home to many regional CSOs. These share many of the characteristics of the national NGOs, and their organisations are also mostly issue based. In this region, the prominent NGOs are usually those that are identified in their work towards democratisation, promotion of human rights and advocacy against globalisation. The Asian Forum for Human Rights and Development (FORUM-ASIA) based in Bangkok, Thailand, has been at the forefront in the campaign against human rights abuses in the region. There is also the Asian Cultural Forum for Development (ACFOD), again based in Bangkok, which works on human rights and social issues.

Among the high-profile NGOs that have been continually campaigning against globalisation is Focus on the Global South, based at Chulalongkorn University in Thailand, which has been prominent in research and publication, networking and advocacy work. There is also the Asian Regional Exchange for New Alternatives (ARENA), a network of Asian scholar-activists that aims to foster exchange among scholars and formulate alternative development perspectives to counter corporate-led globalisation. Similar NGOs also include the Third World Network, which was first established in Penang, Malaysia, and has now become an international NGO with offices globally, and the Southeast Asian Resource Institute for Community Education (SEARICE), which has been active in international campaigns against biotechnology (Tadem and Tadem, 2002).

Labour-based regional NGOs include the Asian Migrant Center (AMC), which focuses particularly on the plight of migrant workers, and the Asia Monitor Resource Center (AMRC), which initially started as a monitoring group for transnational corporations (TNCs). ISIS International, with headquarters in Manila, deals with gender and women's issues, and the Committee for Asian Women (CAW) regularly undertakes studies and conducts seminars on gender issues.

One could therefore argue that the CSOs in Southeast Asia not only are increasing in number, but also have become equally vibrant. This is indeed significant, given the fact that in the early 1980s many states in the region were characterised as semi-authoritarian states that stifled the development of CSOs. This was the period when the notions of state power and legitimacy were very much predicated on economic growth and development – otherwise known as 'performance legitimacy'. The rapid regional economic growth and development largely made up for the absence of effervescent CSOs in many states in the region. There were of course exceptions to this picture, as in the case of the Philippines, which went through a difficult transition from martial law to democracy, aggravated by poor economic growth.

Thus, it was only during the 1997–1998 economic crisis that the number of CSOs rose dramatically and their visibility increased. While there were already national and regional CSOs that had been struggling against the nature and social consequences of neoliberal approaches to economic development, it was with the onset of the regional economic crisis that their views and influence became popular and widely disseminated (Tadem and Tadem, 2002). With the notion of 'performance legitimacy' losing its credence, and the growing dissatisfaction with prevailing neoliberal policies, many CSOs in Southeast Asia joined the 'Battle of Seattle' demonstration in 1999 with their own protests against the World Trade Organisation (WTO), the World Bank, the International Monetary Fund (IMF) and even the Asian Development Bank (ADB).

As CSOs began to form coalitions and networks nationally, regionally and globally, their strategies of engagement also became more sophisticated, aided by the advances in information and communications technology. While the latter made many prominent NGOs media-savvy, the significance of building coalitions and networks has led to the 'transnationalisation' of CSOs. As noted by Wilkin,

> The emergence of transnational network of civil society groups has brought together a wider range of NGO work in the fields of peace, security and development across national boundaries against both the interests and exploitation of the global forces of production and finance. These transnational NGO networks begin to ensure meaningful participation of civil society associations in international decision-making. In addition to advancing resistance to the

current orthodoxy of neo-liberalism, these emerging transnational networks of voluntary organizations are actively involved in creating alternative routes for development.

(Wilkin, 1995)

This emerging trend of transnationalisation not only has increased the visibility of the CSOs in all levels, but has made them significant actors in the arena of decision-making where they were once excluded. Because of their increasing numbers and spread across the globe, CSOs have now been described as powerful countervailing forces against states and markets.

To sum up, in spite of the increased visibility of CSOs, questions still remain with regard to their influence in policymaking and governance. At least in this region, the achievements of CSOs beyond the process of engagement of state-actors to actual policy inputs are at best anecdotal. Since CSOs first made their presence felt in this region, many of the challenges they face in engaging the centres of power – not least, having to cope with a hostile and strictly regulated environment – still remain. A constant dilemma for CSOs relates to finding appropriate mechanisms to remain actively engaged in the arena of contestation among power centres (state and market) while continuing with the enterprise of coalition-building and networking. As we track models of constructive engagement – *modi vivendi* between CSOs and state/market – that are aimed at improving governance and attaining security, the emergence of the APA provides an interesting case.

The APA: a mechanism for regional governance and security in Southeast Asia

If civil society is the space between the state and the market, what this space includes and who occupies it is a question that should be of interest in the study of CSOs. In this regard, the genesis of the APA provides some interesting insights into the kinds of actors and processes at work in the establishment of this emerging transnational civil society organisation, specifically with regard to their approaches to regional governance and security.

The genesis of the APA

The idea of organising a people's assembly in ASEAN had been floated around for many years and had been a subject of discussion in both Track 1 and Track 2 meetings. In particular, many in the Track 2 circles in the region had been pushing this agenda of a people-driven mechanism for some time, as it had always felt that while Track 2 meetings and interactions with the ASEAN governments had increased and intensified, very rarely had NGOs had the opportunity to interact with Track 2 actors. Interactions with Track 1 actors had been even more rare. More importantly, NGOs had been excluded from the agenda-setting and decision-making in ASEAN.

Although ASEAN was set up to enhance economic development and economic cooperation in the region, as well as to foster political security among member states, the organisation has always been regarded as a 'club of elites', disconnected from the people of the region. A good indication of this state of affairs is the fact that while ASEAN, at the time of writing, was well into its thirty-sixth year, it remains an unknown entity for most of the peoples of Southeast Asia (Hernandez, 2002). As such, ASEAN-ISIS undertook, as one of its missions, to continuously push for the idea of a people's assembly in its interactions with Track 1 officials in ASEAN and in the various Track 2 fora, particularly at its annual Asia Pacific Roundtable meetings in Kuala Lumpur. The opportunity finally presented itself at the ASEAN Ministerial Meeting in Brunei in 1995, when the foreign minister of Thailand called for the establishment of a 'congress of ASEAN peoples'. The Thai Foreign Ministry through ISIS Thailand assigned ASEAN-ISIS to conceptualise the modalities and procedures for such an assembly. The original idea of a people's group was for it to be a kind of a regional interparliamentary union.

But ASEAN-ISIS came up with a different version and shaped its own concept paper, 'An assembly of the peoples of ASEAN'. According to the principal author of the concept paper, given the fact that NGOs in the region had already organised activities parallel to and often opposed to those held by governments, it was critical to come up with a regional mechanism that could develop common responses to common challenges.[6] The ASEAN-ISIS concept paper had argued that setting up a group similar to an interparliamentary union would not be appropriate, since its idea of a multi-sectoral representation of a people's assembly would include

> national and local government officials in their private capacity; academia; business; culture and the arts; relevant rural-based groups; village leaders and community leaders; media; labour; sectors concerned with women and children; other professionals; undergraduate and graduate students; religious organizations; and other sectors as are relevant to individual ASEAN member states.

Moreover, it was envisaged that the assembly would be expanded on a step-by-step basis to include 'all sectors of ASEAN societies'.

APA was to be established with the objectives of (a) promoting greater awareness of an ASEAN community; (b) promoting mutual understanding and tolerance for the diversity of culture, religion, ethnicity, social values, political cultures and processes, and other elements of ASEAN diversity; (c) obtaining insights and inputs on how to deal with socio-economic problems affecting ASEAN societies; (d) facilitating the bridging of gaps between ASEAN societies through confidence-building measures; and (e) assisting in the building of an ASEAN community of caring societies as sought by the ASEAN Vision 2020 (see *Report of the First ASEAN People's Assembly*, 2001).

For ASEAN-ISIS, the APA was to be this regional mechanism, which was 'meant to create a regular people's gathering where they would meet on a regular basis, discuss issues they consider timely, important and relevant; seek solutions for them and make recommendations to government on these matters'. ASEAN-ISIS would serve as the 'convenor of APA, its fund-raiser, its facilitator, its spokesperson, its driving force in the initial years, until it takes a life of its own' (Hernandez, 2002). ASEAN-ISIS envisaged that this Track 2 and 'Track 3' collaborative process would benefit ASEAN heads of state and heads of government since APA 'is meant to be more sensitive to the practical realities of ASEAN and is intended to be held every year to coincide with the regular and informal summits of ASEAN'. The timing of the holding of APA is therefore crucial to enable APA to provide inputs to ASEAN leaders on issues that are of concern to the people of the region and how APA thinks these can be addressed.

The launching of APA

The ambitious APA project took about four years to be realised, and during this period it encountered several setbacks that jeopardised its launching. First, there was the problem of funding. Although ASEAN officials endorsed in principle the idea of an APA, the ASEAN Foundation, the donor agency that was approached by ASEAN-ISIS for funding support turned down its application twice, in 1999 and 2000. Decisions for funding grants of the ASEAN Foundation were made by ASEAN senior officials, who decided on the basis of consensus. The fact that the application was denied twice was indicative of the reservations that some ASEAN governments had about the launching of APA. The attitude of certain ASEAN governments therefore became its second and most difficult obstacle. Ironically, the ASEAN Foundation was set up to promote the ASEAN 2020 project, which had as its critical component 'building a community of caring societies' (see ASEAN 1997). Moreover, when the ASEAN Foundation held its round of consultations about priority projects, there was apparently a consensus that APA would be one of these. It was therefore interesting that the implementation of this 'consensus' turned out to be problematic.

Third, the failure of ASEAN-ISIS to get funding from the ASEAN Foundation also revealed the lack of success and influence that some members of this Track 2 body had with their own governments in pushing for this idea. This setback, however, did not deter some members within the ASEAN-ISIS network from pressing ahead and seeking for alternative funding. Encouraged by the fact that the APA project had the support of the ASEAN Secretary-General and the Japanese foreign ministry, ASEAN-ISIS looked for partners outside the region.[7] By mobilising its own networks, key players within ASEAN-ISIS lobbied hard and sought funding from outside sources, which included, among others, the Canadian International Development Agency (CIDA)-funded Southeast Asia Cooperation Project, Japan Official Development Assistance, the Open Society, Batam Industrial Authority and the Asia Foundation. ASEAN-ISIS successfully persuaded these agencies to back the APA project despite the lack of official blessing from the ASEAN governments.[8] Its success in doing so indicated that these donor agencies saw the potential of APA as a people-empowering mechanism.

Without much fanfare, the first APA was held in Batam, Indonesia, on 24–25 November 2000. The choice of the date and the place to hold the APA was indeed symbolic. The launching of APA was set to coincide with the fourth ASEAN summit meeting, which was held in neighbouring Singapore on 22–25 November 2000. Batam was less than an hour's ferry-ride from Singapore, and while it would have been more convenient to hold the meeting in Singapore, it was not possible to do so, for political reasons.

In spite of its initial setbacks, the APA 2000 managed to bring together about 300 representatives of NGOs, grassroots leaders and activists, members of think tanks, and businesspeople. ASEAN-ISIS also managed to persuade some of the prominent regional NGOs such as Forum Asia and Focus on the Global South to attend its inaugural meeting, as well as a few government officials who came in their private capacity.[9] These were former Indonesian president Abdurrahman Wahid, former Indonesian foreign minister Ali Alatas and former national security adviser of the Philippines Jose Almonte. The ASEAN Secretary-General, Rodolfo Severino, also attended.

The issues that were tabled for discussions covered a wide range of social, political and economic issues. They included:

- the role of the people in setting ASEAN's agenda;
- the impact of globalisation;
- the power of women and their empowerment;
- the role of the media;
- the possibility of a regional human rights mechanism;
- the role of civil society;
- efforts to address poverty;
- the limits and opportunities of environmental management;
- events in Myanmar and East Timor;
- policies for education system reform;
- ASEAN's role in regional community-building.

The dynamics of bringing together for the first time a diverse set of CSOs was best depicted in a piece written by a Malaysian participant of APA 2000, who described the Assembly as

> packed with 70 speakers into an intense couple of 14-hour days . . . audiences nonetheless attentive; floor speakers often outshone panellists . . . it was at times an incoherent babble of voices. . . . The fact of it having been success-fully convened at all was, for the moment, enough encouragement for the 'people-to-people' connection now seen as a critical element of ASEAN's interrelationships.
>
> (Rashid, 2001: 237–240)

Inspired by its first success, ASEAN-ISIS convened the second APA two years later on 30 August – 1 September 2002 in Bali, Indonesia. Following its first theme of *An ASEAN of the People, by the People and for the People*, APA-II adopted *We the ASEAN Peoples and Our Challenges* as its second theme. Now that APA had gathered enough momentum, the third APA was held in Manila on 25–27 September 2003. This time the theme was *Towards an ASEAN Community of Caring Societies*, and one of the highlights of the meeting was the ASEAN People's Declaration on the 'Principles of Good Governance'. The statement was APA's attempt to help bring about the ASEAN Security Community and the ASEAN Economic Community on the basis of the people's perspectives. The declaration was also aimed at providing inputs into the policy process of ASEAN and its member states.

Prospects for becoming a regional mechanism for governance and security

Since the launching of APA in 2000, its progress has reflected salient developments that should not be missed in the study of civil society in this region. I shall highlight some of these in what follows.

First, the very fact that an assembly took place with the participation of a wide range of NGOs and other CSOs is in itself testimony to a remarkable feat by those involved. But even more remarkable is the fact that in spite of the 'babble of incoherent voices and the cacophony', a multi-sectoral regional mechanism has emerged comprising different actors who will find their relevant niches in and contribute to governance and human security.

Second, the establishment of these multi-sectoral and transnational CSOs also indicates the emergence of yet another ideational network bound together by the need to be a part of a dynamic global system and the desire to help shape what that global system should be, based on the shared ideals and aspirations of a just and democratic system.

Third, in examining the dynamics of bringing different actors together, APA is significant in that it showed how a Track 2 initiative could succeed in gaining the endorsement of Track 3 actors. Its significance becomes more palpable given that ASEAN-ISIS has been perceived in certain circles as being too close to government, an exclusive 'elite' club and 'sometimes a gatekeeper for expanded popular participation in ASEAN concerns'. As noted by Carolina Hernandez, the head of the ASEAN-ISIS counterpart in the Philippines, who has been a key player of the APA process,

> APA must have been seen as a window of opportunity to get the people's views heard beyond their usual circles, never mind if through ASEAN ISIS. It must also be a sign of the times – one characterised by an increasing willingness by actors in the second and third tracks to engage including the unlike-minded for the achievement of the goals they cannot obtain in isolation from or in hostile opposition to each other. It can also be a sign of the level of trust earned by these actors within each track for those in the other track. Or it might have been a case of simply giving the APA initiative a chance.
>
> (Hernandez, 2002)

Fourth, the dynamics between these two tracks reflects their appreciation of the fact that while there are many different and specialised CSO networks in the region, there was still the need for a horizontal dialogue among networks, across different sectors. Equally important was the cognisance of the need to include such CSOs at the ASEAN level to make ASEAN better known and more accountable to its people – hence highlighting the importance of a vertical dialogue among state and non-state actors. If the capacity to govern requires giving emphasis to pluralities and incoherence, as well as to the horizontal and vertical coordination of public policies in ways that 'are more sensitive to the societal environment than the traditional mode of governing' (Kazancigil quoted in Niraya, 2001: 7), then APA can become a mechanism that could contribute to the quality of regional and global governance.

In this regard, the initiative of APA to produce a regional Human Development Report (HDR) is important. There is yet to be an HDR for Southeast Asia, although the six other regions in the world have one. The Southeast Asia HDR (SEA-HDR), which is patterned after the global Human Development Report, will develop a regional annual report by working on a set of measurable indicators to assess selected goals of ASEAN's Vision 2020. This initiative, which was conceived at APA-II, has already caught the interest and support of the Philippine Office of the United Nations Development Programme (UNDP).[10] The objectives of this project are twofold: to develop a group of CSOs that will be engaged in monitoring the performance of ASEAN's developmental goals, at both the country and the regional levels; and, through the discussion and the dissemination of the report, to use the SEA-HDR as a major vehicle for influencing official policies in ASEAN.

Last but certainly not least, APA reflects the broad agreement among CSOs on strategies for engagement with the centres of power. This is in contrast to the difficulties APA had with agreeing to a common set of issues to be pursued. Given the diverse set of actors, it is often unavoidable that some CSOs would push for more attention to be given to certain issues – for example, human rights abuses in Myanmar – rather than issues of internal displacement due to land reclamation. Nevertheless, the preferred approaches found in APA encourage peaceful participation and constructive dialogue while shunning extremism and violence.

Conclusion

Since its inception, APA has set in place an ambitious APA Action Plan that highlights the human security issues of the people in this region. The Action Plan identifies seven areas that deserve greater attention, more in-depth examination and follow-up action by civil society groups (see *Second APA 2002 Report*, 2003: 7). These are:

1   developing a human rights scorecard;
2   eveloping a framework to evaluate the progress of gender mainstreaming;
3   dentifying threats to democracy by developing 'democracy promoting indicators and/or democracy eroding indicators';
4   developing a code of ethics for (governance in) NGOs;
5   promoting cooperation in tackling HIV/AIDS;

6   promoting cooperation among media groups; and
7   developing the Southeast Asian Human Development Report (SEA-HDR).

Currently, some ASEAN-ISIS members are already coordinating specific areas of the action plan. For example, ISDS Philippines is coordinating the SEA-HDR, together with ISIS Thailand and CSIS Jakarta; while CSIS Jakarta, in collaboration with Forum Asia and ISDS, is developing the human rights scorecard.

In assessing the prospects of APA as a regional mechanism for governance and security, it would be realistic at this stage to be more cautious and not offer definitive views. To be sure, much remains to be seen as to the way the APA process will unfold. Likewise, many other issues will arise with regard to the effectiveness and sustainability of this emerging transnational CSO. One of these is the question of participation. For certain countries in the region that have no democratic foundation (as in the case of Myanmar), the question of participation arises. One would ask how their CSOs – or for that matter their governments – can participate and be part of the APA process. The other complex issue is the question of independence and commitment of CSOs that comprise APA. APA is, to all intents and purposes, a platform for CSOs in the region to come up with a common agenda for human development and security. For countries that were perceived to be initially reluctant to the idea of creating an APA, how can they be prevented from possibly co-opting their CSOs or putting obstacles in APA's way? There is also concern that, while the APA concept is a novel mechanism for regional governance, the voices of the ASEAN peoples may yet fall on deaf ears.

To the sceptics, many more questions will occur. But one could argue that what is more important is to be aware that a mechanism has emerged which has brought together different interest groups in this region. APA therefore offers a novel approach in the larger picture of myriad initiatives that share the common objectives of redefining security and promoting the all-embracing concept of human security.

Notes

1 The first definitive articulation of this concept can be found in the *UNDP Human Development Report 1994* (1994). Since then, several scholars have attempted to define this concept; see, for example, Suhrke (1999).
2 These categories of 'human security' essentially encompass the UNDP's definition of what human security is.
3 ASEAN-ISIS comprises the Institutes of Strategic Studies in ASEAN countries. These are: Policy and Strategic Studies (BDIPSS), Brunei Darussalam; the Cambodian Institute for Cooperation and Peace (CICP), Cambodia; the Centre for Strategic and International Studies (CSIS), Indonesia; the Institute of Foreign Affairs, Laos; the Institute of Strategic and International Studies (ISIS), Malaysia; the Institute for Strategic and Development Studies (ISDS), the Philippines; the Singapore Institute of International Affairs (SIIA), Singapore; the Institute of Security and International Studies (ISIS), Thailand; and the Institute for International Relations (IIR), Vietnam.
4 The literature on civil society is voluminous. Most definitions of civil society refer to John Keane's definition as that social realm distinct from the state and the market.

5 It appears that, by default, civil society has become synonymous with NGOs. See Niraya (2001).
6 The information on the genesis of APA is drawn largely from Carolina Hernandez's account of the processes involved in establishing APA in 'A People's Assembly: A Novel Mechanism for Bridging the North-South Divide in ASEAN' (unpublished manuscript, cited here with permission from the author).
7 The Japanese Foreign Ministry wanted to use half of the Japanese government's contribution to the ASEAN Foundation Fund for the APA project but could not do so, owing to bureaucratic procedures (author's interview with Carolina Hernandez, president of the Institute of Development and Strategic Studies (ISDS), the Philippine counterpart of ASEAN-ISIS, 3 September 2003).
8 The lack of ASEAN official endorsement did not, however, stop the then Thai foreign minister, Surin Pitsuwan, and the deputy foreign minister from openly endorsing APA.
9 For a full documentation of APA 2000, see *Report of the First ASEAN People's Assembly* (2001).
10 ISDS Philippines, along with its partner institutions, is currently developing the modalities of SEA-HDR.

References

ASEAN (1997) *ASEAN Vision 2020*, Jakarta: ASEAN Secretariat.

Bunbongkarn, Suchit (2001) 'Civil Society in Thailand', in Tadashi Yamamoto (ed.) *Governance and Civil Society in the Global Age*, Tokyo: Japan Center for International Exchange.

Commission on Human Security (2003) *Human Security Now: Protection and Empowering People*, New York: Commission on Human Security.

Coronel-Ferrer, Miriam (1997) 'Civil Society: An Operational Definition', in Maria Serena Diokno (ed.) *Democracy and Citizenship in Filipino Political Culture*, Quezon City: Third World Studies Center.

Fine, Robert (1997) 'Civil Society Theory, Enlightenment and Critique', in Robert Fine and Shirin Rai (eds) *Civil Society: Democratic Perspective*, London: Frank Cass.

Hadiwinata, Bob (2003) *The Politics of NGOS in Indonesia*, London: RoutledgeCurzon.

Hall, John A. (ed.) (1995) *Civil Society*, Cambridge: Polity Press.

Hernandez, Carolina G (2002) 'A People's Assembly: A Novel Mechanism for Bridging the North–South Divide in ASEAN' (unpublished manuscript).

Jumbala, Prudhisan (2000) 'Civil Society and Democratisation in Thailand', in Mely Anthony and Jawhar Hassan (eds) *Beyond the Crisis: Challenges and Opportunities*, Kuala Lumpur: Institute of Strategic and International Studies.

Keane, John (1995) *Civil Society: Old Images, New Visions*, Cambridge: Polity Press.

Kumar, Krishna (1993) 'Civil Society: An Inquiry into the Usefulness of an Historical Term', *British Journal of Sociology*, 44 (3): 375–395.

Lee Hock Guan (2004) 'Introduction: Civil Society in Southeast Asia', in Lee Hock Guan (ed.) *Civil Society in Southeast Asia*, Singapore: Institute of Southeast Asian Studies.

Lizee, Pierre (2000) 'Civil Society and Regional Security: Tensions and Potentials in Post-Crisis Southeast Asia', *Contemporary Southeast Asia*, 22 (3): 550–569.

Niraya, Gopal Jayal (2001) 'Civil Society in India', in Tadashi Yamamoto (ed.) *Governance and Civil Society in a Global Age*, Tokyo: Japan Center for International Exchange.

Putnam, Robert (1993) *Making Democracy Work: Civic Traditions in Modern Italy*, Princeton, NJ: Princeton University Press.

Report of the First ASEAN People's Assembly (2001) Jakarta: Centre for Strategic and International Studies.

Rashid, Rehman (2001) 'Agenda Malaysia: The ASEAN People's Assembly', in *Report of the First ASEAN People's Assembly*, Jakarta: Centre for Strategic and International Studies.

Ronas, Malaya (2000) 'Civil Society in the Asia-Pacific: Development, Challenges and Prospects', in Mely Caballero-Anthony and Jawhar Hassan (eds) *Beyond the Crisis: Challenges and Opportunities*, Kuala Lumpur: Institute of Strategic and International Studies.

Second APA 2002 Report: Challenges Facing the ASEAN People (2003) Jakarta: Centre for Strategic and International Studies.

Serrano, Isagani R. (1994) *Civil Society in the Asia-Pacific Region*, Washington, DC: Civicus, World Alliance for Citizen Participation.

Suhrke, Astri (1999) 'Human Security and the Interests of States: Reviving the Oslo–Ottawa Axis', *Security Dialogue*, 30 (3): 265–275.

Tadem, Teresa S. and Tadem, Eduardo C. (2002) 'Anti-globalisation Movements in Southeast Asia', in Samir Amin and François Houtart (eds) *Mondialisation des Resistance*, Paris: L'Harmattan.

UNDP Human Development Report 1994 (1994) New York: Oxford University Press.

Wilkin, Peter (1995) 'New Myths for the South: Globalization and the Conflict between Private Power and Freedom', in Peter Wilkin and Caroline Thomas (eds) *Globalization and the South*, New York: St Martin's Press.

Yamamoto, Tadashi (ed.) (1995) *Emerging Civil Society in the Asia-Pacific Community*, Tokyo and Singapore: Institute of Southeast Asian Studies.

—— (2000) 'The Future of Civil Society in Asia', in Mely Caballero-Anthony and Jawhar Hassan (eds) *Beyond the Crisis: Challenges and Opportunities*, Kuala Lumpur: Institute of Strategic and International Studies.

13 Japan, East Asian regionalism and the politics of human security

Hiro Katsumata

Introduction

The leaders of the Association of Southeast Asian Nations (ASEAN) and Japan announced that they would seek to build an 'East Asian community' in their Special Summit held in Tokyo in December 2003 (ASEAN and Japan, 2003a). This announcement cemented the two parties' cordial relations, and demonstrated the rise of regionalism in East Asia.[1] The notion of East Asia, encompassing Northeast and Southeast Asia, has been under the spotlight in recent years. The development of the ASEAN Plus Three (APT), participated in by the members of ASEAN plus Japan, China and South Korea, has attracted much attention. The first summit meeting of the APT was held in November 1997, and at the second meeting, in December 1998, the leaders agreed to regularize the event. What can be regarded as an East Asian institution is, however, a web of bilateral and multilateral arrangements placed within the framework of the APT. When the ASEAN members hold their annual summit meeting, they also host an East Asian meeting, inviting the three Northeast Asian countries – Japan, China and South Korea – known as 'ASEAN Plus Three'. They also hold separate meetings with each of these three countries, known as 'ASEAN Plus One'. Furthermore, the three Northeast Asian countries meet among themselves as well. In addition, within the framework of the APT, not only annual summit meetings but also ministerial ones in various areas are convened at different times of the year. It should be mentioned that the APT, the core of these meeting arrangements, is not an international organization established on the basis of a treaty. It is, rather, an arena within which participants put forward their international initiatives and agendas for regional cooperation.

Given the backdrop of these trends in East Asian regional institutional development, this chapter is mainly concerned with the manner in which the governance of economic security has unfolded at the East Asian regional level, and explores the ways in which economic security issues have been addressed through East Asian regional cooperation. What is notable about East Asian cooperation is that a major economic power, Japan, is involved. Japan is the largest economy in East Asia, and its activities may have a significant impact on economic security issues in the region. Thus, this chapter is interested in the role of Japan in East Asian cooperation, and especially its contribution to the economic security of Southeast Asian countries in the region.

Helen Nesadurai points out in Chapter 1 that the domestic dimension is an essential aspect of economic security. She argues that for many countries in the developing world, sustaining a particular level of growth *and* socio-economic development is critical for maintaining social cohesion and the integrity of the state. The Asian financial crisis in the late 1990s demonstrated the plausibility of such a claim. For the Southeast Asian countries that were severely damaged by this crisis, many of which are still engaged in the process of economic development, economic security is a crucial concern. It is in this context that this chapter explores the impact of Japanese diplomacy on East Asian regionalism more generally, and on the economic security of the Southeast Asian countries in particular. The central claim of this chapter is simply that Japan plays an important role in the development of East Asian regionalism and in the governance of economic security at the East Asian regional level. Yet such a simple claim encompasses many issues, and it is these issues that constitute the focus of discussion in this chapter.

To summarize, this chapter argues that there is an identity gap between Japan and ASEAN, the two engines of East Asian regionalism. While the former identifies itself as a member of the advanced industrialized democracies, this identity has not been shared by the Southeast Asian countries. The common identity of these countries as ASEAN is based on their own diplomatic principles, associated with the ASEAN Way. This has led to differences between the Southeast Asian states on the one hand, and Japan on the other hand, over who participates in East Asian regional cooperation, the agendas to be pursued and the manner in which these agendas are pursued. This 'identity gap' assumes especial significance in the context of human security, a key plank of Japan's foreign policy. Japan's pursuit of human security agendas in Southeast Asia had the potential to cause tension between the two parties, since the aspect of human security that emphasizes people's 'freedom from fear' is a sensitive issue in Southeast Asia, owing to its close relationship with human rights and democracy. Japan has, however, limited its means of pursuing human security to offers of official development assistance (ODA), effectively concentrating on the 'freedom from want' aspect of human security. This sits better with Southeast Asian governments. While Japan sees itself as an advanced industrialized democracy, its self-identification as a part of Asia has led it to be sympathetic to the special concerns of its regional neighbours regarding state sovereignty. This accommodation, this chapter suggests, is the key to the future consolidation of East Asian regionalism.

The first part of the chapter investigates the impact of Japanese diplomacy on the economic security of Southeast Asian countries by studying the overall development of East Asian cooperation. The concordant relations between ASEAN and Japan are explored. Next, the chapter considers some potential problems in these two parties' joint efforts to promote East Asian regionalism. Following this, the chapter focuses on one key issue resulting from the ideational difference between ASEAN and Japan: the latter's pursuit of human security agendas. In principle, the pursuit of such agendas contributes to economic security; however, in Southeast Asia, human security is a sensitive issue for governments, and Japan's activities in this area may cause tension. Thus, the study goes on to explore the implications of Japan's human security diplomacy for the economic security of the Southeast Asian countries. In the concluding section, broader issues of governance are discussed, and the role of Japan in East Asian cooperation is identified.

ASEAN–Japan concordance: promoting East Asian regionalism

Japan and ASEAN have been the engines of East Asian regionalism. What can be regarded as an East Asian institution was constructed and has been strengthened through the development of cooperation between these two parties. Japan's contribution to the economic security of the Southeast Asian countries may be understood in terms of the development of a regional institution in East Asia, within which Japan carried out various support measures after the onset of the Asian financial crisis.

It was in the mid-1990s that East Asian regionalism began to develop. A plan for a summit meeting between Asia and Europe facilitated East Asian cooperation (Maswood, 2001: 9; Webber, 2001: 357). ASEAN and the European Union agreed that the first meeting – which would later be named the Asia–Europe Meeting (ASEM) – be held in March 1996, and the Asian line-up was left to ASEAN to decide (*The Straits Times*, 5 May 1995: 1). ASEAN decided to invite the three Northeast Asian countries – Japan, China and South Korea – to attend the meeting. Then, in the second half of 1995 and early 1996, several meetings among these four parties, at the senior official and ministerial levels, were held to prepare for the ASEM meeting (Yamakage, 2001: 66–67).

Another important factor which facilitated East Asian regional cooperation was Japan's intention to strengthen its relations with ASEAN countries. These countries were important economic partners for Japan; moreover, the importance of ASEAN had become significant in political terms as well. At this time, for Tokyo, its relations with Beijing were an important part of the political agenda. The fact that a region-wide security dialogue was initiated by ASEAN in the early 1990s made Japan reconsider the importance of the Southeast Asian association. The ASEAN Regional Forum, a multilateral framework involving China, was established within the framework provided by ASEAN. For Japan, stronger relations with ASEAN could lead to wider East Asian cooperation.

With the aim of strengthening Japan's relations with ASEAN, Prime Minister Ryutaro Hashimoto visited Brunei, Malaysia, Indonesia, Vietnam and Singapore in January 1997, the year in which ASEAN celebrated its thirtieth anniversary. In these countries, he proposed that summit meetings be held between ASEAN and Japan on a regular annual basis (Ministry of Foreign Affairs of Japan [hereafter, MOFA Japan], 1997). The ASEAN countries welcomed Hashimoto's proposal in principle (*Nikkei Shimbun* [hereafter, *Nikkei*], 20 January 1997: 8). Yet they sought even broader regional cooperation. In the summer, they decided to invite not only Japan but also China and South Korea to their summit meeting scheduled to be held in Kuala Lumpur in December of that year (ASEAN, 1997).

Soon after the first summit meeting at the East Asian regional level was scheduled, the Asian financial crisis broke out. The crisis dealt a serious blow to the economic security of countries in the region. Retrospectively, it can be said that East Asian regionalism developed dramatically through Japan and ASEAN's joint efforts to deal with this major economic security challenge. Several weeks after the start of the crisis in July 1997, Japan sought to establish an Asian Monetary Fund (AMF). Yet the AMF plan was not implemented, because of opposition from the United States and the International Monetary Fund (IMF). Recovery measures were carried out within the framework of the latter, to which Japan made financial contributions. However, as the situation showed no significant sign of improvement, a sense of frustration and resentment began to grow in Asia against the Washington-sponsored IMF. Then Japan put forward its own initiative in October 1998: the New Miyazawa Initiative. This initiative included up to US$30 billion in financial support, based on bilateral arrangements with Asian countries. The plan was emphasized by Prime Minister Keizo Obuchi during his policy initiative speech, which he delivered before attending the APT meeting in Hanoi in December 1998. In the speech, he acknowledged the 'ever-increasing economic interdependence' between Japan and other Asian countries (MOFA Japan, 1998). In 1998, for example, Japan's exports to Thailand, Indonesia, Malaysia and the Philippines had decreased by 32 per cent from the previous year (Ministry of International Trade and Industry, Japan, 1999: 63). The recovery of the Asian economies was clearly essential to the Japanese economy.

At the APT meeting in Manila in November 1999, the East Asian leaders issued their 'Joint Statement on East Asian Cooperation'. Their statement underscored the prominence of the notion of East Asia, as shown in expressions such as 'interaction', 'closer linkages', 'people' and 'mutual understanding' in East Asia (ASEAN, 1999). One of the most remarkable achievements of the APT has been an agreement reached in May 2000 at the finance ministers' meeting to build a regional network of currency swap agreements, called the Chiang Mai Initiative. Significantly, the agreement extended ASEAN's currency swap network to Japan, which holds a large amount of foreign currency reserves. The previous swap agreement among ASEAN countries had been far from adequate (Soesastro, 1998: 375). What developed after the Chiang Mai meeting was a regional mechanism aimed at preventing another crisis. This mechanism was aimed at deterring speculative attacks by providing an international liquidity mechanism to respond to such attacks, and should be seen as one of the central pillars of economic security governance in East Asia.[2]

In addition to the economic area, the significance of the APT should also be recognized in the political/security field. Regional stability is a prerequisite for any cooperative initiatives, including those for economic security, and the APT serves as an arena for a security dialogue aimed at enhancing mutual understanding and trust. In the 1999 joint statement, the leaders expressed their commitment to promote not only monetary and financial cooperation, but also security dialogue and other cooperative agendas (ASEAN, 1999). During the 1999 meeting, they devoted much time to discussing security issues, such as the Korean Peninsula problem and Indonesia's destabilization resulting from the financial crisis. At this time, the territorial disputes in the South China Sea were not addressed. Nonetheless, East Asian cooperation developed thereafter, and in November 2002, ASEAN and Beijing signed the 'Declaration on the Conduct of Parties in the South China Sea', a political document stipulating a code of conduct in this area (ASEAN and People's Republic of China, 2002). This should be regarded as another achievement of cooperative efforts in East Asia.

East Asian regionalism has emerged through the development of cordial relations between ASEAN and Japan, as demonstrated above. This of course does not mean that the roles of other countries, in particular China, are unimportant. Yet Beijing's active involvement in East Asian regionalism has begun only in recent years. It is ASEAN and Japan that have led regional cooperation since the mid-1990s. The announcement at the ASEAN–Japan Special Summit in Tokyo in December 2003 that they would seek to build an East Asian community is significant in this regard. Japan's commitment to East Asian cooperation has promoted the construction of the first East Asian institution, and Tokyo's activities have contributed to regional efforts to address the economic security issues associated with the financial crisis. Nevertheless, there are some potential problems in their joint effort to promote East Asian cooperation. Such problems concern the notion of East Asia itself.

ASEAN–Japan discord: problematising an East Asian identity?

Who are the East Asians? What sort of agendas should be pursued through East Asian cooperation, and in what way should those agendas be pursued? The answers to these questions from ASEAN and from Japan may differ. The discord between the two parties concerns issues of identity. In an East Asian community, which they intend to construct, members should be able to share a 'we-feeling' or a sense of 'we-ness' (Deutsch *et al.*, 1957). A sense of community involves a common identity as members of East Asia. However, there is an identity gap between the two engines of East Asian regionalism.

Japan is undoubtedly an Asian country in a geographical sense, and shares much with its Asian neighbours in historical and economic terms; nonetheless, Tokyo identifies itself as a member of the advanced industrialized democracies, which share liberal values such as freedom, human rights, democracy and a market economy. Such an identity has been expressed in various diplomatic documents, including Japan's *Diplomatic Bluebook* 2001, the first issue of the new century. The first page of this book states, 'The curtain has been raised on the 21st century. . . . As a principal member of the advanced industrialized democracies . . . Japan is being called on to meet its global responsibilities' (MOFA Japan, 2001a: 1).

However, Tokyo's key partners in East Asian cooperation, the ASEAN countries, do not share such an identity with Japan and with other advanced industrialized democracies. The Southeast Asian countries hold a set of unique diplomatic principles associated with the so-called ASEAN Way of diplomacy, as is elaborated on later in the chapter. They have developed these principles through their interaction over decades, and their common identity as ASEAN has been constructed upon these principles (Khong, 1997; Acharya, 1998: 207–214; 2001a: 26–28, 71, 202; Bessho, 1999: chapter 3). Such an identity gap between Japan and ASEAN may be a source of discord, which may be problematic for the development of East Asian regionalism and the creation of a community.

ASEAN and Japan appear to have different understandings of the notion of East Asia and that of an East Asian community. When Tokyo talks about an East Asian community, its perspective encompasses Australia and New Zealand, which are also advanced industrialized democracies. The Japanese perspective was expressed in Prime Minister Junichiro Koizumi's speech in Singapore in January 2002, in which Japan for the first time articulated its desire to develop a community in East Asia:

> Our goal should be the creation of a 'community'. . . . The first step is to make the best use of the framework of ASEAN+3. . . . I expect that the countries of ASEAN, Japan, China, the Republic of Korea, Australia and New Zealand will be core members of such a community.
>
> (MOFA Japan, 2002a)

The Japanese idea of starting a community-building process on the basis of the APT is shared by ASEAN. However, the question of whether Australia and New Zealand should be considered members of East Asia remains controversial. Hence, the 'Tokyo Declaration', issued at the ASEAN–Japan Special Summit in December 2003, was vague on this point. With regard to the plan for an East Asian community, the leaders of the two parties could not specify the geographical scope of such a community. The declaration ambiguously stated that the APT process was an 'important channel to promote cooperation', while maintaining that a community should be 'outward looking' (ASEAN and Japan, 2003a).

Indeed, the lack of shared understanding between the two parties has been apparent for several years. In 1995, they disagreed over which countries should represent 'Asia' in the summit between Asia and Europe, scheduled for the following year. Tokyo held that Australia and New Zealand should take part. However, as the initiator of the summit, ASEAN decided to invite only the three Northeast Asian countries – Japan, China and South Korea – and suggested that the association might hold the summit without Japan if the latter insisted on the participation of Canberra and Wellington (Jiji Press, 1995).

Japan's concern with Australia and New Zealand cannot be understood purely in security and economic terms. In the security area, the levels of interdependence between Japan and these two countries are by no means high. In the economic field, it is difficult to claim that Tokyo has special relations with them while other Asian countries do not. Take, for example, the volume of trade with Australia as a percentage of total volume of trade: Indonesia's figures are higher than those of Japan, in both exports and imports. The export figures of Malaysia, Thailand and Singapore are higher than that of Japan, while their import figures are lower. Although the Philippines' figures for both exports and imports are lower than those of Japan, it can be said that, overall, it is not the case that Japan's relationship with Canberra is an exceptional one (International Monetary Fund, 2002).

Moreover, there may be discord between ASEAN and Japan over questions of what sort of cooperative agendas should be pursued, and the way in which such agendas should be pursued. A comment by an anonymous ASEAN official at the APT in October 2003 aptly summarizes the potential problems. The official noted that although Japan puts forward the largest number of proposals among the APT participants, there was a gap between its proposals and what ASEAN would like to pursue (*Mainichi Shimbun*, 8 October 2003: 7). To be sure, ASEAN is not a monolithic entity, and disagreements between its members often arise. Yet within the association, there is a common understanding that decisions should be made on a consensual basis, and ASEAN should pursue common policies in its dealings with external powers. However, in the case of ASEAN–Japan relations, there is no common understanding in this regard, and thus things may simply go wrong.

The APT meeting in Brunei in November 2001 is a case in point. At this meeting, which was held a few months after the September 11 attack in the United States, the lack of unity between ASEAN and Japan was apparent in the treatment of issues related to terrorism. At the preparatory stage of the meeting, Japan actively sought an anti-terrorism declaration to be adopted by the participants (*Asahi Shimbun*, 6 November 2001: 3). For Japan, the attack against the United States, another representative of the advanced industrialized democracies, was undoubtedly a crucial global issue, and Japan believed that some kind of action should be taken by East Asians as well. Nonetheless, Tokyo's efforts bore no fruit, owing to the lack of a common understanding of terrorism issues between Japan and ASEAN.

The ASEAN members did not intend to discuss these issues with Japan in depth. At the APT meeting, Japan's prime minister, Junichiro Koizumi, spent most of his allocated time discussing these issues, exploring the possibilities of international cooperation against terrorism; however, few Asian leaders joined the discussion (ibid.; *Nikkei*, 6 Nov 2001: 2). What ASEAN members did instead was to address terrorism issues within the Southeast Asian association. At the ASEAN summit, which was held before the APT, the Southeast Asian countries issued their own anti-terrorism declaration, which reflected their particular concern over attributing terrorism to religious and racial factors (ASEAN, 2001). Subsequently, ASEAN told Tokyo, which was seeking an APT declaration, that there was no need to issue a separate one (*Nikkei*, 6 November 2001: 2).

This kind of discord between ASEAN and Japan over the question of agendas in East Asian cooperation may have some implications for economic security. Issues associated with the concept of 'human security' are significant in this regard. The rest of this chapter focuses on the case of human security issues.

The human security controversy

Human security is a global agenda pursued in the United Nations (UN) by various agencies and actors, including the UN Development Programme (UNDP) and the

UN High Commissioner for Refugees. The 1994 *Human Development Report* of the UNDP elaborated on this concept. According to the UNDP, human security is 'people-centred' and 'concerned with how people live and breathe in a society'. There are two major components of human security: freedom from *fear* and freedom from *want*. Thus, human security concerns how freely people exercise their many choices, whether they live in conflict or in peace, and how much access they have to market and social opportunities (1994: 23–24; 1995: 229–230).

Economic security, then, is one of the main components of human security, along with other aspects such as food, health, environmental, personal, community and political security (UNDP, 1994: chapter 2; 1995). The concept of economic security should not be conflated with that of human security. Yet the latter covers people's right to economic resources. The distinction between these two concepts concerns their scope, not the principle behind them. Given that human security is a broad concept that encompasses economic security, efforts to enhance human security should in principle contribute to economic security. However, in Asia such efforts may entail a set of problems.

The principles of human security, emphasizing people's freedom from fear and want, resonate well with Japan's political values and identity. Its *Diplomatic Bluebook 2001* emphasizes the notions of 'freedom, democracy, respect for basic human rights' as a set of values and institutions to which Japan and other advanced industrialized democracies adhere (MOFA Japan, 2001a: 2). It is said that when new ideas resonate well with existing ones, the former can be promoted smoothly and effectively (Keck and Sikkink, 1998: 204–205; Checkel, 1999; Bernstein, 2000). Thus, Japan has been one of the strongest proponents of human security agendas in the international sphere. It has been attentive to the discourse of human security in the global setting, as its discussion of human security customarily focuses on the activities of the UN (MOFA Japan, 2001b; 2001c: 2–3). The UNDP encouraged the international community to endorse the 'concept of human security as the key challenge for the 21st century' (1994: 39; 1995: 236). Reflecting on such discourse, the diplomatic bluebook mentioned above notes that 'positioning human security as the cornerstone of international cooperation in the 21st century, Japan is working to make the new century a human-centered century' (MOFA Japan, 2001a: 50).

However, for ASEAN, human security is a sensitive agenda. This is because ASEAN politics is traditionally state centred, while human security is people centred. The principles of the ASEAN Way of diplomacy include mutual respect for state sovereignty and non-interference in the internal affairs of other countries. These principles themselves are not peculiar to Southeast Asia; however, the Southeast Asian countries' practice of these principles should be understood in the ASEAN context (Katsumata, 2003). Until the middle of the twentieth century, all the ASEAN countries with the exception of Thailand had been under colonial rule. Historical memories of a common colonial past have made all the ASEAN countries very respectful of one another's sovereignty (Katzenstein, 1997: 32). More importantly, the principle of non-interference has been fostered on the basis of the governments' belief that they should concentrate on nation-building without interference from others. In Southeast Asia, with the possible exception of

Thailand, the state came before the nation (Nathan, 1998: 547). For the post-independence governments that inherited from the colonial powers a multi-ethnic political entity with a weak economic basis, nation-building and the achievement of domestic stability were crucial tasks.

ASEAN's state-centred diplomatic style is ill suited to the pursuit of people's security. In particular, in terms of the two aspects of human security – that is, people's freedom from fear and freedom from want – issues associated with the former can be controversial in Southeast Asia. Examples of such issues include human rights, democracy and numerous problems arising from conflicts. Measures to deal with these issues may become intrusive in the political/security field. However, any form of external interference is unacceptable to the governments of the Southeast Asian states. ASEAN itself also plays little role in addressing the domestic issues of its member countries, especially in the political/security area.

Human security undoubtedly involves issues of human rights and democracy, as the UNDP notes that 'people should be able to live in a society that honours their human rights' (1994: 32; 1995: 233). The Human Security Network, initiated by Canada and Norway in the late 1990s, emphasizes these issues: 'Human security is advanced . . . by protecting and promoting human rights, the rule of law, democratic governance and democratic structures' (Human Security Network, 1999). Yet, in Southeast Asia, some governments see human security as another attempt by the West to impose its liberal values (Acharya, 2001b: 1).

An even more difficult issue is the question of intervention (ibid.: 15; Anwar, 2003: 555–563). Today, some countries call for military measures in order to protect people's rights. Canada, another strong advocate of human security, goes as far as arguing that '[e]nsuring human security can involve the use of coercive measures, including sanctions and military forces' (Axworthy, 1999). Under the rubric of human security, Canada sends missions, deploys troops and carries out peacekeeping operations – or what Ottawa calls 'peace support operations' – under the auspices of international organizations such as the UN and the Organization for Security Cooperation in Europe (see Axworthy, 1999; Department of Foreign Affairs and International Trade, n.d.).

In Southeast Asia, the principles of human security do not resonate, although they do in Japan. Thus, the countries of Southeast Asia have not pursued human security agendas in depth. The joint communiqués of the ASEAN Ministerial Meeting have not focused on such agendas. The ASEAN Concord II in 2003 put forward the concept of an 'ASEAN Security Community'. Although various security agendas, including security dialogue, approaches to conflicts and maritime security, were considered under this new concept, human security was not mentioned (ASEAN, 2003). The Asian financial crisis, which caused a pervasive sense of economic, political and social insecurity, was an event that signalled the relevance of the concept of human security (Acharya and Acharya, 2002: 329–333). Thus, after the crisis Thailand proposed that a caucus on human security issues be set up (Surin 1998). However, the Thai proposal was modified, and ASEAN decided to consider a caucus on 'social safety nets', whose focus would be on social and economic issues, including poverty, disease and illiteracy (*The Nation*, 29 July

1998). This idea was incorporated into the activities of the ASEAN Foundation (Soesastro, 1998: 380). Overall, it can be said that in ASEAN diplomacy the notion of human security has been neglected, although social and economic issues are considered important.

Given that Japan is among the strongest proponents of human security agendas while ASEAN is rather reluctant to pursue them, this could be a cause of discord between the two parties. Thus, it is worth exploring whether and in what way Japan has pursued these agendas in East Asia, while considering the implications of Japan's diplomacy for the economic security of the Southeast Asian countries.

Japan in Asia: human security and economic security

Japan has been pursuing human security agendas in Southeast Asia for several years. Indeed, this is the region where Tokyo's human security diplomacy first started. Yet despite the sensitivity of the issue, Japan's diplomacy has not caused any tension or discord. Rather, the Southeast Asian countries welcome Japan's activities, which contribute to the enhancement of their economic security. In this respect, it should be emphasized that Japanese human rights diplomacy mainly addresses issues concerning people's freedom from want, rather than freedom from fear.

Remarkably, Tokyo has limited its means of pursuing human security to the offering of its official development assistance (ODA), and concentrated on areas related to development, such as poverty, education, health and the environment (MOFA Japan, 2003a: 84, 149).[3] Its aim is to develop local communities and to enhance individuals' abilities. For example, under the rubric of human security, Tokyo's ODA is used to reduce poverty, develop local economies, enhance agricultural infrastructures, build schools and hospitals, as well as to provide education for children and vocational training for adults. Japan's efforts in these areas would enhance the economic security of recipient countries, in particular, if the domestic dimension of economic security were being emphasized.

Moreover, in Japan's human security policies based on its ODA, issues that are deemed to be sensitive in Southeast Asia, such as human rights and democracy, are not addressed extensively. Tokyo seems to have avoided linking these issues to its human security policies. Japan's ODA White Paper 2002 mentions areas on which it intends to focus in its human security assistance, including poverty, education, medical care and healthcare generally, water and sanitation, the environment and the like. Issues of human rights and democracy are not raised here (ibid.: 84, 149, 634).[4] Tokyo's pursuit of human security agendas, unlike Canada's, does not involve any intrusive measures in the political/security field. If issues related to conflicts were to be addressed, Tokyo's main focus would be on post-conflict rehabilitation and redevelopment, instead of the prevention and resolution of conflicts, which might entail political and or military measures. It is worth noting that human security is discussed mainly in Japan's ODA White Papers, and to a limited extent in its Diplomatic Bluebooks. In its Defence White Papers, the phrase 'human security' hardly appears (ibid.; MOFA Japan, 2002b; Japan Defense Agency, 2002).

Why has Japan's focus been limited to the development area? This is because, while Japan sees itself as a member of the advanced industrialised democracies, it also identifies itself as belonging to Asia, and thus has been sympathetic to the special concern of its fellow countries over state sovereignty. According to the director-general of the Multilateral Cooperation Department of Japan's Foreign Ministry, Hideaki Ueda, the Japanese government does not support the idea of intervention under the rubric of human security, given that there are many developing countries that hold to a traditional conception of sovereignty. Ueda highlights his government's dialogue with developing countries in which the latter expressed their concern that developed countries might intervene in their domestic affairs under the pretext of human security. Furthermore, he notes that Japan's approach in its Asian diplomacy is based not on pressure, but on dialogue (Ueda, 2000: 71–73). Such discourse on the part of Japanese officials is common. Another high-ranking official of the same department emphasizes the concerns on the part of developing countries over the developed countries' attempts to interfere and impose their own values through human security activities (Minami, *et al.*, 2003: 28).

Japan's concern for Asian countries is based on its identity as a part of Asia. Such an identity has long been embraced by the Japanese, as reflected in the discourse of its political leaders. Prime Minister Takeo Fukuda delivered a speech in Manila in 1977 in which he proposed the so-called Fukuda doctrine. He noted that both Japan and the Southeast Asian countries are members of Asia, and should foster 'heart-to-heart' relations (MOFA Japan, 1977).[5] Having pursued such cordial relations with other Asian countries, Japan has been sensitive to those countries' anxiety over human security issues. For Japan, any failure to build such relations would result in a sense of alienation.

One might disagree with the above claim and argue that Tokyo's concern for these countries merely reflects the pursuit of its economic interests through ODA. It is true that critics are prone to view economic assistance from developed countries as an attempt to expand their markets or to secure sources of energy. However, such criticism mainly applies to assistance for infrastructure and energy projects. In Japan's human security ODA, with its aim of reducing poverty and enhancing education and healthcare, no substantial economic stakes are involved. Hence, it is hard to explain Japan's special concern for Asian countries without making reference to its identity as a part of Asia.[6] In addition, others might even deny the claim that Japan is attentive to the Asian countries' anxiety, and attribute Japan's non-intrusive approach to its pacifist constitution and norms, which discourage active diplomacy in the political/military area. However, since the early 1990s Japan's diplomacy has actually become active in these areas. Tokyo has sought to make greater international contributions in the political/security area.[7] Yet with respect to the human security issues deemed to be sensitive in Southeast Asia, Japan has limited its focus to the development area. This should be understood in terms of Japan's concern for its fellow Asian countries, the basis of which is a common identity as Asians. In sum, with regard to human security, Japan's multiple identities have served to mitigate the potential negative consequences of its identity gap with ASEAN.

It was in the late 1990s that Japan announced its intention of advancing human security in Southeast Asia by offering ODA. This was part of Japan's efforts to assist the countries that had been affected by the economic crisis. In December 1998, when he visited Hanoi to attend the APT, Prime Minister Obuchi delivered a speech that elaborated on his policy initiatives. Obuchi stated that Japan would address human security by utilizing its ODA (MOFA Japan, 1998).

ODA has been one of the main components of Japanese foreign policy for decades, and Southeast Asia has been the priority area. Hence, it is not surprising that for all the Southeast Asian recipient countries – that is, all the ASEAN members except for Brunei and Singapore – Japan is the largest donor (MOFA Japan, 2003a: 300; Organisation for Economic Co-operation and Development, 2003). What is remarkable is the fact that, in recent years, Tokyo has made human security one of the core elements of its ODA policies, and extended its economic assistance to people of the developing countries, either directly or through its contribution to the UN Trust Fund for Human Security. Its 'Medium-Term Policy on ODA', announced in 1999, incorporated the notion of human security. It can be said that the underlying principles of its mid-term policy address an essential element of economic security. While emphasizing its human security perspective, Tokyo maintained that it would 'provide assistance for balanced economic growth *and* social development' (MOFA Japan, 1999; emphasis added).

Japan's ODA has been extended not only to governments, but also to local communities and individuals. It aims at narrowing the gap between rich and poor (see MOFA Japan, 2003b). Such an approach has largely been welcomed by the Southeast Asian countries. The 'Tokyo Declaration' issued at the ASEAN–Japan summit noted 'the significant contribution of Japan in the area of development assistance' (ASEAN and Japan, 2003a). Even more remarkably, the 'ASEAN–Japan Plan of Action' went as far as to state that both parties will '[c]onsider jointly promoting human security through various projects including those which Japan will support through . . . the Grant Assistance for Grassroots/Human Security Projects' – that is, one element of Japan's ODA policies (ASEAN and Japan, 2003b).

Conclusions

Japanese diplomacy has had a significant impact on the development of East Asian regionalism and on the economic security of the Southeast Asian countries. The first regional institution in East Asia, centred on the ASEAN Plust Three (APT), was constructed and has been strengthened through the development of cordial relations between ASEAN and Japan. The latter's activities after the outbreak of the Asian financial crisis have contributed to regional efforts to enhance economic security. Moreover, Tokyo has been able to address the domestic dimension of the Southeast Asian countries' economic security through its efforts to promote human security on the basis of its ODA policies. It has focused on the development of local communities and the enhancement of individuals' abilities in such areas as poverty, education and health.

However, there is an identity gap between the two engines of East Asian regionalism. While Japan identifies itself as a member of the advanced industrialized democracies, this identity has not been shared by the Southeast Asian countries. The common identity of these countries as ASEAN members is based on their own diplomatic principles. As a result, there may be disagreement between these two parties over questions of which countries should be included in the process of East Asian cooperation, what sort of agendas should be pursued in this process, and in what ways those agendas should be pursued. Yet with regard to human security, despite the sensitivity of this issue in Southeast Asia, Japan's activities have not caused any tension between the two parties. This is because Tokyo also identifies itself as a part of Asia, and thus has been sympathetic to the special concern of its fellow countries over state sovereignty. In other words, with regard to human security, Japan's multiple identities have served to mitigate the potential negative consequences of its identity gap with ASEAN.

On the basis of the study of the human security case, it can be said that the key to addressing the problem of an identity gap within the framework of East Asian cooperation is Japan's own orientation. In this regard, the direction of Japanese diplomacy is one of the key determinants of the future of regionalism in East Asia. East Asian regionalism has emerged only in recent years. The experience of the Southeast Asian countries demonstrates that the construction of a regional identity is a long process. The history of these countries' relations should be understood as their quest for a Southeast Asian identity (Acharya, 2000). This took a long time, during which countries that were politically, economically and culturally diverse have come to terms with each other's differences, and developed their common identity and diplomatic principles. As a result of their lengthy efforts, today ASEAN is seen as a community of friendly nations (Snitwongse, 1995: 520; Khong, 1997; Acharya 1998, 2001a; Bessho, 1999: chapter 3). In East Asia, although the leaders of ASEAN and Japan have recently announced their intention to form a community, regional cooperation is still at an early stage. The East Asian leaders should regard their announcement as the starting point of their quest for an East Asian identity.

Finally, it is worth considering the broader issue of governance, and identifying the position of Japan in East Asian cooperation. Achieving governance does not necessarily require a centralized authority in the form of governments or supranational organizations (Rosenau and Czempiel, 1992; Young, 1994: 12–19). International governance is achievable through countries' efforts to create international regimes or broader cooperative arrangements covering multiple areas. Yet in East Asia, one needs to be careful not to overemphasize multilateral activities under the framework of the APT. A web of bilateral and multilateral arrangements placed within the APT is simply an arena within which participants put forward their cooperative agendas. Mechanisms for economic security at the East Asian regional level comprise a network of bilateral arrangements and a set of economic measures on a bilateral basis. The New Miyazawa Initiative emphasized Japan's bilateral financial support for Asian countries. The Chiang Mai Initiative is based on a network of bilateral currency swap agreements, and Japan's ODA policies are not conducted through multilateral arrangements in East Asia. The development of regional mechanisms for governance is still at an early stage, and such mechanisms largely rely on various bilateral arrangements. After all, East Asian regionalism is still at an incipient stage, and a solid East Asian regional identity has not yet been constructed.

The prominence of the bilateral arrangements brings Japan to the centre stage in regional economic security efforts. It is said that Tokyo cannot assume leadership in East Asia for historical reasons, and because of its rivalry with Beijing (Webber, 2001). Nevertheless, in reality it plays a significant role on a bilateral basis. It is the biggest economic power in East Asia, as shown by the extent of its financial support to the Southeast Asian countries after the economic crisis. The amount of its ODA to these countries is the largest in the world. Moreover, the importance of Japan's role should be understood in ideational terms. Japan's own orientation, concerning its identity as a part of Asia, is the key to addressing the problem of an identity gap in East Asian regionalism. Therefore, in both economic and ideational terms the role of Japan is highly significant in the development of East Asian regionalism and in the governance of economic security.

Notes

1   In this chapter, the term 'regionalism' refers to the development of regional cooperation, which may be either formal or informal. Regional cooperation may entail the creation of a formal institution, yet it can also be based on a looser structure, involving patterns of regular meetings (see Hurrell, 1995: 38–39, 42). The notion of East Asia is an ambiguous and contested one, as is demonstrated in this chapter.

2   To be sure, the currency swap agreements are arranged in coordination with the IMF. Yet even so, they are measures offered by Asians for Asian countries.

3   With regard to Japan's efforts in this area, it has incorporated the human security perspective in its overall ODA policies. Moreover, it has strengthened its assistance measures for grassroots projects and renamed it Grant Assistance for Grassroots Human Security Projects. Furthermore, it established the Trust Fund for Human Security in the United Nations in 1999, and has supported various projects within the framework of the UN (MOFA Japan, 2001c: 7).

4   It is notable in this regard that although Tokyo claims to consider the human rights conditions of recipient countries in its overall ODA policies, Japan's approach in this area is rather practical and non-confrontational (Watanabe, 2001; Lam, 2001: 122–125).

5   In addition, Japan's sense of affinity with Asia has been reflected in speeches of political leaders. See, for example, MOFA Japan (1998). For Japan's identity as a member of Asia, see also Hein and Hammond (1995) and Bessho (1999: ch. 1).

6   Furthermore, it is worth mentioning that countries may strengthen their trade and investment relations without being sensitive to each other's diplomatic concerns, as the 'Western' countries' relations with the Southeast Asian countries demonstrate.

7   For example, in June 1990 Japan hosted a meeting of four Cambodian factions in Tokyo. Thereafter, Japan's active participation in the Cambodian peace process continued, as it contributed its defence forces to the UN peacekeeping operation in 1992.

References

Acharya, A. (1998) 'Collective Identity and Conflict Management in Southeast Asia', in E. Adler and M. Barnett (eds) *Security Communities*, Cambridge: Cambridge University Press, pp. 198–227.

—— (2000) *The Quest for Identity: International Relations of Southeast Asia*, Oxford: Oxford University Press.

—— (2001a) *Constructing a Security Community in Southeast Asia: ASEAN and the Problem of Regional Order*, London: Routledge.

—— (2001b) *Human Security: East versus West?*, Working Paper No. 17, Institute of Defence and Strategic Studies, Singapore.

Acharya, A. and Acharya, A. (2002) 'Human Security in Asia: Conceptual Ambiguities and Common Understandings', *Man and Development*, 24 (4): 325–342.

Anwar, D. F. (2003) 'Human Security: An Intractable Problem in Asia', in M. Alagappa (ed.) *Asian Security Order: Instrumental and Normative Features*, Stanford, CA: Stanford University Press, pp. 536–567.

ASEAN (1997) Joint Communiqué, Thirtieth ASEAN Ministerial Meeting, Subang Jaya, Malaysia, 24–25 July.

—— (1999) Joint Statement on East Asian Cooperation, Manila, 28 November.

—— (2001) ASEAN Declaration on Joint Action to Counter Terrorism, 5 November.

—— (2003) Declaration of ASEAN Concord II, Bali, Indonesia, 7 October.

ASEAN and Japan (2003a) Tokyo Declaration for the Dynamic and Enduring ASEAN–Japan Partnership in the New Millennium, Tokyo, 12 December.

—— (2003b) The ASEAN–Japan Plan of Action, Tokyo, 11–12 December.

ASEAN and People's Republic of China (2002) Declaration on the Conduct of Parties in the South China Sea, Phnom Penh, 4 November.

Axworthy, L. (1999) 'Human Security: Safety for People in a Changing World', Department of Foreign Affairs and International Trade, Ottawa, 29 April.

Bernstein, S. (2000) 'Ideas, Social Structure and the Compromise of Liberal Environmentalism', *European Journal of International Relations*, 6 (4): 464–512.

Bessho, K. (1999) *Identities and Security in East Asia*, Adelphi Paper No. 325, Oxford: Oxford University Press; London: International Institute for Strategic Studies.

Checkel, J. T. (1999) 'Norms, Institutions, and National Identity in Contemporary Europe', *International Studies Quarterly*, 43 (1): 83–114.

Department of Foreign Affairs and International Trade (n.d.) Canada's Human Security website, http://www.humansecurity.gc.ca/menu-en.asp (accessed 1 January 2004).

Deutsch, K. W., Burrell, S. A. and Kann, R. A. (1957) *Political Community and the North Atlantic Area: International Organization in the Light of Historical Experience*, Princeton, NJ: Princeton University Press.

Hein, L. and Hammond, E. H. (1995) 'Homing In on Asia: Identity in Contemporary Japan', *Bulletin of Concerned Asian Scholars*, 27 (3): 3–17.

Human Security Network (1999) A Perspective on Human Security, Chairman's Summary of the first Ministerial Meeting, Lysøen, Norway, 20 May.

Hurrell, A. (1995) 'Regionalism in Theoretical Perspective', in L. Fawcett and A. Hurrell (eds) *Regionalism in World Politics*, Oxford: Oxford University Press, pp. 37–73.

International Monetary Fund (2002) *Directory of Trade Statistics Yearbook 2002*, Washington, DC: IMF.

Japan Defense Agency (2002) *Defense of Japan 2002*, Tokyo: Japan Defense Agency/Urban Connections.

Jiji Press (1995) 'ASEAN to Exclude Aussie from Summit with EU', Washington, DC, 28 July.

Katsumata, H. (2003) 'Reconstruction of Diplomatic Norms in Southeast Asia: The Case for Strict Adherence to the ASEAN Way', *Contemporary Southeast Asia*, 25 (1): 104–121.

Katzenstein, P. (1997) 'Introduction: Asian Regionalism in Comparative Perspective', in P. J. Katzenstein and T. Shiraishi (eds) *Network Power: Japan and Asia*, Ithaca, NY: Cornell University Press, pp. 1–44.

Keck, M. E. and Sikkink, K. (1998) *Activists beyond Borders: Advocacy Networks in International Politics*, Ithaca, NY: Cornell University Press.

Khong, Y. F. (1997) 'ASEAN and the Southeast Asian Security Complex', in D. A. Lake and P. M. Morgan (eds) *Regional Orders: Building Security in a New World*, University Park: Pennsylvania State University Press, pp. 318–339.

Lam, P. E. (2001) 'Japan's Diplomatic Initiatives in Southeast Asia', in S. J. Maswood (ed.) *Japan and East Asian Regionalism*, London: Routledge, pp. 118–131.

Maswood, S. J. (2001) 'Japanese Foreign Policy and Regionalism', in S. J. Maswood (ed.) *Japan and East Asian Regionalism*, London: Routledge, pp. 6–25.

Minami, H., Yuge, A., Yamauchi, M. and Waki, Y. (2003) 'Nihon Gaikou-no Kidou-ryoku To-shi-te: Naze Ningen-no Anzenhosho Na-no-ka [As mobile power of Japanese diplomacy: why human security]', *Gaikou Forum* 185, December: 20–31.

Ministry of Foreign Affairs of Japan (MOFA Japan) (1977) Fukuda Takeo Souridaijin-no Manira-ni-okeru Spiichi [Speech by Prime Minister Takeo Fukuda at Manila], Manila, 18 August.

—— (1997) Press Conference by Prime Minister Ryutaro Hashimoto on the Occasion of His Visit to the Association of Southeast Asian Nations, Singapore, 13 January.

—— (1998) 'Toward the Creation of a Bright Future of Asia', Policy Speech by Prime Minister Keizo Obuchi, Hanoi, 16 December.

—— (1999) 'Japan's Medium-Term Policy on Official Development Assistance', 10 August.

—— (2001a) *Diplomatic Bluebook 2001*, Tokyo: Ministry of Foreign Affairs.

—— (2001b) *Human Security: For the 'Human Centered' 21st Century*, Tokyo, March.

—— (2001c) *The Trust Fund for Human Security: For the 'Human Centered' 21st Century*, Tokyo, November.

—— (2002a) 'Japan and ASEAN in East Asia: A Sincere and Open Partnership', Speech by Prime Minister of Japan, Junichiro Koizumi, Singapore, 14 January.

—— (2002b) *Diplomatic Bluebook 2002*, Tokyo: Ministry of Foreign Affairs.

—— (2003a) *Seifu Kaihatsu Enjo (ODA) Hakusho 2002* [White Paper on Official Development Assistance 2002], Tokyo: Ministry of Foreign Affairs.

—— (2003b) Japan's Official Development Assistance Charter, 29 August.

Ministry of International Trade and Industry, Japan (1999) *Tsu-sho Hakusho 1999* [White Paper on International Trade 1999], Tokyo: Ministry of International Trade and Industry.

Nathan, K. S. (1998) 'Malaysia: Reinventing the Nation', in M. Alagappa (ed.) *Asian Security Practice: Material and Ideational Influences*, Stanford, CA: Stanford University Press, pp. 513–548.

Organisation for Economic Co-operation and Development (2003) 'Aid at a Glance: Aid Charts for Recipient Countries and Territories', February [Online] http://www1.oecd.org/dac/htm/aid_recipients.htm (accessed 1 January 2004).

Rosenau, J. N. and Czempiel, E. O. (eds) (1992) *Governance without Government: Order and Change in World Politics*, Cambridge: Cambridge University Press.

Snitwongse, K. (1995) 'ASEAN's Security Cooperation: Search for a Regional Order', *The Pacific Review*, 8 (3): 518–530.

Soesastro, H. (1998) 'ASEAN during the Crisis', *ASEAN Economic Bulletin*, 15 (3): 373–381.

Surin, P. (1998) Statement at the PMC 9 + 10 Session, Agenda Item 2 (a)–(c), Manila, 28 July.

Ueda, H. (2000) 'Ima Naze "Ningen-no Anzenhosho" Na-no-ka [Why "human security" now]', *Gaikou Forum*, February: 64–73.

UNDP (1994) *Human Development Report 1994*, New York: Oxford University Press.

—— (1995) 'Redefining Security: The Human Dimension', *Current History* 94 (592): 229–236.

Watanabe, A. (2001) 'Japan's Position on Human Rights in Asia', in S. J. Maswood (ed.) *Japan and East Asian Regionalism*, London: Routledge, pp. 68–89.

Webber, D. (2001) 'Two Funerals and a Wedding? The Ups and Downs of Regionalism in East Asia and Asia-Pacific after the Asian Crisis', *The Pacific Review*, 14 (3): 339–372.

Yamakage, S. (2001) 'Nihon-no Tai-ASEAN Seisaku-no Henyou [Changes in Japan's policies towards ASEAN]', *Kokusai Mondai*, 490: 57–81.

Young, O. R. (1994) *International Governance: Protecting the Environment in a Stateless Society*, Ithaca, NY: Cornell University Press.

Index